FROMM
EasyGuide
To
PARIS

By
Margie Rynn

Easy Guides are ✦ Quick To Read ✦ Light To Carry
✦ For Expert Advice ✦ In All Price Ranges

FrommerMedia LLC

Published by
FROMMER MEDIA LLC

ISBN 978-1-62887-080-0 (paper), 978-1-62887-081-7 (e-book)

Editorial Director: Pauline Frommer
Editor: Pauline Frommer
Production Editor: Heather Wilcox
Cartographer: Elizabeth Puhl
Cover Design: Howard Grossman

For information on our other products or services, see www.frommers.com.

Frommer Media LLC also publishes its books in a variety of electronic formats. Some content that
appears in print may not be available in electronic formats.

Manufactured in the United States of America

5 4 3 2 1

AN IMPORTANT NOTE

The world is a dynamic place. Hotels change ownership, restaurants hike their prices, museums
alter their opening hours, and busses and trains change their routings. And all of this can occur
in the several months after our authors have visited, inspected, and written about these hotels,
restaurants, museums, and transportation services. Though we have made valiant efforts to keep
all our information fresh and up-to-date, some few changes can inevitably occur in the periods
before a revised edition of this guidebook is published. So please bear with us if a tiny number
of the details in this book have changed. Please also note that we have no responsibility or liabil-
ity for any inaccuracy or errors or omissions, or for inconvenience, loss, damage, or expenses suffered by anyone as a result of assertions in this guide.

A foreword TO THIS EASY GUIDE TO PARIS

BY
ARTHUR FROMMER

It always happens. Toward the end of every TV, radio, or newspaper interview, I am asked, "If you could vacation in only one place in the world, where would it be?" And I disappoint the questioner by responding not with an exotic or colorful choice—such as New Guinea or Montevideo—but simply with the city of Paris. And while the deflated interviewer changes the subject, I go babbling on about how Paris never fails to enchant.

Let Me Count the Ways

It's true—I can never get enough of the City of Light. To me, Paris is on the frontier, the leading edge, of every touristic activity. It rules the roost not only in cuisine—who could deny that?—but also in art and museums; in concerts, dance, and opera; in political discourse and intellectual debate (scan the newspaper headlines if you doubt that); in monuments and history (from the Pantheon to the Tomb of Napoleon); in fashion and shopping; in its cafes and bars (where you can spend the entire afternoon sipping a single glass of wine and not be asked to move on); in the availability of its civic services (get sick and a roaming ambulance with a doctor on board will almost instantly be at your side); in its luscious-looking open-air markets; in the excitement of its student life; in literature and economics (its resident novelists, philosophers, scientists, and scholars are legendary); and in every other field and endeavor I can name. Return to it for the second time or even the fiftieth—it still seems new.

So obviously, a guidebook series such as ours must have an important volume devoted to Paris. And this one, by American-turned-Parisienne Margie Rynn, is surely among the leading examples.

Margie came to Paris some 14 years ago, and she never left. She married a kind and understanding Frenchman (they have a delightful, 12-year-old son who knows every corner of the French capital), and while enjoying the delights of her adopted city, she proceeded to carve out a career as a distinguished travel journalist whose writings about Paris and France have appeared in numerous prestigious magazines.

Although her *Easy Guide to Paris* devotes more-than-sufficient space to organized commercial tours of Paris (including the fabled Bateaux Mouches riverboats), it's clear from the text that she primarily regards Paris as a walking city, to be explored on your own, often while wandering at random. Here, after all, is a metropolis so built to human scale, so lovely in its architectural design, so lined with small shops with their dynamic proprietors, that there is never an uninteresting block in it. Let me repeat: *You can walk its ancient streets for hours and you will never be uninterested.*

I hope that your decision to carry a light-and-manageable Easy Guide will greatly assist you in your enjoyment of Paris, and that Margie Rynn's own special perspectives will make your visit full of joy—and memorable.

Cordially,

Arthur Frommer

CONTENTS

ABOUT THE AUTHOR

Margie Rynn has been living and writing in France for more than 14 years, mostly in Paris. The author of "Pauline Frommer's Paris," she has also written features for several travel publications, including "Budget Travel Magazine," "EasyJet Inflight," "Ryanair," and "Wiz-zit," as well as other magazines, such as "Time Out New York," "The Amicus Journal," and "Yoga Journal." In a previous New York life, she acted in a Broadway play and performed her own one-woman show at the HERE performance space. Margie is married to a kind and understanding Frenchman, and they have a lovely 12-year-old son.

ABOUT THE FROMMER'S TRAVEL GUIDES

For most of the past 50 years, Frommer's has been the leading series of travel guides in North America, accounting for as many as 24% of all guidebooks sold. I think I know why.

Although we hope our books are entertaining, we nevertheless deal with travel in a serious fashion. Our guidebooks have never looked on such journeys as a mere recreation, but as a far more important human function, a time of learning and introspection, an essential part of a civilized life. We stress the culture, lifestyle, history, and beliefs of the destinations we cover and urge our readers to seek out people and new ideas as the chief rewards of travel.

We have never shied from controversy. We have, from the beginning, encouraged our authors to be intensely judgmental, critical—both pro and con—in their comments, and wholly independent. Our only clients are our readers, and we have triggered the ire of countless prominent sorts, from a tourist newspaper we called "practically worthless" (it unsuccessfully sued us) to the many rip-offs we've condemned.

And because we believe that travel should be available to everyone regardless of their incomes, we have always been cost-conscious at every level of expenditure. Although we have broadened our recommendations beyond the budget category, we insist that every lodging we include is sensibly priced. We use every form of media to assist our readers and are particularly proud of our feisty daily website, the award-winning Frommers.com.

I have high hopes for the future of Frommer's. May these guidebooks, in all the years ahead, continue to reflect the joy of travel and the freedom that travel represents. May they always pursue a cost-conscious path, so that people of all incomes can enjoy the rewards of travel. And may they create, for both the traveler and the persons among whom we travel, a community of friends, where all human beings live in harmony and peace.

Arthur Frommer

THE BEST OF PARIS

Paris is a magnificent city, worthy of all the superlatives that have been heaped upon it for centuries. Its graceful streets, soaked in history, really are as elegant as they say. Its monuments and museums really are extraordinary, and a slightly world-weary *fin-de-siècle* grandeur really is part of day-to-day existence. But Paris is so much more than a beautiful assemblage of buildings and monuments. It is the pulsing heart of the French nation.

If you look beyond its beautiful facade, you'll see that this is a city where flesh-and-blood people live and work and a place where there is a palpable urban buzz. Not only is Paris the capital of the country, but if you include the suburbs, it is home to 20% of the country's population and the source of almost all French jobs. Paris is France's financial, artistic, and cultural center.

Not all that long ago, Paris was not only the navel of France but the shining beacon of Europe. All the continent's greatest minds and talents clamored to come here: The city seduced Nietzsche, Chopin, Picasso, and Wilde, just to name a few. Since the end of World War II, the city has lost some of its global luster. Parisians often moan about France's place in the world and whether or not globalization is a good thing; behind the hand-wringing are some very legitimate concerns about a disappearing way of life.

But despite these concerns, or maybe because of them, Paris is still a bastion of the best of French culture. The culinary legacy alone is enough to fill several books. You can eat your way to nirvana in the city's restaurants, gourmet food stores, and bakeries. The architecture ranges from the lavish opulence of **Place Vendôme** (p. 115) to the contemporary madness of **Musée du Quai Branly** (p. 149). The city is also home to some of the world's greatest museums, including the legendary **Louvre** (p. 112). And let's not even get into the city's concert halls, nightspots, parks, gardens, and cafes—at least not just yet. Even if you have time to see only a fraction of what you'd like to see, in the long run, it really won't matter. What counts is that you'll have been to Paris, sampled its wonders, and savored the experience—and that counts for a lot.

MOST unforgettable
PARIS EXPERIENCES

○ **Seeing the city from above:** Whether it's from the top of the **Eiffel Tower** (p. 145), in front of **Sacré Coeur** (p. 131), or next to a gargoyle on **Notre-Dame** (p. 103), seeing the city from aloft will make your heart sing. There are no skyscrapers in the city center (okay, there's the **Tour Montpar-nasse,** but we try to forget) and you can scan the cityscape and see many of the most famous monuments poking out above the elegant Haussmannian buildings.

o **Strolling across the Pont Neuf:** The view from here is dramatic. To one side, you'll see the **Ile de la Cité,** to the other, the **Eiffel Tower** and the **Louvre.** It's a little like standing in the navel of the Parisian universe, and in fact, you are: The island that this bridge straddles dates back to the city's earliest beginnings.

o **Walking along the Seine at night:** Paris is beautiful in the daytime, but at night, when many of the monuments are lit up, it's positively bewitching. Strolling along the banks of the Seine at night is about as romantic as it gets. A **nighttime** boat cruise (p. 151) is another great way to enjoy the magic.

o **Sipping an apéro at a sidewalk cafe at sunset:** After work or before play, Parisians love to meet up to have an *apéritif,* a mildly alcoholic drink, like a glass of port, or a nice Belgian beer—or just a soda—on a cafe terrace. Join the locals in this early evening ritual and feel like a real Parisian.

o **Soaking up the atmosphere at a farmer's market:** All kinds of Parisians frequent the city's many **covered and open-air markets** (p. 177), which sell all kinds of fresh fruits, vegetables, meats, cheeses, and other goodies. Don't be afraid to plunge into these noisy places; you'll be participating in a tradition that goes back centuries. Just don't touch the merchandise unless directed otherwise; the vendors do the selecting here.

o **Riding a bike:** Yes, you heard me right—ever since the advent of the **Velib'** low-cost bike rental program (p. 226) a few years ago, Paris has been in the process of becoming a two-wheeler city. Sign-up online for a week's worth of bike access and buzz around like a local—the city is small enough and flat enough that riding is a snap. But please, wear a helmet, as traffic can be hairy.

PARIS'S best ARCHITECTURAL LANDMARKS

o **Best monuments to La Gloire (the glory of France):** The **Arc de Triomphe**—the world's largest triumphal arch (p. 125)—is about as grandiose as it gets, at least until you arrive at the magnificent **Place de la Concorde** (p. 131), another grandiose national gesture. If that's not enough, the church of **La Madeleine** (p. 126) was originally meant to be a temple to military glory, and the **Panthéon** (p. 141) is a church made into a crypt for the nation's heroes.

o **Best monuments to spiritual glory:** Despite the French obsession with keeping the Republic secular, the capital harbors some of the world's most exquisite churches. No matter what your views are on religion, you'll be bowled over by the soaring arches of the **Cathedral of Notre-Dame** (p. 103) the stained glass of **Sainte-Chapelle** (p. 116), or the superb rood screen at **St-Etienne du Mont** (p. 142).

o **Best monuments to human ingenuity:** Extraordinary engineers and architects have spent time in this city, leaving behind some amazing buildings in their wake. Most famously, the **Eiffel Tower** (p. 145), gracefully reaches for the sky, while exerting minimal pressure on the ground. The land under the Belle Époque wonder that is the **Palais Garnier** (p. 118) is stabilized by a man-made underground lake. Modern architects have also made their mark, mostly on the city's museums, be it the inside-out structure of the **Centre Pompidou** (p. 119) or the dilating windows at the **Institute du Monde Arabe** (p. 140).

PARIS'S best RESTAURANTS

o **Best for romance:** Thinking of popping the question? Think no more, just reserve a table at **Lasserre** (p. 73) and get it over with for once and for all. With its retractable ceiling, legendary kitchen, and elegant décor, there's no better setting.

o **Best for families:** Set inside the Buttes Chaumont park, at **Rosa Bonheur** (p. 84) parents can enjoy tapas on a large, outdoor terrace while their kids play in the grass. French fry freaks and their meat-eating parents will love **Le Relais de l'Entrecôte** (p. 92), where delicious steak-frites with a special sauce is the only thing on the menu.

o **Best splurge:** If you are planning to pull all the stops out, do it at **L'Arpège** (p. 94), where elegance meets excellence both on the plate and in the décor. Alain Passard deftly creates miracles with vegetables that come from his own gourmet farm, as well as other fresh, top-quality ingredients.

o **Best value:** For a taste of bistronomy (as in, gourmet, modernized bistro food) at a reasonable price, look no farther than **Mangetout** (p. 92). For an affordable meal with authentic regional flavor (Brittany), try **Crêperie Josselin** (p. 98).

o **Best classic bistro:** For once, the critics seem to agree on something: **Bistrot Paul Bert** (p. 81) is one of the best bistros in the city, and that's saying a lot in a city with as many great bistros as this one.

o **Best mom-and-pop restaurant:** One of the last of a dying breed in the city center, **Au Petit Bar** (p. 68) has resisted gentrification. Nothing seems to have changed for decades at this tiny family owned restaurant, which serves cheap, old-fashioned comfort food.

o **Best for tapas:** Yes, tapas now can have a French accent, especially when the chef comes from the southwest, near the Spanish border, as is the case at **Pinxo** (p. 68) one of super-chef Alain Dutournier's more recent enterprises.

o **Best for wine enthusiasts:** If what's in your glass is just as important as what's on the plate, saunter over to **Les Papilles** (p. 89), where the walls are covered with shelves of the best bottles, and the knowing staff will guide you in your search for the ultimate elixir.

PARIS'S best HOTELS

o **Best view:** You won't want to get up in the morning at **Hôtel Brighton;** you'll be happy just staying in bed and gazing at the panorama, which depending on which room you are in, might include the Louvre, Tuileries gardens, and the Eiffel Tower. See p. 34.

o **Best for families:** A terrific value near the Montparnasse train station, **Hôtel Des Bains** offers pretty connecting rooms and family suites at very affordable rates. See p. 59.

o **Best splurge:** It's hard to say if the décor is modern or period at **Relais St-Germain,** but it doesn't really matter because it's simply beautiful. Dark wood, plush fabrics, and priority seating at Le Comptoir du Relais downstairs. See p. 54.

o **Most charming period piece: Hôtel Caron de Beaumarchais** recreates the ambience of 18th-century Paris, when the hotel's namesake, the author of the Barber of Seville, was cavorting in the neighborhood. A bit of Old France right in the middle of the trendy Marais neighborhood. See p. 38.

o **Most eco-friendly:** Just next to the Canal St-Martin, **Le Citizen** recycles all waste, stocks locally sourced filtered tap water, serves organic breakfasts, and its rooms tout bedding made from organic fair-trade cotton and water-conserving toilets and showers. See p. 48.

o **Best for a hilarious honeymoon:** See-through showers, floating "levitation" beds, feather covered ceilings, a fake diamond studded bathtub—**Hotel Seven** has all this and more in its wacky yet wonderful suites that are clearly designed with couples in mind. See p. 49.

o **Best value:** Blessed with a terrific location in the Marais on a lovely and leafy square, **Hôtel Jeanne d'Arc le Marais** is a terrific budget option. See p. 40.

PARIS'S best MUSEUMS

o **Musée du Louvre:** One of the world's largest and best museums, this colossus of culture has its share of masterpieces, including the Mona Lisa, the Venus de Milo, and Winged Victory. But aside from these three famous ladies, there are mountains of other incredible works to see, from ancient Egyptian sculptures to Renaissance masters to stunning gems and jewelry. See p. 112.

o **Musée d'Orsay:** A breathtaking collection of pre-, post-, and just plain old Impressionists deck the walls of this museum, including Renoir, Van Gogh, Manet, Degas, Gauguin and a slew of other masters of 19th-century art. Not only is the artwork incredible, but the building itself, a transformed Belle Epoque train station, is a delight. See p. 148.

o **Musée Rodin:** A prolific genius, Auguste Rodin created so many beautiful sculptures that you could probably fill several mansions like this one. Aside from seeing roomfuls of legendary works like "The Kiss" and "Adam and Eve," you can also go outside and see "The Gates of Hell" in a paradisiacal garden. See p. 149.

o **Musée Jacquemart-André:** Set in a gorgeous 19th-century mansion, this small museum offers a chance to see both exquisite art and how the other half lived. Highlights include a beautiful winter garden, a collection of Italian Renaissance masters, and a magnificent tearoom with a Tiepolo on the ceiling. See p. 128.

o **Musée du Quai Branly:** One of the more recent additions to the Parisian museum scene, this ultra-modern museum gives center stage to artworks that are often overlooked: those of traditional societies in Africa, Asia, and even North America. You'll find everything from a shaman's cloak from Papua New Guinea to Australian aboriginal art, as well as delicate carvings, intricate weavings, and other masterpieces. See p. 149.

THE best FREE & DIRT CHEAP PARIS

o **Attending a free concert:** Every summer the Parc Floral (in the Bois de Vincennes) hosts a bevy of free concerts: first the Paris Jazz Festival in June and July, and then Classique au Vert in August. See p. 156.

o **Picnicking in the Luxembourg Gardens:** You couldn't get richer surroundings if you were at a three-star restaurant, and yet you only paid a few euros for a sandwich. Sometimes being cheap is the best revenge. See p. 143.

o **Seeing Paris from a city bus:** Make your own tour of Paris by bus—for the price of a Métro ticket. Some of the municipal bus lines' routes would put a professional tour bus to shame, like routes Nos. 63 and 87, which hit many of the city's major sites. Visit www.ratp.fr for route maps.

o **Dawdling over a coffee in a cafe:** Okay, you might pay 2.50€ for a cup of coffee, but that means you can sit for hours watching the world go by in an atmospheric cafe, and have an authentically Parisian experience to boot.

o **Enjoying the newly refurbished banks of the Seine, "Les Berges":** What used to be a stretch of noisy roadway between the Musée d'Orsay and the Pont d'Alma is now a place for walking, running, and holding hands, with picnic areas, food and drink, floating gardens, and sports activities, as well as lounge chairs for taking an impromptu siesta. See p. 155.

THE best NEIGHBORHOODS FOR GETTING LOST

o **Montmartre:** If you get away from the crowds at the Sacré Coeur, this mythic neighborhood a great place to wander up and down winding lanes, tilt at windmills, admire the view, and cafe hop. You could also take my walking tour (p. 160).

o **The Latin Quarter:** Once again, the trick here is to ditch the crowds on rue de la Huchette and take off for the less trampled corners of this historic student quarter, like near the universities on rue Erasme, the food shops on **rue Mouffetard,** or down by the delightful **Jardin des Plantes.**

o **The Marais:** Get lost in style in this trendy neighborhood, known as much for its delightful boutiques and hip restaurants as for its magnificent 17th- and 18th-century *hôtels particuliers,* aristocratic mansions, many of which have been turned into terrific museums. See my walking tour on p. 165.

o **Belleville:** You'll see another side of Paris in this diverse, working-class district, where a combination of artists and immigrants have made it into one of the city's most vibrant neighborhoods. **Parc de Belleville** offers wonderful views of Paris; around **rue de Menilmontant** you'll find cool bars and vintage shops. Further east is the romantic **Père-Lachaise** cemetery (p. 134).

THE best UNEXPECTED PLEASURES IN PARIS

o **Dance at a floating club:** Dance the night away at **Batofar** (p. 201), a bar/club in boat docked on the Seine.

o **Sunbathe on the Seine:** Enjoy the sand and sun at **Paris Plage** (p. 155), an annual summer fiesta where the riverbanks become a beach, and concerts, snack bars, tea dances, and other activities are open to one and all.

o **Eat excellent Japanese food:** Experience the pleasures of *okonomiyaki* at **Aki** (p. 68), one of the many Japanese restaurants and noodle shops lining rue Ste-Anne, just off the boulevard de l'Opéra.

o **Watch weavers make tapestries:** At the **Manufacture des Gobelins** (p. 140), you can take a tour and see skilled artists at their giant looms creating magnificent woven works.

o **Sip mint tea in a Moroccan tearoom:** Dream you're in the Kasbah at the tearoom at the **Mosquée de Paris** (p. 99), which is covered in beautiful mosaic tiles.

PARIS'S best GREEN SPACES

- o **The best gardens:** It's hard to choose between the grand geometry of the **Tuileries** (p. 109), the relaxed elegance of the **Luxembourg Gardens** (p. 143), and the colorful palette of **Giverny** (p. 215).

- o **The best parks:** The **Bois de Boulogne** (p. 155) has lakes, gardens, and even a small amusement park (the **Jardin d'Acclimatation;** p. 158) for your rambling pleasure. While there's no amusement park at the Bois de Vincennes, there is a medieval castle, the **Château de Vincennes,** complete with ramparts and a keep (p. 157) as well as the newly re-opened zoo, the **Parc Zoologique de Paris** (p. 133).

- o **The best primrose promenade:** The **Promenade Plantée** (p. 133) must be the world's skinniest garden: Because it's set atop a former train viaduct, you can stroll among the flowers and greenery from the place de la Bastille all the way to the Bois de Vincennes.

PARIS IN CONTEXT

Before there was Paris, there was the Seine. Much wider than it is today, the river looped and curved through the region, and at one point, split into two branches. One branch eventually dried up, leaving a wide band of marshlands to the north, while the other, sprinkled with islands, remained. This swampy bog offered little indication that it had potential for urban grandeur. Yet one day it would become the lifeline of one of the greatest cities in the world.

THE MAKING OF PARIS

Origins

Prehistoric Paris did have two things going for it: a river that led all the way to the Atlantic and those strategically placed islands, which offered both protection and shelter. The largest one, the core of what would one day become the **Ile de la Cité,** attracted the attention of a tribe of Celtic people called the Parisii, who fished and traded along its banks somewhere around the 3rd century B.C. Though they weren't the first Parisians (traces of human habitations have been found that date back to Neolithic times), they were the first to firmly implant themselves in the area, and they made ample use of the river not only as a source of food, but as a trade link. Their island had the good fortune of being on the "Pewter Route," a trade route that stretched from the British Isles to the Mediterranean. As a consequence, the Parisii's wealth was such that by the 1st century B.C., they were minting their own gold coins.

Roman Rule (1st C. B.C.–2nd C. A.D.)

There is no recorded history of Paris before the Romans showed up in 52 B.C., but when Caesar and his boys marched in, the Parisii numbered several thousand and the island bustled with activity. Soon thereafter, however, the Parisii's main activity would be trying to get rid of the Romans. Though they fought valiantly, after a ferocious battle they were massacred by Caesar's troops, and a new Roman town was built both on the island and on the Left Bank, on the slopes of the **Montagne St-Genevieve** (where the Panthéon now stands; p. 141). The new town, for reasons that remain unclear, was baptized Lutécia, and ran along a ramrod-straight north-south axis; the line of this road survives in today's **rue St-Jacques.** (The Parisii would eventually get their due, however, as the city would be renamed Civitas Parisiorum in the 4th c., which eventually was whittled down to Paris.) Though there were only around 8,000 inhabitants, by the 2nd century the town boasted three **Gallo-Roman baths** (you can see the ruins of the largest of these at the corner of boulevards St-Michel and St-Germain) and a vast amphitheater (a piece of which can be seen at the **Arènes de Lutèce,** just off rue Monge in the Latin Quarter).

Barbarian Invasions (3rd–5th C.)

By the 3rd century, the city was subject to waves of barbarian invasions. Most of the population took refuge on the Ile de la Cité, which was then encircled by ramparts. Somewhere around this time, St-Denis was decapitated when he was martyred up on a nearby hill, which in time would be dubbed **Montmartre** (p. 160). Legend has it that the saint picked up his severed head and walked with it for several kilometers, preaching all the while; the **Basilica of St-Denis** (just north of Paris) was built on the place where he finally dropped. The event, which supposedly happened around 250, coincides with Christianity's first appearance on the Parisian scene. Another particularly pious Christian, a young nun named Geneviève, was credited with turning Attila the Hun away from Paris in 451. Alerted that the barbarians were approaching, the citizenry was in a state of panic; Geneviève reassured them, telling them that God was with them. In the end, the Huns didn't march on Paris, but on Orléans; the grateful population, convinced it was Geneviève's doing, made her into the city's patron saint. A church was raised in her honor on the hill that's now known as the **Montagne-Ste-Geneviève;** it was pulled down and replaced by a magnificent new one, commissioned by Louis XV in the 18th century, which was subsequently turned into a national mausoleum after the Revolution and renamed the **Panthéon** (p. 141).

Merovingian & Carolingian Dynasties (6th–10th C.)

At the end of the 5th century, the Franks (a Germanic people) invaded and established the Merovingian dynasty of kings; the first, Clovis, made Paris the capital of his new kingdom in 508. The Merovingians were ardent Catholics; under their rule the city sprouted dozens of churches, convents, and monasteries. Childebert I, the son of Clovis, inaugurated a small basilica that would soon be dubbed **St-Germain-des-Prés** after the saint was buried there in 576. Over time, this church would grow into a powerful abbey and intellectual center that would dominate much of the Left Bank up until the Revolution. Even after the abbey was dismantled, and many of its buildings burned, the church lived on, as did the name of the neighborhood. Though the city enjoyed a certain amount of prosperity during this time, it was short-lived; the Merovingians, who were known as the "do-nothing" kings, were eventually toppled, and by the 8th century, a new dynasty, the Carolingians, had replaced them.

The most famous member of this clan was Charlemagne, who went on to conquer Italy and was crowned emperor by the Pope in 800. Arts and letters thrived during this period, and the city began to build up on the Right Bank, around the church of **St-Gervais–St-Protais,** and the Port du Grève, where the **Hôtel de Ville** (p. 121) now stands. Starting in the mid–9th century, the city was periodically ravaged by Normans and Vikings, who would sack Paris on their way to plundering Burgundy. The Normans were particularly persistent; after a barricade was erected on the Seine to keep their boats from passing in 885, they laid siege to the city for an entire year. It was only after King Charles the Simple signed a treaty in 911 giving the Normans Normandy that life returned to normal; but by then Paris was in ruins. The age of the Carolingians was drawing quickly to a close.

The Founding of the Capetian Dynasty (11th C.)

In 987, Hugues Capet, the Count of Paris, was crowned king of France; his direct descendants ruled the country for 3½ centuries, and two branches of the Capetian dynasty, the Valois and Bourbons, would continue to rule (with a brief pause during the Revolution) until 1792. With the Capetians came stability, and Paris rebuilt and grew, particularly on the Ile de la Cité and the Right Bank. The Left Bank, flattened by the Normans, was left as it was; little by little it was covered with fields and vineyards. The 12th century was a period of economic growth; it saw the birth of **Les Halles** (p. 106), the city's sprawling central market, around which a new commercial quarter developed. In 1163, Bishop Maurice de Sully decided Paris deserved a new cathedral, and ground was broken on the **Cathédral de Notre-Dame de Paris** (p. 103); finished 200 years later, it remains one of the world's most exquisite examples of medieval architecture.

It was around this time that that mushy, marshy strip of land on the Right Bank, known as the **Marais** (or swamp), was partially drained and carpeted with farms. Philippe Auguste, before taking off on a crusade, had a sturdy rampart built around the newly extended city limits; fragments of this wall can still be seen today (see "Walking Tours," p. 165). Philippe's grandson, Louis IX (St-Louis), added another architectural jewel to the cityscape: the **Sainte-Chapelle** (p. 116), a small church whose upper-story walls are almost entirely made of brilliantly colored stained glass. Louis had it built to house a treasure he bought from the debt-ridden Byzantine emperor: Christ's crown of thorns and some fragments of the holy cross (the relics are now in Notre-Dame).

Medieval Glory & Gore (12th–14th C.)

By the 12th century, Paris boasted a population of around 200,000, much larger than other European capitals, as well as a burgeoning reputation as an economic as well as intellectual center. Quality fabrics, leather goods, and metalwork were produced in Paris, as well as art objects. The University of Paris was slowly coming into being, and colleges were popping up all over the left bank; in 1257, Robert de Sorbon established the small theological college that became the **Sorbonne.** The city seemed unstoppable.

But the 14th century would, in fact, put an end to this fruitful period. When the last Capetian king, Charles IV, died in 1328, the succession to the throne was disputed, in part because the closest descendent was Edward III, king of England, who also presided over a chunk of southwestern France. This and many other gripes exploded into the Hundred Years War, which devastated France for over a century. Expansion in Paris came to an abrupt halt, the endless wars and riots wore down the populace, and in 1348 the Black Plague killed tens of thousands. In the early 1400s Paris was hit by famine and a string of extremely cold winters: Between one disaster and another, the city lost about half of its population during this period. In 1420, the English occupied Paris; despite the efforts of Joan of Arc and Charles VII, who laid siege to the city in 1429, troops loyal to the Duke of Bedford (the English Regent) didn't leave until 1437. This same duke was responsible for having Joan burned at the stake in Rouen in 1431.

Renaissance Renewal (16th C.)

Slowly, the city came to life again. The population increased, as did commercial and intellectual activity. The invention of the printing press spread new ideas across Europe; the primary trend, Humanism, would find a home in Paris. Great thinkers were drawn to city's universities, such as Erasmus, and John Calvin. More colleges emerged from the academic landscape: In 1530, François I established a school that would become the prestigious **College de France,** and in 1570 the **Académie Française** was founded by Charles IX. If the Renaissance made its mark on the intellectual life of the city, it had little impact on its architectural legacy. The Renaissance kings liked Paris but lived and did their building elsewhere. François I, the most construction-happy among them, brought some of the greatest masters of the Italian Renaissance, like Leonardo da Vinci and Benvenuto Cellini, to France, but their genius was mostly displayed in François' châteaux on the Loire and at **Fontainebleau** (p. 216), not in the capital. The king's primary contribution to the cityscape was the remodeling of the **Louvre** (p. 112) and construction of the **Hôtel de Ville** (p. 121), designed by the Italian architect Boccador. The latter building was burned down in 1871 during the fall of the Paris Commune; the existing edifice is a fairly faithful copy erected in 1873. Two glorious churches, **St-Etienne-du-Mont** (p. 142) and **St-Eustache** (p. 116), were also built during this period; their decoration attests to the jubilant spirit of the times.

War interfered once again with the city's development in 1557 when the bloody struggle between the country's Protestants and Catholics morphed into the Wars of Religion. Even the marriage of the future king, Henri of Navarre, a Protestant, to Marguerite de Valois, a Catholic, did not diffuse the conflict: A week after their wedding, August 24, 1572, the bells of **St-Germain l'Auxerrois** (p. 117) signaled the beginning of the St-Bartholomew's Day massacre, which resulted in the deaths of between 2,000 and 4,000 Parisian Protestants. When in 1589, Henri was declared King of France (as Henri IV), Parisians would not let the Protestant monarch enter the city. After 4 months of siege, the starving citizens relented and in the end, to show his good will, the King converted, famously declaring that "Paris is worth a mass."

Henri IV lived on to be an enormously popular king, whose structural improvements left a lasting mark on the city. He was the force behind the **Pont Neuf** (p. 120), which straddles the Right and Left Banks, as well as the Ile de la Cité. To create the bridge, two small islets off the western tip of the Ile de la Cité were filled in and made part of the larger island; the tranquil **place Dauphine** was also created during this time. Henri also conceived the strikingly harmonious place Royale (now called **Place des Vosges;** p. 124). The King would not live to see it finished; in 1610, when the royal carriage got stuck in a traffic jam on rue de la Ferronerie, he was stabbed by Ravaillac, a deranged Catholic who was convinced that Henri was waging war against the Pope.

The Age of Louis XIV (17th C.)

There was a building frenzy amongst the aristocracy of the 17th century. Marie de Médicis built the Italian-style **Palais du Luxembourg** in 1615, around the same time that the **Marais** (p. 119) was inundated with splendid palaces and *hôtels particuliers,* or mansions. The new **Ile St-Louis,** made from the joining of two previously uninhab-ited islets to the east of the Ile de la Cité, was filled with stately mansions that only the rich could afford. After Marguerite de Valois moved in to the neighborhood, the **St-Germain** quarter also became a place to see and be seen. Finally, in 1632 the powerful Cardinal Richelieu built a huge palace, now called the **Palais Royal** (p. 115), near the Louvre, which encouraged yet another new neighborhood to develop.

In 1643, a 5-year-old boy named Louis XIV acceded to the French throne, where he would stay for the next 72 years. One of the most influential figures in French history, Louis XIV's early years were spent in Paris, under the protection of his mother, Anne of Austria. It was not a happy time: The city was writhing under a nasty rebellion called La Fronde, instigated by cranky nobles trying to wrest control back from the powerful prime minister, Cardinal Mazarin, and the young monarch and his mother were chased from one royal residence to the next. When he grew up and things calmed down, he settled into the **Louvre,** commanding his team of architects, led by Le Vau, to finish up the **Cour Carrée** and other unfinished parts of the palace. The spectacular colonnade on the eastern facade dates from this period. Louis eventually decided to build his own castle, however; one that was far enough from the noise and filth of the capital, and big enough to house his entire court—the better to keep a close eye on their political intrigues. The result was the **Château of Versailles** (p. 209), a testament to the genius of Le Vau, as well as master landscape architect André Le Nôtre.

Even if Louis XIV didn't live in the city, he certainly added to its architectural heritage. He was responsible for construction of **Les Invalides** (p. 146), a massive military hospital, as well as two grand squares, **place des Victoires** and place Louis-le-Grand, which today is known as **Place Vendôme** (p. 115). Two gigantic entryways, celebrating Louis' military victories, were built at the city gates; the **Porte St-Denis** and the **Porte St-Martin.** Both of these triumphal archways still hover over parts of the 10th arrondissement, looking somewhat out of place in this working-class district.

From Enlightenment to Revolution

Paris continued to grow, and the population density increased. At the turn of the 18th century, there were 500,000 Parisians crammed into a vast network of narrow, mostly unpaved streets. Sewers were nonexistent and clean drinking water a luxury. While life in the rarified atmosphere of the aristocratic salons of the **Marais** was brimming with art, literature, and deep thought, down on the ground it was filled with misery. Poverty and want were the constant companions of the vast majority of Parisians. On an intellectual level, the city was soaring—under the reign of Louis XV, Paris became a standard-bearer for the Enlightenment, a school of thought that championed reason and logic and helped construct the intellectual framework of both the American and French Revolutions. Salons—regular meetings of artists and thinkers in aristocratic homes—flourished, as did cafes; drawn in by the wildly popular new drink called coffee, they were the ideal meeting place for philosophers, writers, and artists, as well as a new breed of politicians with some revolutionary ideas. Political debates were particularly passionate in the cafes in the galleries of the **Palais Royal** (p. 115), which had been filled with shops and opened to the public by Duke Louis Philippe d'Orléans.

Meanwhile, back in Versailles, the court of Louis XVI seemed to be utterly oblivious of the mounting discontent in the capital. As the price of bread skyrocketed and more and more Parisians found themselves on the street (there were more than 100,000 homeless people in the city in 1789, out of an overall population of between 600,000 and 700,000), the disconnect between the aristocracy and the common man threatened to rupture into a bloody conflict. Amazingly, Louis XVI and his wife Marie Antoinette continued to live their lives as if the civil unrest in the capital didn't concern them. A financial crisis in the royal treasury prompted a meeting of the Estates-General in Versailles in May 1789, a representative body that had not been convened since 1616. The assembly began demanding a more democratic system of taxation, and better representation of the Third Estate (the people). When the King tried to close down the proceedings, the group, which had renamed itself the National Assembly, dug in its heels and wrote a constitution. The royals kept dithering and trying to break up the assembly, until finally, the Revolution erupted on July 14, 1789, when an angry mob stormed the Bastille prison. There were only 7 prisoners in the fortress, but no matter—the genie was out of the bottle, and the pent-up anger of the populace was unleashed.

Not only was the royal family imprisoned and beheaded, but after the initial euphoria faded and the high ideals were set down on paper, the leaders of the Revolution began to squabble, and the factional skirmishes became increasingly deadly. The events of the Revolution are too many to relate here, but within a few years, not only were aristocrats being sent off to the guillotine, but just about anyone who disagreed with the ruling powers, including many of the leaders who wrote the rules. Finally, Robespierre, who directed the bloodiest phase of the Revolution, known as "the Terror," had his turn at the guillotine, and a new government was set up. Called the Directory, this unsuccessful attempt at representative government met its end when a general named Napoleon Bonaparte staged a coup in 1799.

The Empire

Under Napoleon, Paris slowly put itself back together. The economy restarted, and the Emperor turned his attentions to upgrading the city's infrastructure, building bridges (**Pont St-Louis, Pont des Arts, Pont d'Iéna,** and **Pont d'Austerlitz**), improving access to water (the **Canal de l'Ourcq**), and creating new cemeteries, like **Père-Lachaise** (p. 134) because the old ones were so crowded that they had become public health hazards. Napoleon was also responsible for the **rue de Rivoli,** a wide east-west boulevard, the first of several that would be laid down later on in the 19th century. The collection of the **Louvre** was greatly enhanced by all the booty the Emperor acquired during his many military campaigns. Napoleon's love of war would eventually be his undoing; after his defeat by the English at Waterloo he was exiled to the isle of Ste-Helena, where he died in 1821. Paris sports huge monuments to his memory, in particular the **Arc de Triomphe** (p. 125), which honors the Imperial Army.

The Restoration & Urban Renewal

Incredibly, after all the blood that was spilled in the name of the Republic, Louis XVI's brother (Louis XVIII) became King of France in 1814. What's more, another brother, Charles X, became king after Louis XVIII's death. What both brothers had in common is that they tried to bring back the old days of absolute monarchy, while the citizenry had become accustomed to the reforms of the Revolution and the relatively benign rule of Napoleon. This, coupled with the continuing poverty of many Parisians resulted in two serious uprisings, *"Les Trois Glorieuses,"* the 3 "glorious" days in July of 1830, and the Revolution of 1848. In fact, it is these two uprisings, and not the Revolution itself, that are honored on the column in the **Place de la Bastille** (p. 133), the site of the infamous prison. After Charles, a republic was declared, and Napoleon's nephew, Louis-Napoleon, ran for and won the presidency. He liked being president so much that he didn't want to give up power at the end of his term, so he staged a coup and declared the birth of the Second Empire, calling himself Napoleon III.

Under Charles X, the unhygienic state of the city center started to cause serious alarm, particularly after a cholera epidemic in 1832 devastated the population. Many residents fled to the outer limits of the city, away from the overcrowded poor quarters where the filthy streets were often completely clogged with traffic. City administrators began to draft plans for new avenues, in particular the prefect, Rambuteau, who went ahead and started laying down wide boulevards, like the one named after him.

But it was Napoleon III who really changed the face of Paris, when he gave urban planner Baron Haussmann free rein to "modernize" the city. Not only did Haussmann lay down wide boulevards that eased congestion and opened up vistas, he cleverly arranged them so that if ever there was yet another popular uprising, they would facilitate military maneuvers and make it tough for citizens to set up barricades. Over half of the city was ripped up and rebuilt; Haussmann instituted strict regulations for the height of the new buildings and the style of their facades. The result was the elegant buildings and boulevards you see today. On the plus side, the city finally got a decent sewage system and water access, and the squalid slums were knocked down. Several parks were created, such as **Buttes Chaumont** (p. 137) and the **Bois de Boulogne** (p. 155) as well as grand plazas like the **Place de la République** (p. 132) and **place du Trocadéro.** On the other hand, the character of the city was completely changed, and much of its social fabric was pulled down with the houses. Working-class Paris has been slowly disappearing ever since.

From the Commune to the Belle Epoque

The boulevards were put to the test during the Paris Commune of 1870, a brief, but bloody episode that was yet another attempt of the French people to construct a democratic republic. The boulevards did their job: The rebellion was crushed and at least 20,000 communards were executed. When the smoke cleared, a new government was formed, and to everyone's surprise it was a republic. The National Assembly had intended to form a constitutional monarchy, but the heir to the throne had no interest in the word "constitutional." As a stopgap measure, a temporary republic was set up—little did anyone know that it would last for 60 years.

There must have been an audible sigh of relief from Parisians, who would finally enjoy a little peace and harmony—or at least enough of a break from war and woe to have a good time. And so they did. During the "Belle Epoque," the years at the end of the 19th century and the beginning of the 20th, the arts bloomed in Paris. Groundbreaking art expositions introducing new movements like Impressionism (around 1874) and Fauvism (around 1905) changed people's ways of seeing painting. Up in **Montmartre,** an entire colony of artists and writers (Picasso, Braque, Apollinaire, and others) were filling cafes and cabarets in their off hours. The Lumière brothers and Léon Gaumont showed their newly hatched films in the city's first movie theaters. The city hosted a number of World's Fairs including that of 1889, which created the **Eiffel Tower** (p. 145), and 1900, which left behind the **Pont Alexandre III bridge,** as well as the **Grand and Petit Palais** (p. 125 and 130). Another great moment in 1900 was the inauguration of the Paris Métro's first underground line.

The World Wars

The fun came to an abrupt halt in 1914 with the outbreak of World War I, which killed 8.4 million Frenchmen. Calling all Parisians to arms, General Gallieni and his troops fought off the approaching German army (the Battle of the Marne) and saved Paris from occupation. The city did get bombarded however; on Good Friday, 1918, the church of **St-Gervais–St-Protais** took a direct hit and over 100 people died. The city rebounded after the war, both economically and culturally, especially during the 1920s, *"Les Années Folles"* (The Crazy Years). Paris became a magnet for artists and writers from all over. Americans, in particular, came in droves—F. Scott Fitzgerald, Henry Miller, Ernest Hemingway, and Gertrude Stein were some of the better-known names. They and other European expats like Marc Chagall, James Joyce, and George Orwell gathered in **Montparnasse** cafes like **Le Dôme, Le Select,** and **La Coupole.**

The 1930s brought economic depression and social unrest—a dreary backdrop for the approaching war. The Germans were re-arming, and Hitler was rising to power; in May 1940 Germany invaded the Netherlands, Luxembourg, and Belgium and broke through France's defensive Maginot line. The Germans occupied Paris on June 14, and for 4 years the city would know hunger, curfews, and suspicion. The Vichy government, led by Marchal Pétain, in theory governed unoccupied France, but in fact, collaborated with the Germans. One of the darkest moments of the occupation was in July of 1942, when the French police rounded up 13,152 Parisian Jews, including 4,115 children, and parked them in a velodrome before sending them off to Auschwitz; only 30 survived. General Charles de Gaulle became the leader of the Free French and organizer of the Resistance; after the Allies landed in Normandy in 1944, Paris was liberated and de Gaulle victoriously strode down the **Champs-Élysées** before a wildly cheering crowd. He would later become president of the country (1958–69).

Post-War Paris

Writers and artists filtered back to the cafes once the war was over (some had never left), and the **Café de Flore** (p. 100) and **Les Deux Magots** (p. 101) were headquarters for existential all-stars like Jean-Paul Sartre and Simone de Beauvoir. But the late 1940s was also the beginning of the end of French colonial rule, which was punctuated by violent clashes, including a revolt in Madagascar and a war in Indochina that would eventually entangle the United States. In North Africa, Morocco and Tunisia won their independence relatively peacefully, but France would not let go of Algeria without a long and bloody fight, with repercussions that are still being felt today. The war in Algeria led to the collapse of the French government; de Gaulle was asked to start a new one in 1958. Thousands of Algerian refugees flooded France, with many settling in the Paris region; Algeria finally gained its independence in 1962.

The writer André Malraux was de Gaulle's minister of cultural affairs from 1958 to 1969 and was responsible for protecting and restoring many endangered historic districts like the **Marais.** Elsewhere, modern architects were putting their own questionable stamp on the city, like the doughnut shaped **Maison de Radio France** in the 16th arrondissement, and the vaguely "Y"-shaped **Maison de UNESCO** in the 15th. The late 1960s also marked Paris in less concrete ways. In May 1968, students, hoping to reform the university system, joined a general workers strike that was in the process of paralyzing the nation. The police invaded **La Sorbonne** to calm the protests, and more students and sympathizers took to the streets. The confrontations became violent, with students attacking police with cobblestones—**boulevard St-Michel** was subsequently paved with asphalt. This was a period of profound social change; those who participated still proudly refer to themselves as *soixante-huitards* (68ers).

The 1970s was a period of architectural awkwardness—horrified by the idea of becoming a "museum city," then-president Georges Pompidou decided to modernize. One of his ideas that, thankfully, never came to fruition was to pave over the Canal St-Martin to make way for a freeway that would cut through the center of the city. The dismal **Tour Montparnasse** dates from this period, as does the destruction of the old Les Halles marketplace, which was replaced with an unpleasant underground shopping mall (**Forum des Halles,** which mercifully is being rebuilt). Pompidou's one "success" is the nearby **Centre Pompidou** (p. 119), whose strange, inside-out design provoked howls of outrage when it was built but now has been accepted as part of the Parisian landscape. When François Mitterrand became president in 1981, he too wanted to leave an architectural legacy, and the list of his *grands projets* ("big projects") is lengthy. Fortunately, most were considerably more palatable than his predecessor's. It is to Mitterrand that we owe the **Musée d'Orsay,** the **pyramid** (and underground shopping complex) at the Louvre, and the ultra-modern **Bibliothèque**

National **François Mitterrand,** as well as the **Institute du Monde Arabe** (p. 140) and the **Opéra Bastille.** President Jacques Chirac was the force behind the excellent **Musée du Quai Branly** (p. 149), which opened in 2006.

PARIS TODAY

In the last decade or so, life has been relatively calm in Paris, with the notable exception of the terrorist attacks on Métro stations in 1995, a year that also brought paralyzing transportation strikes. Tourism has become one of the city's major sources of wealth, with about 29 million tourists visiting Paris each year.

Paris has been looking slicker and cleaner in the last few years. Renovation of historic buildings is ongoing and a vigorous anti-dog doo campaign has even made inroads on cleaning up the notoriously messy sidewalks. The city has continued to evolve, in large part thanks to the dynamic and imaginative leadership of **Bertrand Delanoë,** the city's socialist (and openly gay) mayor, who was elected back in 2000. More than any mayor in recent history, and even more than the last couple of presidents, he has changed the face of the city, and given it a much-needed shot of energy. Paris feels younger these days, with refreshed public spaces, like the new and improved **Place de la République** (p. 132) and the delightfully pedestrian-ized **banks of the Seine** (see Les Berges; p. 155), which now include floating gardens, picnic areas, and yoga classes.

The advent of the **Velib' bike program** in 2007 (p. 226) is slowly transforming Paris into a bike-friendly place. Since then, the city has backed a host of other green measures, including bus lanes, pedestrian-friendly riverbanks, and Autolib', a Velib'-like program where you can rent an electric car to toodle around the city. Other innovative initiatives from city hall include the ever-popular **Paris Plage**—who would have thought of dumping sand on the banks of the Seine making a beach?—and **Nuit Blanche,** an annual all-night cultural party.

In 2014, Delanoë stepped down and his protégé, **Anne Hidalgo,** was elected Paris' first female mayor. It's too early to tell what her impact will be in the city, but chances are she will continue in the footsteps of her predecessor.

When he left office in 2012, Nicolas Sarkozy had not really left his mark on the capital—though his wife's (ex-model Carla Bruni) fashion sense has impacted the wardrobe of many a Parisienne. The current president, François Hollande, seems to have too much on his plate right now with France's economic woes to give much thought to leaving an architectural legacy in the capital.

But despite the dour economic forecast (which seems as interminably cloudy as the city's weather forecast), on the surface at least the capital seems to be in the pink of good health. Paris has managed to carefully conserve its architectural heritage and its traditional way of life while making a serious effort to enter the modern world. Paris is, after all, the capital of France and one of the major players in the European Union, and a certain dynamism comes with the territory—even if it is framed in Belle Epoque swirls and Mansard roofs. Yet even if the pulse of life in the capital ticks faster than it once did, it still allows for aimless intellectual discussions in cafes, leisurely Sunday strolls through Parisian parks, and relaxed lunches over glasses of wine. And maybe it is exactly that gentle aesthetic that makes the city one-of-a-kind. It is rare in today's turbulent world to find a city that so harmoniously mixes tradition and modernity, without enslaving itself to either one.

SUGGESTED ITINERARIES & NEIGHBORHOODS

3

Paris is an embarrassment of riches—there are so many wonderful things to see, it's hard to know where to begin. And while you are standing there thinking about it, the clock is ticking and your precious time is withering away. In this chapter, I'll offer up detailed itineraries so you can see the city's highlights in a short time without wearing yourself to a frazzle, as well as a couple of custom tours for particular interests. I'll also give you an overview of the city layout and break down the neighborhoods one by one, so you can design an itinerary of your own.

ICONIC PARIS IN 1 DAY

If you have just 1 day in Paris, your biggest challenge will be trying not to spend the whole day wishing you had more time. Here's an itinerary that will give you at least a taste of the city, and give you ideas for your next trip. *Start: The Champs de Mars, 7th arrond, Métro: Ecole Militaire, RER: Champs de Mars–Tour Eiffel.*

---

1 **The Eiffel Tower ★★★**
Hopefully you've gotten there early on a weekday and it won't take too long to go up and take a gander at the splendid view of the city from the second floor. If lines are long, skip the view and cross the bridge (Pont d'Iéna), heading up to the esplanade at the **Palais de Chaillot ★**, where you can admire the Iron Lady in all her splendor. See p. 145.

If you haven't done so already, cross the bridge (Pont d'Iéna) and head up to the Palais de Chaillot and the Place du Trocadéro. Hop on the no. 63 bus (direction Gare de Lyon), which will cruise past Les Invalides, and down boulevard St-Germain. Get off at the church of St-Germain-des-Prés.

2 **St-Germain-des-Prés ★★★**
After visiting the church (p. 144), cross the square to at least stroll by **Les Deux Magots ★** and the **Café de Flore ★** (p. 100), two legendary cafes that were the home base of Sartre and De Beauvoir and scores of other artists and intellectuals. The cafes are crowded and pricey for lunch, so here's another option:

Lunch at Marché St-Germain 🍴
If you wander a little further down boulevard St-Germain and take a right on rue Mabillon, you'll find yourself at the Marché St-Germain, a covered market that is half shops and half market stalls filled with delectable goodies. Either pick up the fixings for a picnic here, or try one of the dozens of restaurants that surround the market. A personal favorite is **Le P'tit Fernand** (p. 92).

Walk back out to boulevard St-Germain and turn right and continue to rue de l'Ancienne Comédie and turn left to Carrefour de Buci, then veer right on rue Dauphine and continue down to the Seine (admiring the galleries and antiques shops as you go). When you reach the river, cross the Pont Neuf.

3 Ile de la Cité ★★

Admire the view from the **Pont Neuf** ★ (p. 120) which straddles the island. Wander around the pretty **Place Dauphine** ★ (you'll find the entrance at the very tip of the island), and stroll along the quays of this island, which was once the center of Parisian life.

4 Notre-Dame ★★★

Visit the cathedral, and if you have the energy, climb the steps to the tower to take in yet another gorgeous view (and ogle some cute gargoyles). See p. 103.

Cross over to place du Châtelet. If you are tired, you can take the No. 7 Métro from here to Palais-Royal–Musée du Louvre. Otherwise, you can walk another 10 minutes or so down the Quai de la Mégisserie (past a row of pet stores) to the Louvre.

5 The Louvre ★★★

Spend what's left of the afternoon admiring the outsides of the buildings (save the museum for the next trip) and wandering through the **Tuileries Garden ★★★**. See p. 109.

Stroll west through the gardens until you arrive at the place de la Concorde.

6 Place de la Concorde ★★★

From this vantage point, you cannot only take in the place itself (p. 131), but also peer down the **Champs-Élysées ★★** and see the **Arc de Triomphe ★★★** (p. 125) in the distance.

If you still have energy in the evening, finish your visit with an **evening cruise** along the river (see "Boat Tours," p. 151), from which you can admire just about all of the above gussied up in elegant lighting effects.

ICONIC PARIS IN 2 DAYS

Now you have a little more space to breathe. This itinerary also starts at the Eiffel Tower, but then takes off in another direction. *Start: The Champs de Mars, 7th arrond, Métro: Ecole Militaire, RER: Champs de Mars–Tour Eiffel.*

Day 1

1 The Eiffel Tower ★★★

Go up directly to the second floor (the first one is closed); if you like thrills, visit the third as well. See p. 145.

Take the RER C to St-Michel–Notre Dame.

2 The Latin Quarter ★★★

Admire the Place St-Michel and the Boul' Mich (boulevard St-Michel) and try to imagine it all filled with long-haired students throwing *pavés* (paving stones) during the heady days of May 1968, when protesters brought the country to a standstill. Then wander up the boulevard and consider stopping in at the **Musée de Cluny ★★** (p. 141). After, continue up past the dome of **La Sorbonne** (one of France's oldest universities, founded in 1257) to the **Luxembourg Gardens ★★★** (p. 143). Either picnic here or settle down at a nearby table:

Paris Neighborhoods

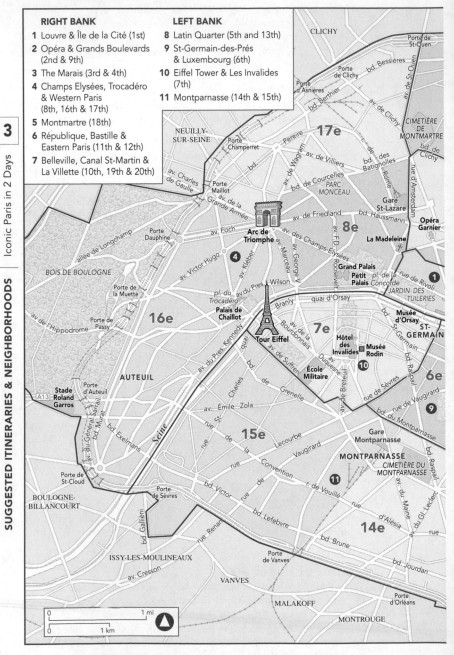

RIGHT BANK

1 Louvre & Île de la Cité (1st)
2 Opéra & Grands Boulevards (2nd & 9th)
3 The Marais (3rd & 4th)
4 Champs Elysées, Trocadéro & Western Paris (8th, 16th & 17th)
5 Montmartre (18th)
6 République, Bastille & Eastern Paris (11th & 12th)
7 Belleville, Canal St-Martin & La Villette (10th, 19th & 20th)

LEFT BANK

8 Latin Quarter (5th and 13th)
9 St-Germain-des-Prés & Luxembourg (6th)
10 Eiffel Tower & Les Invalides (7th)
11 Montparnasse (14th & 15th)

3

Iconic Paris in 2 Days

SUGGESTED ITINERARIES & NEIGHBORHOODS

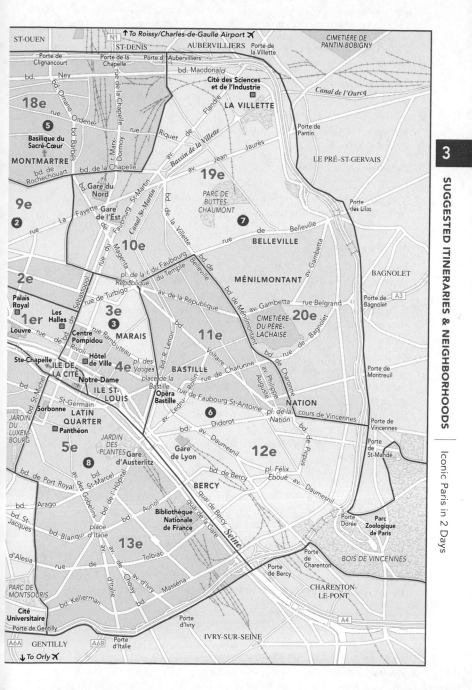

Lunch near the Luxembourg Gardens ☕

If it's a weekday and you are hungry, enjoy a terrific meal at **La Ferrandaise** (p. 91), about a block away. If you just want something light, and/or La Ferrandaise is closed, stop in for a *croque-monsieur* (a French version of a grilled cheese sandwich) or a salad at Le Rostand, a Belle Epoch cafe with a lovely terrace just across the street from the gardens (6 place Edmond Rostand, 6th arrond.; ℃ **01-43-54-61-58; RER: Luxembourg).

Either walk or hop on any bus going down boulevard St-Michel to the Ile de la Cité, get off at Cité–Palais de Justice.

3 Ste-Chapelle ★★★

Marvel at the kaleidoscope of colors in this tiny church's magnificent stained-glass windows.

Walk down rue de Lutèce and turn right on rue de la Cité.

4 Notre Dame ★★★

Visit the cathedral and if the line is not long and you are not too tired, climb the stairs to see the view from the towers.

Walk across the Pont d'Arcole to the Right Bank and the place de l'Hôtel de Ville.

5 The Marais ★★★

By now you deserve a break from cultural icons and are ready to shop or just sit in a cafe in this trendy—and beautiful—neighborhood. If you had the strength, you could visit one of the many museums here, but you probably don't, so save it for another day/trip. Around sunset, stop by **place des Vosges ★★★** (p. 124) for a pre-dinner *apéritif* before you hunt down a restaurant.

Day 2

1 The Louvre ★★★

Start your day as early as possible at this mega-museum, which should keep you going until at least lunchtime, when you can either call it quits or simply take a nice long break and eat at one of the restaurants recommended on p. 61–102. If you are in a hurry to get back to the artwork, there are two tasty sandwich counters under the pyramid. After the Louvre, you can recover in the **Tuileries Garden ★★★**.

Le Nemours ☕

If you are in need of refreshment after the Louvre (and who isn't?), this beautiful cafe on the Place Colette (right next to the Palais Royal) is an excellent choice. Great pastries too. See p. 102.

Stroll west through the gardens until you arrive at the place de la Concorde.

2 Place de la Concorde ★★★

From this grandiose plaza (p. 131), you can look down the **Champs-Élysées ★★** and see the **Arc de Triomphe ★★★** (p. 125) in the distance.

Take the bus no. 84 or 94, or Métro line 12 (direction Mairie d'Issy) to the 6th arrondissement.

3 St-Germain ★★★

End your day in this delightful neighborhood, where you can visit a church (**St-Germain-des-Prés**, p. 144; **St-Sulpice**, p. 145), check out famous cafes

(**Les Deux Magots,** p. 101, **Café de Flore,** p. 100), or shop 'til you drop. Then find a restaurant (p. 61), after which you can explore the nearby nightlife.

ICONIC PARIS IN 3 DAYS

Now that you've seen all the absolute must-sees, you have time to explore some of the great stuff you've missed. Here is a third day of discovery. *Start: Musée d'Orsay, Métro: Assemblée Nationale, RER: Musée d'Orsay.*

Day 3

1 Musée d'Orsay ★★★

Spend the morning enjoying this incredible collection of Impressionist paintings (p. 148), and then break for lunch at one of the museum's three restaurants (light snacks, chic cafeteria, or full-on Belle Epoque restaurant). If Impressionists aren't your thing, you could start the day at **Musée du Quai Branly ★★★** (p. 149).

Leave the museum and take the steps down to the banks of the Seine. If you are starting from Musée d'Orsay, turn left (west); if you are coming from Musée du Quai Branly, turn right (east).

2 Les Berges ★★★

Weather willing, enjoy the newly restored riverbanks (see sidebar on p. 155), strolling westward. Once a busy roadway, this embankment is now a delight for pedestrians with floating gardens, running lanes, and gourmet snack bars (May–Oct only).

At the Pont des Invalides, go up the stairs and admire the winged horses hovering above before going down into the Métro and taking line 13 (direction Asnières or St-Denis) and changing to line 12 (direction Porte de la Chapelle) at Gare St-Lazare. Get off at place des Abbesses. Take the elevator up (don't get smart and take the stairs, it's a looong way up).

3 Montmartre ★★★

While away the rest of the afternoon on top of this scenic hill ("La Butte"), clambering around the cobbled streets and perhaps taking a walking tour (p. 160). If your feet have had enough, take the **Montmartrobus,** a small bus run by the transit authority that will take you all over the Butte with a regular bus ticket (for a route map, go to www.ratp.fr). Visit the **Musée de Montmartre** (p. 132) to find out more about the artists and poets who made this neighborhood famous. Around sunset, take in the panorama in front of the **Sacré Coeur,** and bid adieu to Paris with a drink at one of the cafes on **place des Abbesses.**

AN ITINERARY FOR FAMILIES

Paris can be a challenge with kids and parents may be frustrated because there are so many wonderful grown-up things to see. The trick is to admit to yourself that you just won't see as much as you'd like to, and schedule lots of playtime. In the end, everyone will be less stressed out and happier, even if you didn't get to see all 14 of those museums you had planned to see.

Day 1

Spend the morning at the **Luxembourg Gardens,** where your offspring can go wild at the huge **playground, sail boats** in the fountain, **ride a pony,** or just run around and have fun. Depending on your situation, parents can take turns sneaking off to visit nearby attractions, like the **Panthéon, Musée Zadkine,** and **St-Etienne-du-Mont,** or find peace and quiet in a **Latin Quarter** cafe. Then walk down to **St-Germain-des-Prés** (p. 144) and peek into the church before lunching at **Le Relais de l'Entrecôte** (p. 92). After lunch, walk back up to **St-Sulpice** (p. 145) and catch the no. 87 bus to the **Champs de Mars,** where you will visit the **Eiffel Tower** (p. 145). After that, everyone will be pooped. Thankfully, the **boat ride on the Seine** leaves right down by the river.

Day 2

Start your day at the **Jardin des Plantes** (p. 137), where you can choose between the **Museum National d'Histoire Naturelle** (p. 140), the **Ménagerie** (a small zoo; p. 140), and the **playground.** There's also a fun boxwood **labyrinth** at the top of a little hill. Lunch at the nearby **Mosquée de Paris** (p. 99), a lovely tearoom attached to the Paris Mosque with an outdoor enclosed patio. If there are science geeks in your crew, head to the **Musée des Arts et Métiers** (p. 124) after lunch. Otherwise spend the afternoon at the **Palais de Tokyo** (p. 130), a contemporary art museum that is so wacky both kids and parents are sure to have a blast.

Day 3

Kids may not appreciate the view at **Sacré Coeur** (p. 131), but they will enjoy the ride in the **funicular** that you take to get there (follow the signs from the Abbesses Métro stop). Once you are up there, there is plenty of space to run around on the esplanade, and lots of buskers for entertainment. After toodling around Montmartre, grab a bite to eat at **Milk** (p. 80), a kid-friendly tearoom just south of the basilica. After lunch, wander around the **covered passages** off the Grands Boulevards (see "Arcadia," p. 173), where you can window shop without worrying about anyone running off into the street, and reward everyone's good behavior with a visit to **Grévin,** a fun wax museum just off the Passage Jouffroy. If everyone is still in a good mood, take the number 4 Métro all the way back to Cité and for an early evening visit to **Notre-Dame,** when the crowds will have thinned.

PARIS FOR ROMANTICS

Paris must be the honeymoon capital of the world, and for good reason—it seems like every time you turn a corner you see something (or someone) beautiful. Here is a 2-day itinerary for a romantic getaway, or for just for hopeless romantics. *Start: Pont Neuf, in front of the statue of Henri IV.*

Day 1

This itinerary starts in front of a statue of one of France's great romantic kings, Henri IV, who was known for his good humor and love of wine, women, and song (among other things). Walk down the steps to the pretty **Square du Vert Galant,** a quiet garden at the very tip of the island where you can contemplate the fantastic view and/or make out without anyone bothering you (in general, make-out sessions are well tolerated, and even applauded, in public parks here). From here, you can walk to the **Louvre** (p. 112) and take in endless representations of people in love, from all eras. If you can afford it, splurge on lunch at **Le Grand Véfour** (p. 64), a gourmet restaurant in the **Palais Royal** (p. 115) with a magnificent 18th-century decor. If you are on a tight budget, a nice picnic in the **Tuileries Garden** (p. 109) should do the trick. After lunch, drift over to the **Place Vendôme** (p. 115) to look at the high-end jewelry displays. Then wander over to the **Place de la Concorde** (p. 131), and stroll up the **Champs-Élysées.** At this point, you'll be in need of refreshment, so you can stop into **Ladurée** (p. 99) for tea and *macarons.* Now it's time to think about dinner. You could opt for either elegant tapas at **Pinxo** (p. 68) or more affordable fusion food at **Le Fumoir** (p. 65). As the night falls, the obligatory romantic stroll is on the **Pont des Arts** (p. 120), where hundreds of fellow romantics attach locks inscribed with their loved one's name, and throw the key in the Seine.

Day 2

After sleeping in, start your day with a late breakfast at **Le Petit Cler** (p. 96), an adorable cafe on rue Cler. After, mosey over to the **Musée Rodin** (p. 149), where you can contemplate, and even imitate, Rodin's famous marble sculpture, "The Kiss." Be sure to amble about the beautiful gardens after the museum. If it's nice out, grab a **Velib'** (p. 226) and cycle down to the recently **remodeled banks of the Seine** (p. 155) where you can cycle or stroll free and easy by the river below the Quai d'Orsay. If the weather is bad, take the no. 13 Métro up to Miromesnil and have tea at the beautiful **tearoom at the Musée Jacquemart-André** (p. 98). If you are up for it, visit the museum after (p. 128). Otherwise, it's time to start thinking about the evening's activities. A true romantic will have bought tickets to something at the **Palais Garnier** (p. 118) but others will be just fine with **La Bellevilloise** (p. 198), where you can eat, drink, and dance.

CITY LAYOUT

One of the nice things about Paris is that it's relatively small. It's not a sprawling megalopolis like Tokyo or London. Paris *intramuros,* or inside the long-gone city walls, measures about 87 sq. km (34 sq. miles) excluding the large exterior parks of Bois de Vincinnes and the Bois de Boulogne and counts a mere 2.2 million habitants. The suburbs, on the other hand, are sprawling.

Getting around is not difficult, provided you have a general sense of where things are. The city is vaguely egg shaped, with the Seine cutting a wide upside-down "U" shaped arc through the middle. The northern half is known as the **Right Bank,** and the southern, the **Left Bank.** To the uninitiated, the only way to remember is to face west, or downstream, so that the Right Bank will be to your right, and the Left to your left.

The city is neatly split up into 20 official ***arrondissements*** or districts, which spiral out from the center of the city. The lower the number of the arrondissement, the closer you'll be to the center. As the numbers go up, you'll head toward the outer city limits. The lower numbered arrondissements also correspond to some of the oldest parts of the city, like the Louvre and the Ile de la Cité (1st arrondissement), or the Marais (3rd and 4th arrondissements). Note that the arrondissements don't always correspond to historical neighborhoods.

Even if you're only in the city for a week, it's worthwhile to invest in a purse-size map book (ask for a "Paris par Arrondissement" at bookstores or larger newsstands), which costs around 8€. The book should include a street index and a detailed set of maps by arrondissement—one of the best is called "Le Petit Parisien," which includes separate Métro, bus, and street maps for each district. To get a general sense of where the arrondissements are, see the map on the inside front cover of this book.

Paris is old, so the logic of its **streets and avenues** is often as contorted as the city's history. That said, there are some major boulevards that function as reference points. On the Left Bank, boulevard St-Michel acts as a more or less north–south axis, with boulevard St-Germain cutting a vaguely east–west semicircle close to the city center and boulevard Montparnasse cutting a larger one farther out. On the Right Bank, boulevard de Sebastopol runs north–south, with rue de Rivoli crossing east–west near the river. As rue de Rivoli heads east, it turns into rue de St-Antoine; to the west, it jogs around the place de la Concorde and becomes the Champs-Élysées. Farther north, a network of wide boulevards crisscrosses the area, including boulevards Haussmann, Capuccines, and Lafayette.

There are also several enormous star-shaped traffic roundabouts, where several large avenues converge: On the Left Bank place Denfert-Rochereau and place d'Italie are major convergence points; on the Right Bank place de la Bastille and place de la République reign to the east, and place de Charles de Gaulle (also called Etoile), home of the Arc de Triomphe, commands to the west.

NEIGHBORHOODS IN BRIEF

Paris is a city for walkers. One lovely neighborhood after another unfolds along its sidewalks, punctuated by plazas and monuments that are best experienced at ground-level. At every turn there seems to be an intriguing area that begs to be explored.

The Right Bank
LOUVRE & ILE DE LA CITE (1ST ARRONDISSEMENT)

Best for: Museums, historic sights, architecture, transportation hubs

What you won't find: Evening entertainment, quiet streets

This is the heart of the city, and the oldest part of Paris, though you'd never know it to see it now. In the 19th century, Baron Haussmann, Napoleon's energetic urban planner, tore down almost all of the medieval houses that once covered this area. **The Ile de la Cité** is where the city first emerged after Gallic tribes started camping out here in the 3rd century B.C. By the 1st century A.D., the Romans were building temples, and by the Middle Ages, a mighty fortress sat across the river on the Right Bank. The fortress has long since been incorporated into the majestic buildings of the **Louvre,** which along with the **Jardin des Tuileries** takes up a big chunk of the neighborhood. Today, the Ile is mostly visited for the soaring **Cathedral of Notre Dame** and the gemlike **St-Chapelle,** along with the historic **Conciergerie.** *Note:* To avoid confusion, I've included the entire Ile de la Cité in this section, even though the eastern half is technically in the 4th arrondissement.

While the major museums and sites are to the west, the people's part of this neighborhood is on its eastern edge, near **Les Halles** and **place du Châtelet.** Stuffed with stores, particularly along the bustling **rue de Rivoli** and around the **Forum des Halles** (which is still open despite the massive remodeling job going on above), Parisians descend on this area for their shopping needs. While the spooky gardens are currently

Baron Haussmann: A Man with a Plan

The Paris you see before you was radically transformed in the late 19th century by a pugnacious urban planner named Georges-Eugène Haussmann. Before Haussmann got his hands on it, Paris was a mostly medieval city of tiny streets and narrow alleyways—and major sanitation problems. Everyone agreed that something needed to be done to facilitate traffic and clean up the city, but no one managed to come up with a solution. Enter Baron Haussmann. Named prefect of the Seine by Napoleon III, Haussmann pushed through wide boulevards (Malsherbes, Haussmann, and Sebastapol, among others), demolished dozens of old neighborhoods, and encouraged promoters to build new buildings, following, of course, his strict rules on the style of the facades and the height of the structures. The result was the elegant "Haussmannian" architecture that lines most of the city's streets, as well as

the system of central arteries that collect in star-shaped intersections at various strategic points. The boulevards were strategically placed—one of the reasons for their creation was to make it easier to crush rebellions in the worker's quarters, and garrisons were set up at crucial intersections. Streets were also now too wide in most areas to be easily barricaded. Haussmann also accessorized his new neighborhoods and streets; the famous kiosks, benches, and lampposts you'll see around the city also date from this epoch. While there's no denying his projects improved traffic, sanitation, and security and gave a pleasing architectural unity to the cityscape, Haussmann's take-no-prisoners approach has been criticized for having neutered the personality of entire neighborhoods (the Ile de la Cité, for example, was almost entirely razed) and destroying important historical buildings.

closed, Les Halles is still not the safest area and it's worth avoiding at night. The same is true of the seedy rue St-Denis, just to the east, as this is one of Paris's red-light districts.

OPERA & GRANDS BOULEVARDS (2ND & 9TH ARRONDISSEMENTS)

Best for: Good restaurants, covered passages, boutiques

What you won't find: Major monuments and museums, green spaces

When the Grands Boulevards were plowed through the city in the 19th century (see box above), they created a new opportunity for stylish Parisians to stroll, see, and be seen, while theaters and cafes flourished. Times changed and so did fashion, and for decades this area was considered a has-been. In recent years, the area has undergone a transformation, particularly in the 9th arrondissement, where cafes, boutiques, and restaurants have popped up in between the church of St-Georges and place Clichy, in an area that used to be known as "New Athens." Many artists of the 19th-century Romantic movement, like George Sand and Eugène Delacroix, lived and worked here. The 9th is also the home of the **Grand Magasins** (big-name department stores), which are located on boulevard Haussmann near Gare St-Lazare, as well as the grandiose **Palais Garnier,** home of the Opéra de Paris. You'll notice lots of men and women bustling about in business suits in the 2nd arrondissement, which is the home of the **Bourse,** the French stock exchange. To the east, the trendy set descends on **rue**

Montorgueil, a picturesque, cobbled market street, and the pedestrian area around **rue Etienne Marcel,** which has gained a reputation as a hip fashion district. This also is the arrondissement with the greatest concentration of *passages,* **19th-century covered shopping arcades** that were the forefathers of today's shopping malls (but much prettier; see "Arcadia," p. 173).

THE MARAIS (3RD & 4TH ARRONDISSEMENTS)

Best for: Restaurants, nightlife, window shopping, 17th-century mansions, museums

What you won't find: Bargain shopping, iconic sights, open spaces

What was once marshy farmland (*marais* means "marsh" or "swamp") quickly became a seat of power when the Knights Templar decided to build a fortress here in the Middle Ages. Other religious orders followed suit, and after King Charles V decided to build a royal residence here in the 14th century, there was a real-estate boom that produced a slew of mansions and palaces. In the 17th century, King Henri IV created a magnificent square bordered by Renaissance-style townhouses, today called the **place des Vosges.** If the Marais was hot before, then it was positively on fire. Nobles and bourgeois pounced on the neighborhood, each one trying to outdo the other by constructing more and more resplendent *hôtels particuliers,* or private mansions.

The overstuffed quarter was already falling out of fashion by the time the Revolution flushed out all its aristocrats in the 18th century. The magnificent dwellings were abandoned, pillaged, partitioned, and turned into stores, workshops, and even factories. The new residents were working class, with more immediate concerns than saving historic patrimony. The neighborhood fell into disrepair, and unfortunately periodic attempts on the part of the city to "clean up" resulted in the destruction of many architectural gems.

The area underwent a real renovation in the 1960s, and today several of the most **magnificent mansions** have been restored and are open to the public in the form of museums like the **Carnavalet, Musée Cognac-Jay,** and the **Musée Picasso.** The architecturally odd **Centre Pompidou** is also located here.

Today the area is terribly *branché* (literally, "plugged in"), and you'll see some of the hippest styles in boutique windows here, as well as dozens of happening restaurants and bars lining its narrow streets. The neighborhood is still a mix though—jewelry and clothing wholesalers bump up against stylish cafes and shops. The vibrant gay scene on rue Vielle du Temple intersects with what's left of the old Jewish quarter on **rue des Rosiers.**

CHAMPS-ÉLYSÉES, TROCADÉRO & WESTERN PARIS (8TH, 16TH & 17TH ARRONDISSEMENTS)

Best for: Serious strolling (on the Champs-Élysées), museums, monuments, chic restaurants and stores

What you won't find here: Affordable eateries or hotels, regular folk

The **Champs-Élysées** cuts through this area like an asphalt river—it's the widest boulevard in Paris. Crossing the street here feels a bit like traversing a raging torrent (be sure to wait for the light). There are fans and foes of this epic roadway. Some find its lights and sparkles good clean fun, while others find it crass and commercial. However you feel about the street itself, you're bound to be impressed by the **Arc de Triomphe,** which lords over the boulevard from its western tip. To the south of the Champs are some of the most expensive stores, restaurants, and homes in the city (particularly around Ave. Montaigne). To the north, a largely residential area extends up to the beautiful **Parc Monceau,** which is surrounded by some equally delightful museums, like the **Musée Jacquemart-Andrée** and the **Musée Nissim de Camondo.**

To the west, the illustrious Seizième (sez-ee-*em,* sixteenth), is the most exclusive arrondissement of the city. Laying on the outer western edge of the city, this residential area is packed with magnificent 19th-century residences and apartment houses, as well as many fine parks and gardens. In fact, the arrondissement shares its western border with the **Bois de Boulogne,** one of the city's two huge wooded parks. While the 16th might be pretty dull on the whole, it's also graced with a terrific array of museums. The **Palais de Chaillot** shelters the **Cité de l'Architecture,** just down the street is the vast **Musée Guimet,** and a little farther on there are two modern art museums in the **Palais de Tokyo,** not to mention a half a dozen others (like the **Marmottan** and the **Baccarat**) sprinkled around the arrondissement. And a stop at the esplanade on the **place du Trocadéro** is a must. Between the two wings of the Palais de Chaillot is a superb **view** of the Eiffel Tower, which you can walk to by strolling down the hill through the **Jardins du Trocadéro.**

MONTMARTRE (18TH ARRONDISSEMENT)
Best for: Restaurants, nightlife, atmosphere

What you won't find here: Monuments (with the exception of Sacré-Coeur), major museums, grand architecture

Once a village overlooking the distant city, Montmartre is now as inseparable from Paris as the Eiffel Tower, which means it's a major target for the tour-bus crowd. And crowded it is, especially in the area immediately around the **Basilica of Sacré-Coeur** and the overdone **place du Tertre.** Yet, Montmartre is also home to an increasingly hip crowd, who stick to the more authentic area around the **place des Abbesses.** The narrow cobbled streets that climb past the two remaining **windmills** are peppered with boutiques and cute restaurants frequented by a cool combo of young professionals and budding artists.

In the east of the 18th is the lively immigrant quarter of **Barbès,** which is home to large communities from Africa, India, and the Maghreb (North Africa). Here you'll find a jumble of inexpensive stores selling everything from long-necked teapots to pajama-like salwar trousers, as well as tiny restaurants that offer exotic delicacies.

RÉPUBLIQUE, BASTILLE & EASTERN PARIS (11TH & 12TH ARRONDISSEMENTS)
Best for: Nightlife, good restaurants, Revolutionary history, arty boutiques

What you won't find here: Major monuments and museums, high-end shops

These two arrondissements were pretty much off the tourist radar until 1989, when the new **Bastille opera house** provoked an explosion of bars and restaurants in the surrounding streets. Though the shine has already worn off the **nightspots** of rue de Lappe and rue de la Roquette, just off the place de la Bastille, the nocturnal life of the 11th arrondissement is far from dull, as new clubs and cafes have opened further north on rue de Charonne and **rue Oberkampf.** Now even Oberkampf has become thoroughly saturated, and intrepid partiers are staking out new ground in Menilmontant in the 20th.

North of the **place de la Bastille** is the vast pedestrian-friendly **place de la République.** To the south is the Faubourg St-Antoine, a historic workers' quarter that has been inhabited by woodworkers and furniture makers since the 13th century. After a few centuries the density of underpaid, overburdened workers made St-Antoine a breeding ground for revolutionaries. The raging mob that stormed the Bastille prison in 1789 originated here, as did those of the subsequent uprisings of 1830, 1848, and the Paris commune.

Today, aside from the shops and night life on rue de Charonne and Oberkampf, this area is relatively mellow. While the architecture here is nowhere near as grand as elsewhere in Paris, the neighborhood has retained an authenticity that's rarely found in the more popular parts of the city. There are still a large number of furniture stores and *ébénistes* (woodworkers) tucked into large interior courtyards accessible by covered passages off rue du Faubourg St-Antoine. Make a point of wandering down one of these; you'll be rewarded with a look at a way of life that has survived the centuries. This quarter extends all the way past the **Viaduc des Arts** to the **Gare de Lyon** train station, a magnificent example of Belle Epoque architecture. At the western end is the **Bois de Vincennes,** one of the city's two wooded parks.

BELLEVILLE, CANAL ST-MARTIN & NORTHEAST PARIS (10TH, 19TH & 20TH ARRONDISSEMENTS)

Best for: Nightlife, restaurants, strolling (along the Canal), arty boutiques

What you won't find here: Major monuments, museums, and architectural wonders

For a long time, no one seemed to care about these arrondissements. They were too far from the center of the city, too working-class to be of interest to the trendy set, and too monument-less to appeal to tourists. Then, with real estate skyrocketing, young professionals and artists began to move in. Suddenly, the forgotten **Canal St-Martin** was blooming with cafes and restaurants and the streets around it were full of trendy shops. Artists looking for studio space discovered multi-ethnic **Belleville,** a cultural melting pot of immigrants from North Africa (both Jewish and Muslim), Asia (this is Paris's biggest Chinatown), and other parts of the world. The vast park and cultural venues of **La Villette** have also attracted new interest away from the center. Happily, these areas aren't gentrified (yet) and parts are infused with a certain youthful energy that's hard to come by in other areas of the city. These areas are relatively tourist-free and offer an opportunity to see a more local side of the city.

Aside from the **Parc de la Villette,** there are two other green havens here: the **Parc des Buttes Chaumont** and the **Père-Lachaise Cemetery,** where the likes of Jim Morrison, Edith Piaf, and Chopin are buried. There are also several good bars and music venues around **Menilmontant** to the north of the cemetery and around **place St-Blaise** to the south.

The Left Bank

LATIN QUARTER (5TH ARRONDISSEMENT)

Best for: Affordable dining, student bars, art house movie theaters, museums, Jardin des Plantes

What you won't find here: Good shopping, quiet (at least not in the environs of place St-Michel)

Since the Middle Ages, when the **Sorbonne** and other academic institutions were founded, this has been a student neighborhood. (It earned its name as the "Latin" Quarter because back in the old days, all classes were taught in Latin.) Today the area still harbors the highest number of colleges and universities in the city, and you'll certainly see plenty of students and professors hanging around the inexpensive restaurants and cafes around here. You'll also see plenty of tourists, who tend to swarm around the warren of tiny streets that lead off of the place St-Michel. Avoid Rue de la

Huchette (except for the great swing-dancing club, **Le Caveau de la Huchette**), which is lined with garish restaurants of questionable quality. **Boulevard St-Michel,** a legendary artery that once was lined with smoky cafes filled with thinkers and rabble-rousers, has now fallen prey to chain stores, though a few big bookstores have held on. The boulevard also harbors the **Musée de Cluny,** a terrific collection of medieval art and Roman ruins.

For a more authentic taste of this neighborhood, wander east and upward, around the windy streets on the hill that leads to the **Panthéon,** the church of **St-Etienne-du-Mont** and around rue Monge, toward lovely the **Jardin des Plantes.** Surrounded by the city's **natural history museum,** this botanical garden is a lovely place to relax. Down by the Seine, the **Institut du Monde Arabe** is a fascinating museum housed in a spectacular building by architect Jean Nouvel.

ST-GERMAIN-DES-PRÉS & LUXEMBOURG (6TH ARRONDISSEMENT)

Best for: Fine dining, historic cafes, shopping, parks (the Jardin du Luxembourg)

What you won't find here: Penniless intellectuals and artists, low prices

The church of St-Germain-des-Prés, the heart of this neighborhood, got its name (St. Germain of the Fields) because when it was built in the 11th century, it was in the middle of the countryside. What a difference a millennium makes. The church became the nucleus of a huge and powerful abbey, which would later constitute an autonomous minacity complete with a hospital and a prison. The Revolution cut the church down to its current size, and an elegant collection of apartment houses, squares, and parks grew up around it, making it one of Paris's most appealing areas to live in (as real-estate prices will attest). If the neighborhood has always had aristocratic airs (it was a favorite haunt of the nobility during the 17th and 18th c.), during the last part of the 19th century up to the mid–20th century it was also a magnet for penniless artists and intellectuals, who hung out in legendary cafes like the **Café de Flore** and **Les Deux Magots.**

Today few struggling creative types can afford either the rents or the price of a cup of coffee around here, and young artists and thinkers have moved north and east to cheaper parts of town. Though the ambiance is decidedly bourgeois these days, the neighborhood is still dynamic, and the cafes and shops along the boulevard St-Germain are crowded with a mix of politicians, gallery owners, and editors. This is also a fun neighborhood for shopping—there's everything here from 500€ pumps on chic rue des St-Pères to 20€ sundresses on the more plebian rue des Rennes. And when you've tired yourself out, you can stroll over to the magnificent **Jardin du Luxembourg** for a timeout by the fountain.

EIFFEL TOWER & LES INVALIDES (7TH ARRONDISSEMENT)

Best for: Iconic monuments, majestic avenues, grand vistas, museums

What you won't find here: Affordable restaurants or shopping, nightlife

The **Eiffel Tower** reigns over this swanky arrondissement, where the streets that aren't lined with ministries and embassies are filled with elegant apartment buildings and prohibitively expensive stores and restaurants. A large portion of the neighborhood is taken up by the **Champs de Mars,** a park that stretches between the tower and the **Ecole Militaire,** and by the enormous esplanade in front of the **Invalides,** which sweeps down to the Seine with much pomp and circumstance. Some of the city's best museums are around here, including the **Musée d'Orsay,** the **Musée Rodin,** and the

Musée du Quai Branly, whose wacky architecture has added some spice to this very staid area.

While there's certainly a lot to see here, the neighborhood is a little short on human warmth—this is not the place to come to see regular Parisians in their natural habitat. One exception is the area around the pedestrian **rue Cler,** a market street that is home to many delightful small restaurants and food stores. Word is out about this cozy corner, however, so expect to see plenty of tourists when you go into that cute *boulangerie* for a couple of croissants.

MONTPARNASSE (14TH & 15TH ARRONDISSEMENTS)

Best for: Shopping, historic cafes, nightlife

What you won't find here: Extraordinary architecture, museums, monuments

In the early 1970s, government officials decided the time had come to make Paris a modern city. Blithely putting aside concerns for historic patrimony and architectural harmony, the old Montparnasse train station and its immediate neighborhood were torn down and a 58-story glass tower and shopping complex was erected in its place. A new train station was constructed behind the tower, as well as a barrage of modern apartment buildings and office blocks. Fortunately, even ugly contemporary architecture didn't manage to kill the neighborhood—at the foot of the **Tour Montparnasse,** life goes on as it always has. A few steps away from the station, tiny old streets are still lined with stores, cafes, and *crêperies* (crêpe restaurants), these last being an outgrowth of the large Breton (that is, from Brittany) community that still inhabits this area. Farther down boulevard Montparnasse, you'll find legendary brasseries like **La Coupole** and **Le Select,** where Picasso, Max Jacob, and Henry Miller used to hang out in the 1920s. For a bit of calm, take a walk around the **Cimetiére de Montparnasse,** where artists like Charles Baudelaire and Constantin Brancusi are buried, as well as Colonel Alfred Dreyfus. In the evenings, crowds pour into the many movie theaters around the station, as well as the many restaurants in the area.

To the south, the arrondissement takes a more residential turn, with the exception of rue Daguerre, a lively market street a block south of the cemetery, and farther south, rue d'Alésia, a discount shopper's mecca.

WHERE TO STAY

There are more than 1,500 hotels in Paris, from palaces fit for a pasha to tiny family-run operations whose best features are their warm welcome and personal touch. In theory, you should be able to find something in line with your budget, your timeframe, and your personal tastes. But if you can't find the hotel of your dreams in the list below, don't despair—at the end of this chapter I list alternative lodging options, like bed and breakfasts and short-term apartment rentals.

WHAT TO EXPECT

Parisian lodgings can be many things: charming, opulent, cozy, homey, and even outrageous. But keep in mind the following: **Parisian hotel rooms tend to be small.** Why do I stress this? Because inevitably, tourists who come from countries where hotel rooms are often staggeringly big (does anyone actually need two king-size beds in a double room?) are shocked when they check in to tiny, family hotels in ancient buildings. And its not just budget lodgings—even nifty boutique hotels can have snug rooms. After weathering years of complaints, many Parisian hotel owners are convinced that all Americans have bedrooms the size of the Astrodome.

Don't be too hard on the management; most historic Parisian buildings are protected by city regulations that make it difficult, if not impossible, to make structural changes. If you absolutely need room to stretch out, ask for a triple, or even a quadruple room (if they're available). Otherwise, consider an international chain hotel, where space and extra amenities are usually not a problem.

Amenities

Unless you are staying in a hotel in our "expensive" category, you should be prepared for **minimal amenities.** Washcloths are scarce, toiletries are few, and a few of the smaller hotels still don't have elevators (and when they do, they're often closet size). Assume that most guest rooms are large enough to live in comfortably, but not spacious enough to do yoga. All of the rooms in the hotels listed below have in-room bathrooms with toilets, unless otherwise mentioned.

Now that I've prepared you for the worst, let me tell you what Parisian hotels do have (besides charm and personality, *bien sûr*). Almost all have in-room TVs with cable channels, telephones, and hair dryers in the bathrooms. Irons, fax machines, and hair dryers (if they are not in the room) can usually be found at the reception desk. Almost all have hotel-wide Wi-Fi.

Most hotel rooms have air-conditioning. That said, since normal Parisian weather is anything but tropical—June and July can be sweater weather—your chances of encountering sweltering heat are low. Still, if

Though the listings below show room rates for two people, single rooms are often available for solo travelers at reduced rates. The best tactic is to ask the hotel directly, as they don't always advertise their smallest rooms, even on their own websites. While some singles are comparable to a regular double, others might be tiny, and the toilet facilities may be on the landing.

Parisian Hotels & Accessibility

Hotels in centuries-old buildings may be full of charm, but they also often feature narrow staircases and/or tiny elevators, so if accessibility is a concern, be sure to check when you reserve. Parisian hotels are evolving: Most hotels in the moderate and expensive categories now have at least one wheelchair-accessible room.

4

WHERE TO STAY | Practical Matters

you're coming in the summer months, check; you may want to think twice about taking a room on a non-air-conditioned top floor or facing a noisy street that makes it impossible to open the windows at night.

While a continental **breakfast** (juice, coffee, or tea, and a croissant and/or baguette) is still the standard, many hotels now offer a more generous morning meal that may include yogurt, ham, cereal, juice, and sometimes even eggs and bacon. If you are planning on eating breakfast at the hotel, find out what it includes, because you could end up paying up to 9€ for an uninspired continental breakfast, when you could have paid less and had more fun munching on a croissant on a sidewalk terrace at a cafe. On the other hand, romantics will appreciate the fact that at most hotels, you can have your breakfast delivered to your room for no extra charge.

PRACTICAL MATTERS
When to Reserve

Paris is one of the world's top travel destinations, and hotels book up fast. Even during what should be a slow month, the city might be completely booked up because of a trade show or festival that you are not aware of.

Make sure you understand the cancellation policy—most hotels take at least 1 night's stay as a deposit, which they will keep if you don't show up. What's more, cancellation policies vary depending on what type of rate or package you end up with. Read the fine print: In some cases you have to cancel as much as 5 days in advance in order not to lose the deposit.

High & Low Season

Parisian hotel rate fluctuations are a little like the weather—it's difficult to distinguish one season from the other. Everyone seems to agree that August is the lowest of low season. That's when most of France heads for the beach, and hotels are desperate for business. The rest of the year is a free-for-all, heavily dependent on the scheduling of tradeshows. For the nitty-gritty on trade show dates, visit www.salons-online .com and search for "Paris," but in general, September and October are usually high

GETTING THE best rate

In recent years, the quest for a good room rate has become a challenge equal to that of hunting for airfare bargains. Prices on hotel and aggregator websites vary radically from day to day, depending on availability, season, and the vagaries of the market. Many of the hotels listed here have rates that vary by as much as 50% depending on when you book and how far in advance. Some even offer further reductions for non-refundable bookings.

While online travel booking sites like Expedia, Priceline, and booking.com may offer considerable discounts on room rates, often the best place to look is the hotel's official website, particularly in the case of smaller, affordable hotels. Why? Those aggregator sites charge hotels fees as much as 20%, a percentage that many hotels feel obliged to pass on to the customer. Smaller establishments can afford to be more generous on their own websites. Some hotels listed below have simply refused to jump on the Internet booking bandwagon, both for financial and moral reasons:

They don't feel the random rate hikes are fair (and fear scaring away their return customers). But for most hotels, Internet surfing to find affordable prices.

The up side is that if you are willing to do a bit of legwork, there are some great deals to be had, especially for properties in the higher price range. A nice boutique hotel that you thought was completely out of your budget might have rates that are not so different from middle or even low-price lodgings—if you reserve several months in advance or happen on a seasonal promotion. Many hotels offer discounts for stays of over 3 nights; if they don't offer one up front, it's worth asking.

Perpetually fluctuating prices make it difficult to fix rates in guidebooks; the prices quoted here attempt to offer a realistic range, with the top price reflecting the rack rate (maximum "official" rate) and the lower figure corresponding to the average discount Internet rate. **Note:** Rates almost never include breakfast.

Seeing Stars

French hotels are graded by a government-regulated system that hands out 0 to 5 stars, which the hotels then must post at the entrance to their establishment. Unfortunately, the criteria used often has more to do with quantity than quality. Rooms are rated on things like size, number of beds, and the presence or absence of items like hair dryers and minibars—overall atmosphere and charm are not necessarily a factor. So it's possible to end up in a darling two-star hotel that's much nicer than a three-star down the

street with big rooms and a minibar with all the ambience of a rehab center. What's more, the recent addition of a fifth star prompted everyone to try to jump up a notch, so the most basic hotel might now have three stars. One thing is sure, the more stars it has, the more a hotel is allowed to charge. My advice: Use the French star system as a rough estimate of quality, then do some homework on your own. By the way, the stars besides the listings below are our own, and have no relation to the French star system.

season, while November, December, and January are low season (except for Christmas and New Year's). Once spring arrives, prices tend to rise.

price CATEGORIES

Expensive	300€–500€
Moderate	150€–300€
Inexpensive	Under 150€

THE RIGHT BANK

Louvre & Ile de la Cité (1st Arrondissement)

It was here that Paris began, and it is here that you will still find a great number of the city's most famous sites—and the highest concentration of tourists. The area surrounding the Louvre is littered with hotels, most of which are dreadfully overpriced. Even modest budget hotels, with no visible amenities or charm, charge high prices and get away with it because many visitors are convinced that this neighborhood is the best spot to set up camp. Admittedly, if you only are in town for 1 or 2 days, a central locale is key, since time will be of the essence. But if you have a little more time, you'll find much more comfortable lodgings, at lower prices, a 10-minute walk away.

EXPENSIVE

Hotel Brighton ★★★   Did someone say "view"? How about a panorama of the Louvre and the Tuileries gardens from your bed? Or maybe a glimpse of the Eiffel Tower looming above it all? While not every room in this gracious hotel has the jackpot view, those in the "deluxe" and "executive" categories do, and all have a subdued, classic decor with elegant fabrics draping the windows and tasteful decorative touches. In short, this classy establishment belongs under the arcades of the rue de Rivoli, and if it is not quite as grand as the Meurice (just down the block), it is also about one-third the price. Rooms are spacious and airy, with reproduction and real antiques and roomy bathrooms. Understandably, those with views book up early.

218 rue de Rivoli, 1st arrond. ℰ **01-47-03-61-61.** www.hotel-britannique.com. 61 units. 239€–450€ double; 399€–460€ suite. Métro: Tuileries. **Amenities:** Bar, concierge, laundry service, room service, Wi-Fi (free).

MODERATE

Hôtel Britannique ★★   When you step into the salon off the lobby here, you'll be tempted to immediately throw yourself into one of the plush armchairs and order a cup of tea. Decidedly British in decor and atmosphere, these lodgings are located on a remarkably quiet street, considering it is about a minute away from the busy Place du Châtelet. The immaculate, soundproofed rooms are comfortably and conservatively furnished, with gentle swags of drapery hanging over the bed and windows. Rooms facing the street are the most pleasant, with large windows that offer views of the Théâtre du Châtelet across the street; rooms on the courtyard are larger though, and can be made into triples. There are adjoining rooms for families and one suite that sleeps four. A good value, considering the quality of the lodgings and the central location.

20 ave. Victoria, 1st arrond. ℰ **01-42-33-74-59.** www.hotel-britannique.fr. 39 units. 190€–266€ double; 335€–394€ for suite 2 to 4 people. Métro: Châtelet. **Amenities:** Bar, room service after 6pm, Wi-Fi (free).

Hôtel Thérèse ★★★ Just a few steps from the Palais Royal and a few more from the Louvre, these recently overhauled lodgings combine old-fashioned Parisian charm with modern Parisian chic. Soft grey/teal blues highlight a creative decor that complements the building's history instead of clashing with it. Comfy sofas invite you to relax in the lobby, whose stylish decor includes lots of mirrors, bookcases, and unique lighting fixtures. The comfort factor extends to the rooms, many of which have very high ceilings, interesting drapery fabrics, and upholstered headboards.

5–7 rue Thérèse, 1st arrond. ℰ **01-42-96-10-01.** www.hoteltherese.com. 40 units. 180€–390€ double. Métro: Palais-Royal or Pyramides. **Amenities:** Concierge, library/bar, Wi-Fi (free).

INEXPENSIVE

Hôtel du Cygne ★ Chock-full of exposed beams and stone walls (not to mention narrow stairways—there is no elevator), this 17th-century building has been carefully restored, and the simple lodgings receive ongoing tender loving care from Isabelle Gouge, the friendly owner. Most of the rooms are predictably small, but are cheerfully decorated with fresh white walls, floral bedspreads, and the owner's personal touch. If you can handle the climb to the top floor, you'll be rewarded with a roomy suite that can sleep three. The hotel is located near Les Halles (a little seedy at night) and the Montorgueil neighborhood (very hip at night). There is no elevator.

3–5 rue du Cygne, 1st arrond. ℰ **01-42-60-14-16.** www.cygne-hotel-paris.com. 18 units. 100€–132€ double; 147–167€ suite. Métro: Etienne Marcel. RER: Les Halles. **Amenities:** Wi-Fi (free).

The Marais (3rd & 4th Arrondissements)

Centuries ago, this neighborhood was a swamp (*marais*), but now it's merely swamped with stylish boutiques, restaurants, and people who seem to have just stepped out of a hair salon. Stunning 16th- and 17th-century mansions, which had fallen into disrepair, have been scrubbed down and fixed up over the past few decades, and they shine like pearls along the narrow streets of this fashionable area where clothing stores, cool bars, and clubs are quickly closing in on what's left of Paris's historic Jewish quarter. There are many excellent museums here, including the Musée Picasso and the Musée Carnavalet. In short, this is a great area to stay in, so much so that in recent years it has become swamped with savvy travelers. You might not hear a lot of French in some of those cute cafes on rue Vielle du Temple.

EXPENSIVE

Hôtel du Petit Moulin ★★ Famed designer Christian Lacroix has turned one of the oldest bakeries in Paris into a hip hotel with a artistic soul. While its 19th-century facade hasn't changed since it sold baguettes, the inside now reflects the lovely, if idiosyncratic, world of Mr. Lacroix. Rooms feature surprising juxtapositions of colors, periods, and patterns that somehow blend together in elegant harmony. Some of the artwork on the walls is by the Master himself. The cozy "honesty bar" in the salon is a quirky mix of ancient artwork and colorful modern paintings. This stylish address (in the upper Marais) draws a well-heeled, knowing crowd, so reserve well in advance.

29–31 rue du Poitou, 3rd arrond. ℰ **01-42-74-10-10.** www.hoteldupetitmoulin.com. 17 units. 215€–350€ double, 430€–450€ junior suite for up to 4 people. Parking 20€. Métro: St-Sebastien Froissart. **Amenities:** Concierge service, honesty bar, laundry service, room service, Wi-Fi (free).

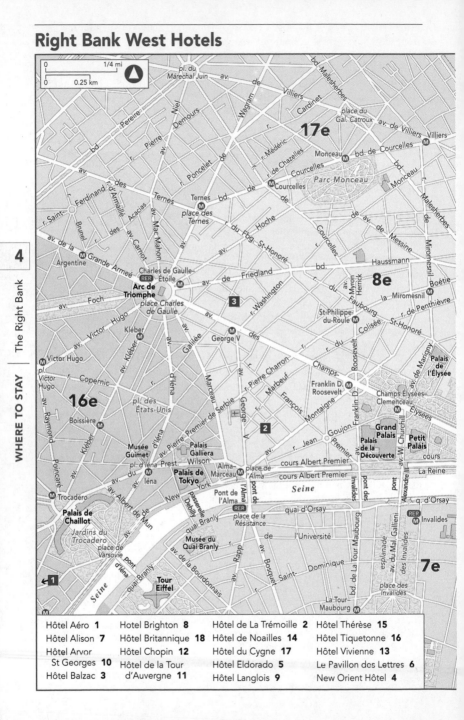

Hôtel Aéro **1**	Hotel Brighton **8**	Hôtel de La Trémoille **2**	Hôtel Thérèse **15**
Hôtel Alison **7**	Hôtel Britannique **18**	Hôtel de Noailles **14**	Hôtel Tiquetonne **16**
Hôtel Arvor St Georges **10**	Hôtel Chopin **12**	Hôtel du Cygne **17**	Hôtel Vivienne **13**
	Hôtel de la Tour d'Auvergne **11**	Hôtel Eldorado **5**	Le Pavillon des Lettres **6**
Hôtel Balzac **3**		Hôtel Langlois **9**	New Orient Hôtel **4**

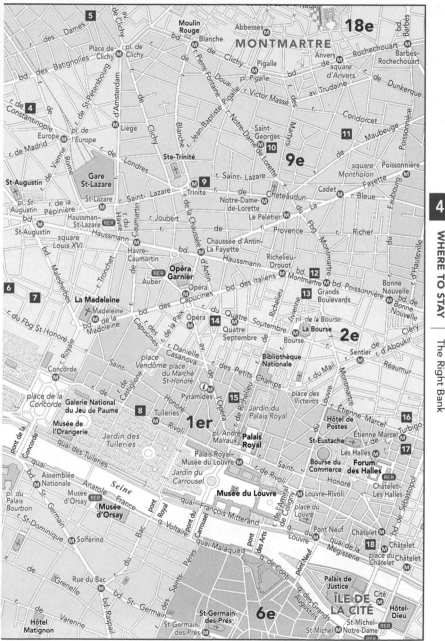

Pavillon de la Reine ★★★ Just off the place des Vosges, this "Queen's Pavilion" harkens back to the days when the magnificent square was the home of royalty. You certainly feel like a noble as you pass through an arcade into a small formal garden, and enter this elegant mansion, which is set back from the hustle bustle of the Marais. Despite its 54 rooms, the hotel feels small and intimate, like a lord's private hunting lodge in the country. The decor is a suave combination of subtle modern and antique history: Dark period furniture blends with rich colors on the walls and beds and choice objects and historic details abound. Several of the deluxe rooms are duplexes with a cozy sleeping loft. There is also a full spa for guests, with a sauna, steam room, and fitness room, as well as massages and beauty treatments.

28 place des Vosges, 3rd arrond. ℂ **01-40-29-19-19.** www.pavillon-de-la-reine.com. 54 units. 385€–550€ double; 600€–1,200€ suite. Métro: Bastille. **Amenities:** Bar, concierge, fitness room, laundry service, room service, sauna, spa, Wi-Fi (free).

MODERATE

Hôtel de la Bretonnerie ★★ This popular and affordable hotel, located smack in the middle of the Marais, has a remarkably high charm factor. Rooms feature exposed beams, pretty period prints, and high ceilings, as well as large windows that let in light from either the small street or the courtyard. Romantics on a budget will appreciate the rooms with four-poster beds; those who need to stretch out will enjoy the spacious junior suites and duplexes. The manager is passionate about her work and the service is excellent. *Note:* Rooms are prettier than the photos on the website.

22 rue Sainte Croix de la Bretonnerie, 4th arrond. ℂ **01-48-87-77-63.** www.hotelbretonnerie.com. 29 units. 150€–185€ double; 210€–235€ junior suites and duplexes for up to 4 people. Métro: Hôtel de Ville. **Amenities:** Computer in lobby, Wi-Fi (free).

Hôtel Caron de Beaumarchais ★★★ In the 18th century, Pierre August Caron de Beaumarchais—author of The Barber of Seville and the Marriage of Figaro—lived near here, and this small hotel celebrates both the playwright and the magnificent century he lived in. The walls are covered in high-quality reproductions of period fabrics; rooms are furnished with authentic antique writing tables and ceiling fixtures; and period paintings and first edition pages of The Barber of Seville hang on the walls. You half expect Pierre Auguste himself to come prancing through the door. The rooms are smallish, but the high ceilings (with exposed beams) and tall windows let in lots of light making them feel spacious. Unlike other parts of the Marais, there are food stores, buses and metro stops close by, and it's a short walk to the Seine. Room rates are reasonable year-round.

12 rue Vieille-du-Temple, 4th arrond. ℂ **01-42-72-34-12.** www.carondebeaumarchais.com. 19 units. 145€–198€ double. Métro: St-Paul or Hôtel de Ville. **Amenities:** Wi-Fi (free).

Hôtel Saint-Louis en l'Isle ★★ Set on the tiny main drag of the tranquil Ile Saint-Louis, this friendly place has a prime location on one of the city's most desirable pieces of real estate. The impeccable rooms are done up in a low-key modern style with historic touches: beige walls, stone floors, dark wood furniture, and many framed etchings of 17th- and 18th-century nobles from days of yore. The street-side rooms are quiet but a little dark; if you want a lot of light ask for a corner room, or splurge on one of the rooms on the top floor, which have small balconies and nicer

Right Bank East Hotels

Cosmos Hotel **7**
Hôtel Caron de
  Beaumarchais **2**
Hôtel de la
  Bretonnerie **3**
Hôtel de la
  Porte Dorée **12**
Hôtel du Petit
  Moulin **4**
Hôtel Jeanne d'Arc
  le Marais **10**
Hôtel Résidence
  Alhambra **8**
Hôtel Saint-Louis
  en l'Isle **1**
Le Citizen **5**
Le Pavillon Bastille **11**
Pavillon de la Reine **9**
St Christopher's Paris
  Hostel - Canal **6**

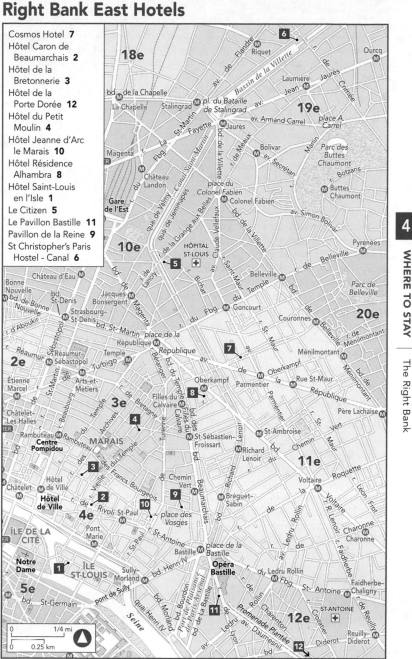

views. The elevators stop at landings between floors, so you'll have to be able to manage stairs here. There is one handicap-accessible room on the ground floor.

75 rue St-Louis-en-l'Ile, 4th arrond. © **01-46-34-04-80.** www.saintlouisenlisle.com. 20 units. 179€–199€ double, 249€ double on top floor; 289€ triple. Métro: Pont Marie. **Amenities:** Wi-Fi (free).

INEXPENSIVE

Hôtel Jeanne d'Arc le Marais ★★★ Considering its prime location in the southern Marais, right next to the leafy place du Marché St-Catherine, this cozy hotel is an incredible deal. While definitely not luxurious, the rooms are in excellent shape, decked out in warm colors and old-fashioned prints; several have been given a more modern makeover and new bathrooms. Families will be interested in the reasonably priced quads as well as the two communicating rooms on the sixth floor. Rooms book up months in advance, especially for fashion weeks (Feb, Mar, July, and Sept). Note: There is another hotel with the same name in the 13th arrondissement—make sure you are in contact with hotel in the Marais when you reserve, or you will be in for an unpleasant surprise.

3 rue de Jarente, 4th arrond. © **01-48-87-62-11.** www.hoteljeannedarc.com. 35 units. 110€–150€ double; 180€ triple; 220€ quad. Métro: St-Paul. **Amenities:** Computer in lobby, Wi-Fi (free).

Champs-Élysées, Trocadéro & Western Paris (8th, 16th & 17th Arrondissements)

Even grander than the 7th arrondissement, the area around the Champs-Élysées is positively mythic. To the south of the boulevard, along avenues Montaigne and George V, are the most exclusive designer shops in the city; to the north, elegant buildings, shops, and restaurants stretch up to lovely Parc Monceau, which has some excellent museum neighbors, including Musée Nissim de Camondo and Musée Jacquemart-André. As you head north and east, towards the Gare St-Lazare train station, the neighborhood becomes more proletarian. Affordable lodgings are scarce around here, especially near the Champs and the Arc de Triomphe, where the high prices often have more to do with the location than the quality of the accommodations. Ironically, the location is not particularly central; it's a good hike from here to Notre-Dame.

EXPENSIVE

Hôtel Balzac ★★★ Chandeliers and yards of rich fabric await you in the lobby of these luxurious lodgings, which were built for the director of the Paris Opéra in 1853. Just a few steps away from the Champs-Élysées, this classy townhouse features spacious rooms with huge beds, high thread-counts, and more swags of chiffon and velour around the bed and windows. The ambiance is classic and very French, with reproduction antiques, high ceilings, and subtle colors. Visiting dignitaries can opt for a Royal or Presidential Suite with views of the Eiffel Tower; lesser mortals will be happy with the junior and "regular" suites that feature separate sitting areas and dressing rooms. There's a covered interior courtyard where you can enjoy a drink on a plush sofa; if you're itching to get out, Louis Vuitton and Fouquet's are just around the corner. For luxury on a personal scale, this is an excellent choice; the service is impeccable without being haughty, and the hotel is small enough to still feel intimate. Pierre Gagnaire, a Michelin three-star gourmet pleasure palace, is in the same building.

6 rue Balzac, 8th arrond. ✆ **01-44-35-18-00.** www.hotelbalzac.com. 69 units. 320€–600€ double; 450€–1,300€ suite and junior suites; 2,000€–3,000€ Royal and Presidential suites. Métro: George V. **Amenities:** Restaurant, bar, business center, dry cleaning, room service, concierge, private parking (23€), Wi-Fi (free).

Hôtel de La Trémoille ★★★   Just off the hyper-sophisticated avenue George V and steps away from the Champs-Élysées, this classy hotel is as refined and elegant as its surroundings, and has a lovely young staff to attend to your (almost) every need. The spacious rooms have exceptionally high ceilings (except for those on the sixth floor), tall windows, and a subtly modern decor. The white walls have kept their 19th-century trimmings, while the curtains, bedsteads, and covers are all rich fabrics in shades of prune, teal, and gold. Rooms include a full complement of designer toiletries, as well as iPod docks and a heated trouser press. Those on the second and fifth floor have small balconies; the suites are vast, by Paris standards.

14 rue de la Trémoille, 8th arrond. ✆ **01-56-52-14-00.** www.hotel-tremoille.com. 93 units. 360€–750€ double; 565€–1,250€ suite. Métro: Alma-Marceau. **Amenities:** Restaurant, bar, concierge, exercise room, sauna, spa, room service, Wi-Fi (free).

Le Pavillon des Lettres ★★   Just around the corner from the Élysées Palace (headquarters of President François Hollande) and across the street from the powerful Ministry of the Interior, this tastefully chic hotel is located in the navel of the French political universe. However, the theme here is literature. Each of the 26 rooms is designated by a different letter of the alphabet and linked to a famous author. If you are in room Z, for example, you might find a copy of Zola's "Nana" on the bedside table and some of the author's text on the wall behind the headboard. The room design is serenely hip: The colors are sober, but the materials are soft and comforting, in subtle shades of grey, olive green, beige, and mauve. While the rooms are a little small, the ceilings are mostly high and the bathrooms are spacious.

12 rue des Saussaies, 8th arrond. ✆ **01-49-24-26-26.** www.pavillondeslettres.com. 26 units. 265€–355€ double; 420€–515€ junior suite. Métro: Madeleine. **Amenities:** Lounge, library, room service, iPads for guests, Wi-Fi (free).

MODERATE

Hotel Aéro ★★   Located in what used to be the village of Passy (before it got gobbled up by the 16th arrondissement), these colorful lodgings lie on a cute pedestrian market street. The soundproofed rooms are just upstairs from the hotel's restaurant, which features a large outdoor terrace that sprawls out onto a leafy square. True, it's a little out of the city center, but if you are looking for calm and quaint (and chic boutiques), this neighborhood has it all. Despite the decorator's fondness for fuchsia, the room decor is pleasantly subdued, with lots of warm wood colors and arty mosaic tiles in the bathrooms. Everything is in tip-top condition, and double paned windows keep out most street noise. If you are a light sleeper, ask for a room on the courtyard.

3 place de Passy, 16th arrond. ℰ **01-46-47-10-00.** www.parishotelaero.com. 14 units. 150€–230€ double. Métro: Passy or La Muette. **Amenities:** Restaurant, bar, concierge service, Wi-Fi (free).

Hôtel Alison ★★ While the lobby decor at this comfortable, family-run hotel hasn't changed since at least 1982 (think Almodóvar movies), it is impeccably clean and shiny, as are the relatively spacious rooms. There's nothing frumpy or musty about these crisp lodgings. The owners simply haven't felt the need to update the shiny white ceilings in certain rooms, or the square black headboards in others. However you feel about beige walls and chocolate carpets, you should be pleased with the generally high level of comfort here and the excellent location around the corner from the Madeleine and a short stroll to the Champs-Élysées and the Place de la Concorde. The owners are art fans and the paintings hung throughout the hotel belong to their private collection; not surprisingly, their clientele includes a lot of people from the art world.

21 rue de Surène, 8th arrond. ℰ **01-42-65-54-00.** www.hotel-alison.com. 34 units. 129€–185€ double; triple 185€–205€; family suite 230€. Métro: Charles-de-Gaulle–Etoile or George V. **Amenities:** Bar, Wi-Fi (free).

INEXPENSIVE

New Orient Hôtel ★★★ Here is a good example of why you shouldn't pay too much attention to the French hotel star system. This lovely hotel, which offers comfortable rooms with high ceilings, 19th-century moldings, and antique headboards and armoires, only gets two stars, while a drab hotel nearby with a fraction of the charm has four. While it may not be on top of the Champs-Élysées, it's not far, and it's close to stately Parc Monceau and a quick trot to the Saint Lazare train station. The friendly owners, who are inveterate flea market browsers, have refinished and restored the antique furniture themselves. Rooms (many of which have small balconies) are in tip-top shape, and bathrooms sparkle. Though there's an elevator, you'll have to negotiate stairs to get to it. The low rates remain are stable here throughout the year.

16 rue de Constantinople, 8th arrond. ℰ **01-45-22-21-64.** www.hotelneworient.com. 30 units. 130€–180€ double, 168–205€ family room for 4. Métro: Villiers, Europe, or St-Lazare. **Amenities:** Computer in lobby, Wi-Fi (free).

Opéra & Grands Boulevards (2nd & 9th Arrondissements)

The area just north of the Grands Boulevards (those wide throughways that Baron Haussman plowed through Paris in the 19th c.) and just below Montmartre is a lovely mix of hip bars and restaurants and old-time Paris, with a good sprinkling of small museums for a dose of culture. While there are not too many big monuments around here, the area's upsides include lower room rates and a more neighborhood-y feel (at least, away from the boulevards).

EXPENSIVE

Hôtel de Noailles ★★ The giant pink and blue snails in the lobby might not be to everyone's liking, but most will appreciate the otherwise low-key feel of these hip accommodations. Very sleek, the rooms feature lots of varnished wood, padded headboards, and bathrooms with glass walls (with curtains for the shy). Some rooms on the sixth floor feature private terraces. There are three handicap-accessible rooms on the ground floor. The curious works of art in the lobby are a legacy of the hotel's periodic art exhibits; there is a loungelike bar area with a fireplace as well as an open-air terrace where you can breakfast in nice weather.

9 rue de la Michodière, 2nd arrond. ℂ **01-47-42-92-90.** www.paris-hotel-noailles.com. 56 units. 171€–400€ double; 380€–600€ suite. Métro: Quatre-Septembre or Opéra. RER: Auber. **Amenities:** Bar; concierge; sauna; fitness room; room service; Wi-Fi (free).

MODERATE

Hôtel Arvor St Georges ★★★   These spiffy lodgings are located in the charming "New Athens" neighborhood, where 19th-century Romantics like George Sand and Frédéric Chopin lived and worked. Maybe that's why Mme. Flamarion, of the famous French publishing house, decided to open this arty yet relaxed hotel, where fresh white walls show off modern photography and Daniel Buren graphics. Rooms are a little small, but simple and chic, with white walls, a splash of color and a distinctive table or armchair. Those on the upper floors have nice rooftop views, and some of the spacious suites offer a glimpse of the far-off Eiffel Tower. The airy lobby area, with large windows and bookshelves, is an invitation to kick back and read or sip a cup of tea. The tasty breakfast is served here or outside in the flower-filled patio when the weather is nice. The friendly staff will point you to great nearby restaurants.

8 rue Laferrière, 9th arrond. ℂ **01-48-78-60-92.** www.hotelarvor.com. 30 units. 139€–220€ double; 207€–280€ suite. Métro: St-Georges. **Amenities:** Bar; Wi-Fi (free).

Hôtel de la Tour d'Auvergne ★   For a little style at an affordable price, try this small inn just down the street from hip rue des Martyrs. The decor is a little eccentric but very stylish, with bold colors and interesting juxtapositions of old and new. While some decors are in quiet shades of grey and beiges, others can be a little overwhelming (like the one in pink and black). There's a cozy bar and Internet corner. Despite its resolutely modern look, this building holds a lot of history: Modigliani rented a room here for 6 months, and Victor Hugo and Auguste Rodin lived on this street. Though the views over the back courtyard are uninspired, some guests prefer the quiet of the rear rooms.

10 rue de la Tour d'Auvergne, 9th arrond. ℂ **01-48-78-61-60.** www.hoteltourdauvergne.com. 26 units. 135€–200€ double. Métro: Cadet. **Amenities:** Bar; room service; Wi-Fi (free).

Hôtel Langlois ★★   You won't be surprised to learn that this unusual hotel was once a bank: The lobby ceiling is so high you could easily walk around on stilts. The rooms are truly spacious, and some include bathrooms that are downright huge. The other atypical feature here is the furniture—many of the rooms have gorgeous Art Nouveau fittings that would make an antiques dealer foam at the mouth. All but one have pretty tiled fireplaces, and most have retained their old ceiling moldings. An antique wrought-iron elevator running up the center of the building adds another authentic Parisian touch. It's no wonder that this hotel is a favorite for magazine photo shoots. *Note:* Although the rooms are large, the beds can be small; those lovely old bedsteads were made before king-size mattresses came into style.

63 rue St-Lazare, 9th arrond. ℂ **01-48-74-78-24.** www.hotel-langlois.com. 27 units. 150€–190€ double; 240€ suite. Métro: Trinité. **Amenities:** Wi-Fi (free).

The Right Bank

INEXPENSIVE

Hôtel Chopin ★ Nestled at the back of the delightful Passage Jouffroy, this budget hotel has remarkably quiet rooms considering its location in the middle of the rush and bustle of the Grands Boulevards. The staircase is a little creaky (you will have to climb a flight to get to the elevator) and the decor is nothing to write home about, but rooms are clean and colorful and bathrooms are spotless. Rooms on the upper floors get more light; many have nice views of Parisian rooftops. Across the street from the Passage Jouffroy entrance is Passage des Panoramas, a maze of hip bistros and shops.

10 bd. Montmartre or 46 passage Jouffroy, 9th arrond. ℰ **01-47-70-58-10.** www.hotel-chopin.com. 36 units. 102€–123€ double; 145€ triple. Métro: Grands Boulevards or Richelieu-Drouot. **Amenities:** Wi-Fi (free).

Hôtel Tiqutonne ★★ Possibly one of the best deals in the city, these cute, if basic lodgings are just around the corner from the chic Passage du Grand Cerf. This is definitely a budget hotel: The doors feel a little light and the carpets are a little worn, but the paint is fresh, the ceilings are high, and the atmosphere is homey. The old-fashioned bedspreads lay over firm mattresses, and rooms on the upper floors get lots of light. This is one of the few hotels left in Paris that still has cheap rooms with toilets on the landing; doubles with just a sink go for 50€. (There's a shower in the hall for 5€.) For an in-suite toilet and shower, you'll pay just 65€. At these prices, don't expect TVs or toiletries. The hotel is just steps away from Les Halles and a block or so from the restaurants and food shops of rue de Montorgueil. Reserve well in advance.

6 rue Tiquetonne, 2nd arrond. ℰ **01-42-36-94-58.** www.hoteltiquetonne.fr. 45 units. 50€–65€ double. Métro: Etienne Marcel; RER: Les Halles. **Amenities:** Wi-Fi (free).

Hôtel Vivienne ★★★ Right around the corner from Passage des Panoramas, this family-run hotel offers comfortable, renovated, spotless lodgings at terrific prices. About half the hotel is decorated in a classic, if old-fashioned style with floral prints, the other rooms have been given a modern makeover with shades of grey and tasteful stripes. A few rooms have balconies with space for a small table; some have communicating doors, and there are some large suites that are great for families. If you don't mind sharing a toilet, there are several doubles that go for 85€. The hotel is located on a street filled with shops for stamp and coin collectors; the location may not be exactly central, but it's only a 10-minute stroll to the Palais Royal. If you are a light sleeper, ask for a room facing the courtyard as the street can be a little noisy.

40 rue Vivienne, 2nd arrond. ℰ **01-42-33-13-26.** www.hotel-vivienne.com. 44 units. 101€–160€ double; 196€ suite for 2–3. Métro: Grands Boulevards or Richelieu–Drouot. **Amenities:** Wi-Fi (free).

Montmartre (18th Arrondissement)

If you're looking for a romantic setting, you can't do much better than Montmartre. Once you get away from the tourist hoards that invade the Sacre-Coeur and Place du Tertre, you'll find lovely little lanes and small houses, harkening back to the days when Picasso and the boys were at the Bateau Lavoir. Unfortunately, the pickings are a bit slim if you want to actually sleep here. If you are determined to stay up on the Butte (a high hill) book early, as the few quality lodgings are generally in high demand. Another consideration: Though Montmartre is charming, it's on the northern edge of the city, so you'll need to budget extra time to get down the hill to the center of town.

Montmartre Hotels

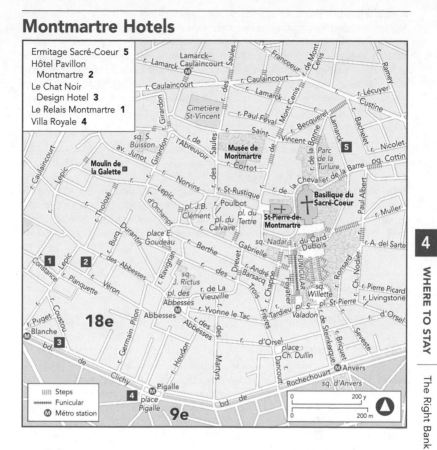

Ermitage Sacré-Coeur **5**
Hôtel Pavillon
  Montmartre **2**
Le Chat Noir
  Design Hotel **3**
Le Relais Montmartre **1**
Villa Royale **4**

EXPENSIVE

Villa Royale ★★ If your vision of Paris involves the scarlet-toned settings once associated with the Moulin Rouge and the paintings of Toulouse-Lautrec, this unusual hotel might be for you. The decor evokes a cross between a mansion and a bordello, with lots with rococo gewgaws, jewel-toned walls, velvet and velour upholsteries, and TV screens that are sometimes encased in gilded frames. "Classic" rooms are the smallest, with space for a tiny table and chairs; the larger "Royal" suites are ideal for the honeymoon crowd, with Jacuzzis or fireplaces, or both. For some, this hotel could be a horror, for others a hoot. The hotel faces Place Pigalle; expect some noise on the weekends. Room rates fluctuate wildly here, so book far in advance; sometimes you can get a small double for as little as 165€.

2 rue Duperré, 9th arrond. ⓒ **01-55-31-78-78.** www.villa-royale.com. 31 units. 200€–530€ double. Métro: Pigalle. **Amenities:** Room service, Wi-Fi (free).

MODERATE

Le Chat Noir Design Hotel ★ Located two steps from the Moulin Rouge in the heart of Paris's red light district, this modern hotel is named after one of the favorite haunts of painter Henri de Toulouse-Lautrec, which used to be next door. The spacious and spotless contemporary rooms have lots of white walls with decorative accents in red and black, and big windows that let in lots of light. The triples are particularly spacious, and there are two large handicap-accessible room. The only problem here is the neighborhood: Only stay here if you don't mind being in the middle of a strip of sex shops. Rooms facing the boulevard can be noisy on weekend nights. On the upside, you are only a few minutes downhill from the heart of Montmartre.

68 bd. de Clichy, 18th arrond. ℂ **01-42-64-15-26.** www.hotel-chatnoir-paris.com. 39 units. 180€–300€ double, 230€–350€ triple. Métro: Blanche. **Amenities:** Room service, Wi-Fi (free).

Le Relais Montmartre ★★ These comfortable lodgings include small, but impeccable rooms decked out in light, warm colors and a classic decor. Nothing is particularly hip or stylish here, but these are quality accommodations in tasteful floral prints and reliable service. The one decorative quirk was the decision to paint the exposed beams on the ceilings shades of lavender or blue. The hotel is located on a peaceful little side street, right around the corner from a delicious stretch of food shops on Rue Lepic. There are adjoining rooms for families, and a lovely little patio for breakfasting in good weather.

6 rue Constance, 18th arrond. ℂ **01-70-64-25-25.** www.hotel-relais-montmartre.com. 26 units. 176€–259€ double, 218€–289€ triple. Métro: Blanche. **Amenities:** Concierge service, laundry service, iPad for guests, Wi-Fi (free).

INEXPENSIVE

Ermitage Sacré-Coeur ★★★ Built in 1890 by a rich gentleman for his mistress, this beautifully preserved townhouse has been lovingly converted into an intimate hotel. There may not be room service (although the complimentary breakfast is served in your room) or much by way of amenities, but the ambiance is unique. Tucked behind the Sacre-Coeur, this small mansion still feels like a private home. In fact, it virtually is: The Canipel family has run these unconventional lodgings for over 40 years. Each of the 5 rooms is decorated with different period prints and draperies, as well as some beautiful antique bedsteads and armoires. The hallways and entry are done up in deep blues and gold leaf; wall murals and paintings are the works of a local artist. There is no elevator and no TVs in the rooms. The Canipels also rent nearby studios and apartments that sleep one to four.

24 rue Lamarck, 18th arrond. ℂ **01-42-64-79-22.** www.ermitagesacrecoeur.fr. 5 units. 115€–120€ double; 150€ triple; 170€ quad. Rates include breakfast. No credit cards. Métro: Lamarck-Caulaincourt. Parking 20€. **Amenities:** Wi-Fi (free).

Hôtel Eldorado ★★ Though it's right outside the border, the soul of this quirky hotel belongs in Montmartre. Funky and imaginative, the decor is the work of the owner-artist who likes to use bright colors and offbeat details mosaic mirror frames and tiny sparkly chandeliers. The largest and most atmospheric rooms are in the "pavilion," a small, separate house behind the main building, with high ceilings and large windows. However, these rooms are separated by a pretty garden patio used by their restaurant, Bistrot des Dames, which means that there can be noise until midnight in the warmer months. If you are a stickler for tidiness, you may not appreciate the occasional chipped paint or loose floor tiles; if you are young at heart, you will love the bohemian charm factor. There is no elevator and no TV or telephone in the rooms.

18 rue des Dames, 17th arrond. ℂ **01-45-22-35-21.** www.eldoradohotel.fr 33 units. 65€–94€ double; 82€–102€ triple. Métro: Place de Clichy. **Amenities:** Bar, restaurant, Wi-Fi (free).

4

WHERE TO STAY | The Right Bank

Hôtel Pavillon Montmartre ★   Smack in the middle of downtown Montmartre, these spotless lodgings will please those who prefer clean efficiency to eccentric charm (see above). Beds are firm, bathrooms look new, windows are double-glazed. The decor, on the other hand, is pretty boring, but who cares when rue des Abbesses is just around the corner? Most rooms get plenty of sunlight, but there are a few on the courtyard that are slightly below street level and get less—if light is an issue for you, be sure to request an upstairs room when you reserve.

5 rue Aristide Bruant, 18th arrond. ℭ **01-42-52-89-80.** www.paris-hotel-pavillonmontmartre.com. 30 units. 70€–145€ double, 95€–170€ triple, 110€–190€ quad. Métro: Blanche or Abbesses. **Amenities:** Wi-Fi (free).

République, Bastille & Eastern Paris (11th & 12th Arrondissements)

Just north of the Marais, this area offers low rates and proximity to the nightlife around Rue Oberkampf. Nearby, the Faubourg St-Antoine area has nice lodging options, even if it's less than central. This historic workers neighborhood was where revolutionary fervor came to a head on July 14, 1789 when its irate citizens stormed down the boulevard and took over the Bastille prison. Things have calmed down considerably since then, and outside of the heated nightlife scene around the Bastille and rue de Charonne, it's a pretty sleepy neighborhood.

MODERATE

Le Pavillon Bastille ★   Just across the way from the Opéra Bastille and about a block east of the Place, this unpretentious hotel offers relatively spacious, contemporary rooms at reasonable rates. This is a practical choice as it is very convenient to public transportation (including the Gare de Lyon train station) and an easy walk to the lively Bastille/Charonne and Marais neighborhoods. It's also a good bet for families, as there are several adjoining rooms. However, there is little charm here, due to the fact that most rooms look out over a busy boulevard (even if the double-paned windows keep out most noise).

65 rue de Lyon, 12th arrond. ℭ **01-43-43-65-65.** www.paris-hotel-pavillonbastille.com. 25 units. 125€–240€ double. **Amenities:** Wi-Fi (free).

INEXPENSIVE

Cosmos Hotel ★★   Just around the corner from the animated Oberkampf neighborhood, this budget option is one of the best deals in town. The modern rooms are generally spotless, and everything from the bed linens to the floor covering looks spanking new. And such a deal: only 68€ to 75€ a double. Furthermore, the staff is friendly and helpful. The only downside is that there can be some noise on weekend nights as people spill out of the busy nearby bars and restaurants.

35 rue Jean-Pierre Timbaud, 11th arrond. ℭ **01-43-57-25-88.** www.cosmos-hotel-paris.com. 36 units. 68€–75€ double; 85€ triple; 94€ quad. Métro: Parmentier. **Amenities:** TV, hair dryer, Wi-Fi (free).

Hôtel de la Porte Dorée ★★★   True, it's a little out of the way, but these lovely lodgings are well worth the Métro fare. Period prints, antique headboards, high ceilings, wood floors, and original curlicue moldings are all part of the package at this hotel, which is owned by a friendly Franco-American couple. The hotel goes the extra mile for both the environment (ecologically correct policies) and babies (toys, playpens, and even potty seats available). And you'll pay less for all this than you will for something utterly basic in the center of town. While the location is not central, it is right next to the verdant Bois de Vincennes, where you can rent bikes or picnic. The nearby Métro will get you to the city center in about 15 minutes.

273 ave. Daumensil, 12th arrond. ℂ **01-43-07-56-97.** www.hoteldelaportedoree.com. 43 units. 95€–190€ double; 110€–210€ triple. Métro: Porte Dorée. **Amenities:** Wi-Fi (free).

Hôtel Résidence Alhambra ★★   Recently reopened after a complete overhaul, this budget classic now sports a lobby in chic shades of gray. Rooms are sleek and polished, with splashes of bright color. Regardless of what you think of the new decor (I find it a bit cold), you should be happy with the top-quality materials and the delightful courtyard garden, which has thankfully stayed as lovely as ever. Tucked in the crook of this L-shaped hotel, the garden is large and leafy, with tables for breakfast alfresco. You can even bring your own eats and picnic there after 10am. Eight of the guest rooms on the bottom floor open directly onto a balcony over the garden; about half of the others face onto it. Requests for garden views will be taken but the hotel won't promise anything.

13 rue de Malte, 11th arrond. ℂ **01-47-00-35-52.** www.hotelalhambra.fr. 53 units. 124€–200€ double; 169€–249€ triple; 209–299€ quad; 209€–259€ family suite Métro: Oberkampf. **Amenities:** Computer and printer in lobby, Wi-Fi (free).

Belleville, Canal St-Martin & La Villette (10th, 19th & 20th Arrondissements)

When historic arty neighborhoods like St-Germain and Montmartre became far too expensive for up-and-coming artists, many of them immigrated to these more proletarian neighborhoods, giving the area a funky, bohemian feel. Though it's gentrifying, Belleville is still known for artists' studios, while dozens of hip cafes and restaurants now line the Canal St-Martin and the Bassin de la Villette. The young and adventurous will appreciate this part of town, but it is a commute to the city center.

MODERATE

Le Citizen ★★   Maybe it's the smiling young staff in jeans or the ecological ethos, but there's something alternative in the air at this adorable boutique hotel on the Canal St-Martin. While the rooms are on the small side, they are light and airy, with lots of blonde wood clean lines, and they all look out on the tree-lined canal. There are only two rooms per floor, ranging from the snug "City" to the spacious "Suite Zen" which can to sleep a couple with two children. On some floors, two rooms can be connected to form a large "apartment." When you check in, you'll be handed an iPad loaded with information and apps on Paris, as well as restaurant recommendations. Minibar and a buffet breakfast are included in your room rate.

96 quai de Jemmapes, 10th arrond. ℂ **01-83-62-55-50.** www.lecitizenhotel.com. 12 units. 189€–269€ double, 299€329€ suite, 480€ apartment. Rates include breakfast. Métro: Jacques Bonsergent. **Amenities:** Room service, minibar (free), iPad, Wi-Fi (free).

St Christopher's Paris Hostel–Canal ★   This behemoth hostel, located on the picturesque Bassin de la Villette, boasts 346 beds, most of which are in dormitories for 6 to 12 hostelites. Dorms can be big or small, mixed sex or female-only, and with or without in-suite bathrooms, which accounts in part for the wide variety of rates (they also fluctuate with the seasons). If you are shy, there are 21 private rooms, but for 80€–100€ you can probably do better at a budget hotel. The dorms are filled with young, mostly English-speaking travelers doing their post-college European tour. The hostel includes a British-style bar, club, onsite launderette, and Internet cafe. This may not be the most authentic Parisian experience (the staff is mostly British), but it is certainly a cheap and practical one. St Christopher's has a second gargantuan hostel next to the Gare du Nord; see the website for details.

159 rue Crimée, 19th arrond. ℭ **01-40-34-34-40.** www.st-christophers.co.uk/paris-hostels. 346 beds, 21 private rooms. 20€–39€ per person in dormitories; 80€–100€ double. Rates include breakfast. Métro: Crimée or Laumière. **Amenities:** Restaurant, bar, nightclub, bicycle rental, luggage lockers, Laundromat, day trips, towel rental, Wi-Fi (free).

THE LEFT BANK
Latin Quarter (5th & 13th Arrondissements)

Central and reasonably priced, the Latin Quarter is a long-time favorite for travelers in search of affordable accommodations. As a consequence, a few corners of this famously academic neighborhood are overrun with tourists and trinket shops. The streets immediately surrounding the place St-Michel (especially around rue de la Huchette) are where you'll find the worst tourist traps, both hotel and restaurant-wise; better prices and quality are to be had in the quieter, and more authentic areas around the universities (College de France, La Sorbonne, Faculté de Sciences), a little farther from Notre-Dame but still in easy walking distance.

EXPENSIVE

Hotel Seven ★★★   Weird and wonderful, this luxury concept hotel is made for lovers in search of a night to remember. Mirrors and transparent showers abound here, as do huge beds, theatrical lighting and large sofas. Each of the creatively designed rooms and suites has a different theme: Some rooms are romantically space-age, with mobiles, pinpoint lights and in-room transparent double showers, while the suites go all out: "Sublime" is all white with a round double bed under a feathery ceiling; "The Black Diamond" features a faux crocodile headboard and a black bathtub studded with Swarovski synthetic diamonds. Most have "levitation" beds, which are suspended horizontally. The hotel's a bit out of the way, at the southern end of the Latin Quarter.

20 rue Berthollet, 75005 Paris. ℭ **01-43-31-47-52.** www.sevenhotelparis.com. 35 units. 217€–397€ double; 477€–877€ suite. Métro: Les Gobelins. **Amenities:** Bar, room service, laptop loans, massages by appointment, wine cellar, concierge, Wi-Fi (free).

MODERATE

Hôtel Design De La Sorbonne ★★   In the thick of the student quarter facing La Sorbonne, this cozy boutique hotel combines comfort with an unusual, but classy decor. Period furniture is covered in lively green, blue and dark brown stripes; colorful wall fabrics put a modern spin on Victorian patterns, and excerpts from French literary classics are woven into the carpets. Each room has a desk with an iMac for guest's use. As pretty as they are, the rooms are small, and some have bathrooms that are downright tiny. If you need space, opt for a deluxe with a bathtub or the large room on the top floor with a view of the Sorbonne and the Pantheon.

6 rue Victor Cousin, 5th arrond. ℭ **01-43-54-58-08.** www.hotelsorbonne.com. 38 units. 130€–370€ double; 200€–400€ top floor double. Métro: Cluny–La Sorbonne. RER: Luxembourg. **Amenities:** Wi-Fi (free).

Hôtel des Jardins du Luxembourg ★   Just around the corner from its glorious namesake, these intimate lodgings are tucked away on a quiet impasse, an excellent hideaway for a romantic honeymoon or cozy retreat. The building's claim to fame is that Sigmund Freud stayed here on his first visit to Paris; perhaps this has something to do with the 1930s and 1940s touches to the decor. The Art Deco ambiance of the lobby and reading lounge invites deep reflection, or at least a nice rest in one of the plush armchairs. Most of your resting, of course, will be in the rooms, which are decorated with a good deal of class. While the standard rooms are quite pretty, with curly wrought-iron headboards and puffy comforters, the superior rooms, which cost only 10€ more, have nicer views, small balconies, snazzy bathrooms, and designer-fabric covered walls.

5 impasse Royer-Collard, 5th arrond. ℂ **01-40-46-08-88.** www.les-jardins-du-luxembourg.com. 26 units. 110€–205€ double. Métro: Cluny–La Sorbonne. RER: Luxembourg. **Amenities:** Bar, Wi-Fi (free).

Hôtel Saint-Jacques ★★   The spacious rooms in this delightful hotel retain lots of architectural details from its Belle Epoque past. Most of the ceilings are adorned with masses of curlicues, and some have restored 18th-century murals to gaze at while you laze in bed. Modern reproductions of famous French paintings hang on the walls, and Second Empire-themed murals decorate the lobby and breakfast room. The romantic decor has a light, feminine feel, in shades of light blue, cream, and grey—considerably more inviting than when the hotel served as a set for the Audrey Hepburn/Cary Grant classic, Charade. There are two very pretty wheelchair-accessible rooms on the ground floor.

35 rue des Ecoles, 5th arrond. ℂ **01-44-07-45-45.** www.paris-hotel-stjacques.com. 26 units. 137€–326€ double; 217€–312€ triple. Métro: Maubert-Mutualité. **Amenities:** Babysitting, bar, Wi-Fi (free).

Minerve Hôtel ★★   If there is a more dedicated hotel owner than Eric Gaucheron, I have yet to meet him. Every detail at this hotel has been scrupulously considered, from the carved cherry wood headboards to the swags of period fabrics on the windows, to the antiques that decorate many rooms. Some have exposed beams, others have marble bathrooms, and those on the second, fifth, and sixth floors have small balconies with nice views of the Latin Quarter. In his eternal quest to keep his clientele happy, Gaucheron has had the walls of the small interior courtyard painted with blue skies and country scenery so that those without a view don't have to suffer. There's a family suite with two adjoining rooms.

13 rue des Ecoles, 5th arrond. ℂ **01-43-26-26-04.** www.parishotelminerve.com. 54 units. 146€–182€ double; 202€ triple; 222€–364€ suite up to 4 pers. Parking 25€ per day. Métro: Jussieu or Cardinal Lemoine. **Amenities:** Wi-Fi (free).

INEXPENSIVE

Familia Hôtel ★   Next door to the Minerve (see above) is another hotel owned by the same hyperenthusiastic management. Similar in look and feel to its sister hotel, the Familia's rooms are smaller and a touch less luxurious, and consequently, less expensive. The same penchant for details is evident here, with carved and monogrammed doors and hand-painted wall murals.

11 rue des Ecoles, 5th arrond. ℂ **01-43-54-55-27.** www.familiahotel.com. 30 units. 110€–147€ double; 186€ triple; 209€ quad. Métro: Jussieu or Cardinal Lemoine. **Amenities:** Wi-Fi (free).

Hôtel des Grandes Ecoles ★★★   Tucked into a private garden on the slope of the Montagne St-Geneviève, this lovely hotel gives you the impression you have just walked out of Paris and into the countryside. A path leads to a flower-bedecked interior courtyard, where birds chirp in the trees; the reception area adjoins an inviting

Left Bank Hotels (Eiffel Tower Area)

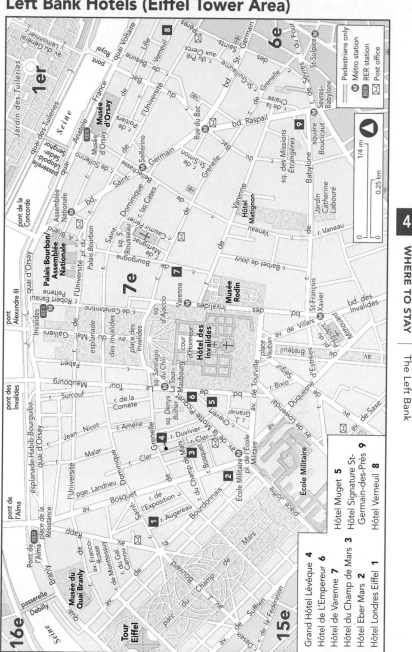

Grand Hôtel Lévêque **4**
Hôtel de L'Empereur **6**
Hôtel de Varenne **7**
Hôtel du Champ de Mars **3**
Hôtel Eber Mars **2**
Hôtel Londres Eiffel **1**
Hôtel Muget **5**
Hôtel Signature St-Germain-des-Prés **9**
Hôtel Verneuil **8**

Left Bank Hotels (Latin Quarter, St-Germain, Montparnasse)

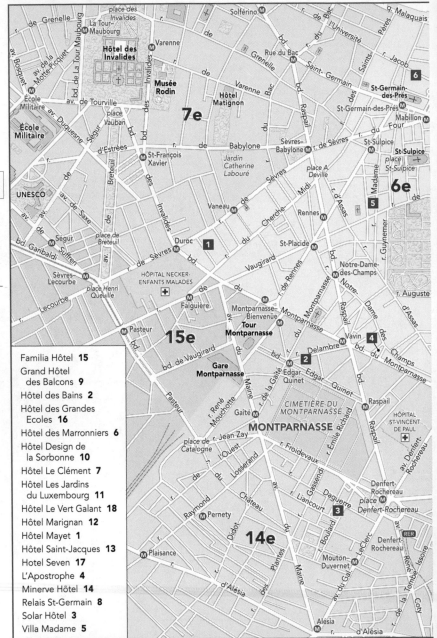

Familia Hôtel **15**

Grand Hôtel
des Balcons **9**

Hôtel des Bains **2**

Hôtel des Grandes
Ecoles **16**

Hôtel des Marronniers **6**

Hôtel Design de
la Sorbonne **10**

Hôtel Le Clément **7**

Hôtel Les Jardins
du Luxembourg **11**

Hôtel Le Vert Galant **18**

Hôtel Marignan **12**

Hôtel Mayet **1**

Hôtel Saint-Jacques **13**

Hotel Seven **17**

L'Apostrophe **4**

Minerve Hôtel **14**

Relais St-Germain **8**

Solar Hôtel **3**

Villa Madame **5**

3e

MARAIS

r. des Francs Bourgeois

pl. des Vosges

M Châtelet

Châtelet

quai de la Mégisserie

pont Neuf

q. de Conti

q. des Grands Augustins

q. de Gesvres

Hôtel de Ville

r. de Rivoli

St-Paul

r. St-Antoine

Palais de Justice

Cité
M

ÎLE DE LA CITÉ

Hôtel de Ville

Hôtel de Ville

Pont Marie

r. de Fourcy

r. St-Paul

r. de Seine

bd.

Odéon
M

St-Michel M

quai St-Michel

Cluny–La Sorbonne

St-Michel–Notre-Dame

quai de Montebello

Cathédrale Notre-Dame

q. de la Tournelle

ÎLE ST-LOUIS

quai des Célestins

Sully–Morland

bd. Henri IV

7

8

Saint-

r. du Petit Pont

St-Michel

r. des

Germain

pont de Sully

bd. Morland

quai Henri IV

bd. Bourdon

9

Musée de Cluny

Maubert-Mutualité

bd. St- Germain

Institut du Monde Arabe

Seine

Vaugirard

r. de Médicis

r. de Tournon

12

Sorbonne

Lagrange

r. des Écoles

14 15

r. des Fossés St-Bernard

quai

pont d'Austerlitz

Palais du Luxembourg

10

13

LATIN QUARTER

Monge

r. Lemoine

r. Jussieu

CAMPUS DE JUSSIEU

St- Bernard

place Valhubert

JARDIN DU LUXEMBOURG

RER

r. Souflot

Cardinal Lemoine

16

Jussieu

Cuvier

Ménagerie

Luxembourg

Panthéon

r. du Card

Jussieu

r. Linné

JARDIN DES PLANTES

Gare d'Austerlitz

Comte

l'Observatoire

11

Gay

Lussac

r. Lacépède

Place Monge

Monge

Geoffroy

Muséum National d'Histoire Naturelle

Buffon

Gare d'Austerlitz

Gare d'Austerlitz

5e

Grande Mosquée de Paris

Port-Royal

Église du Val-de-Grâce

St-

Jacques

Claude

Bernard

Censier-Daubenton

St-Hilaire

GROUPE HOSPITALIER PITIÉ-SALPÊTRIÈRE

bd.

de

VAL-DE-GRÂCE

17

r. Berthollet

Port

Royal

Les Gobelins

Marcel

St-Marcel

MATERNITÉ PORT-ROYAL

Fbg. St-Jacques

Glacière

av.

des

r. Le Brun

l'Hôpital

HÔPITAL COCHIN

Santé

bd. Arago

Arago

r. du Banquier

Campo Formio

Observatoire de Paris

la

de

Gobelins

13e

Saint-Jacques

bd.

St- Jacques

de

Glacière

square René Le Gall

18

Croulebarbe

Place d'Italie

place d'Italie

Vincent

Auriol

Nationale

r. Edmond Gondinet

Auguste

Blanqui

Corvisart

Bobillot

av. d'Italie

HÔPITAL SAINTE-ANNE

| 0 | | 1/4 mi |
| 0 | 0.25 km | |

breakfast room with potted plants and an upright piano. The spotless rooms are filled with country-style furniture and papered in old-fashioned prints; crocheted bedspreads and framed etchings of flowers complete the look. Views from most windows are of either the garden or surrounding trees. The calm is such that the hotel has nixed TVs. What's more, this unique ambience comes at a reasonable price. Rooms in the "Garden Building" are more modern with newer bathrooms; families will appreciate the six suites that can sleep four.

75 rue de Cardinal-Lemoine, 5th arrond. ℰ **01-43-26-79-23.** www.hotel-grandes-ecoles.com. 51 units. 130€–160€ double, 180€ family room. Parking 30€. Métro: Cardinal Lemoine or Place Monge. **Amenities:** Wi-Fi (free).

Hôtel Le Vert Galant ★★   Located in a quiet green corner near the Manufacture des Gobelins, this lovely haven is wrapped around a small garden. All the rooms in this family-run operation look out on greenery, and the hotel has an unfussy, country feel. Rooms have recently been renovated and now sport oak floors, Italian tiled showers, and fresh wallpaper. The Basque restaurant next door, Auberge Etchegorry, is run by the same management. You may feel like you have left the city center, but the hotel is only minutes away from rue Mouffetard and three Métro lines.

41 rue Croulebarbe, 13th arrond. ℰ **01-44-08-83-50.** www.vertgalant.com. 15 units. 100€–150€ double. Métro: Corvisart, Gobelins, or Place d'Italie. **Amenities:** Restaurant, Wi-Fi (free).

Hôtel Marignan ★★   A budget classic, these simple lodgings cater to travelers looking for reasonable, centrally located lodgings, who don't mind a little noise in the hallways. Not only is the price right, but there are extras like free washing machines and kitchen access (after your free breakfast is served). Though still pretty basic, the rooms have recently been renovated, with new bedcovers and furniture. The pretty carved ceiling moldings have been left intact, and the newly tiled bathrooms are spotless. Room sizes range from comfortable to enormous—this is one of the few hotels in Paris to offer rooms for up to five people. The cheapest rates involve sharing a toilet and/or shower. You can reserve by e-mail, but not online. There is no elevator.

13 rue du Sommerard, 5th arrond. ℰ **01-43-54-63-81.** www.hotel-marignan.com. 30 rooms. 72€–121€ double; 102€–140€ triple; 120€–161€ quad; 133€–170€ quint. Continental breakfast included in room rate. Métro: Cluny–La Sorbonne. **Amenities:** Wi-Fi (free).

St-Germain-des-Prés & Luxembourg (6th Arrondissement)

Sleek boutiques and restaurants abound in this legendary (and expensive) neighborhood; historic cafes and monuments lend plenty of atmosphere. Unlike some other Parisian neighborhoods, this one is lively even late at night; it is also centrally located and in walking distance to many top sights. The highest concentration of noise and tourist traps is around boulevard St-Germain and Carrefour de l'Odéon; once you turn down a side street, things quiet down considerably.

EXPENSIVE

Relais St-Germain ★★★   Fashioned out of three adjoining 17th-century townhouses, this intimate hotel mixes old world charm and jazzy modern ideas. Exposed beams abound in the spacious rooms, even the smallest of which are equipped with a comfortable sitting area. And yet, there is nothing fussy or boring about the decor, which artfully blends period furniture with modern prints, like a Louis XV armchair covered in zigzagged leather. The effect is both stylish and deeply comforting. You'll want to fling yourself onto the king-sized bed, cover yourself with a fake-fur throw, and just stare out the window (all of which look out on the lovely Carrefour de l'Odéon). There are some extra stairs between floors, so if you have mobility issues, make that clear when you reserve. Guests have priority at the hotel's restaurant, Le Comptoir (p. 91), where you might otherwise wait 6 months for a reservation. Rooms book up far in advance here.

9 Carrefour de l'Odéon, 6th arrond. ℂ **01-44-27-07-97.** www.hotelrsg.com. 22 units. 285€–370€ double; 395€ suite. Rates include breakfast if you reserve on the hotel's website. **Amenities:** Restaurant, Wi-Fi (free). Métro: Odéon.

Villa Madame ★★   These sleek lodgings offer spacious, modern rooms in subdued tones with a large dose of Parisian elegance. A few on the upper floors have balconies overlooking the neighborhood, which is just a short walk from the Jardin du Luxembourg; there is one large suite with a roomy terrace. Downstairs, there is a handicap-accessible room, as well as an interior courtyard where you can have breakfast or just lounge around with a drink in the evening surfing on the house iPad. When it's nippy out you can have tea by the fireplace in the salon.

44 rue Madame, 6th arrond. ℂ **01-45-48-02-81.** www.hotelvillamadameparis.com. 28 units. 200€–400€ double, 400€–520€ suite. Métro: Rennes or St-Sulpice. **Amenities:** Bar, concierge service, laundry service, room service, Wi-Fi (free).

MODERATE

Hôtel des Marronniers ★★   Just a few minutes away from the church of St-Germain-des-Prés, these cozy lodgings are nestled in the back of a quiet courtyard behind the galleries and antique stores of chic rue Jacob. All of the rooms have been renovated recently and feature rich fabrics, bright colors, and reproduction antiques; many have exposed beams on their high ceilings. Guests are invited to take tea or just relax in the lovely garden behind the hotel; if it's raining you can do the same on the covered veranda. Three- and four-person bedrooms are available for families.

21 rue Jacob, 6th arrond. ℂ **01-43-25-30-60.** www.paris-hotel-marronniers.com. 36 units. 155€–225€ double; 230€–270€ triple; 270€–340€ quad. Métro: St-Germain-des-Prés. **Amenities:** Wi-Fi (free).

Hotel Mayet ★★   The lobby here sports two murals, one by American graffiti artist JonOne and the other by his French counterpart, André. Rooms are snug, but colorful, with white walls and touches of bright orange. The decoration includes a light-hearted North African theme, with paintings of camels in the desert and vintage photos of beautiful Moroccan movies stars. This family-run enterprise also has an apartment for rent next door that sleeps four with a kitchen and washer dryer.

3 rue Mayet, 6th arrond. ℂ **01-47-83-21-35.** www.mayet.com. 23 units. 102€–200€ double; 157€–240€ triple. Métro: Duroc. **Amenities:** Bar, Wi-Fi (free).

INEXPENSIVE

Hôtel Le Clément ★★   These charming lodgings offer affordable comfort about 2 blocks away from St-Germain-des-Prés. Facing the restaurant-lined Marché St-Germain, there's plenty going on at night; light sleepers should be advised that the least-expensive doubles all face the street. That said, all of the impeccably maintained rooms are air-conditioned and double-paned windows keep out most noise. Walls are covered in traditional prints, and beds are decked out in white quilted spreads. Doubles tend to be small, but the mini-suites are good for families. Service can be slightly frosty, but is generally discrete and helpful.

6 rue Clément, 6th arrond. ℂ **01-43-26-53-60.** www.hotelclementparis.com. 28 units. 119€–165€ double; 167€–185€ triples and suites. Métro: Mabillon. **Amenities:** Wi-Fi (free).

Grand Hôtel des Balcons ★   For the neighborhood, the rooms in this plain and simple hotel are remarkably spacious. Most also have small balconies, the better to enjoy the view of the lovely Odéon neighborhood. The roomy triples and quads are a good bet for families, and there is a handicap-accessible room on the ground floor. The lobby has an old-fashioned Art Nouveau feel and the rooms are well-kept and impeccably clean, if not particularly stylish.

3 rue Casimir Delavigne, 6th arrond. ℂ **01-46-34-78-50.** www.balcons.com. 49 units. 135€–240€ double; 240€ triple or quad. Métro: Odéon. **Amenities:** Wi-Fi (free).

Eiffel Tower & Nearby (7th Arrondissement)

For some reason, many visitors to Paris clamor for hotels that are right near the Eiffel Tower, perhaps under the mistaken impression that this is a central location. It isn't. Not only that, the 7th arrondissement is one of the grandest in Paris, filled with government ministries and posh residences—not exactly a place where you are likely to experience a typical slice of Parisian life. That said, there's no denying it's a beautiful, quiet area, and that there is something magical about wandering out of your hotel in the morning and seeing the Eiffel Tower looming in the background.

EXPENSIVE

Hôtel de Varenne ★★   There is an atmosphere of refined serenity at this hotel, which caters to the ministerial crowd that frequents the area. Set back from the street, rooms are very quiet, and there is a lovely garden patio for breakfast alfresco in the warmer months. The decor is stately, without being stuffy; the custom-made furniture is inspired by Louis XVI and Empire styles. Entirely restored in 2014, infinite care has been taken to ensure that every inch of each room is in top condition, and there is now a handicap-accessible suite on the ground floor. Considering the quality of the lodgings and the self-importance of the neighborhood, the rates here are very reasonable.

44 rue de Bourgogne, 7th arrond. ℂ **01-45-51-45-55.** www.hoteldevarenne.com. 26 units. 157€–287€ double. 267€–327€ triple, 337€–387€ suite. Métro: Varenne or La Tour Maubourg. **Amenities:** Wi-Fi (free).

Hôtel Verneuil ★★★   This intimate hotel feels like a chic private home. Shelves filled with books line the walls, a low sofa invites, and comfortable furniture is scattered around the lobby. While the hallways of this 17th-century townhouse are painted in somber shades of brown and beige, the rooms are bright, friendly and modern, if a little small. The feeling is cozy and personal, with a creative jumble of antique charm and contemporary class. If you need to stretch out, go for the deluxe room which has space for a desk and chairs to relax in; there are a few adjoining rooms for families. Guests can use iPads and make free international calls from their rooms.

8 rue de Verneuil, 7th arrond. ℂ **01-42-60-82-14.** www.hotel-verneuil-saint-germain.com. 26 units. 179€–360€ double. Métro: St Germain-des-Prés or Rue du Bac. **Amenities:** Bar, babysitting, business corner with printer, massages by appt., laundry service, room service, Wi-Fi (free).

Hôtel Muget ★★   Known for its impeccable service and comfort level, the lovely rooms at this personable hotel are fitted with faux-antique furniture, big wood headboards hand-painted with a lily-of-the-valley (muguet) motif, and pretty bathrooms with old-fashioned wood washstands and mirror frames. Rooms are relatively large for Paris, and the triples are downright spacious. Five doubles have a great view of the Eiffel Tower, three others of Les Invalides; needless to say they book up months in advance. The others, which are equally comfy and less expensive, look out on either the quiet street or the airy courtyard. Three rooms on the ground floor look directly into a small but lush garden.

11 rue Chevert, 7th arrond. ℰ **01-47-05-05-93.** www.hotelmuguet.com. 43 units. 165€–280€ double, 250€–350€ triple. Métro: Varenne or La Tour Maubourg. **Amenities:** Computer and printer in lobby, Wi-Fi (free).

Hôtel Signature St-Germain-des-Prés ★★★   Run by the friendly Prigent family (who are also at the helm of the Hôtel Londres Eiffel; see below), this new boutique hotel has both stylish interiors and a homey charm. Bright colors on the walls blend harmoniously with subdued bedsteads and linens; smart mid-century reproduction furniture and faux antique phones take edge off sleek modern lines. The "Prestige" rooms cost more, but are especially roomy (30 sq. m/323 sq. ft.), a rarity even in upscale Parisian hotels. In addition to particularly attentive service, this hotel is also blessed with an excellent location for shopping addicts: It's just down the street from Bon Marché.

5 rue Chomel, 7th arrond. ℰ **01-45-48-35-53.** 26 units. 220€–350€ double; 380€ triple; family suite 500€. Métro: Sèvres-Babylone or St-Sulpice. **Amenities:** Concierge service, Wi-Fi (free).

MODERATE

Hôtel de L'Empereur ★★   All the rooms facing the street in this perfectly manicured hotel (run by the same meticulous management as the Muguet; see below) have great views of the nearby golden dome of Les Invalides, which hovers over the tomb of Napoleon (hence the name of the hotel). The best views are from the fifth and sixth floors. If views aren't your priority, consider the larger rooms facing the courtyard, which get lots of light, less street noise, and are less expensive. The plush rooms are decorated with a modern take on Empire style. There are communicating rooms for families here.

2 rue Chevert, 7th arrond. ℰ **01-45-55-88-02.** www.hotelempereur.com. 31 units. 140€–290€ double. 225€ triple. Métro: Ecole Militaire. **Amenities:** Concierge service, guest computer, Wi-Fi (free).

Hôtel Eber Mars ★★   When you walk in the door, chances are you will be greeted by none other than Monsieur Eber himself, who has spent the last 10 years lovingly renovating his hotel. Eber has opted for a 1930s-era decor that is low-key and specifically Parisian. Walls in the spacious rooms are papered in subtle period patterns in neutral colors, lit by authentic art-deco hanging fixtures picked up at antiques fairs. Old-fashioned radiators have been scraped and lacquered; prints dating from the Universal Exposition of 1889 (which unveiled the Eiffel Tower—another decor theme) are hung on the walls. Rooms in this hotel are unusually large for Paris; the triples and communicating suites are ideal for families. Breakfast is served all day.

117 ave. de la Bourdonnais, 7th arrond. ℰ **01-47-05-42-30.** www.hotelebermars.com. 25 units. 120€–280€ doubles; 200€–300€ triples. Métro: Ecole Militaire. **Amenities:** Bar, Wi-Fi (free).

Hôtel Londres Eiffel ★★★   From the moment you enter, you feel like you are in a private home here, and you'll probably be greeted by the friendly owners, the Prigents. Polished iron and wood banisters lead up spiral staircases to narrow hallways and cozy rooms with a personal touch to the decor. There is an old-fashioned, yet modern feel here; walls are covered with fabrics printed with tasteful 19th-century kitsch motifs, 1940's-style furniture, and a terrific comfort level. A few of the rooms have views of the Eiffel Tower (which is just steps away), but they book up early. For even more quiet and intimacy, ask for a room in the Pavillion, a small elevator-less building in the back with just six rooms. Adjoining rooms are available for families.

1 rue Augereau, 7th arrond. ℂ **01-45-51-63-02.** www.londres-eiffel.com. 30 units. 150€–275€ double; 330€ triple. Métro: Ecole Militaire. **Amenities:** Wi-Fi (free).

INEXPENSIVE

Hôtel du Champ de Mars ★★ An adorable and affordable little inn right around the corner from the food shops of rue Cler—what more could you ask for? The impeccably maintained rooms are tastefully decorated with the kind of care people generally reserve for their own homes: thick cotton bedspreads, framed etchings, and printed fabrics in warm colors on the walls and windows. Two rooms have a tiny courtyard, while those on the upper floors get lots of light. All of the comfortable doubles cost 130€.

7 rue du Champ de Mars, 7th arrond. ℂ **01-45-51-52-30.** www.hotelduchampdemars.com. 25 units. 130€ double. Métro: Ecole Militaire. **Amenities:** Laptop loan for guests, Wi-Fi (free).

Grand Hôtel Lévêque ★ This budget classic had a modern makeover a few years ago and the bright rooms are as clean and tidy as ever. While purple and beige may not be everyone's favorite color combination, the decor is basic and direct, and some of the rooms are quite large. The hotel is on rue Cler, a delightful pedestrian street lined with food stands, cafes, and cute shops.

29 rue Cler, 7th arrond. ℂ **01-47-05-49-15.** www.hotel-leveque.com. 50 units. 100€–169€ double; 126€–220€ triple. Métro: Ecole Militaire. **Amenities:** Computer and printer in lobby, Wi-Fi (free).

Montparnasse & Nearby (14th & 15th Arrondissements)

Montparnasse is more centrally located than it might seem—it's right on the border of St-Germain and close to the Luxembourg gardens. Also, the train station is a major transit hub for a bundle of Métro lines and bus routes. Though the utterly unaesthetic Tour Montparnasse now casts a shadow over this ancient artists' haunt (Henry Miller, Man Ray, Chagall, Picasso . . .) the neighboring streets are still full of personality.

EXPENSIVE

L'Apostrophe ★★ Honoring the neighborhood's literary history (Henry Miller wrote across the way at La Coupole and Hemmingway set up shop at Closerie des Lilas down the street), this "poem hotel" is dedicated to the beauty and mystery of writing. The decor is a little off the wall, but very tastefully so, starting with an impressive silhouette of a tree on the hotel's facade. Inside, rooms are themed: "Caligraphy" has Chinese characters splashed on royal blue walls, "Musique" features stenciled sheet music, instruments, and giant piano key, and "Paris–Paradis" pays homage to the writer Jules Renard and the city's skyline. The larger rooms include a Jacuzzi bathtub right in the room—very romantic, but not for anyone who doesn't want to get naked in front of their roommate (the toilet is private).

3 rue de Chevreuse, 6th arrond. ℂ **01-56-54-31-31.** www.apostrophe-hotel.com. 16 units. 169€–310€ standard double; 220€–353€ double with a Jacuzzi. Métro: Vavin. **Amenities:** Bar, Wi-Fi (free).

INEXPENSIVE

Hôtel des Bains ★★★   With cute, comfortable rooms and excellent rates, this friendly hotel is one of the best deals on the Left Bank, especially for families. This hotel offers several good-size, two-room suites for up to four people as well as comfortable doubles with high ceilings. The decor is simple with original objects and artwork from the art market that takes place on the nearby square every Sunday (where there is also an open-air market Wed and Sat mornings). Most rooms have wood floors and a few have tiny balconies. The elevator stops at a landing between floors, so you will need to be able to manage a few stairs.

33 rue Delambre, 14th arrond. ⓒ **01-43-20-85-27.** www.hotel-des-bains-montparnasse.com. 42 units. 103€ double; 135€–170€ suites for 2–4 people. Métro: Vavin, Edgar Quinet, or Montparnasse. **Amenities:** Wi-Fi (free).

Solar Hôtel ★   Declaring itself "the first ecological, economical, and activist hotel," these basic lodgings feature compact florescent lighting, composting, and recycling. The bright blue rooms have a hostel-like feel (though they are private), but the mattresses are firm and everything is clean and tidy. There is a nice garden for sipping your fair trade tea and bicycles for guests' use. The location is excellent, just around the corner from rue Daguerre, an adorable pedestrian market street, and a short walk from airport buses and transit at Denfert-Rochereau. There are two buildings, one with free Wi-Fi in the rooms, one with Wi-Fi only in the common areas, where there are guest computers. Rooms are a great deal at 79€, including an organic breakfast.

22 rue Boulard, 14th arrond. ⓒ **01-43-21-08-20.** www.solarhotel.fr. 34 units. 79€ double. Rates include breakfast. Métro/RER: Denfert-Rochereau. **Amenities:** Wi-Fi (free), bicycles and computers with Internet access (free).

ALTERNATIVE ACCOMMODATIONS

Hotels are all very well and good, but for some, nothing beats staying in a private home or apartment, particularly if you are a family on a budget. Fortunately, there are several options for travelers with an independent streak, including short-term rentals, bed & breakfasts, and "aparthotels," that is, short-term apartments with some hotel services.

Short-Term Rentals

In recent years there has been a boom in short-term rentals, and there are now dozens of agencies proffering hundreds of apartments smack in the center of the City of Light. Though the rates for two people are sometimes (but not always) significantly less than what you'd pay at a hotel, the advantages are many, not the least of which is the fact that you can cook some of your meals at home and save yourself a ton of time and money. Other benefits are privacy, independence, and a chance to see what it's like to live like a Parisian, even if it's just for a week.

If you are more than two, and especially if you are traveling *en famille,* the benefits can be huge. Family suites and/or adjoining rooms are rare in Parisian hotels, and you will almost always end up paying for two doubles—that is, somewhere around 250€ to 450€ per night—whereas you could rent a one-bedroom apartment with a foldout couch and/or extra bed in the living room for around 1,000€ to 1,400€ per week, or 143€ to 200€ per night.

In most cases, you will deal with the agency (not the owners), and the minimum stay is 4 days to 1 week. There are hundreds of agencies on the Internet, but here are a few well-established ones:

- **Parisian Home** (© 01-45-08-03-37; www.parisianhome.com)
- **France Lodge** (© 01-56-33-85-85; www.francelodge.fr)
- **Appartement de Ville** (© 01-42-45-09-08; www.appartementdeville.com)
- **Paris Attitude** (© 01-42-96-31-46; www.parisattitude.com)
- **Paris Appartements Services** (© 01-56-33-85-85; www.paris-appartements-services.com)

Another less conventional agency option is the wildly popular **Airbnb** (www.airbnb.com), a vast network of accommodations offered directly by local owners. Its Paris page has hundreds of offers for rooms (shared or private) and entire apartments.

Bed & Breakfasts

Though bed-and-breakfasts *(chambres d'hôtes)* are extremely common in the French countryside, in the big city, where privacy and anonymity are treasured, the idea of strangers living in one's home generally fills Parisians with horror. This is a city where despite the high rents, roommates are virtually unheard of, and poverty-stricken students would prefer to live in an attic, alone, rather than share an apartment with nonfamily members.

A terrific way to find a quality B&B is to visit the city's official B&B website: **Hôtes Qualité Paris** (www.hotesqualiteparis.fr). A partnership with Paris' most well-established and trusted B&B agencies, the site offers a wide range of rooms for about 50€ to 140€ per person per night, based on double occupancy. A couple of other recommended agencies are:

- **Alcôve & Agapes** (© 01-44-85-06-05; www.bed-and-breakfast-in-paris.com)
- **Good Morning Paris** (© 01-47-07-28-29; www.goodmorningparis.fr)

Aparthotels

Mostly designed for business travelers, these utilitarian lodgings are a cross between a hotel and an apartment. Short on charm, *aparthotels* are decidedly practical, as each unit comes with a kitchenette as well as hotel services such as fresh towels, dry cleaning, and a reception desk. Rates are generally higher than short-term rentals, but you do have the comfort of knowing you are dealing with a large company (if that makes you comfortable), with standardized apartments, organized websites, and customer service.

The best-known *aparthotel* company is **Citadines** (© 01-41-05-79-05; www.citadines.com), which offers clean, comfortable units in excellent locations around the city. The cheapest rentals are the studios with pullout beds, which range from 110€ to 320€ a night depending on the season and location.

Alternative Accommodations

WHERE TO STAY

WHERE TO EAT

Everywhere you look in Paris, someone is doing their best to ruin your waistline. *Boulangeries* (bakeries) with buttery croissants and decadent pastries lurk on every street corner, open-air markets tempt the senses, and terrific restaurants with intriguing menus sprout up on every block. Below is just a sampling of Paris's gourmet delights. The best cafes, tearooms, and other places to find sinful sweets are listed at the end of this chapter.

In France, food is not a pastime; it's an art. Eating and drinking is a topic of serious discussion, the subject of radio shows, newspaper columns, and even feature films. So it's not surprising that Paris, navel of the French universe, should boast some of the best food on Earth. Fortunately, you don't have to have a king-size budget to dine like royalty. But you do have to choose wisely. Once upon a time, you could wander into just about any restaurant in Paris and sit down to a good meal; today, this is no longer the case. Try not to notice all the fast-food places that have popped up around the city, and don't even think about eating in one of the ubiquitous Chinese restaurants that serve a bland version of this marvelous Asian cuisine.

Fortunately, the guardians of good food are fighting back. Sick of the pressure and fuss of the temples of *haute cuisine,* about 10 years ago a bunch of famous chefs like Christian Constant and Yves de Camdeborde started what is now known as the "bistronomy" movement, opening dressed-down bistros that serve modern versions of traditional worker's cuisine at prices that a worker might be able to afford (at least, for a night out on the town). Since then, a plethora of "neo-bistros" have opened up all over town, serving classic bistro dishes with a dash of contemporary *je ne sais quoi.* While not exactly cheap, in general these restaurants are affordably hip, and serve excellent food. One outgrowth of this movement is the obsession with "noble" ingredients, such as high-quality, regional produce or products, often from a specific small-scale farm or artisan, sometimes organic, but always in keeping with the oldest and best traditions.

A French version of the Spanish tapas bar has recently appeared on the Parisian scene, where the tapas often come with a southwestern or Basque accent. And *pourquoi pas?* As lunch is usually the big meal of the day, Parisians are happy to nibble something light at night, especially with a nice glass of wine.

There's also a puzzling interest in American food. Gourmet hamburgers are ubiquitous on bistro menus, and you'll find bagels and smoked salmon at "le brunch."

PRACTICAL MATTERS
Eating Hours & Annual Closings

In Paris, unless you see a sign that says SERVICE NONSTOP, meals are usually severely restricted to set hours. This is one of the reasons it's a good idea to reserve, if you can (the other is that dining rooms tend to be small). Don't expect to wander in someplace for a bowl of soup at 4pm. Lunch is generally served between noon and 2pm (sometimes 2:30pm), and dinner is served from 7:30 to 10:30pm (sometimes 11pm). Many restaurants are closed on Sundays and/or Mondays; some have started serving brunch on Sundays, which is served from 11am to 2pm. Cafes and restaurants with a bar tend to stay open between mealtimes serving drinks and coffee; if you are starving, you can usually order a light sandwich, or a *croque-monsieur* (a French take on a grilled ham and cheese sandwich). Some brasseries serve late into the night. For late-night dining options, see p. 71. Many restaurants close in August, and some between Christmas and New Year's; see listings for details. *Tip:* If you didn't reserve and you want to avoid waiting in line, try to arrive at the very beginning of the service, noon or around 7:30pm. Most French people eat later than that, so you'll avoid the rush.

Reservations

Most restaurants in Paris are small, so if you have your heart set on eating at one in particular, reserving ahead, even if it is the same day, is essential. If you are looking

Practical Matters

WHERE TO EAT

To Tip or Not to Tip?

In France, waiting tables is a time-honored profession, one that comes with paid vacation and retirement benefits. That said, no one gets rich being a French waitperson. Tipping is not required, or even expected, but it is a nice thing to do, especially if you've been at the table for several hours, or enjoyed good service. While the price you see on the menu includes tax and service, if you feel so inclined, leave a small tip (about 50¢ for drinks, a euro or two after meals in mid-range cafes or restaurants). Of course, no one will mind if you leave more.

Useful Websites for Foodies

o **Paris by Mouth** (www.parisbymouth.com) provides insider information (in English) on dining in the capital.

o **The Fork** (www.thefork.com) allows you to reserve restaurants online for free (according to area and type of food), and supplies a list of restaurant promotions—sometimes up to 50% off (check restrictions before you book).

o **Le Fooding** (www.lefooding.com) has a terrific list of Parisian restaurants as well as food-oriented events and news. French, with some English translations.

o **David Lebovitz** (www.davidlebovitz.com) is a pastry chef and cookbook author who has a rocking website that discusses everything from restaurants and recipes to shopping and travel tips. A personal favorite.

to dine at one of Paris's hip neo-bistros or famous gourmet temples, you may have to reserve even months in advance. Ask your hotel receptionist to help if you can't manage the telephone, or try reserving online through www.thefork.com (which also offers discounts). Otherwise, you can often reserve on the restaurant's site via e-mail.

price CATEGORIES

Expensive Main dishes 30€ and up
Moderate Main dishes 15€–30€
Inexpensive Main dishes under 15€

Dejeuner sur L'Herbe (Picnics)

Although restaurants are all very well and good, there's a lot to be said for a quick and easy outdoor meal in one of Paris's many lovely parks and squares. Picking up picnic ingredients is a pretty easy affair, though there's a bit of terminology you should be familiar with. For good takeout food, look for the nearest *charcuterie* (these specialize in smoked meat, pâtés, and other pork products) or *traiteur* (a store that sells prepared takeout dishes and salads). At almost any *boulangerie* (bakery), you can find what may well be **the best lunch bargain in the city:** their lunch *"formule,"* or set menu. For around 7€, you can get a long sandwich (usually half a baguette), amply filled with chicken, ham, or tuna and *crudités* (tomato, lettuce, and other saladlike items), a drink, and a fresh pastry. Often you can substitute a slice of quiche for a sandwich. *Formules* and sandwiches are usually only available from 11am to 2pm. **Eric Kayser** (www.maison-kayser.com) and **Paul** (www.paul.fr) are standout local bakery chains, serving delicious salads, sandwiches, and even hot dishes. But your best bet is to use your *nez* and find a place on your own. Just be careful in tourist areas, like the Eiffel Tower, where you might find a dud.

Choosing a Restaurant

Below is a very selective list of restaurants, wine bars, and tearooms that serve good, honest food. But seeing as how there are thousands of restaurants in Paris, you just might wander into something wonderful and unexpected on your own. Finding a good

Good Healthy Meals to Go or to Stay

Over the past few years, many sandwich bars have popped up all over town:

o **Cojean** (22 locations; www.cojean.fr). These airy, modern boutiques serve fresh, healthy food, including innovative salads, quiches, sandwiches, and fresh-squeezed juices. Many veggie options. You can eat on site at comfortable tables. Open until 4 or 5pm in most locations.

o **Exki** (10 locations; www.exki.com). This Belgian chain (pronounced "exkey," like the French word for

"exquisite") offers a terrific array of healthy sandwiches, soups, and desserts (including vegetarian choices), usually until 9 or 10pm. They use lots of organic, free-trade ingredients, and have a low ecological footprint.

o **Boco** (3 locations; www.boco.fr). This one is almost too good to be true. Organic take-out by Michelin-starred chefs for under 15€. Hot food, cold food, light meals, and desserts until 8 or 10pm. Main dishes 7 to 10€.

When people ask me about the legendary rudeness of Parisian wait staff, I have to fight the urge to do the French shrug. It really depends. As in most places in the world, in tourist restaurants you will not find the best service. On the other hand, there is no denying that Parisian customer service can be particularly frosty. Here's the way I see it: With Parisians, you are guilty until proved innocent. If you can weather the initial chilly blast and show them you are not easily flustered, they'll usually warm up, and before you know it they will be charming your socks off.

restaurant is extremely subjective, taking into account any number of variables and a good dose of what the French call "le feeling." That said, I recommend you take some precautions. Unfortunately, it is all too easy to waste time and money on tourist restaurants that shovel out food that is at best, unmemorable, and at worst, indigestible. Look for the places that are full of happy customers, where there's a line even. Or maybe just follow your nose, and let yourself be tempted by those delicious smells coming out of the kitchen.

5 THE RIGHT BANK

Louvre & Ile de la Cité (1st Arrondissement)

Dining near the Louvre can be expensive and frustrating. Since almost every tourist visiting the city comes to this part of town, it's rife with overpriced, mediocre tourist restaurants boasting menus in at least five languages. However, if you poke around some of the smaller streets away from the museum, there are plenty of little restaurants where you can eat well without blowing a royal budget.

EXPENSIVE

Le Grand Véfour ★★★ CLASSIC FRENCH   Back in the day, when the galleries of the Palais Royal were known for drinking, gambling, and revolutionary plotting (p. 115), what was then called the Café de Chartres was the place to see and be seen. Napoleon, Hugo, Colette, and Cocteau all dined in this magnificently preserved 18th-century dining room. Today, eating here is still a memorable event. Guy Martin, chef and owner for the past decade, continues to serve his signature dishes like Prince Rainier III pigeon and truffled oxtail parmentier, alongside sublime new creations that feature more contemporary flavors like sumac and star anise. The desserts are always incredible, especially the *palet* (a thick biscuit) with milk chocolate and hazelnuts, served with caramel and sea-salt ice cream. Reserve at least 2 weeks in advance; note that the lunch fixed-price menu is a third of the price of dinner.

17 rue de Beaujolais, 1st arrond. © **01-42-96-56-27.** www.grand-vefour.com. Main courses 88€–108€; fixed-price lunch 98€, fixed-price dinner 298€. Mon–Fri 12:30–1:45pm and 8–9:45pm. Closed Aug. Métro: Louvre–Palais-Royal or Pyramides.

Spring ★★★ MODERN FRENCH   One of the city's most talked about restaurants has a chef who is—gasp—American! Chef Daniel Rose, native of Chicago, pays utmost respect to all things French, while adding a dash of Yankee derring-do to his superb creations. The menu changes all the time, but it might start with quail eggs with lemony eggplant caviar, followed by filet of sole with mussels, smoked ham and green tomatoes. Desserts might include a crustless lemon tart or berries floating in a tea made from the pit of a peach. You must order the four-course fixed-price menu, but that doesn't seem to be a problem for diners, who fight for a seat here. Reserve around 3 months in advance.

6 rue Bailleul, 1st arrond. ℰ **01-45-96-05-72.** www.springparis.fr. Fixed-price dinner 84€. Tues–Sat 6:30–10:30pm. Closed second week in Aug. Métro: Louvre-Rivoli.

MODERATE

La Brasserie de l'Ile Saint-Louis ★ TRADITIONAL BRASSERIE Owned by the same family for three generations, this lovely, old-fashioned brasserie serves healthy portions of classic Alsatian dishes, like choucroute garni—a small mountain of sauerkraut topped with slices of ham, sausage, and other smoked meats—in a relaxed atmosphere. If sauerkraut isn't your game, try other classic brasserie fare like a tender entrecote (rib steak) or a breaded fillet of haddock. The decor is rustic without being kitsch. Despite the location, many of the diners are regulars. Eating's not a requirement; if you want, you can just enjoy a Mutzig (Alsatian beer) on the terrace and soak up a splendid view of the buttresses of Notre-Dame. Service is "nonstop."

55 quai de Bourbon, 4th arrond. ℰ **01-43-54-02-59.** www.labrasserie-isl.fr. Main courses 19€–32€. Thurs–Tues noon–11pm. Closed in Aug. Métro: Pont Marie.

La Tour de Montlhéry–Chez Denise ★★ TRADITIONAL FRENCH/ BISTRO One of the last remnants of the bustling atmosphere that used to surround the old Les Halles central market, Chez Denise stays open until the early hours of the morning and serves sturdy platters of *côte de boeuf* (a giant rib steak), grilled marrow bones, and brochettes of grilled meat so long they look like swords. The long-aproned waiters are used to encountering English speakers, but that hasn't changed the vibe, which is local and lively. If you are not a carnivore, there are a few fish dishes, and you can always enjoy the homemade fries, which are delicious.

5 rue des Prouvaires, 1st arrond. ℰ **01-42-36-21-82.** Main courses 22€–30€. Mon–Fri noon–3pm and 7:30pm–5am. Closed July 15–Aug 15. Métro: Les Halles.

Le Fumoir ★★ MODERN FRENCH With its high ceilings, subdued lighting, and large windows, this understatedly hip spot is a good place to regroup. During the day (except at lunchtime) dawdling is encouraged: Magazines and newspapers are available at the front entry, and there's a small lending library/book exchange in the back

Let's Do Lunch

Many restaurants in Paris serve a set-price menu at lunch that is considerably cheaper than the same food served at dinnertime. It is not at all unusual to find a two- or three-course lunch prix-fixe, called alternately a *formule* or a menu for 16€ to 25€. The only downside is that your choice of dishes will usually be limited on the *formule*. **Note:** Set lunches are usually only served Monday through Friday.

Right Bank West Restaurants

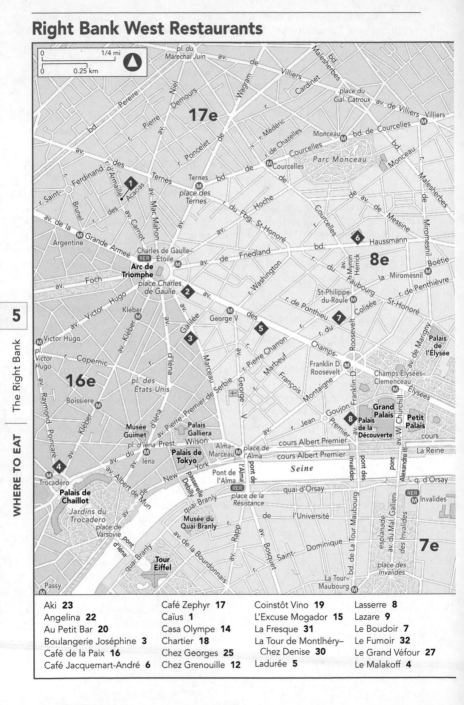

Aki **23**	Café Zephyr **17**	Coinstôt Vino **19**	Lasserre **8**
Angelina **22**	Caïus **1**	L'Excuse Mogador **15**	Lazare **9**
Au Petit Bar **20**	Casa Olympe **14**	La Fresque **31**	Le Boudoir **7**
Boulangerie Joséphine **3**	Chartier **18**	La Tour de Montlhéry–	Le Fumoir **32**
Café de la Paix **16**	Chez Georges **25**	Chez Denise **30**	Le Grand Véfour **27**
Café Jacquemart-André **6**	Chez Grenouille **12**	Ladurée **5**	Le Malakoff **4**

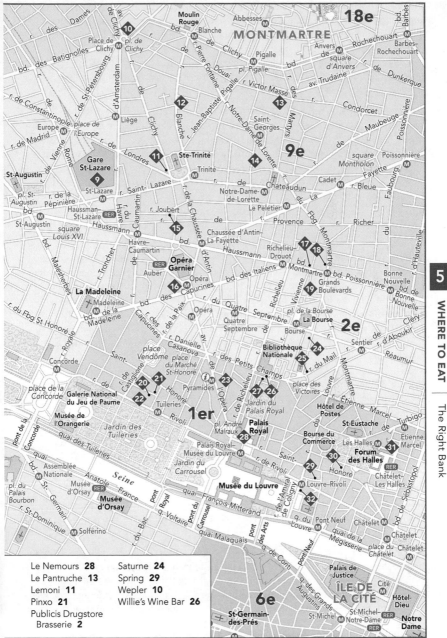

Le Nemours **28**
Le Pantruche **13**
Lemoni **11**
Pinxo **21**
Publicis Drugstore
 Brasserie **2**

Saturne **24**
Spring **29**
Wepler **10**
Willie's Wine Bar **26**

room. At night, well-dressed 30-somethings crowd around the magnificent wood bar—which in a former life stood in a Philadelphia speakeasy—as they wait for their table. Like the surroundings, the seasonal menu has an international flair: The offerings might include pork sautéed with cabbage and kimchi or raviolis with Corsican *broccio* cheese and wild garlic pesto. On Sundays, there's a 26€ brunch complete with pancakes and eggs Benedict.

6 rue de l'Amiral Coligny, 1st arrond. ℂ **01-42-92-00-24.** www.lefumoir.com. Main courses 15€– 26€; fixed-price menu lunch 23€–26€, fixed-price menu dinner 34€–38€.Daily 11am-2am, lunch served noon–3pm, dinner 7–11pm. Métro: Louvre-Rivoli.

Pinxo ★★★ MODERN FRENCH/TAPAS Get a taste of renowned chef Alain Dutournier's exquisite cooking in a relaxed atmosphere at this modern tapas restaurant where food is made to be shared (each dish is priced per person on the menu). Dishes include things like lobster ravioli with artichoke emulsion, nuggets of lamb with cépes (wild mushrooms), or organic marinated salmon with herring and fennel. The best way to wash it all down is with a glass of wine (of course)—choose from 120 bottles, many of which are available by the glass.

9 rue d'Alger, 1st arrond. ℂ **01-40-20-72-00.** www.alaindutournier.com. Portions per person 6€–9€, meal per person 35€–40€. Mon–Fri 12:15–2:15pm and 7–10:30pm, Sat 7–10:30pm. Closed Aug. Métro: Tuileries.

Willi's Wine Bar ★ MODERN BISTRO/WINE BAR Contrary to what you may expect, Willi was a dog. The owner's basset hound to be exact. But he graciously lent his illustrious name to this wine bar, which has been thrilling taste buds for over 30 years. You'll hear a lot of English spoken here, but don't let it scare you—in addition to a terrific selection of wines, you can indulge a variety of delicious dishes like roasted cod with fresh peas and sherry or veal with preserved lemons and ginger. If you'd just like to nibble something with your glass of wine, there's a selection of Spanish ham and finger food too.

13 rue des Petits Champs, 1st arrond. ℂ **01-42-61-05-09.** www.williswinebar.com. Main courses 16€–23€; fixed-price lunch 20€; fixed-price dinner 36€. Mon–Sat noon–2:30pm and 7–10:30pm; wine bar noon–midnight. Closed 2 weeks in Aug. Métro: Pyramides or Bourse.

INEXPENSIVE

Aki ★★ JAPANESE There are several Japanese restaurants on rue Ste-Anne (see box), and while quality varies, some of them are excellent, like this one, which specializes in *okonomiyaki*. This delicious dish is a sort of grilled omelet topped with meat or seafood and a yummy sauce. Watch the cooks create yours on a griddle in the open kitchen, before diving into your meal. You can also sample udon or soba noodles here. Get here early or be prepared to stand in line.

11bis rue Sainte Anne, 1st arrond. ℂ **01-42-97-54-27.** Main courses 11€–15€. Mon–Sat 11am– 10:45pm. Métro: Pyramides.

Au Petit Bar ★★ TRADITIONAL FRENCH Tucked on a small street right behind the illustrious Rue de Rivoli, this old-fashioned, mom-and-pop restaurant has somehow survived the onslaught of chic that has inundated the neighborhood. Mom and Pop are really in the kitchen, while their son is behind the bar bantering with the customers, most of whom he knows by name. The food is simple and solid—you might start with mackerel in white wine, followed by steak frites, and finish up with a chocolate mousse, for example. Prices are extremely reasonable, considering the

The Right Bank

WHERE TO EAT

Right Bank East Restaurants

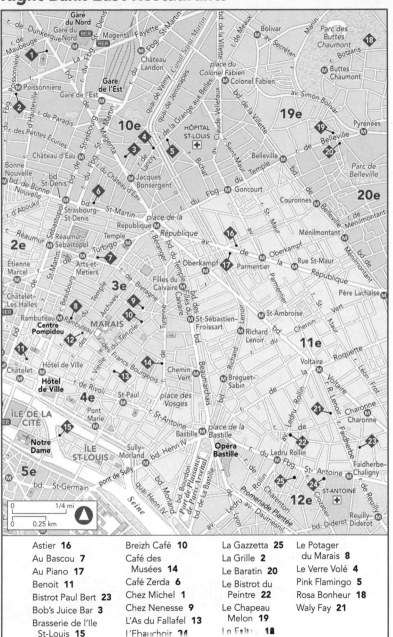

Astier **16**	Breizh Café **10**	La Gazzetta **25**	Le Potager
Au Bascou **7**	Café des	La Grille **2**	du Marais **8**
Au Piano **17**	Musées **14**	Le Baratin **20**	Le Verre Volé **4**
Benoit **11**	Café Zerda **6**	Le Bistrot du	Pink Flamingo **5**
Bistrot Paul Bert **23**	Chez Michel **1**	Peintre **22**	Rosa Bonheur **18**
Bob's Juice Bar **3**	Chez Nenesse **9**	Le Chapeau	Waly Fay **21**
Brasserie de l'Île	L'As du Fallafel **13**	Melon **19**	
St-Louis **15**	l'Ebauchoir **24**	Lo Eolo **18**	

You are wandering around the streets near the Opéra, when you take a sharp turn onto the rue Ste-Anne. Suddenly, everything is in Japanese, and there are noodle shops everywhere! Plunge into a bowl at one of these restaurants:

o **Udon Jubey,** 39 rue Ste-Anne, 1st (✆ 01-40-15-92-54; Métro: Pyramides), makes some of the best Udon noodles in town; slurp at the counter or jump on one of the limited number of tables.

o **Higuma,** 32 bis rue Ste-Anne, 1st (✆ **01-47-03-38-59;** Métro: Pyramides), features an open kitchen, ramen soups, and a long line out the front door.

o **Aki Boulangerie,** 16 rue Ste-Anne, 1st (✆ **01-40-15-63-38**), is a bakery-tearoom run by the same management as the restaurant (described above). Excellent Japanese teas and savory goodies, as well as terrific Franco-Japanese pastries, such as asuki bean tarts, and matcha tea éclairs.

close proximity to the ritzy place Vendôme; in fact, this is probably one of the cheapest cups of coffee on the Right Bank. No credit cards accepted.

7 rue Mont Thabor, 1st arrond. ✆ **01-42-60-62-09.** Main courses 7.50€–12€. Mon–Sat 7am–9pm. Closed Aug. Métro: Tuileries.

La Fresque ★ MODERN FRENCH   Named for its frescoed walls, this cozy, centrally located favorite serves modern bistro cuisine with plenty of vegetables (and vegetarian choices). While packed with business folk and shoppers at lunchtime, at night it draws a cooler crowd, ready to tuck into hearty dishes like rabbit pâté, duck leg in orange sauce, and chocolate mousse. Located on a pedestrian street, the outdoor terrace fills up quickly on sunny days.

100 rue Rambuteau, 1st arrond. ✆ **01-42-33-17-56.** www.restaurant-la-fresque-paris.fr. Main courses 12€–17€, fixed-price lunch 15€. Mon–Sat noon–3:30pm and 7pm–midnight. Closed 1 week in Aug. Métro: Les Halles. RER: Châtelet–Les Halles.

Le Marais (3rd & 4th Arrondissements)

You should have no trouble finding good things to eat in the Marais. Between its working-class roots and its more recent makeover there is a wide range of choices, from humble falafel joints to trendy brasseries. Unlike the shops here, which have become so hip it hurts, there are still a good selection of midrange restaurants that attract both the sleek set and just regular folks.

EXPENSIVE

Benoit ★ TRADITIONAL FRENCH   This historic restaurant had hosted a century's worth of Parisian notables when renowned chef Alain Ducasse took the helm in 2005. The venerable dining room is still lined with mirrors, zinc, and tiles, while the classic menu has been given an extra dash of pizzazz. Escargots (snails) in garlic butter, and brill braised with Jura wine share the stage with roasted milk-fed lamb from the Pyrenées and sautéed scallops *grenobloise*. Save room for the Armagnac baba with whipped cream.

20 rue St-Martin, 4th arrond ✆ **01-42-72-25-76.** www.benoit-paris.com. Main courses 26€–49€; fixed-price lunch 38€. Daily noon–2pm and 7:30–10pm. Closed first 3 weeks of Aug. Métro: Hôtel-de-Ville.

There aren't many restaurants that stay open until the wee hours of the Parisian night, but there are a few stalwarts around Les Halles. **Le Tambour,** 41 rue de Montmartre, 2nd arrond. (✆ **01-42-33-06-90;** Métro: Les Halles), serves reliable dishes like steak frites (mains 14€–18€) from noon to 5:30am every day in a dining room filled with kitschy Paris memorabilia. Nearby, **Au Pied de Cochon,** 6 rue Coquillière, 1st arrond.

(✆ **01-40-13-77-00;** Métro: Les Halles), is a brasserie open 24/7 that specializes in pork and more pork, but they also serve seafood and other dishes (mains 20€–50€). Their restorative onion soup is ideal at 4am after a night on the town. For a late-night meat fix, head to **La Tour de Montlhéry–Chez Denise** (p. 65; open until 5am), where the steak is as juicy as it is huge.

MODERATE

Au Bascou ★★ BASQUE   Basque cuisine, like the province, is not entirely French. Using lots of tomatoes, onions, and sweet Espelette pepper, the dishes have a decidedly different tang to them. But while the name of this restaurant refers to Basque country, the menu covers the entire southwest. Traditional Basque dishes like *pipérade* (a tasty omelet loaded with peppers and onions) and *axoa* (a stew of veal shoulder, peppers, and onions) mingle with southwestern classics like duck foie gras and roast *palombe* (wood pigeon). Everything is handled with great care by the chef, who used to be the right hand man of Alain Sederens.

38 rue Réaumur, 3rd arrond. ✆ **01-42-72-69-25.** www.au-bascou.fr. Main courses 18€; fixed-price lunch menu 18€–25€. Mon–Fri noon–2pm and 8–10:30pm. Closed in Aug. Métro: Arts-et-Métiers.

Café des Musées ★ TRADITIONAL FRENCH/BISTRO   Weary culture vultures who've tried to do both the Picasso museum and the Musée Carnavalet on the same day will appreciate this bustling corner cafe with its appealing sidewalk tables. This is not just any old corner cafe, mind you, but one where the young chef does terrific things with bistro classics like steak frites and *andouillette* (tripe sausage) as well as lighter fare like fresh vegetable casserole with basil oil, or shrimp with Thai curry. The lunch fixed-price menu is particularly good value.

49 rue de Turenne, 3rd arrond. ✆ **01-42-72-96-17.** www.cafedesmusees.fr. Main courses 12€–21€; fixed-price lunch 17€, dinner 27€. Daily noon–3pm and 7–11pm. Closed mid-Aug to early Sept. Métro: St. Paul or Chemin Vert.

Le Potager du Marais ★ VEGETARIAN   Not just vegetarian, this organic haven is downright vegan—something you won't find on every Parisian street corner. The shoe-box sized dining room fills up quickly with fans of its delicious veggie offerings, which include *seitan bourguignon,* mushroom pâté, and pumpkin parmentier. Many items are gluten-free. Finish off with a simple but scrumptious apple compote.

22 rue Rambuteau, 3rd arrond. ✆ **01-57-40-98-57.** www.lepotagerdumarais.fr. Main courses 16€–19€. Wed–Sun noon–3pm and 7–10:30pm. Closed first 2 weeks of Sept and last 3 weeks of Jan. Métro: Rambuteau.

INEXPENSIVE

Breizh Café ★★ CRÊPERIE   After wandering off to Japan, where he found both a wife and professional success, Chef Bertrand Larcher started opening hugely

France is a meat-loving, carnivorous country. The most common reaction to those announcing a non-meat-eating status will be a blank stare of amazement mixed with horror. Don't worry, there are many ways of getting around the problem. Scan menus for *salades composées*, meal-size salads that often come in meat-free versions. If you eat fish, most restaurants offer at least one or two selections. And there are vegetarian restaurants here. I've listed a few (**Bob's Juice Bar, p. 83; Le Potager du Marais**, p. 71; and **Jardin des Pâtes**, p. 89), but space limitations make it hard to go in depth. For more options, visit The Happy Cow (www. happycow.net), a veggie online network with extensive listings for Paris.

popular crêperies, first in Tokyo and then back in the home country. His Paris version is a warm and modern wood-paneled space decorated with funky Japanese art that offers both friendly service and great food. Start with oysters or head straight for a savory buckwheat *galette,* crisp and nutty and filled with high-quality organic ingredients, such as farm fresh eggs, Bordier butter, and seasonal produce. Sip on one of the artisanal ciders, and save room for a sweet crepe, drizzled with chocolate or salted butter caramel. It gets very crowded here, so try to reserve ahead.

109 rue Vieille du Temple, 3rd arrond. ℂ **01-42-72-13-77.** www.breizhcafe.com. Main courses 7.50€–14€. Wed–Sat 11:30am–11pm; Sun 11:30am–10pm. Closed last 3 weeks in Aug. Métro: Filles du Calvaire.

Chez Nenesse ★★★ TRADITIONAL BISTRO   This neighborhood haunt has stayed true to its proletarian roots in a frighteningly hip part of the northern Marais. At lunchtime, the chef sends out traditional bistro fare (such as blanquette de veau, or rump steak) into the busy dining room, while dinner comes with a change in menus and ambience—the checked plastic tablecloths are traded for white linen, and *magret de canard au cassis* (duck breast with cassis liqueur) and *filet d'agneau a l'estragon* (lamb steak with tarragon) take center stage. Thursday is steak-frites day, when regulars crowd in at lunch for their weekly dose of the yummy house fries.

17 rue Saintonge, 3rd arrond. ℂ **01-42-78-46-49.** Main courses lunch 11€–12€, dinner 16€–20€. Mon–Fri noon–2:30pm and 8–10:15pm. Closed Aug and from Christmas to New Years. Métro: Filles de Calvaire or Oberkampf.

L'As du Fallafel ★★ FALAFEL/ISRAELI   This Marais institution place offers, without a doubt, the best falafel in Paris. And they're kosher, yet. True, falafel joints are scarce in this city, but that doesn't take away from the excellence of these overstuffed beauties, brimming with cucumbers, pickled turnips, shredded cabbage, tahini, fried eggplant, and those crispy balls of fried chickpeas and spices. Other arrangements of similar ingredients *sans* pita can be found in the *assiettes* (platters). Wash it down with an Israeli beer. Service is fast and furious, but basically friendly—just be prepared to deal with hoards of tourists and locals at lunch. Closed Friday afternoon and all day Saturday.

34 rue des Rosiers, 4th arrond. ℂ **01-48-87-63-60.** Main courses 8€–20€. Sun–Thurs 11am–midnight; Fri 11am–3pm. Métro: St. Paul.

Le Felteu ★★ TRADITIONAL BISTRO It's easy to walk right by this unassuming restaurant, where locals crowd in to the shabby, but clean dining room for copious portions of excellent food. You'll usually find either Brigitte or her husband Jerry, the long-time owners, behind the bar chatting with the regulars. Meanwhile in the kitchen, their intense young chef will be doing magical things with grilled lamb, or blood sausage *(boudin)* and sautéed apple and potato cubes or some other traditional bistro fare. Each dish is garnished with the vegetable du jour and/or a hearty portion of potato gratin. No credit cards.

15 rue Pequay, 4th arrond. ℂ **01-42-72-14-51.** Main courses 15€–22€. Mon–Fri 12:30–2:15pm and 8–10:30pm, Sat 8–10:30pm. Closed Aug. Métro: Rambuteau or Hôtel de Ville.

Champs-Élysées & Western Paris (8th, 16th & 17th Arrondissements)

Mobbed with tourists, oozing with opulence, the Champs-Élysées is a difficult place to find a good meal, unless you are willing to spend a lot of money. Mediocre chain restaurants abound on the grand avenue itself, kebab joints mingle with frighteningly expensive gourmet palaces on the surrounding side streets. If you have no strings attached to your wallet, you can explore dinners in the many two- and three-Michelin star restaurants in the area; if you are like the rest of us, consider splurging on lunch in one of these same eateries for half the price.

EXPENSIVE

Caïus ★★★ MODERN FRENCH You would never know from the subdued tones of the wood-paneled dining room that the chef here is a fan of spices and herbs from faraway lands. That said, Jean-Marc Notelet's subtle and delicious cuisine also makes use of more local products, in particular, high-quality regional ingredients like mussels from Brittany, veal from Corrèze, and free-range pork brought up on apples and acorns. Menu must-haves include cod with lemon grass and combava, grilled duck with sumac, and beef confit with tonka beans and niora. All those exotic elements blend beautifully with French dishes, as the full dining room attests; this place is a favorite for business lunches and dinners, and draws a devoted local clientele.

6 rue d'Armaillé, 17th arrond. ℂ **01-42-27-19-20.** www.caius-restaurant.fr. Main courses 20€–25€; fixed-price dinner 42€. Mon–Fri noon–2pm and 7:30–10:30pm. Closed 3 weeks in Aug. and last week in Dec. Métro: Argentine.

Lasserre ★★★ GOURMET FRENCH André Malraux, Salvador Dali, Audrey Hepburn, Marlene Dietrich . . . the list of celebrities who have dined at this legendary restaurant is understandably long—what famous person wouldn't want to eat in this superb dining room, where the ceiling opens when the weather is willing, and the food will send you swooning? A silk-draped, arch-windowed affair, the room glistens with fine porcelain, silver knickknacks, and crystal candelabras. When it's closed, you can still admire the ceiling, which is painted with white clouds and a cerulean sky. Along with the restaurant's classics, like Challans duck and filet of beef Rossini, you can find more modern creations, like sea bass with vegetables in chardonnay, and roasted lamb confit with artichokes and apples. Reserve at least 2 weeks ahead. Dinner jackets required for men.

17 ave. Franklin D. Roosevelt, 8th arrond. ℂ **01-43-59-02-13.** www.restaurant-lasserre.com. Main courses 85€–120€; fixed-price lunch 90€ and 120€, fixed-price dinner 220€. Thurs–Fri noon–2pm; Tues–Sat 7–10pm. Closed mid-July through Aug. Métro: Franklin Roosevelt.

MODERATE

Lazare ★★★ MODERN BISTRO   Before the Gare St-Lazare train station had its recent makeover, about the only thing you could get to eat was a limp sandwich. Today, you can eat like a king as you wait for your train to come in, and I'm not talking about the Burger King that opened up on the main level. Eric Frechon, one of those Michelin-starred chefs, is the great mind behind this gourmet enterprise, which serves as cafe, bar, and restaurant. The lofty ceilings, wood furnishings, and white walls give the place relaxed air, as does the menu, which features French comfort food like boeuf bourguignon, cod *brandade* (a sort of fish shepherd's pie), and Toulouse sausage with mashed potatoes. Don't be fooled, though, granny is definitely not in the kitchen. A gaggle of young intense cooks bustle about, preparing each dish with the best ingredients and designing each plate with care. Breakfast is served from 7:30–11am and tea time is 3–6pm.

Inside the Gare St-Lazare shopping gallery, 8th arrond. ℂ **01-44-90-80-80.** www.lazare-paris.fr. Main courses 19€–42€; fixed-price lunch (Sun only) 39€. Daily 7:30-midnight, lunch served noon–3pm, dinner 7–11pm. Métro: Gare St-Lazare.

Le Boudoir ★★ TRADITIONAL FRENCH   This intimate restaurant features three different settings for your gustatory pleasure: a chic restaurant in shades of red, a cozy dining room upstairs, and a *fumoir*, or cigar salon, where you can smoke without driving your neighbors mad. But the main event here is the food which reaches gourmet heights at a relatively earth-bound price. A minimalist menu features French classics like Chateaubriand Rossini and sautéed scallops cooked to perfection and served with intriguing vegetable accompaniments like squash risotto. If you can't decide, order the tasting menu (evenings only, 55€) and sample two appetizers, two main courses, and a desert. On Saturday nights, Le Boudoir becomes a wine bar, serving tapas and charcuterie to go along with your glass of red (or white, or rosé . . .).

25 rue du Colisée, 8th arrond. ℂ **01-43-59-25-29.** www.boudoirparis.fr. Main courses 26€–35€; fixed-price lunch 30€–35€, fixed-price dinner 55€. Mon–Fri noon–2pm and 8–10pm, Sat (wine bar only) 8–10pm. Closed Aug. Métro: St-Philippe-du-Roule.

Le Malakoff ★ BRASSERIE   While the brasseries on the Place du Trocadéro are generally overpriced and sniffy, this one is accessible, both in terms of price and service. The menu is standard Parisian brasserie fare—steak tartare, grilled chicken, *choucroute garni*, steak frites—executed with skill, and supplemented with a wide variety of tasty *salades composées* (meal-sized salads). Best of all, you get a front row view of the grandiose Place and the Palais de Chaillot (and if you lean over, the Eiffel Tower). The same management runs **Le Wilson,** a smaller operation at 2 place du Trocadéro at the corner of ave. du Président Wilson, which offers a similar menu.

6 place du Trocadéro, 16th arrond. ℂ **01-45-53-75-27.** www.le-malakoff.com. Main courses 13€–25€. Mon–Fri 7:30am–1am, Sat–Sun 8:30am–1am. Métro: Trocadéro.

Publicis Drugstore Brasserie ★★ MODERN BRASSERIE   You won't find toothpaste at this "drugstore," whose name comes from a former 1950s incarnation that consisted of a warren of shops, restaurants and services "à l'americaine." This ultra-modern, oh-so-chic complex has replaced the funky original, keeping the multi-functional concept in tact with shops, restaurants, and a cinema. The Brasserie is the most accessible eating option—a light-filled expanse with an incredible street-side view of the Champs and the Arc de Triomphe. The food is high-end casual, featuring items like gourmet hamburgers, grilled fish, steak tartare, and fillet of sole delivered by a young and beautiful wait staff. Meals are served non-stop until 2am, a good bet for a late night meal after sampling nearby nightlife. There's a terrific buffet brunch on Sundays from 11am–4pm.

133 ave. des Champs-Élysées, 8th arrond. ℰ **01-44-43-77-64.** www.publicisdrugstore.com. Main courses 19€–39€; fixed-price lunch 20€–25€; Sunday brunch 36€. Mon–Fri 8am–2am. Sat–Sun 10am–2am Métro: Charles de Gaulle–Etoile.

INEXPENSIVE

Boulangerie Joséphine ★ BAKERY/SANDWICHES/FRENCH   This terrific bakery near the Arc de Triomphe does double duty as a lunch spot, with a nice outdoor terrace and a pretty upstairs dining room that fills quickly with local office workers and business people. You can buy sandwiches and salads (and desserts, of course) to go or sit down for table service, which gives you the option of trying one of the excellent daily specials, like stuffed vegetables, roast chicken, or osso buco. Also open for breakfast from 8am.

69 avenue Marceau, 8th arrond. ℰ **01-47-20-49-62.** www.josephine-boulangerie.com. Main courses 5€–15€. Mon–Fri 8am–8pm. Closed for 1 week in mid-Aug. Métro: Charles de Gaulle–Etoile.

Opéra & Grands Boulevards (2nd & 9th Arrondissements)

Buzzing with cafes and theaters in the 19th century, the long-overlooked Grand Boulevards are finally coming back to life, especially where these wide avenues intersect with the Opéra, and the hip and happening part of the 9th arrondissement that borders Montmartre. Less trendy, but also less expensive, the little streets around the Bourse (the French stock exchange) has a wide range of restaurant options, especially at lunchtime. The covered passages that crisscross parts of the 2nd arrondissement (p. 173) also harbor some excellent dining options.

EXPENSIVE

Casa Olympe ★★ MEDITERRANEAN/MODERN FRENCH   Olympe Versini earned a Michelin star in her 20s and has been writing cookbooks and dazzling discerning palates ever since. One of the pioneers of "nouvelle cuisine" in the 1970s, she has since moved on to warmer climes, as the menu at this intimate restaurant shows. There is a distinctly Mediterranean flair to dishes like marinated sardines, sautéed swordfish with almonds, sweetbreads with Pantelleria capers, and roast shoulder of lamb with thyme. If you don't have room for a big dessert, finish off your meal with whipped lemon sherbet with prosecco.

48 rue St-Georges, 9th arrond. ℰ **01-42-85-26-01.** www.casaolympe.com. Main courses 20€–29€; Fixed-price menu lunch 26€, fixed-price menu dinner 39€. Mon–Wed noon–2pm and 7:30–10:30pm; Thurs–Fri noon–2pm and 7:30–11pm; Sat 7:30–11pm. Closed 2nd and 3rd week of Aug. Métro: St-Georges.

Chez Georges ★★ TRADITIONAL FRENCH   A step back in time, this is how Parisian restaurants were before cuisine became nouvelle, or vanilla infusions were allowed to touch a fish dish. The room is crowded and lively; the cooking is old-fashioned and delicious. Many of the customers are regulars who work at the nearby stock exchange. The handwritten menu features beautifully executed classics like fillet of sole, *pot-au-feu* (beef simmered with vegetables), and sweetbreads with morels. Save room for the profiteroles at dessert.

1 rue du Mail, 2nd arrond. ℰ **01-42-60-07-11.** Main courses 20€–41€. Mon–Fri noon–2:30pm and 7–11pm. Closed Aug. and the last week of Dec. Métro: Bourse.

Saturne ★★★ MODERN FRENCH   There are not very many glass-roofed restaurants in Paris, and even fewer with a kitchen like this one. The chef's Scandinavian roots are evident in the decor, with its sleek blonde wood and white walls. But it's what's on the plate that makes it difficult to get a reservation here: exquisitely refined combinations of flavors and textures, described on the menu as a list of ingredients. Resembling works of contemporary art, dishes might combine gnocchi, chestnuts, and truffles, or guinea hen with purple artichokes, and spring garlic, and could be followed with a concoction of carrots, citrus, and olives. At lunch you can choose between a menu of three, five, and seven dishes; and dinner, there's a one fixed-price menu for one and all.

17 rue Notre-Dame-des-Victoires, 2nd arrond. ℰ **01-42-60-31-90.** www.saturne-paris.fr. Fixed-price lunch 40€–65€, fixed-price dinner 65€. Mon–Fri noon–2pm and 8–10:30pm. Closed first 3 weeks of Aug. Métro: Bourse.

MODERATE

Chez Grenouille ★ TRADITIONAL FRENCH   Chef Alexis Blanchard has won prizes for his pâtés and *boudins* (blood sausage), so you'll find all manner of charcuterie on the menu here, plus updated classics such as suckling pig with foie gras, duck parmentier, sweetbreads, oxtail, and pigs' feet, plus a fish dish or two for lighter eaters. Like the menu, the decor goes for a mix of tradition and modernity, though with less success. But it's the food that counts here, and it is hearty and delicious. Finish with a boozy baba au rhum.

52 rue Blanche, 9th arrond. ℰ **01-42-81-34-07.** www.restaurant-chezgrenouille-paris.com. Main courses 25€–36€; fixed-price lunch 23€, fixed-price dinner 35€. Mon–Fri noon–2:30pm and 7–11pm; Sat 7–11pm Métro: Trinité.

Coinstôt Vino ★★ WINE BAR   What's in a name? In this case, an amalgam of French and Italian words for "corner bistro" and "wine," which pretty much sums things up. This tiny place—which sits on the corner of two covered alleyways in the lovely Passage des Panoramas—has a generous and excellent selection of wines. While much of the menu is top-quality nibbles to enjoy while you savor your wine, like oysters, plates of smoked ham, pâté, and cheese, there are also a few *plats du jour* (daily specials) like grilled sea bass and steak with mushrooms. In season, the oysters come from Utah Beach, of Normandy Landings fame. Recently, a pizza chef was imported from Italy, and you can sample his excellent wares with your glass of *vino.*

26 bis passage des Panoramas, 2nd arrond. ℰ **01-44-82-08-54.** www.coinstot-vino.com. Main courses 15€–25€, fixed-price lunch 16€–19€. Mon–Fri noon–2:15pm and 6pm–midnight; Sat 6pm–midnight. Closed first 3 weeks of Aug and last week of Dec. Métro: Grands Boulevards or Bourse.

Le Pantruche ★★ TRADITIONAL FRENCH/BISTRO   The name is old-fashioned slang for Paris, but this little bistro has a decidedly modern feel to it. Maybe it's the mirrored column near the bar. In yet another case of runaway chefs from Michelin-starred restaurants, here you'll find flavorful updated bistro fare like braised sweetbreads with carrots in a licorice glaze, or suckling pig with pears, celery root, and chestnuts. It's hard to resist indulging in desert when the Grand Marnier soufflé is on the menu. Definitely reserve ahead, as the fixed-price menus at lunch and dinner are a terrific value and the tiny dining room fills quickly.

3 rue Victor Massé, 9th arrond. ℰ **01-48-78-55-60.** www.lepantruche.com. Main courses: 14€–25€; dinner 21€–25€; fixed-price lunch 19€, fixed-price dinner 35€ Mon–Fri 12:30–2:30pm and 7:30–9:30pm. Closed first 3 weeks of Aug. Métro: Pigalle.

INEXPENSIVE

Café Zephyr ★ TRADITIONAL BISTRO This large old-fashioned bistro sprawls out on the sidewalk of one of the Grand Boulevards. Nowhere near as hip as the new restaurants in the Passage des Panoramas across the street, the joy of the Zephyr is all in the atmosphere: a friendly, noisy place to stop for a *salade composé* (meal-sized salad) or a steak-frites, or just to sip a drink and watch the world go by. At night, the pool table becomes a focus of attention for some; others come here to eat before seeing a show at the nearby Opéra Comique. There's a nice brunch on Sundays.

12 bd. Montmartre, 9th arrond. ☎ **01-47-70-80-14.** Main courses 11€–15€, brunch 18€. Daily 8am–2am. Métro: Grands-Boulevards or Richelieu–Drouot.

Chartier ★★ TRADITIONAL FRENCH This vast restaurant claims to have served some 50 million meals since it opened in 1896, and considering the fact that the dining room can seat over 300 people, it seems entirely possible. This gargantuan establishment is one of the last of the *bouillons,* or workers' restaurants, that used to be found all over Paris back in the 19th century. The idea was to serve good food at modest prices, an idea that has still speaks to working Parisians over 100 years later, if the line out the door is any indication. You come here for the experience, more than for the food, which is tasty, but certainly won't win any Michelin stars. The menu covers a wide variety of traditional dishes like roast free-range chicken with fries, or rump

---

A Word About Kids in Restaurants

Many foreigners wonder how French people manage to make their kids behave so well in restaurants. While the ritual of long Sunday family lunches probably trains them to sit still at an early age, there's also the fact that childhood rowdiness is not well tolerated in eating establishments. If the kids can't sit still, the parents simply don't eat out with them. It's rare to find crayons, puzzles, and other kid-friendly items in Parisian restaurants, though they usually have high-chairs (*chaise-haute,* shehz-*oht*), if not booster seats (*réhausseur, ray-*hoh-sur). That said, by and large French people are kid-friendly, so small, family-owned restaurants will usually be pretty understanding, as long as you don't let your kids run wild. Ask if there's a child menu (menu enfant). While not particularly nutritious, they'll usually keep small ones busy with plenty of French fries. Below is a short list of

some restaurants that are particularly amenable to the kid contingent:

o **Restaurant Polidor** (p. 93) With its red checked tablecloths and family-style cooking, this is a good place for an introduction to bistro food.

o **Crêperie Josselin** (p. 98) This local favorite (a sit-down restaurant, not a stand on the street) is a great option for kids because they offer early dinner seating and easy prices. What kid doesn't love a crepe?

o **Le Relais de l'Entrecôte** (p. 92) Serving unlimited helpings of steak and fries, this lively place is a no-brainer for the kid set.

o **Rosa Bonheur** (p. 84) Located inside the Parc des Buttes-Chaumont, this cool cafe has a beautiful outdoor terrace where parents can nibble on tapas while watching their kids roll down the hill.

steak with pepper sauce. Service is fast and furious (how could it not be with this many tables?) but it's all part of the atmosphere, which is something that belongs to another time and place. There are no reservations, so be prepared to wait.

7 rue du Faubourg Montmartre, 9th arrond. ℰ **01-47-70-86-29.** www.restaurant-chartier.com. Main courses 8.70€–13€. Daily 11:30am–10pm. Métro: Grands-Boulevards.

Lémoni ★ HEALTHY/MEDITERRANEAN/TAKEOUT For a quick lunch that does not involve grease or excessive carbohydrates, this Franco-Cretan (as in Crete, Greece) cafe is a sure bet. Dedicated to healthy, organic cooking with a Mediterranean bent, this colorful luncheonette offers a delicious selection of homemade soups, salads, hot dishes, juices, and yummy deserts, with plenty of vegetarian options. You can eat onsite or take a meal to go. There is a second Lemoni at 5 rue Hérold in the 1st arrondissement.

5 rue de Clichy, 9th arrond. ℰ **01-74-30-21-37.** www.lemonicafe.fr. Main courses 5€–9.50€. Mon–Fri noon–3pm Metro: Trinité or Saint Lazare.

L'Excuse Mogador ★ CREPES In the hustle bustle of clothing stores and lunch spots that line the streets in this crowded quarter, this tiny crêperie is a standout. The crêpes are generously filled with fresh ingredients like goat cheese, spinach, eggplant, and of course, ham and cheese; the zinc bar and vinyl banquettes make the ambiance that much more Parisian. It's open only at lunchtime, when it fills up quickly with shoppers and office workers.

21 rue Joubert, 9th arrond. ℰ **01-42-81-98-19.** Main courses 6€–10€. Mon–Sat 11:30am–4pm. Closed in Aug and last week in Dec. Métro: Havre-Caumartin.

Montmartre (18th Arrondissement)

When you get away from the tourist traps of Place du Tertre, you start to understand why people love this neighborhood, and why it's become a favorite with the arty-hipster set. To the north and west of the basilica is where you will find the villagey atmosphere you've heard so much about; to the east and south, Montmartre gives way to Barbès, a lively immigrant neighborhood where you are just as likely to see women in Indian saris and African prints as in smart Parisian apparel. Either way, you're bound to come across good food.

MODERATE

Chéri Bibi ★★ TRADITIONAL FRENCH Sitting pretty on the eastern side of the Sacré-Coeur, Chéri Bibi has become the unofficial canteen for the young and artsy Montmartre crowd. The affordable fixed-price two- or three-course menu features classic French fare with modern touches, like a tender flank steak with homemade chutney or beef stew with coriander. The decor is understated hip, with flea-market chairs and exposed stone walls. A crowd often gathers around the restaurant's zinc bar just to sip wine, sometimes spilling out onto the sidewalk on a warm night. Open only in the evenings.

15 rue André del Sarte, 18th arrond. ℰ **01-42-54-88-96.** Fixed-price dinner 26€–29€. Mon–Sat 8–11pm (until 2am for the bar). Métro: Barbes-Rochechouart or Chateau Rouge.

Nansouty ★★★ MODERN FRENCH Just north of the Butte de Montmartre, this popular wine bar will appeal to both gourmets and wine enthusiasts. You'll have a choice of over 100 bottles on the massive blackboard, which you can supplement with top-quality nibbles. Can't make up your mind? Just ask the wait staff, who are wise in

Montmartre Restaurants

Café Burq **1**
Chéri Bibi **3**
Eté en Pente Douce **4**
Milk **2**
Nansouty **5**

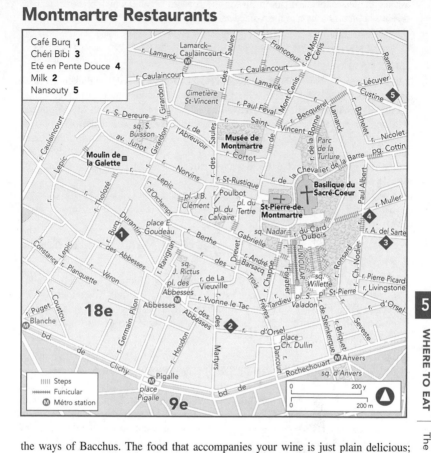

the ways of Bacchus. The food that accompanies your wine is just plain delicious; there's a touch of southern warmth on the menu, which features exquisitely prepared yet simple dishes, like melt-in-your-mouth tuna *ventreche provençal* or a tender slice of veal with puréed potatoes. If the tiramisu is on the blackboard, you are in for a treat.

35 rue Ramey, 18th arrond. (✆ **01-42-52-58-87.** Main courses 18€; fixed-price lunch 17€, fixed-price dinner 30€ Tues–Fri noon–2:30pm and 8–11pm; Sat and Mon 8–11pm. Métro: Lamarck-Caulincourt or Château Rouge.

Wepler ★★ FRENCH BRASSERIE Picasso and Modigliani used to hang out at this venerable brasserie on Place de Clichy, as did writer Henry Miller, who made it his headquarters. "I knew it like a book," he wrote. "The faces of the waiters, the managers, the cashiers, the whores, the clientele, even the attendants in the lavatory, are engraved in my memory as if they were illustrations in a book which I read every day." Today the atmosphere is quite sedate, but it's still a wonderful place to sit and watch the world go by, and the prices are accessible enough that it is still frequented by artists and writers. The menu is classic brasserie (steak tartare, shellfish platters, poached haddock in *beurre blanc*) but with a light, gourmet touch. If you don't want a big meal, ask for the less expensive cafe menu on the covered terrace, which features delicate omelets, a *plat du jour*, and meal-sized salads.

14 place de Clichy, 18th arrond. ℂ **01-45-22-53-24.** www.wepler.com. Main courses 16€–27€; fixed-price lunch 23€–30€, fixed-price dinner 35€. Daily 8am–midnight. Métro: Place de Clichy.

INEXPENSIVE

Milk—Mum in her Little Kitchen ★ TEAROOM/LIGHT MEALS Tired? Hungry? Got kids? This adorable tearoom/snack shop is just the spot to take a load off and entertain the young'uns. Decked out in a sort-of early 1960s kitchen decor, with lots of brightly painted wood and playfully kitsch toys and objects (most of which are for sale), this place speaks to the child in us all, offering him or her treats like cookies and chocolate milk, smoothies, cakes, quiches, salads, and other good stuff. The brunch (served every day), is extremely popular on the weekends, so reserve ahead.

62 rue d'Oursel, 18th arrond. ℂ **01-42-59-74-32.** www.milk-lepicerie.com. Main courses 9.50€, fixed-price lunch 14€, brunch 23€. Mon–Fri 8:30am–4pm, Sat-Sun 8:30am–6:30pm. Closed 2 weeks in Aug. Métro: Abbesses.

République, Bastille & Eastern Paris (11th & 12th Arrondissements)

With a mix of working-class families, hipsters, and *bobos* (bourgeois bohemians), the area between République and Nation is diverse, young, and fun. This might be why there are so many good restaurants around here. This is also a good neighborhood for discovering the flavors of Africa, in restaurants that feature cooking from France's former colonies.

EXPENSIVE

La Gazzetta ★★★ MODERN FRENCH Just down the street from the bustling outdoor food market at Aligre, this beautiful, old-fashioned looking bistro is helmed by a chef whose cooking is anything but traditional. How about spelt risotto with nettles, or mackerel with burnt spring onions, topped off with goat cheese ice cream with roasted apricots for dessert? It may sound strange, but tastes fantastic. Fans of experimental cooking can savor the seven-course tasting menu for 65€. At lunch there's a fixed-price menu with three tiny appetizers and a main dish for 19€, an excellent price for this quality.

29 rue de Cotte, 12th arrond. ℂ **01-43-47-47-05.** www.lagazzetta.fr. Fixed-price lunch 19€; fixed-price dinner 39€–65€. Tues–Sun noon–2pm and 7:30–10pm. Closed in Aug. Métro: Ledru-Rollin.

MODERATE

Astier ★★ TRADITIONAL FRENCH/BISTRO This beautiful old restaurant has kept up its polished wood and checked tablecloths, as well as its classic menu. Wild boar terrine, rabbit in mustard sauce, rib steak with anchovy toasts, pike *quenelles* (a sort of elegant dumpling) and *tarte tatin* (caramelized apple tart), are menu regulars, plus the legendary cheese tray. It's a picture postcard version of a Paris bistro, without the surly waiters. The wine list is delectable too. The fixed-price menu is definitely the way to go here, as the main courses can get pricey on their own.

44 rue Jean-Pierre Timbaud, 11th arrond. ℂ **01-43-57-16-35.** www.restaurant-astier.com. Main courses 22€–26€. Fixed-price lunch 25€–39€; fixed-price dinner 35€–45€. Daily 12:45–2:15pm and 7–10:30pm. In July–Aug, closed Sat and Mon lunch, and all day Sun. Métro: Parmentier or Oberkampf.

Bistrot Paul Bert ★★★ BISTRO/TRADITIONAL FRENCH There are so many beautiful old bistros in this part of town, it's hard to choose, but when in doubt, you can't go wrong at this one. Even the most hardnosed food critics get misty-eyed about this place, which specializes in the kind of cooking that reminds people of the good old days, even if they aren't that old. You might find comfortable classics like *onglet* (a type of beef steak) with shallots, or something a little more challenging, like roast venison with cranberries. This is definitely a meat-eater's hangout, though you can find lighter fare on the ever-changing menu, like roast pigeon or monkfish with creamy rice. The wine list features many unusual and affordable bottles from small wine producers.

18 rue Paul Bert, 11th arrond. ℂ **01-43-72-24-01.** Main courses 27€; fixed-price lunch 19€ and 38€, fixed-price dinner 38€. Tues–Sat noon–2pm and 7:30–11pm. Closed in Aug. Métro: Faidherbe-Chaligny.

INEXPENSIVE

Au Piano ★ MODERN FRENCH A glassed-in sidewalk terrace is what gives this low-key restaurant its airy, relaxed feel—a nice set up for enjoying a juicy cut of steak and fries or a fillet of sea bream with spiced honey sauce. The idea is to offer modern French food at reasonable prices, and as far as I'm concerned, it works. What's more, there's free live music (piano) to accompany your meal. There's enough space here for larger parties, though you should reserve ahead.

32 avenue de la République, 11th arrond. ℂ **09-53-33-56-06.** www.lescantines.com. Main courses dinner 13€–18€; fixed-price menu lunch 15€–16€, dinner 20€–25€. Daily 10am–11pm. Métro: Parmentier.

L'Ebauchoir ★★★ MODERN FRENCH Located in an unlikely corner of the 12th arrondissement, this crowded neighborhood hangout offers a great selection of modern bistro cooking at decidedly reasonable prices. The high ceilings, sunny yellow walls and wooden fixtures create a warm and friendly environment for Mediterranean inspired dishes like roast lamb with sweet garlic, polenta, and olives or grilled bonito with a peach and preserved lemon salad. There's usually a nice vegetarian option here, like layers of eggplant and feta with olives and fresh capers. With one of the last surviving reasonable three-course lunches (15€), this place gets jammed at noon, so try to reserve.

43 rue des Citeaux, 12th arrond. ℂ **01-43-42-49-31.** www.lebauchoir.com. Main courses dinner 19€–24€; fixed-price lunch 13€–27€. Mon 8–11pm, Tues–Fri noon–2:30pm and 8–11pm, Fri–Sat noon–2:30pm and 7:30–11pm. Closed 1 week mid-Aug. Métro: Faidherbe Chaligny or Reuilly Diderot.

Waly Fay ★★ SENAGALESE Take a gastronomic voyage to West Africa at this popular restaurant that has introduced umpteen Parisians to delicious Senegalese cuisine. A former French colony, Senegal has absorbed culinary influences from France, as well as its northern neighbors in the Maghreb. Cool music and candlelight set the scene for some of the best *poulet yassa* (chicken marinated in lime and onions) in Paris; there also several versions of *n'dolé,* spinachlike leaves cooked with peanut sauce and mixed with shrimp, or fish, or meat. Less adventurous eaters might like the marinated brochettes, which are grilled over a wood fire. Fill out the meal with a side order of fried plantains or atéké (manioc, both). There's also a terrific selection of rums here for cocktail hour.

6 rue Godefroy Cavalgnac, 11th arrond. ℂ **01-40-24-17-79.** www.walyfay.com. Main courses 13€–28€. Daily 7pm–midnight.

Belleville, Canal St-Martin & Northeast Paris (10th, 19th & 20th Arrondissements)

Between the two parks of Belleville and Buttes Chaumont and along the Canal St-Martin lie some of the city's most quirky and delightful restaurants. One of the last strongholds of Paris' bohemian set, here you can find both gourmet bistros and funky cheap eats, as well as a good number of wine bars that serve both nibbles and the fruit of the vine.

MODERATE

Café Zerda ★★ NORTH AFRICAN/COUSCOUS Here is where you come for some of the best *couscous* in Paris. A steaming heap of fine couscous (grains of semolina), a savory bouillon with vegetables, and delicately grilled or roasted meat are the three main components of this dish, originally imported from North Africa and now wildly popular in France. Zerda offers a choice of lamb, chicken and *merguez* (spicy lamb sausage) versions; my favorite is the meltingly tender "lamb cooked in sauce," but they are all good. If you prefer one of their scrumptious *tagines* (stews seasoned with such ingredients as dried fruits, olives, or preserved lemons) be patient: They take 20 minutes to prepare. Not only is the food great, but the service is warm and friendly.

15 rue René Boulanger, 10th arrond. ℂ **01-42-00-25-15.** www.zerdacafe.fr. Main courses 15€–21€. Mon and Sat 6:30–11:30pm, Tues–Fri noon–3pm and 6:30–11:30pm. Closed 2 weeks in Aug. Métro: Strasbourg–St-Denis.

Chez Michel ★★★ BRETON/SEAFOOD Diners come from all over Paris, as well as across the channel (via the nearby Eurostar train hub at Gare du Nord) to sample Thierry Breton's superb cooking at an affordable price that has barely budged in a decade. A native of Brittany, Breton improvises on recipes from back home, including lots of seafood dishes like cotriade, a Breton ("Breton" means from Brittany, by the way) fish stew, and fresh crab salad. There's a massive oven in the dining room itself so that diners can order options like braised lamb and other slow-baked specialties. For dessert, try the copious rice pudding or the awe-inspiring Paris-Brest (a choux pastry filled with praline cream).

10 rue de Belzunce, 10th arrond. ℂ **01-44-53-06-20.** www.restaurant-chez-michel.com. Fixed-price lunch 29€, fixed-price dinner 35€. Tues–Fri noon–2pm and Mon–Fri 7pm–midnight. Closed in Aug. Métro: Gare du Nord.

La Grille ★ SEAFOOD/TRADITIONAL FRENCH When you arrive at this tiny restaurant, you understand the name: The entire facade is enclosed by 200-year-old wrought-iron grills. Back in the day, fishermen from Dieppe used this place as a springboard for carousing after delivering their fish to Les Halles market. Today the restaurant is known for its *beurre blanc*, a classic butter sauce made with wine and shallots that is terrific with fish. The signature dish here is an entire turbot (for two) prepared tableside and doused with—yes, you guessed it—*beurre blanc*. Other recommended dishes are duck terrine with hazelnuts, *boeuf bourguignon*, and a brochette of scallops with *beurre blanc*.

80 rue du Faubourg-Poissonnière, 10th arrond. ℂ **01-47-70-89-73.** Main courses 18€–24€. Mon–Fri noon–2pm 7–10pm. Closed 2 weeks mid-Aug. Métro: Poissonnière.

Le Baratin ★★ TRADITIONAL FRENCH/BISTRO For some time, people have been crowding into this bistro to sample the cooking of Argentina-born Chef Raquel

Carena's down-home bistro fare. You can find modern treats like smoked mackerel tartare and duck with ginger and gooseberry jelly, as well as more traditional fare. The lunch fixed-price menu is a great value, only 18€ for a three-course meal There is an impressive wine cellar, managed by Raquel's famously grumpy husband, Philippe Pinoteau.

3 rue Jouye-Rouve, 20th arrond. ℂ **01-43-49-39-70.** Main courses 18€–30€; fixed-price lunch 20€. Tues–Sat noon–2:30pm and 8–11:30pm. Closed last 3 weeks in Aug and first week of May. Métro: Pyrenées.

Le Chapeau Melon ★★ WINE BAR/BISTRO   Wine enthusiasts won't mind the trek up to the heights of Belleville to sample the goods at this wine bar-cum restaurant, not far from the beautiful Parc des Buttes-Chaumont. Specializing in "natural" wines (that is, grown and fermented according to tradition and without additives), you can buy bottles to go or drink them onsite for a small corkage fee. If you'd like some food to go with that wine, you can indulge in the tempting menu, which might include offerings like carpaccio of sea bream with citrus or watercress *quenelles* with asparagus cream.

92 rue Rébeval, 19th arrond. ℂ **01-42-02-68-60.** Main courses 18€–20€, fixed-price dinner 35€. Tues–Fri noon–2pm, Wed–Sat 8–11pm, Sun noon–4pm and 7–11pm. Closed first week of Jan and 3 weeks in Aug. Métro: Pyrenées.

Le Verre Volé ★ WINE BAR/MODERN FRENCH   The sun is shining, the leafy trees are posing prettily along the Canal St-Martin, and you are walking over one of the Japanese-eque bridges that curve over the water. All that's missing is a table and a glass of wine. Luckily, this wine bar/restaurant is on hand to delight you with a vast selection of bacchic and gustatory delights. You could just share a plate of sliced smoked meats and sausage, the usual accompaniment to a glass of red, or you can go ahead and explore the menu, which might include a slice of milk-fed veal or mullet ceviche. Then select a bottle of wine from the shelves that line the walls, and enjoy it (for a nominal corkage fee) in this informal, if crowded, setting.

67 rue de Lancry, 10th arrond. ℂ **01-48-03-17-34.** www.leverrevole.fr. Main courses 15€–23€. Daily 12:30–2pm and 7:30–10:30pm. Métro: Jacques Bonsergent.

INEXPENSIVE

Bob's Juice Bar ★ VEGETARIAN   Hipsters are tripping all over themselves to try "smoossies" (that is, smoothies) these days, and some of the best can be found at this terrific vegetarian restaurant, which has become *the* place to sample muffins, bagels, soups and other delicious vegetarian goodies. The brainchild of Marc Grossman (alias "Bob"), an erstwhile New Yorker, this may not be the most authentically French experience, but it certainly is a tasty one. You can sit down or take out here, or try the larger Bob's Kitchen in the Marais (74 rue des Gravilliers), which is open on weekends.

15 rue Lucien Sampaix, 10th arrond. ℂ **09-50-06-36-18.** Smoothies 4€–5€; main courses 5€–8€. Mon–Fri 7:30am–3pm. Métro: Jacques Bonsergent.

Pink Flamingo ★ PIZZA   This is a pizza delivery you won't forget. Once you've ordered your pizza from the Pink Flamingo's impressive menu (try the Poulidor with goat cheese and sliced duck breast or the Ho Chi Minh with chicken, shrimp, and green coconut curry sauce), you'll be handed a pink helium filled balloon. Then you wander down to a bench by the canal and your pizza is delivered by a bicyclist seeking out pink balloons. The pizzas are also made with the best, freshest ingredients, and the crusts are made with organic flour. There are three other locations at 105 rue Vieille du Temple in the 3rd, 23 rue d'Aligre in the 12th, and 30 rue Muller in the 18th.

67 rue Bichat, 10th. ℭ **01-42-02-31-70.** www.pinkflamingopizza.com. Pizzas 12€–17€. Mon–Thurs 7–11:30pm, Fri–Sun noon–3pm and 7–11:30pm. Métro: Jacques Bonsergent.

Rosa Bonheur ★ TAPAS   This unconventional space is named after an unconventional 19th-century painter/sculptress. Yes, it's a restaurant and tapas bar, but its also a sort of off-the-wall community center, hosting various expositions and events, and has its own chorus and soccer team. Located in an old *buvette* (refreshment pavilion) inside the Parc des Buttes Chaumont that dates from the Universal Exposition of 1900, the restaurant boasts a sprawling terrace and one of the best panoramic views in town. A huge crowd gathers to drink and nibble tapas outside, but the menu also features main dishes such as stuffed and grilled shrimp, lamb and carrot stew, and monkfish with sage sauce. The ambiance is relaxed and friendly, and coming here is a good excuse to stroll through the beautiful Buttes Chaumont park. That park, plus an indoor play area and kids' menu, makes Rosa Bonheur a great family option.

2 allée de la Cascade, 19th arrond. ℭ **01-42-00-00-45.** www.rosabonheur.fr. Tapas 6€–9€; main courses 16€–22€. Thurs–Sun noon–midnight. Closed first 2 weeks in Jan. Métro Botzaris.

THE LEFT BANK

Latin Quarter (5th & 13th Arrondissements)

For over 700 years, this lively neighborhood has been overrun with students, a population that is forever on the lookout for a good cheap meal. As a result, the area is full of inexpensive snack shacks, of varying quality, from souvlaki huts to Vietnamese noodle shops to Breton crêperies. Steer clear of the unbearably touristy area around rue de la Huchette, where you are bound to pay too much for mediocre product, and be wary of rue Moufftard, which was once a good bet for good food, but has since become a victim of its own success. If you want to eat well, you'll need to venture a little farther afield, where innovative restaurateurs have been cultivating a knowledgeable clientele of professors, professionals, and savvy tourists.

VERY EXPENSIVE

La Tour d'Argent ★★★ CLASSIC FRENCH   Although its reputation as the best in Paris has long been eclipsed, dining here remains a memorable event—not necessarily for the food (although the "Silver Tower" has one Michelin star), but for its history, its view, and its incredible service. Five or six different waiters will visit your table at one time or another, accomplishing various tasks (opening wine bottles, pulling out your chair, and even leading you to the bathroom) with utmost professionalism and not a hint of snobbery. They then discreetly disappear into the rich decor as you gaze through the huge windows that give you a first class view of Notre Dame's flying buttresses. By the time you've finished your pressed duck (the signature dish—each duck has been numbered since 1890), you feel like a pasha. The fixed-price lunch is a good way to enjoy this singular experience without ruining your budget. Be sure to reserve at least a week in advance; jackets required for men at dinner.

15–17 quai de la Tournelle, 5th arrond. ℭ **01-43-54-23-31.** www.latourdargent.com. Main courses 70€–140€; fixed-price lunch 80€, fixed-price dinner 180€–200€. Tues–Sat noon–1pm; Tues–Sat 7–9pm. Closed Aug. Métro: St-Michel or Maubert-Mutualité.

Left Bank Restaurants (Eiffel Tower Area)

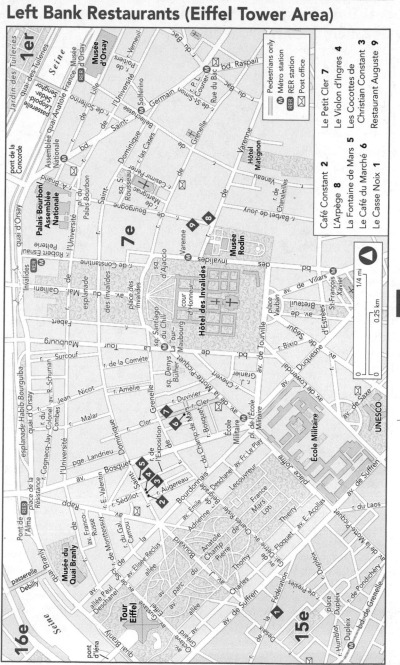

Café Constant **2**
L'Arpège **8**
La Fontaine de Mars **5**
Le Café du Marché **6**
Le Casse Noix **1**

Le Petit Cler **7**
Le Violon d'Ingres **4**
Les Cocottes de
Christian Constant **3**
Restaurant Auguste **9**

- Pedestrians only
- Ⓜ Métro station
- RER RER station
- ☒ Post office

Left Bank Restaurants (Latin Quarter, Saint Germain, Montparnasse)

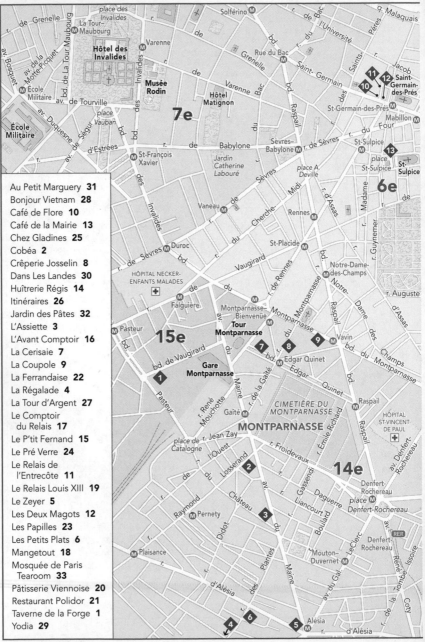

Au Petit Marguery **31**
Bonjour Vietnam **28**
Café de Flore **10**
Café de la Mairie **13**
Chez Gladines **25**
Cobéa **2**
Crêperie Josselin **8**
Dans Les Landes **30**
Huîtrerie Régis **14**
Itinéraires **26**
Jardin des Pâtes **32**
L'Assiette **3**
L'Avant Comptoir **16**
La Cerisaie **7**
La Coupole **9**
La Ferrandaise **22**
La Régalade **4**
La Tour d'Argent **27**
Le Comptoir
   du Relais **17**
Le P'tit Fernand **15**
Le Pré Verre **24**
Le Relais de
   l'Entrecôte **11**
Le Relais Louis XIII **19**
Le Zeyer **5**
Les Deux Magots **12**
Les Papilles **23**
Les Petits Plats **6**
Mangetout **18**
Mosquée de Paris
   Tearoom **33**
Pâtisserie Viennoise **20**
Restaurant Polidor **21**
Taverne de la Forge **1**
Yodia **29**

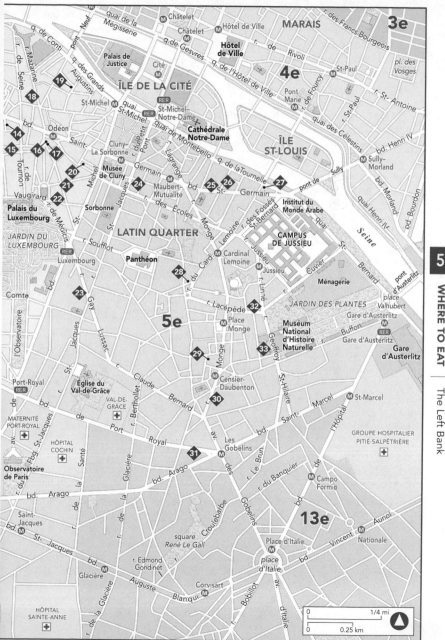

EXPENSIVE

Itinéraires ★★ FRENCH FUSION   After earning acclaim at 24 years old with his tiny tapas bistro in the 11th arrondissement, gifted chef Sylvain Sendra has opened this elegant enterprise devoted to finding the meeting point between French and more fare-flung cuisines. The seasonal menu, which features lots of organic ingredients, might include a lamb confit with sweet spices and cauliflower couscous or poached cod in sage broth with mushrooms and aioli and a Vahlrona chocolate soufflé tart with coffee ice cream for dessert. If everyone in your party is of a like mind, you can order one of the two tasting menus at dinner (everyone shares the chef's choice of dishes).

5 rue de Pontoise, 5th arrond. ℂ **01-46-33-60-11.** www.restaurantitineraires.com. Main dishes 27€–35€; fixed-price lunch 32€ and 38€, fixed-price dinner 55€—85€. Tues–Fri noon–2pm and 7–10:30pm, Sat 7–10:30pm. Closed Aug. Métro: Maubert-Mutualité.

MODERATE

Au Petit Marguery ★★ TRADITIONAL FRENCH/BISTRO   This place has everything you always wanted in a French bistro: antique tile floors, banquettes, vested waiters, and a dark rose color scheme. The menu also reflects the traditions of yester-year, with an emphasis on game dishes in autumn and fresh produce in summer. Appetizers include several different terrines, including home-made foie gras; main dishes feature both meaty items like 7-hour lamb and lighter fare like sea bream with fennel and star anise. Top it all off with a Grand Marnier soufflé (a specialty of the house). The restaurant has a smaller and more relaxed version of itself next door, the **Comptoir Marguery,** where prices are lower and the menu is a little more basic, and there is another outpost of the main restaurant, **Au Petit Marguery Rive Droite,** at 64 avenue des Ternes on the right bank.

9 bd. du Port-Royal, 13th arrond. ℂ **01-43-31-58-59.** www.petitmarguery.com. Fixed-price lunch 19€–37€; fixed-price dinner 31€–37€. Daily noon–2:15pm and 7pm–10:15pm. Métro: Gobelins.

Dans Les Landes ★ SOUTHWESTERN FRENCH/TAPAS   Les Landes is a region in the southwest of France blessed with green forests, sandy beaches, and lots of great food. Chef Julien Duboué takes inspiration from his native homeland and neighboring Basque country to create luscious tapas to be sampled with (many) glasses of great regional wines. Fried *chipirions* (small squid that are crisp, golden, and dusted with smoky pepper), polenta with smoked duck breast, Basque-style mussels—the list is long and tempting. The place is packed at night, so get there early or reserve a table.

119 bis rue Monge, 5th arrond. ℂ **01-45-87-06-00.** Tapas 7€–23€. Daily noon–11pm. Closed last week of Dec, first week of Jan and 3 weeks in Aug. Métro: Censier-Daubenton.

Le Pré Verre ★★ MODERN FRENCH/ASIAN FUSION   This laid-back gourmet wine bar is the work of the Delacourcelle brothers (Philippe is the chef, Marc is the wine maven), trailblazers in the bistronomy movement. One of the first restaurants to offer a reasonably priced, easy-to-understand menu of gourmet goodies, this crowded and convivial place offers dishes that are a scrumptious blend of traditional French and exotic ingredients. Your main course could be a meltingly tender *cochon de lait* (milk-fed pork) served with a smooth cinnamon-infused sauce and a delectably crunchy mass that turns out to be cabbage. Or it might be bark-roasted cod with delicately smoked mashed potatoes. Dessert could follow with an endive tiramisu doused in coffee. The

The Left Bank | WHERE TO EAT

weekday lunch menu is a particularly great deal: appetizer and main dish (chef's choice) plus a glass of wine and coffee for 15€.

8 rue Thenard, 5th arrond. © **01-43-54-59-47**. www.lepreverre.com. Main courses 20€; fixed-price lunch 15€ and 32€, fixed-price dinner 32€. Tues–Sat noon–2pm and 7:30–10:30pm. Closed last week of Dec. Métro: Maubert-Mutualité or Cluny-La Sorbonne.

Les Papilles ★★ BISTRO/WINE BAR Lined with shelves upon shelves of delectable bottles, this bustling wine shop/bistro/gourmet grocery matches simple but excellent fare with terrific samples of the fruit of the vine. At dinnertime, the fixed-price menu offers great value—four courses for 35€—but no choices. If you don't want the menu, try the *marmite du marché*, the stew of the day served in a cast-iron pot. At lunch there is lighter fare: a variety of salads, open-faced sandwiches, and charcuterie plates, or a fixed-price menu combining any of those with a dessert. Wine is available by the glass, but patrons are encouraged to choose a bottle from the nearby shelves and pay just a small corkage fee (7€) above retail price—a great way to try a good bottle without the usual restaurant markup on the wine.

30 rue Gay-Lussac, 5th arrond. © **01-43-25-20-79**. www.lespapillesparis.fr. Main courses 13€–16€. Fixed-price lunch 22€–28€, fixed-price dinner 35€. Tues–Sat noon–2pm and 7–10pm. Closed in Aug and between Christmas and New Year's. RER: Luxembourg.

INEXPENSIVE

Bonjour Vietnam ★★ VIETNAMESE This postage-stamp of a restaurant serves deliciously authentic Vietnamese dishes like *bò bún*, a heap of rice vermicelli, sliced beef, and crispy spring rolls in a tangy sauce, or a steaming bowl of *pho*, beef broth with vegetables and noodles, topped with fresh basil, mint and bean sprouts. The less adventurous might prefer caramel pork or ginger chicken, both featured on the 12€ lunch set menu. Most everyone enjoys the steamed raviolis as a starter. These fresh dishes are made to order, so don't expect instant service.

6 rue Thouin, 5th arrond. © **01-43-54-78-04**. Main courses 12€–14€. Fixed-price lunch 12€. Wed–Mon noon–2:30pm and 7–11pm. Métro: Cardinal Lemoine.

Chez Gladines ★ SOUTHWESTERN Hungry? Come here for enormous and tasty portions of rib-sticking French southwestern specialties. That means crispy duck confit with sautéed potatoes, Basque-style chicken (with tomatoes and bell peppers), *pipérade* (a casserole of eggs with smoked ham, sliced and sautéed potatoes, bell peppers, and a bright tomato sauce), and the like. Even the salads are gargantuan, filled with things like bacon, goat cheese, smoked ham, and foie gras. The success of the original Gladines in the 13th arrondissement (30 rue des Cinq Diamants) has spawned four other locations, including this one and three others: 11 bis rue des Halles, 1st arrond.; 74 bd. des Batignolles, 17th arrond.; and 64–66 rue de Charonne, 11th arrond.

44 bd. St-Germain, 5th arrond. © **01-46-33-93-88**. www.gladines.com. Main courses 9€–14€. Mon–Thurs noon–11pm; Fri–Sat noon–midnight, Sun noon–11:30pm. Métro: Maubert-Mutualité.

Jardin des Pâtes ★ PASTA/VEGETARIAN This light-filled restaurant specializes in pasta. But this is no ordinary pasta—not only are the rice, wheat, rye, and barley noodles made fresh every day, but the organic flour that goes into them is ground daily on the premises. The stress on wholesome ingredients is menu wide; even the ice cream is 100% natural. While you won't find the usual Italian sauces, you will find original creations like rye pasta with ham, cream, sweet onions,

Paris actually has two Chinatowns: the more established one, amongst the ugly apartment towers between avenues d'Ivry and Choisy in the 13th arrondissement (about a 5-min. walk from Place d'Italie) and another newer one in Belleville in the 20th. Neither Chinatown is strictly Chinese, as the population also includes communities from Vietnam, Cambodia, and other Asian countries. There are dozens of good restaurants in this neighborhood. A couple of my favorites for Chinese food are **Imperial Choisy,** 32 ave. de Choisy, 13th arrond. (© **01-45-86-42-40**), and across the street, **Likafo,** 39 ave. de Choisy, 13th arrond. (© **01-45-84-20-45**), for great shrimp ravioli soup.

white wine, and Comté cheese or barley pasta with fresh salmon, leeks, seaweed and crème fraîche. There are lots of vegetarian choices here, and the relaxed atmosphere makes it a good place to bring (well-behaved) kids. Pastas are made to order, so don't be in a hurry.

4 rue Lacépède, 5th arrond. © **01-43-31-50-71.** Main courses 11€–14€. Daily noon–2:30pm and 7–11pm. Métro: Place Monge.

Yodia ★★ CHINESE   While most of the Chinese restaurants that have sprouted up all over Paris are decidedly mediocre (except those in Chinatown, see box below), this tiny place is a standout. For one, it specializes in homemade noodles garnished with ingredients and flavors from Sichuan province. The wheat-based noodles, which are flavored with carrots, beets, or spinach, come in a bouquet of colors, and appear in a variety of dishes like caramelized beef with bean sprouts and chives, or chopped pork, chili sauce, peanuts, and coriander. The staff is young and modern; you might dine to the sounds of Chinese soul or rap music. If the room is full you can get take-out.

3 rue des Patriarches, 5th arrond. © **01-82-09-43-86.** Main courses 7.50€–9€. Mon–Sat noon–3pm and 7–10:30pm. Métro: Place Monge or Censier-Daubenton.

St-Germain-des-Prés (6th Arrondissement)

St-Germain is a mix of expensive eateries that only the lucky few can afford, and smaller bistros that bring back the days when intellectuals and artists frequented the Café de Flore. Overpriced tourist restaurants cluster around Boulevard St-Germain near the Carrefour de l'Odéon; as you head south and north of this major boulevard, your choices will expand. Though the Marché St-Germain has been transformed into a type of mall, the restaurants hugging its perimeter offer a wide range of possibilities.

VERY EXPENSIVE

Le Relais Louis XIII ★★★ TRADITIONAL FRENCH   In an ancient building on the site where Louis XIII was crowned back in 1610, this acclaimed restaurant pays homage to not only the monarch, but also traditional French cuisine at its most illustrious. No tonka beans or reduced licorice sauce here—Chef Manuel Martinez turns his formidable talents on classic sauces and time-honored dishes like sea-bass *quenelles* and roast duck, though he's not opposed to topping off the meal with a little lemon-basil sherbet at dessert. His signature dishes include lobster and foie gras ravioli and braised sweetbreads with wild mushrooms. The atmospheric dining room, crisscrossed with exposed beams and ancient stonework, makes you wonder if the Three Muske-teers might not tumble through the doorway bearing your mille-feuille with Bourbon vanilla cream.

8 rue des Grands-Augustins, 6th arrond. © **01-43-26-75-96.** www.relaislouis13.fr. Main courses 59€; fixed-price lunch 55€; fixed-price dinner 85€–135€. Tues–Sat 12:15–2:30pm, 7:30–10:30pm. Closed last week in Apr, first week in May, and all Aug. Métro: Odéon or St-Michel.

EXPENSIVE

Le Comptoir du Relais ★★★ TRADITIONAL FRENCH/BISTRO   The brain-child of super-chef Yves de Camdeborde, this small and scrumptious bistro is still bringing in the crowds almost a decade after it opened. Camdeborde is often credited with starting the bistronomy movement in the 1990s when he walked out on the Crillon and opened up his own bistro where he could offer the French equivalent of "down home" cooking, using the best ingredients and charging affordable prices. During the day, the Comptoir is a bistro, serving relatively traditional fare, like a slice of lamb with thyme sauce or panier de cochonaille, a basket of the Camdeborde family's own brand of sliced smoked ham, dried sausage, and other pork-based delectables. On week-nights, it's a temple to haute cuisine, with a tasting menu that includes as many as five different dishes. Reserve far (i.e., months) in advance for this fixed-price meal, which changes every night. There are no reservations at lunch, or on the weekends when the bistro menu is served from noon to 11pm, so arrive early or be prepared to wait.

9 carrefour de l'Odéon, 6th arrond. © **01-44-27-07-50.** www.hotel-paris-relais-saint-germain.com. Main courses weekends and weekdays 15€–29€; fixed-price dinner weeknights 60€. Daily noon–11pm. Métro: Odéon.

MODERATE

Huîtrerie Régis ★★ OYSTERS/SEAFOOD   Like oysters on the half shell? Good, because that's all they have here: delicious bivalves that come straight from the Marennes-Oléron region on France's Atlantic coast. The brief and to-the-point menu gives you a choice of middle-sized *fines de claires* or larger speciales *Garniers,* as well as a few sea urchins and organic shrimp. You'll have to order at least a dozen oysters to sit down in the tiny restaurant, considering the price you may as well order a *for-mule,* or fixed-price menu, which include various combinations of oysters, wine, and coffee. These oysters are fresh, oceany mouthfuls of flavor that deserve a good glass of Sancerre.

3 rue de Montfaucon, 6th arrond. © **01-44-41-10-07.** www.huitrerieregis.com. Oysters per dozen 26€–41€; fixed-price lunch or dinner 30€–40€. Tues–Sun noon–2:30pm and 6:30–10:30pm. Closed July 15 to Sept 15. Métro: Mabillon or St-Germain.

La Ferrandaise ★★ TRADITIONAL FRENCH/BISTRO   Named after a particu-larly tasty breed of cow, the beef at this carnivore's paradise comes direct from Puy du Dôme, the center of France's green heartland. The young chef is also a great believer in local products (all vegetables are local and/or organic) and authentic bistro cuisine. Menu highlights could include a *blanquette de veau* (veal stew), or beef served with crushed cauliflower and fresh asparagus, but if meat is not your game, there are also scrumptious fish and poultry dishes. To finish off, try a fresh Auvergne cheese like Saint Nectaire or Fourme d'Ambert. Bring your appetite, as you must take one of the fixed-price menus; there is no à la carte.

8 rue de Vaugirard, 6th arrond. © **01-43-26-36-36.** www.laferrandaise.com. Fixed-price lunch 16€ and 35€, fixed-price dinner 35€ and 48€. Tues–Fri noon–2:30 and 7–10:30pm, Mon and Sat 7–11pm. Closed 3 weeks in Aug. Métro: Odéon.

Le P'tit Fernand ★★ TRADITIONAL FRENCH/BISTRO This tiny slice of restaurant packs a flavorful punch. Red-checked tablecloths provide a homey background for excellent bistro dishes like thick steak with a confit of shallots and creamy mashed potatoes, or duck magret (breast) served with morello cherry sauce. You could start with a nice light beet and rhubarb gazpacho, or go nuts and order the homemade terrine of foie gras. Whatever it is, it will be executed with loving care and quality ingredients, which is why this restaurant has a devoted clientele.

7 rue Lobineau, 6th arrond. ℂ **01-40-46-06-88.** www.lepetitfernand.fr. Main courses 18€–26€. Daily noon–2pm and 7–11:30pm. Métro: Mabillon.

Le Relais de l'Entrecôte ★★ TRADITIONAL FRENCH/STEAK You won't have to trouble yourself with deciding what to eat here: The only thing on the menu is steak. Just tell the waiter how you want it cooked (*bien cuit* for medium-well, *à point* for medium-rare, or *saignant* for rare) and sit back and wait. First comes a fresh green salad, and then the main event: a giant silver platter of steak, doused in an addictive "secret sauce," and served with crispy golden fries. Expect to see your server return with a second helping once you've finished. Desserts, if you can find the strength, are classic and delicious, including profiteroles and crème brûlée. Get here early, as you can't reserve and there is often a line out the door. If the line looks too long, you can try one of the two other locations: 101 bd. Montparnasse in the 6th, or 15 rue Marbeuf in the 8th.

20 rue St. Benoît, 6th arrond. ℂ **01-45-49-16-00.** www.relaisentrecote.fr. Daily noon–3pm and 7–11:30pm. Fixed-price lunch and dinner 27€. Métro: St-Germain-des-Prés.

Mangetout ★★★ MODERN FRENCH This affordable taste treat comes courtesy of Michelin-starred chef Alain Dutournier, the force behind Pinxo (p. 68). For a relative pittance, you can get a delicious two- or three-course set meal that might start with a golden broth decked with fresh shrimp and vegetables, continue with a surprisingly light *blanquette de veau* (veal stew), and finish up with a tourtière, a flakey apple tart that is usually found in the French southwest, Dutournier's home sweet home. The quality of the ingredients and the cooking is superb and the price is right. As the dining room is tiny, diner reservations are essential.

82 rue Mazarine, 6th arrond. ℂ **01-43-54-02-11.** www.alaindutournier.com/wp/mangetout. Main courses 17€–24€, fixed-price lunch 20€–25€, fixed-price dinner 23€. Tues–Sat noon–2pm and 7–10:30pm. Closed in Aug. Métro: Mabillon or Odéon.

INEXPENSIVE

L'Avant Comptoir ★ WINE BAR/TAPAS/CREPES This shoebox-size wine bar-cum-crêpe stand is an outcropping of the venerable Comptoir du Relais next door. Hungry diners descend on the bar and tapas component while waiting for a table at the restaurant; those in search of quick and portable bite can order take-out crêpes and salads (note that if you order from the takeout menu, you give up your right to stand and eat at the counter). There is a decidedly hip atmosphere here, despite the low key "this is just a typical southwestern bar" decor. Goodies include fried croquettes stuffed with Iberian ham, *brandade* (mashed potatoes with cod), oxtail canapés with horseradish cream, and chicken hearts grilled with garlic and parsley.

3 carrefour de l'Odéon, 6th arrond. No phone. www.hotel-paris-relais-saint-germain.com. Hors d'oeuvres 5€–8€. Daily noon–midnight. Métro: Odéon.

Pâtisserie Viennoise ★★ BAKERY Squeezed between two medical schools, this old-fashioned pastry shop gets its share of students and professors in need of a

Even the most stylish locals humbly bow their heads when they step inside this temple of baked goods. The store is tiny and unassuming, but the orders are meted out like communion wafers. You ask for your bread, and wait silently while the baker solemnly counts out the slices (yes, you order by the slice). Then you meekly pay and leave room for the next suppliant.

This isn't just bread, it's history. Pierre Poilâne opened his store in 1932, serving country-style bread made with stone ground flour in a wood-burning oven. Success was such that the recipe hasn't changed an iota and today the round loaves are shipped all over the world. Not many bread makers rub shoulders with the jet set: In 1969, son Lionel even made Salvador Dali a bedroom made out of bread. Today granddaughter Apollonia guides the mothership with a firm hand, making sure the tradition continues. Poilâne is at 8 rue du Cherche-Midi, 6th arrond. (℡ **01-45-48-42-59;** www.poilane.fr; two other locations in the Marais and near the Eiffel Tower).

nosh. And this is a nosher's heaven: There's a huge selection of pastries, including Viennese classics like Linzer torte and strudel, and the hot chocolate is one of the best in the city (3.50€–4€). It's thick and dark and bitter—sugar cubes are provided so you can adjust the sweetness—and if you ask for it *à la viennoise*, it will come with a dollop of real whipped cream. The tiny dining area looks like it hasn't changed in at least 50 years: a collection of wooden booths and small tables that might have been shipped in from Vienna. You can also lunch here on a variety of inexpensive quiches, salads and pasta dishes, including some nice vegetarian choices. No credit cards.

8 rue de l'Ecole de Médecine, 6th arrond. ℡ **01-43-26-60-48.** Main courses 7€–9€; pastries 3€–3.50€. Mon–Fri 8:30am–7:30pm. Closed mid-July through 3rd week of Aug. Métro: Odéon or Cluny La Sorbonne.

Restaurant Polidor ★ TRADITIONAL FRENCH/BISTRO   An unofficial historic monument, Polidor is not so much a restaurant as a snapshot of a bygone era. The decor has not changed substantially for at least 100 years, when Verlaine and Rimbaud, the bad boys of poetry, would come here for a cheap meal. The bistro would continue to be a literary lunch room for decades: In the 1950s it was dubbed "the College of Pataphysics" by a rowdy group of young upstarts that included Max Ernst, Boris Vian, and Eugene Ionesco; André Gide and Ernest Hemingway were reputed regulars. The menu features hefty bistro standbys like boeuf bourguignon and blanquette de veau (veal stew with white sauce), but if you look carefully you'll also find lighter fare like salmon with basil and chicken breast with morel sauce. These days, the arty set has moved elsewhere; you'll probably be sharing the long wood tables with other tourists, along with a dose of locals. Though the food is not particularly memorable, the ambience is unique; a good place to taste a bit of history. No credit cards.

41 rue Monsieur-le-Prince, 6th arrond. ℡ **01-43-26-95-34.** www.polidor.com. Main courses 11€–20€; fixed-price menu 22€–35€. Daily noon–2:30pm; Mon–Sat 7pm–12:30am; Sun 7–11pm. Métro: Odéon.

Eiffel Tower & Nearby (7th Arrondissement)

Crowded with ministries and important people, this neighborhood is so grand, you half expect to hear trumpets blowing each time you turn a corner. While you will have no

5

WHERE TO EAT

The Left Bank

problem finding chic gourmet restaurants, eating here on a budget takes some skill, or at least a bit of insider knowledge. Though this is a rather staid neighborhood, there are a few streets that are fairly lively, namely rue Cler, a pretty market street, and rue St-Dominique, home to some of the best restaurants on this side of the Seine. You're likely to get fleeced if you insist on eating right next to the Eiffel Tower—that is, if you can find a restaurant, as the pickings are pretty slim in the Iron Lady's immediate vicinity. If it's a nice day, buy a sandwich at a bakery and have a picnic on the Champs de Mars, where you can't beat the price or the view.

VERY EXPENSIVE

L'Arpège ★★★ MODERN FRENCH   Chef Alain Passard made waves when he decided to put vegetables, not meat, in the spotlight at his Michelin-three-star restaurant. You can still find meat on the menu, but it takes a backseat to carrots, turnips, sweet peas, or whatever other lovely plant life is in season. This pristine produce, which comes from Passard's farm near Le Mans, is often picked in the morning and ends up on diner's plates the same evening. Uneaten food makes the return journey and becomes compost. Food politics aside, the flavors that Passard coaxes from these vegetables are truly remarkable. The menu comes in two sections: the "grand crus" of the vegetable garden, and the "memory" dishes: milk-fed lamb from the Aveyron with wild celery, or fresh fish from Brittany with lovage and sweet peas. Service is discreet, as one expects at a restaurant frequented by diplomats and executives, and the dining room, with etched glass, burnished steel, and pearwood paneling, is beautiful. Don't miss the *tarte aux pommes bouquet de roses* (a tart composed of apple ribbons rolled into tiny rosettes). Reservations required at least 2 weeks in advance.

84 rue de Varenne, 7th arrond. ✆ **01-47-05-09-06.** www.alain-passard.com. Main courses 110€–225€; fixed-price lunch 140€, fixed-price tasting menu (lunch and dinner) 420€. Mon–Fri noon–2pm and 7–10:30pm. Métro: Varenne.

EXPENSIVE

Le Violon d'Ingres ★★★ TRADITIONAL FRENCH   Decked out in shades of cream and chocolate, this is the most elegant and refined of the three Christian Constant restaurants on rue Saint-Dominque. The menu treats classic dishes with kindness and care, giving each a dash of delicious originality. Menu choices might include roast sea bass in a sliced almond crust with capers and lemon, Pyrénées lamb roasted with spices, and the chef's own *cassoulet*. Top it all off with a vanilla ice cream-filled *macaron* floating in a berry soup.

135 rue St-Dominique, 7th arrond. ✆ **01-45-55-15-05.** www.leviolondingres.com. Main courses 39€–48€; fixed-price menu lunch 41€–47€, fixed-price menu dinner 95€. Daily noon–2:30pm and 6:30–11:30pm. Métro: Invalides or Ecole-Militaire.

Restaurant Auguste ★★ MODERN FRENCH/SEAFOOD   It's not every famous chef that can call himself "Mr. Goodfish." Gael Orieux's love of the sea and everything in it has led him to become spokesperson for an association dedicated to protecting the oceans. Naturally, that means what you see in your plate is not only delicious, but also ecologically correct. Let's hope he makes an impact on his clientele, much of which consists of politicians taking a break from the nearby Assemblée Nationale. Aside from protecting fish, Orieux cooks it, serving some of the best seafood in town served with stunning artistic flair. Your dish might look like artwork, but actually be red mullet with sweet and sour cherries, turnips in coconut sauces, and wild elderberries or turbot with tomatoes, green peppers, and quail eggs. Meat-eaters might appreciate the veal with juniper berries, sweet peas, and rhubarb.

54 rue de Bourgogne, 7th arrond. (C) **01-45-51-61-09.** www.restaurantauguste.fr. Main courses 36€–55€; fixed-price lunch 37€, fixed-price dinner 88€. Mon-Fri noon–2:30pm and 7–10:30pm. Closed 3 weeks in August. Métro: Varenne.

MODERATE

La Fontaine de Mars ★★ BISTRO/SOUTHWESTERN FRENCH   Red and white checks are everywhere at this old-school bistro: on the tablecloths, the wicker chairs, and even the curtains. A venerable institution since it first opened in 1908, it's low-key classy decor and traditional menu attracted the attention of President Obama, who made a surprise appearance here with his wife Michele when he visited France in 2009. The kitchen turns out reliable and succulent southwestern dishes like cassoulet, foie gras, and duck breast with black cherry sauce. Starters include *escargots* (snails) and *oeufs au Madiran* (eggs baked with red wine and bacon), and the dessert list is full of classics such as *île flottante*, crème brûlée, and dark chocolate mousse.

129 rue St-Dominique, 7th arrond. (C) **01-47-05-46-44.** www.fontainedemars.com. Main courses 17€–49€. Daily noon–3pm and 7:30–11pm. Métro: Ecole Militaire.

Le Casse Noix ★★ TRADITIONAL FRENCH/BISTRO   Chef Pierre-Olivier Lenormand brings his high-caliber food to a casual, affordable setting. The decor is nostalgic (note the nutcracker collection and vintage advertisements) and the traditional French cooking is sincere and generous. Perhaps a roast pork shoulder Ibaïona with olive puree will fill the bill? Or why not try a classic *petit salé* (lentils with smoky ham) followed by a crowd-pleasing dessert like *île flottante* ("floating island," a puffy meringue floating on vanilla cream). About a 10-minute walk from the Eiffel Tower, this is a good bet for those looking for a bit of authenticity in an otherwise very touristy neighborhood. At dinnertime, the fixed-price menu is *obligatoire,* as there is no à la carte ordering. Lunch is more flexible.

56 rue de la Fédération, 15th arrond. (C) **01-45-66-09-01.** www.le-cassenoix.fr. Main courses at lunch 19€–23€; fixed-price lunch 21€ and 26€, fixed-price dinner 33€. Mon–Fri noon–2:30pm and 7–10:30pm. Closed in August and between Christmas and New Year. Métro: Dupleix.

INEXPENSIVE

Café Constant ★★★ TRADITIONAL FRENCH/BISTRO   At this relaxed bistro you are quite likely to find Christian Constant himself at the bar smoking a cigar during his off hours. The restaurant serves a modern version of French comfort food like tangy poached cod with aioli, melt-in-your-mouth beef daube (stew) with carrots, or steak with shallots and creamy potato puree. While the low prices and great food are no longer a travel secret (you might be sharing the dining room with Asian and American tourists), that's not a reason not to make the most of it: This is still one of the best deals in town. At lunch on weekdays you can even get a two-course meal (chef's choice) for 16€—a terrific deal for this level of quality. You can even stop in for a croissant and coffee from 7am to noon and between meal service hours you can always come in for a drink. Reservations are not accepted.

139 rue Saint-Dominique, 7th arrond. (C) **01-47-53-73-34.** www.maisonconstant.com. Main courses 16€–26€; lunch fixed-price menu 16€–23€. Daily noon–5pm and 7–11pm. Métro: Ecole Militaire.

Le Café du Marché ★ TRADITIONAL FRENCH/BISTRO   This bustling cafe has one of the nicest sidewalk terraces in the area. Located on the rue Cler, a pedestrian market street, you can do some serious people watching here without inhaling excess car exhaust. The menu features simple bistro dishes like crispy duck *confit* and thick slabs of grilled lamb, as well as more modern turns like salmon brochettes with balsamic vinegar and ginger. Meals are served "non-stop" all day. *Note:* Prices vary by 2 to 3 euros depending what time of day you eat; the fluctuations are detailed on the menu.

38 rue Cler, 7th arrond. © **01-47-05-51-27.** Main courses 10€–15€. Mon–Sat noon–11pm. Sunday noon–3:30pm. Métro: Ecole Militaire.

Le Petit Cler ★ TRADITIONAL FRENCH/BISTRO A mini-version of La Fontaine de Mars (see above), this cute little cafe tumbles out on to the rue Cler pedestrian market street and serves food that of the same high quality as its upscale big sister, but simpler, and at a lower price. While you won't find as many red and white checks, you will find classic cafe fare (steaks with sautéed potatoes, omelets, and tartines—open-faced grilled sandwiches, and the like) as well as a daily special, which might be roast chicken (Sun) or fresh fish (Fri, natch). You can also get a good continental breakfast here.

29 rue Cler, 7th arrond. © **01-45-50-17-50.** www.fontainedemars.com. Main courses 11€–15€. Daily 8am–11pm. Closed 2 weeks in August and from Christmas to New Years. Métro: Ecole Militaire

Les Cocottes de Christian Constant ★★ MODERN FRENCH An affordable version of Chef Christian Constant's cuisine is on offer at this casual restaurant where everyone sits on a stool at the counter or a high table and almost all dishes are served in a cast iron *cocotte* (casserole). The hearty cocottes range from simple concoctions of caramelized potatoes with pig's feet, to gourmet combinations of squab with preserved garlic, artichokes, and thyme-scented sweet peas. There's also a 16€ "cocotte du jour" that changes daily. If you're not that hungry, there are soups, light salads, and "verrines," jam-jar-sized glass containers of pâté or other delicacies. Desserts include an oversized waffle with Chantilly cream and Constant's signature chocolate tarte. There are no reservations, so get here early before there's a line.

135 rue St. Dominique, 7th arrond. No phone. www.maisonconstant.com. Main courses 15€–29€. Daily noon–3:30pm and 6:30–10:30pm. Métro: École Militaire.

Montparnasse & Nearby (14th & 15th Arrondissements)

The famous cafes (Le Dôme, Le Select, La Coupole, and so on) where struggling writers and artists like Picasso, Hemingway, and Chagall, once hung out are now much too expensive for most ordinary mortals, much less struggling artists, so having a drink and soaking up the atmosphere is probably the most affordable way to enjoy them. This is also the most Breton (that is, from Brittany) section of Paris. The trains from Brittany arrive and depart from Montparnasse, and the story goes that between the Wars, fresh-off-the-train Bretons, not knowing where else to go, settled in the immediate vicinity. Hence the high density of crêperies (the crepe having its origins in Brittany). In recent years, the neighborhood has woken up, gastronomically speaking, and a bundle of new gourmet bistros are tantalizing local taste buds.

EXPENSIVE

Cobéa ★★ MODERN FRENCH Gray and white elegance greets the diner when they enter this pretty little house (a throwback to when southern Montparnasse was part of the countryside). Chef Philippe Bélissent invents concoctions that are as delicate and refined as the dining room. Perfectly cooked veal with fava beans and polenta, freshly caught John Dory, or pigeon with artichokes and olives might show up on the mix-and-match menu. The concept at dinner is as follows: There is one menu, from which you decide whether you'd like to try four (70€), six (85€), or eight (105€) courses. Service is impeccable.

11 rue Raymond Losserand, 14th arrond. ℂ **01-43-20-21-39.** www.cobea.fr. Fixed-price lunch 49€–65€, fixed-price dinner 75€–115€. Tues–Sat 12:15–1:15pm, 7:15–9:15pm. Closed in Aug. Métro: Gaîté or Pernety.

MODERATE

La Cerisaie ★ SOUTHWESTERN FRENCH/BISTRO   This shoebox-size dining room near the Tour Montparnasse serves the soul-warming cuisine of southwestern France. Depending on the season, you might start with chestnut soup or home-made foie gras. In autumn and winter, Chef Cyril Lalanne does amazing things with wild game and his menu features every animal in the forest from hare to partridge to boar. Finish with the southwestern take on the classic rum baba, made with the region's Armagnac instead of rum. It's best to reserve ahead, but if you can't, you may have to line up for one of the two seatings, at 7pm and 9pm.

70 bd. Edgar-Quinet, 14th arrond. ℂ **01-43-20-98-98.** www.restaurantlacerisaie.com. Main courses 15€–35€. Mon–Fri noon–2pm and 7–10pm. Closed mid-July to mid-Aug. Métro: Montparnasse-Bienvenüe or Edgar Quinet.

La Régalade ★★★ TRADITIONAL FRENCH/BISTRO   This sweet little bistro, with its cracked tile floors, polished wood, and burgundy banquettes, was one of the first outposts in the bistronomy movement. It is currently owned by chef Bruno Doucet, who has maintained the tradition of simplicity and quality. The menu changes regularly, but starters could include foie gras in asparagus bouillon or marinated sea scallops with basil and Parmesan. Main dishes are generally variations on French comfort food, such as a succulent pork breast with sweet peas, or lively innovations like a creamy squid risotto with sautéed prawns. Dessert could be a stinky Reblochon cheese, a molten Guanaja chocolate cake, or the house specialty, rice pudding. Reserve a week in advance.

14 ave. Jean-Moulin, 14th arrond. ℂ **01-45-45-68-58.** Fixed-price menu 37€. Tues–Fri noon–2:30pm; Mon–Fri 7–11:30pm. Closed first 2 weeks of Aug. Métro: Alésia.

L'Assiette ★ TRADITIONAL FRENCH   There's a whiff of the Belle Epoque in this old-fashioned dining room, which has its share of mirrors and ceiling ornaments. The menu appeals to culinary nostalgia as well, with dishes like home-made cassoulet, pike quenelles (long and delicate fish dumplings) with Nantua sauce, as well as *escargots* (snails) and homemade foie gras for starters. For dessert, indulge in crème caramel made with salted butter, or profiteroles with chocolate sauce. The restaurant also hosts workshops for tea-lovers where you can explore the secrets of gourmet teas (more information at www.thesdelassiette.com).

181 rue du Château, 14th arrond. ℂ **01-43-22-64-86.** www.restaurant-lassiette.com. Main courses 25€–29€; fixed-price lunch 23€. Wed–Sun noon–2:30pm and 7:30–10:30pm. Closed Aug. Métro: Gaité.

Les Petits Plats ★★ MODERN FRENCH/BISTRO   Not especially hungry but you still want to eat well? This friendly bistro offers all of its main courses either in full or half-sizes (at full and half prices). The blackboard lists the day's offerings, which might include a juicy slab of Aubrac beef, lightly sizzled cod with compote of roasted fresh vegetables, or sautéed squid and scallops with black rice. Finish it off with a meltingly rich chocolate *mi-cuit* (a not-quite-cooked cake). The ambiance is relaxed and the young staff is downright charming. At dinner there is a tasting menu of five different dishes for 45€.

39 rue des Plantes, 14th arrond. ℂ 01-45-42-50-52. Main courses 22€–26€; half-dishes 11€–13€; fixed-price lunch 17€. Mon–Sat noon–2pm and 7:30–10pm. Closed 3 weeks in Aug. Métro: Alésia.

INEXPENSIVE

Crêperie Josselin ★★ CREPERIE   This is one of the best of the dozens of crêperies concentrated near the Montparnasse train station. The cook working the griddle knows exactly how to achieve the lacy, golden edges of a perfect galette, and they are not shy with the butter. Josselin's specialty is the "couple" or double crêpe that uses two of these lacy confections in one dish. If you are not starving ask the waiter to make it a "simple." Try to save room for a sweet crêpe after. Tradition demands that this meal be accompanied by a bowl of hard cider (low alcohol content, for adults only). The easy prices, continuous service, and wide range of flavor combinations make this a great option for children. If you hanker for their delicious crêpes on a Monday, when it's closed, just wander down to No. 59, Le Petit Josselin, its sister restaurant (which is closed Sun). No credit cards accepted at either.

67 rue du Montparnasse, 14th arrond. ℂ **01-43-20-93-50.** Main courses 6.50€–11€; fixed-price menu 11€. Tues–Fri 11:30am–3pm and 6–11pm, Sat–Sun noon–11pm. Métro: Montparnasse-Bienvenüe.

Taverne de la Forge ★ ALSATION   The menu and the decor at this woodsy tavern honor Alsace, an eastern region that shares a border with Germany. Decked out with a chalet interior and a wood-burning oven, this cozy restaurant serves up delicious specialties like flammekueches, the Alsatian version of pizza. The delicate, thin crust is dotted with sautéed onions, smoked ham, mushrooms, or a variety of other goodies like potatoes, or smoked salmon. Other regional specialties include variations on the cheese-on-potatoes-and-ham theme, as well as choucroute, smoked meats on a heap of cooked and shredded cabbage, as well as a selection of standard bistro fare. Right next to the Montparnasse station, and with "non-stop" service all day, this is a good place to grab a bite when you are waiting for your train.

63 bd. de Vaugirard, 15th arrond. ℂ **01-43-20-87-10.** Flamekueches 8€–12€, main dishes 14€–21€. Daily 11am–10:30pm. Métro: Montparnasse–Bienvenüe.

THE TOP TEAROOMS

It may surprise you to know that despite their famous cafe culture many French people are closet tea fanatics. So it is only fitting that some of the world's loveliest tearooms are in Paris. Here is a sampling of some of the city's finest tea temples.

Angelina ★★ TEAROOM   This Belle Epoque beauty under the arcades on the rue de Rivoli was once frequented by Proust and Coco Chanel, among other notables. Famous for its hot chocolate and its chestnut-y Mont Blanc pastry, this is also a great spot for a chic breakfast or lunch.

226 rue de Rivoli, 1st arrond. ℂ **01-42-60-82-00.** www.angelina-paris.fr. Main courses 16€–29€, fixed-price breakfast 20€–29€, brunch 39€. Mon–Fri 7:30am–7pm; Sat–Sun 8:30am–7pm. Métro: Tuileries.

Café Jacquemart-André ★★ TEAROOM   Peek up at the Tiepolo ceiling as you sip your tea in what was once the dining room of Edouard André and Nélie Jacquemart. This beautiful tearoom serves excellent teas and delicious pastries from

This is a particularly tough call, since there are new pastry shops opening up all the time, but here are a few classic outlets where not even the sniffiest gourmet will turn their nose up.

o **Dalloyau,** 101 rue du Faubourg St-Honoré, 8th arrond. (℃) **01-42-99-90-00;** www.dalloyau.fr; Métro: St-Philippe du Roule), has been in business since Napoleon was in power and supplies pastries to the Élysée Palace (the French White House). Known for **Le Dalloyau,** a light praline cake filled with almond meringue.

o **Pierre Hermé,** 72 rue Bonaparte, 6th arrond. (℃) **01-43-54-47-77;** www.pierreherme.com; Métro: St-Sulpice). It may look like a chic jewelry store, but the goods are edible here. Exquisite and fashionable pastries include the Ispahan series, based on litchi, rose, and raspberry flavors.

o **Stohrer,** 51 rue Montorgueil, 2nd arrond. (℃) **01-42-33-38-20;** www.stohrer.fr; Métro: Sentier or Les Halles), was opened by Louis XV's pastry chef in 1730. This is the place to sample the ultimate **baba au rhum** (a rum-soaked sponge cake); Stroher invented it in the 18th century.

For a complete run down on where to find delicious goodies, take a look at **The Paris Pastry E-Guide** by local blogger and pastry chef David Lebovitz (www.paris-pastry.com).

Stroher and La Petite Marquise. Lunch (or brunch Sat–Sun) from 11:45 to 3pm, tea and pastries 3–5:30pm. No reservations.

Musée Jacquemart-André, 158 bd. Haussmann, 8th arrond. (℃) **01-45-62-11-59.** www.musee-jacquemart-andre.com. Main courses 15€–20€, fixed-price lunch 18€–24€; brunch 29€. Daily 11:45am–5:30pm. Métro: Miromesnil or Saint-Augustin.

Ladurée ★ TEAROOM This luxury pastry shop has boutiques everywhere these days, but there's nothing quite like a cup of tea and macarons (their famous light-as-air filled cookies) in one of their elegant Parisian tearooms. The rue Royale location, with its original 1862 *boiseries* (decorative wood paneling), and the grandiose Champs-Élysées site with its upstairs salon are the most impressive.

75 ave. des Champs-Élysées, 8th arrond. (℃) **01-40-75-08-75.** www.laduree.fr. Main courses 18€–34€, fixed-price lunch 40€–51€, brunch 40€. Mon–Thurs 7:30am–11:30pm, Fri 7:30am–12:30am, Sat 8:30am–12:30am, Sun 8:30am–11:30pm. Métro: George V.

Mosquée de Paris ★ TEAROOM For an altogether different cup of tea, have a seat at this lovely tearoom attached to the grand Paris Mosque. Sip a glass of sweet mint tea and nibble on a corne de gazelle (a crescent-shaped, powdered sugar–covered delight) or another pastry on the patio or in the beautifully tiled tearoom and dream that you're in the Casbah. Note that the entry is not the same as the one for the mosque.

39 rue Geoffroy St-Hilaire, 5th arrond. (℃) **01-43-31-38-20.** www.la-mosquee.com. Mint tea 2€, pastries 2€. Daily 9am–midnight. Métro: Censier-Daubenton.

THE TOP CAFES

It would be a crime to come to Paris and not stop to have a coffee (or other drink) in a cafe. Cafe life is an integral part of the Parisian scene, and it simply won't do to visit the capital without at least participating once. *Important note:* Cafes are not bars, in the North American sense—though they generally serve alcohol, they are not places where people come to get smashed. They are places where people come to just "be," to sip a drink, to take a break, to read a book, or to simply watch the world go by. Perhaps that's why the great Existentialist himself, Jean-Paul Sartre, spent so many of his waking hours in cafes. Most cafes open very early in the morning, and close between midnight and 2am.

There must be thousands of cafes in Paris, and a thorough run down would easily fill a book. Though you could probably have a primal cafe experience in just about any corner operation, here are a few ideas for your own personal cafe tour.

Historic Cafes

Café de Flore ★★ CAFE   A monument to the St-Germain quarter's intellectual past, Café de Flore is a must-sip on the cafe tour circuit. Seemingly every great French intellectual and artist seems to had his moment here: Poets Apollinaire and André Breton wrote here; artists Zadkine, Picasso, and Giacometti came to take refuge from Montparnasse; literary and theatrical stars came to preen; and of course, philosophers gathered to figure out the meaning (or nonmeaning) of life. During the war, Simone de Beauvoir and Jean-Paul Sartre more or less moved in, and Sartre is said to have written his trilogy "Les Chemins de la Liberté" ("The Roads to Freedom") here. The atmosphere now is less thoughtful and more showbiz, but it still may be worth an overpriced cup of coffee just to come in and soak it up.

172 bd. St-Germain, 6th arrond. ⓒ **01-45-48-55-26.** www.cafedeflore.fr. Daily 7am–2am. Métro: St-Germain-des-Prés.

Café de la Paix ★ CAFE   A Parisian institution ever since it was inaugurated by Empress Eugenie in 1862, this is the home of what is quite possibly the most expensive

---

Coffee Talk

Ordering a cup of coffee in Paris is not quite as simple as it sounds. There is a multitude of delightful caffeinated (and decaffeinated) java possibilities at most any cafe. Here is a miniglossary to help you navigate once your waiter makes it over to your table.

Café (ka-*fay*)—coffee. This is pure, black espresso, albeit lighter than the Italian version, served in a small demitasse cup. Always served with sugar on the side.

Décaf (*day*-ka)—decaf, or decaffeinated coffee. An unleaded version of the above.

Café serré (ka-*fay* sehr-*ay*)—smaller in volume, but packs a bigger punch. Resembles an Italian espresso.

Noisette (nwa-zet)—a café with a dash of steamed milk (my favorite).

Café crème (crem)—a café with an equal amount of steamed milk, served in a larger cup.

Café au lait (ka-*fay* oh lay)—virtually identical to the above, sometimes with a bit more milk. The biggest difference is the time of day; in the morning they call it a café au lait, in the afternoon a crème.

Cappuccinos, by the way, are rare in Parisian cafes, and when you do get one, chances are it won't resemble anything you'd get in Italy. *Important tip:* Drinks at the bar (coffee or otherwise) can cost half what you will pay sitting down at a table.

cup of coffee in the city (6€). Everyone from Emile Zola to Yves Montand has done time at this Second Empire marvel, whose gold leaf and curlicues have recently been meticulously renovated. Its outdoor terrace offers a magnificent view of the Palais Garnier—the perfect place for a drink before a night at the Opéra. It won't be cheap, but it will be memorable.

Corner of Place de l'Opéra and Boulevard des Capucines. © **01-40-07-36-36.** www.cafedelapaix.fr. Daily 9am–midnight. Métro: Opéra.

La Coupole ★★ CAFE   The artistic legacy of this brasserie is almost as vast as its square footage: Marc Chagall, Josephine Baker, Henry Miller, Salvador Dalí, and Ernest Hemingway are just some of the stars that lit up this converted charcoal depot. One of the largest restaurants in France, this Art Deco mastodon first opened in 1927, and has been hopping ever since. Thirty-three immense painted pillars hold up the ceiling; huge murals and paintings cover the walls. Though the food is decent (the lamb curry is the signature dish), it's best to just come here for a drink or a snack, grab a table by the windows, and watch the world go by. It's also a fun place to have breakfast.

102 bd. du Montparnasse, 14th arrond. © **01-43-20-14-20.** www.lacoupole-paris.com. Tues–Sat 8:30am–midnight, Sun–Mon 8:30am–11pm. Métro: Vavin.

Les Deux Magots ★★ CAFE   After the war, de Beauvoir and Sartre moved from Café de Flore to this nearby artists' haunt, where they continued to write and think and entertain their friends for a good chunk of the rest of their lives. The literary pedigree here is at least as impressive as that of its neighbor: Poets Verlaine and Rimbaud camped out here, as did François Mauriac, André Gide, Paul Eluard, Albert Camus, and Ernest Hemingway. Since 1933, Les Deux Magots has been handing out a literary prize (in 1994, the Flore came up with its own). The outdoor terrace is particularly pleasant early in the morning before the crowds wake up.

6 place St-Germain-des-Prés, 6th arrond. © **01-45-48-55-25.** www.lesdeuxmagots.fr. Daily 7:30am–1am. Métro: St-Germain-des-Prés.

Cafes with Decor

Le Bistrot du Peintre ★ CAFE   Artists, hipsters, and other fauna from the bustling rue de Charonne area crowd in to this popular spot, which sports an authentic Art Nouveau interior with the original peeling paint. Lean up against the zinc bar and admire yourself and others in the vast mirror behind the barman, or simply slouch at one of the tiny tables that tumble out onto the sidewalk.

116 ave. Ledru-Rollin, 11th arrond. © **01-47-00-34-39.** www.bistrotdupeintre.com. Daily 7am–2am; Métro: Ledru-Rollin.

Le Zeyer ★★ CAFE   After a hard day of shopping in the discount stores on rue d'Alesia, nothing could be nicer than a steaming cafe crème at this gorgeous Art Deco brasserie. One of the last of its kind that hasn't been turned into a tourist trap, this local hangout has a spacious covered terrace—the perfect spot for a rainy afternoon.

62 rue d'Alesia, 14th arrond. © **01-45-40-43-88.** www.lezeyer.com. 8am–midnight. Métro: Alésia.

Cafes for People-Watching

Café de la Mairie ★ CAFE   What could be nicer than sitting in a wicker chair at a sidewalk cafe on the place St-Sulpice? Relatively car-exhaust free (there is one lane of traffic between you and the place), in good weather tables on the wide sidewalk are much in demand; you may have to hover a while to get one. Indoors, it's a 1970s archetype: Formica bar, boxy chairs, and an odd assortment of pensioners, fashion victims, students, and would-be novelists.

8 place St-Sulpice, 6th arrond. ℂ **01-43-26-67-82.** Mon–Fri 7am–2am; Sat 8am–2am; Sun 9am–2am. Métro: Mabillon or St-Sulpice.

Eté en Pente Douce ★ CAFE   On a delightful corner facing the tranquil eastern side of Sacre-Coeur this colorful cafe features a lovely sidewalk terrace where you can relax away from the tourist hoards. Don't bother with the food here, which is fair to middling, just order a *café,* or a nice cool beer and look out on the greenery and watch people huffing and puffing up the stairs to the basilica. You'll have to huff and puff a little yourself to get here.

23 rue Muller, 18th arrond. ℂ **01-42-64-02-67.** www.parisresto.com. Daily noon–midnight. Métro: Anvers.

Le Nemours ★ CAFE   Cuddled up in a corner next to the Comedie Française, this quintessentially Parisian cafe has a great terrace stretching out onto the Place Colette. It's the ideal spot for a before- or after-theater drink, boning up on your Molière, or just taking a load off after a day at the nearby Louvre.

2 place Colette, ℂ **01-42-61-34-14.** Mon–Fri 7am–midnight; Sat 8am–midnight; Sun 9am–8:30pm. Métro: Palais Royale-Musée du Louvre.

EXPLORING PARIS

6

W
ith more than 130 world-class museums to visit, scores of attractions to discover, extraordinary architecture to gape at, and wonderful neighborhoods to wander, Paris is an endless series of delights. The hardest part is figuring out where to begin. Fortunately, you can have a terrific time in Paris even if you don't see everything. Some of your best moments may be simply roaming around the city without a plan. Lolling on a park bench, dreaming over a drink at a sidewalk cafe, or noodling around an unknown neighborhood can be the stuff of your best travel memories.

Area by area, the following pages will highlight the best that Paris can offer, from iconic sights known the world over to quirky museums and hidden gardens, from 1,000-year-old castles to galleries celebrating the most challenging contemporary art, and from the must-sees to the only-if-you've-seen-everything-else-sees. Here, then, is the best of Paris's attractions.

THE RIGHT BANK
Louvre & Ile de la Cité (1st Arrondissement)

This is where it all started: Back in its misty and uncertain beginnings, the Parisii tribe set up camp on the right bank of the Seine, and then started hunting on the **Ile de la Cité.** Many centuries later, the **Louvre** popped up, first as a fortress, and now as one of the world's mightiest museums. The city's epicenter, this area packs in a high density of must-see monuments and museums, but don't miss the opportunity for aimless strolling in the magnificent **Tuileries Gardens** or over the **Pont Neuf.** This section includes the entire Ile de la Cité, though technically half of it lies in the 4th arrondissement.

Cathédrale de Notre-Dame ★★★ CATHEDRAL   One of France's most brilliant expressions of medieval architecture, this remarkably harmonious ensemble of carved portals, huge towers, and flying buttresses has survived close to a millennium's worth of French history and has served as a setting for some of the country's most solemn moments. Napoleon crowned himself and Empress Josephine here, Napoleon III was married here, and some of France's greatest generals (Foch, Joffre, Leclerc) had their funerals here. In August 1944, the liberation of Paris from the Nazis was commemorated in the cathedral, as was the death of General de Gaulle in 1970.

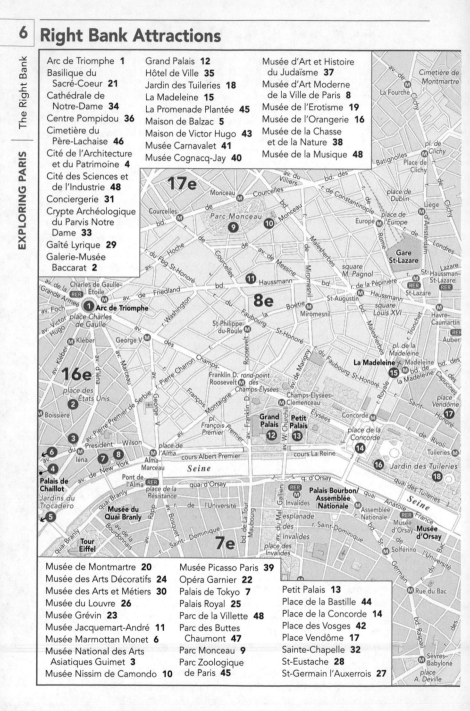

Arc de Triomphe **1**
Basilique du Sacré-Coeur **21**
Cathédrale de Notre-Dame **34**
Centre Pompidou **36**
Cimetière du Père-Lachaise **46**
Cité de l'Architecture et du Patrimoine **4**
Cité des Sciences et de l'Industrie **48**
Conciergerie **31**
Crypte Archéologique du Parvis Notre Dame **33**
Gaîté Lyrique **29**
Galerie-Musée Baccarat **2**

Grand Palais **12**
Hôtel de Ville **35**
Jardin des Tuileries **18**
La Madeleine **15**
La Promenade Plantée **45**
Maison de Balzac **5**
Maison de Victor Hugo **43**
Musée Carnavalet **41**
Musée Cognacq-Jay **40**

Musée d'Art et Histoire du Judaïsme **37**
Musée d'Art Moderne de la Ville de Paris **8**
Musée de l'Erotisme **19**
Musée de l'Orangerie **16**
Musée de la Chasse et de la Nature **38**
Musée de la Musique **48**

Musée de Montmartre **20**
Musée des Arts Décoratifs **24**
Musée des Arts et Métiers **30**
Musée du Louvre **26**
Musée Grévin **23**
Musée Jacquemart-André **11**
Musée Marmottan Monet **6**
Musée National des Arts Asiatiques Guimet **3**
Musée Nissim de Camondo **10**

Musée Picasso Paris **39**
Opéra Garnier **22**
Palais de Tokyo **7**
Palais Royal **25**
Parc de la Villette **48**
Parc des Buttes Chaumont **47**
Parc Monceau **9**
Parc Zoologique de Paris **45**

Petit Palais **13**
Place de la Bastille **44**
Place de la Concorde **14**
Place des Vosges **42**
Place Vendôme **17**
Sainte-Chapelle **32**
St-Eustache **28**
St-Germain l'Auxerrois **27**

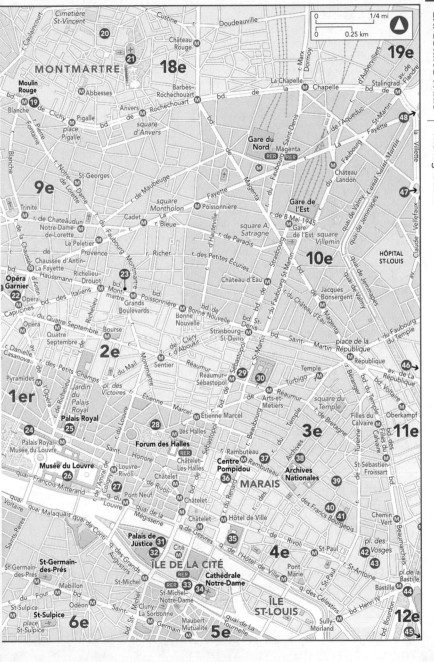

Paris Museum Pass

In recent years, many of the city's major museums, including the **Louvre,** the **Pompidou Center,** and the **Musée d'Orsay,** have joined the many attractions covered by this pass, making it a good deal if you are planning on seeing several museums and/or castles like **Versailles** (also on the list) during a short stay. Take a look at the list of museums included on the website and see if the price is right (42€ for a 2-day pass, 56€ for a 4-day pass, and 69€ for a 6-day pass) for the number of days you are staying. Keep in mind that average adult museum entry fee ranges around 8€ to 13€, and castles like Versailles and Fontainebleau run anywhere from 11€ to 25€. For more information and a list of attractions, visit www.parismuseumpass.com.

The New Les Halles

Famously called "the belly of Paris," **Les Halles** was the city's primary wholesale fruit, meat, and vegetable market for 8 centuries. The smock-clad vendors, beef carcasses, and baskets of vegetables all belong to the past, as the market was relocated to the suburb of Rungis in the early '70s. In a fit of modernity, all the pretty 19th-century pavilions were torn down and in their place a weird, partly underground shopping mall was constructed around a giant hole in the ground: the **Forum des Halles** (1–7 rue Pierre-Lescot, 1st arrond.). Fortunately, in 2010, the city embarked on a massive renovation program to overhaul the shopping center and the surrounding gardens, which is why the entire area has been temporarily transformed into a construction zone. By the end of 2014, the whole thing will be covered by "the canopy," an immense, undulating sheet of glass and metal that will gently float over the Forum. It won't be finished before 2016, but the underground mall remains open and operational during the renovations. For information, visit www.parisleshalles.fr.

The story of Notre Dame begins in 1163, when Bishop Maurice de Sully initiated construction, which lasted over 200 years. (The identity of the architect who envisioned this masterpiece is a mystery.) The building was relatively untouched up until the end of the 17th century, when monarchs started meddling with its windows and architecture. By the time the Revolutionaries decided to convert it into a "Temple of Reason," the cathedral was already in sorry condition—and the pillaging that ensued didn't help. The interior was ravaged, statues were smashed, and the cathedral became a shadow of its former glorious self.

We can thank the famous "Hunchback" himself for saving Notre Dame. Victor Hugo's novel, "The Hunchback of Notre Dame," drew attention to the state of disrepair, and other artists and writers began to call for the restoration of the edifice. In 1844, Louis-Phillipe hired Jean-Baptiste Lassus and especially architect/archeologist/writer/painter Viollet-le-Duc to restore the cathedral, which they finished in 1864. Though many criticized Viollet-le-Duc for what they considered to be overly romantic and unauthentic excesses, he actually took extreme care to remain faithful to the historic gothic architecture. His addition of a 45m (148-ft.) spire, for example, was in fact

Notre-Dame Cathedral

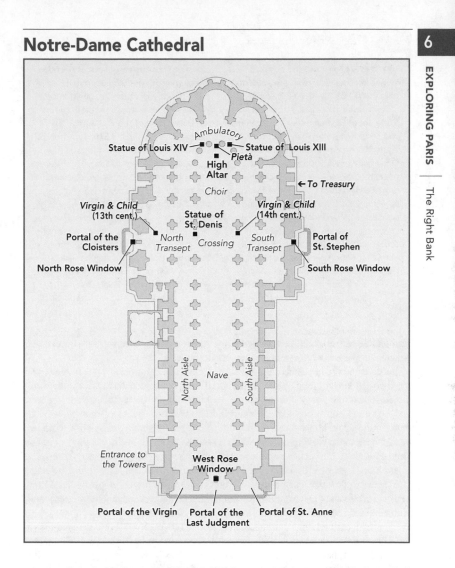

Statue of Louis XIV
Ambulatory
Statue of Louis XIII
Pietà
High Altar
Choir
← To Treasury
Virgin & Child (13th cent.)
Statue of St. Denis
Virgin & Child (14th cent.)
Portal of the Cloisters
North Transept
Crossing
South Transept
Portal of St. Stephen
North Rose Window
South Rose Window
North Aisle
Nave
South Aisle
Entrance to the Towers
West Rose Window
Portal of the Virgin
Portal of the Last Judgment
Portal of St. Anne

a re-creation of one that existed in the 13th century. Made out of lead-covered oak *(chene),* it weighs 750 metric tons (827 U.S. tons).

Begin your visit at **Point Zéro,** just in front of the building on the *parvis* (the esplanade). It is literally the epicenter of French life, the official center of Paris and the point from which all distances relative to other French cities are calculated. Before you are three enormous **carved portals** depicting (from left to right) the Coronation of the Virgin, the Last Judgment, and scenes from the lives of the Virgin and St-Anne. Above is the **Gallery of the Kings of Judah and Israel**—thought to be portraits of the kings of France, the original statues were chopped out of the facade during the Revolution; some of the heads were eventually found in the 1970s and now are in the Musée

The lines are long and the climb is longer, but the view from the **rooftop balcony** (✆ **01-53-40-60-80;** www.monuments-nationaux.fr; 8.50€ adults, 5.50€ under 26, free under 18; Apr–June and Sept 10am–6pm, July–Aug Sun–Thurs 10am–6pm, Fri–Sat 10am–11pm, Oct–Mar 10am–5:30pm) at the base of the cathedral's towers is possibly the most Parisian of all views. After trudging up some 255 steps (a narrow winding staircase with a handrail—not for small children or anyone with mobility concerns), you'll be rewarded with a panorama that not only encompasses the Ile de la Cité, the Eiffel Tower, and Sacré-Coeur, but is also framed by a collection of photogenic **gargoyles.** These fantastic monsters, composed of various portions of apes, birds, and even elephants, came directly from the imagination of Viollet-le-Duc, who placed them during the restoration of the cathedral. One of the most famous is the **Stryga,** a horned and winged beasty holding his head in his hands, pensively sticking his tongue out at the city below. Squeeze around the narrow first balcony to the entrance to the belfry, Quasimodo's old haunt; its massive wood beams hold up a 14-ton bell. Another 147 steps up another narrow stairway lead up to the summit of the **south tower,** from which there is an endless view of Paris. To minimize the wait, come in the morning before the crowds get thick, and avoid weekends.

National du Moyen Age/Thermes de Cluny. Above this is a superb **rose window,** over which soar the two bell **towers** of Quasimodo fame.

Upon entering the cathedral, you'll be immediately struck by two things: the throngs of tourists clogging the aisles, and then, when you look up, the heavenly dimensions of the pillars holding up the ceiling. Soaring upward, these delicate archways give the impression that the entire edifice is about to take off into the sky. Up there in the upper atmosphere are the three remarkable stained-glass **rose windows,** one for each of the west, north, and south ends of the church. The north window retains almost all of its 13th-century stained glass; the other two have been heavily restored. There is an impressive **treasury** filled with relics of various saints including the elaborate cases for the **Crown of Thorns,** brought back from Constantinople by Saint Louis in the 13th century. The crown itself is not on display; however, it can be viewed, along with a nail and some pieces of the Holy Cross, on the first Friday of the month (3pm), every Friday during Lent (3pm) and Good Friday (10am–5pm). For a detailed look at the cathedral, take advantage of the **free guided tours in English** (Wed–Thurs 2pm, Sat 2:30pm) or rent an **audioguide** for 5€.

When you leave, be sure to take a stroll around the outside of the cathedral to admire the other portals and the famous flying buttresses.

Place du Parvis Notre-Dame, 4th arrond. ✆ **01-53-10-07-02.** www.notredamedeparis.fr. Admission free to cathedral. Treasury 4€ adults, 2€ students and seniors, 1€ ages 6–12, free for children 5 and younger. Cathedral Mon–Fri 8am–6:45pm, Sat–Sun 8am–7:15pm. Treasury Mon–Fri 9:30am–6pm; Sat 9:30am–6:30pm; Sun 1:30–6:30pm. Métro: Cité or St-Michel. RER: St-Michel.

Conciergerie ★ HISTORIC SITE   A relic of the darker side of the Revolution, the Conciergerie was where some of its most famous participants spent their final days before making their way to the guillotine. Danton, Desmoulins, Saint-Just, and Charlotte Corday passed through these doors, but perhaps its most famous guest was Marie

Antoinette, who spent her time here in a dismal cell, reading and praying while she awaited her fate. After doing away with the monarchy, the Revolution began to eat itself alive; during the particularly bloody period known as the Terror, murderous infighting between the various revolutionary factions engendered panic and paranoia that led to tens of thousands of people throughout the country being arrested and executed. Twenty-two of the leaders of one of the leading factions, the Girondins, were condemned to death; legend has it that on the eve of their execution they drank and sang until dawn in their cell (now called the Chapelle des Girondins). Eventually Robespierre, the main force behind the Terror, and an ardent advocate for Marie-Antoinette's execution, found himself in the cell next door to the one she stayed in.

Though it's been a prison since the 15th century, the building itself is actually what remains of a 14th-century royal palace built by Philippe le Bel. Even before the Revolution, the Conciergerie was notorious: Henry IV's murderer, Ravaillac, was imprisoned here before an angry crowd tore him apart alive. The enormous **Salle des Gens d'Arms,** with its 8.4m-high (28-ft.) vaulted ceiling, is an impressive reminder of the building's palatial past. As for the prison itself, though the cells have been outfitted with displays and re-creations of daily life (including wax figures), it's a far cry from the dank hell it once was. Fresh paint and lighting make it a little difficult to imagine what it was like in the bad old days, but a few areas stand out, like the **Cours des Femmes** (the women's courtyard), which virtually hasn't changed since the days when female prisoners did their washing in the fountain. **Marie Antoinette's cell** was converted into a memorial chapel during the Restoration; a re-creation of her cell, containing some original objects, is on display. There are some interesting historical exhibits, including a list of the names of all those guillotined during the Revolution, 2,780 in Paris alone.

2 bd. du Palais, 1st arrond. ℂ **01-53-40-60-80.** www.monuments-nationaux.fr. Admission 8.50€ adults, 5.50€ ages 18–25, free for 17 and younger. Daily 9:30am–6pm. Métro: Cité, Châtelet, or St-Michel. RER: St-Michel.

Crypte Archéologique du Parvis Notre-Dame ★ ARCHEOLOGICAL SITE Back in the 1960s, construction of an underground parking lot revealed a vast array of archeological ruins under the esplanade in front of Notre-Dame. Specialists were called in and the site was preserved and made accessible to visitors. The ruins are a jumble of centuries of Parisian history, including Roman baths, medieval ramparts, and an ancient port. Explanatory displays have been translated into English, but seeing as how it is difficult for even archeologists to make sense of the layers of stonework, spiffy 3D displays have recently been installed that show what Paris looked like during various epochs, bringing parts of the ruins to life. For some it'll still be just a pile of rocks, for others, a fascinating look into the city's history.

7 parvis Notre-Dame, 4th arrond., entrance at the western end of the esplanade in front of Notre-Dame. ℂ **01-55-42-50-10.** www.crypte.paris.fr. Admission: 4€ adults, 3€ over 60, 2€ ages 14–26, free ages 13 and under. Tues–Sun 10am–6pm. Métro: Cité or St-Michel, RER: St-Michel-Notre-Dame.

Jardin des Tuileries ★★★ PARK This exquisite park spreads from the Louvre to the place de la Concorde. One of the oldest gardens in the city—and the first to be opened to the public—it's also one of the largest. In the Middle Ages, there was a factory here that made clay tiles *(tuiles),* a word that was incorporated into the name of the palace that Catherine de Medicis built at the far end of the Louvre in 1564. Such a grand palace needed equally splendid Italian gardens; later in the mid-1600s,

Louis XIV gave master landscape artist André Le Nôtre—the man behind the gardens of Versailles—the job of giving them a more French look. Le Nôtre's elegant geometry of flowerbeds, parterres, and groves of trees made the Tuileries Gardens the ultimate stroll for well-to-do Parisians.

Though the Tuileries Palace burned down during the Paris Commune in 1871, the landscaping lived on. During World War II, furious fighting went on here, and many statues were damaged. Little by little in the post-war years the garden put itself back together. Seventeenth- and 18th-century representations of various gods and goddesses were repaired, and the city added new works by modern masters such as Max Ernst, Alberto Giacometti, Jean Dubuffet, and Henry Moore. Rodin's "The Kiss" and "Eve" are here, as well as a series of 18 of Maillol's curvaceous women, peeking out of the green **labyrinth** of hedges in the Carousel Gardens near the museum.

Pulling up a metal chair and sunning yourself on the edge of the large **fountain** in the center of the gardens (the **Grande Carrée**) is a delightful respite for tired tourists after a day in the Louvre; cranky tots will enjoy playing with one of the wooden **toy sailboats** that you can rent from a stand (2.50€ for a half-hour).

Near place de la Concorde, 1st arrond. ℭ **01-40-20-90-43.** Free admission. Daily Apr–May 7am–9pm; June–Aug 7am–11pm; Sept 7am–9pm; Oct–Mar 7:30am–7:30pm. Métro: Tuileries or Concorde.

Musée de l'Orangerie ★★ MUSEUM   Since 1927, this former royal greenhouse has been the home of Monet's stunning "Nymphéas," or water lilies, which he conceived as a "haven of peaceful meditation." Two large oval rooms are dedicated to these masterpieces, in which Monet tried to replicate the feeling and atmosphere of his garden at Giverny. He worked on these enormous canvases for 12 years, with the idea of creating an environment that would soothe the "overworked nerves" of modern men and women—in what could be called one of the world's first art installations.

The other highlight here is the Guillaume collection, an impressive assortment of late-19th- and early-20th-century paintings. The collection is on the lower level, where the first, light-filled gallery displays mostly portraits and still-lifes, like Renoir's glowing, idyllic "Femme Nu dans un Paysage," and Cézanne's rather dour looking "Madame Cézanne." The rest of the collection is under artificial lights: slightly sinister landscapes by Rousseau, enigmatic portraits by Modigliani, distorted figures by Soutine, as well as some kinder, gentler Picassos ("Les Adolescents" bathed in pink and rust tones). This collection has a stormy history—after Guillaume's death, his rather flamboyant wife rearranged the collection to her own taste, selling off some of the more "difficult" paintings. The result is a lovely collection that lacks a certain bite—truly impressive works by these masters can be seen elsewhere.

Jardin des Tuileries, 1st arrond. ℭ **01-44-77-80-07.** www.musee-orangerie.fr. Admission 10€ adults, 7.50€ ages 18–25, free ages 17 and younger. Wed–Mon 9am–6pm. Métro: Concorde.

Musée des Arts Décoratifs ★★ MUSEUM   Possessing some 150,000 items in its rich collection, this fascinating museum offers a glimpse of history through the prism of decorative objects, with a spectrum that ranges from medieval traveling trunks to Philippe Starck stools. The collection is organized in more or less chronological order, so on your journey you will pass by paintings from the First Italian Renaissance, through a room filled with exquisite 15th-century intarsia ("paintings" made out of intricately inlaid wood), before gaping at huge, intricately carved 17th-century German armoires. Other highlights include a tiny room covered in gilded woodwork from an 18th-century mansion in Avignon, a 19th-century courtesan's bedroom, and a

Louvre

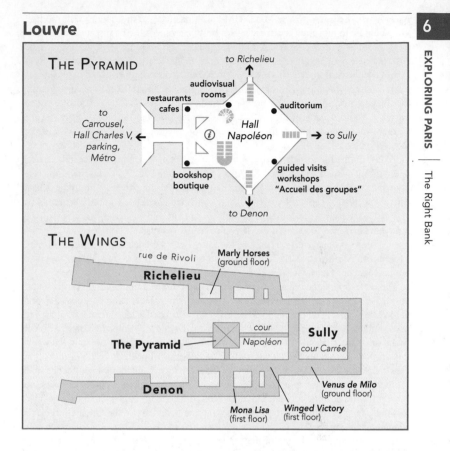

stunning Art Nouveau dining room. While the objects themselves are beautiful, the link between style and historic context is illuminating; the endless curlicues of the rococo style, which perfectly reflected the excesses of Louis XV's court, for example, gives way to more puritanical neo-classicism, which developed during the Enlightenment, when unrestrained frivolity began to look degenerate.

The collection weakens after 1930; it's hard to tell whether this is due to a lack of imagination on the part of the museum or on the part of 20th-century designers. The chronological sequence can be hard to follow; the visit starts on the third floor.

If you still have the strength, there are two other museums in the building: the **Musée de la Publicité,** which takes on the history of advertising, and the **Musée de la Mode et du Textile,** which hosts temporary exhibits on the many facets of clothing, including the works of famous couture houses like Jean-Paul Gaultier and Dior (both have the same hours as the main museum and are included in price of ticket to Arts Décoratifs).

Palais du Louvre, 107 rue de Rivoli, 1st arrond. (𝒞) **01-44-55-57-50.** www.lesartsdecoratifs.fr. Admission 11€ adults, 8.50€ ages 18–25, free for children 17 and younger. Tues–Sun 11am–6pm. Métro: Louvre-Palais-Royal or Tuileries.

Musée du Louvre ★★★ MUSEUM   The best way to thoroughly visit the Louvre would be to move in for a month. Not only is it one of the largest museums in the world, with over 35,000 works of art displayed over 60,000 sq. m (645,835 sq. ft.), but it's packed with enough artistic masterpieces to make the Mona Lisa weep. Rembrandt, Reubens, Botticelli, Ingres, and Michelangelo are all represented here; subjects range from the grandiose (Antoine-Jean Gros's gigantic "Napoleon Bonaparte Visiting the Plague-Stricken in Jaffa") to the mundane (Vermeer's tiny, exquisite "Lacemaker"). You can gape at a diamond the size of a golf ball in the royal treasury or marvel over exquisite bronze figurines in the vast Egyptian section. There's something for everyone here.

Today, the building is divided into three wings: Sully, Denon, and Richelieu, each one with its own clearly marked entrance, found under I.M. Pei's glass pyramid. Get your hands on a museum map, choose your personal "must-sees," and plan ahead. There's no way to see it all, and you'll be an instant candidate for early retirement if you try. Mercifully, the museum is well organized and has been very reasonably arranged into color-coded sections. If you're really in a rush, or you just want to get an overall sense of the place, you can take the introductory guided tour in English (1½ hr.; 11:15am and 2pm Wed–Mon; 12€). You won't see as much as you would on your own, but at least you'll know what you are seeing.

The museum's three biggest stars are all located in the Denon wing. "La Joconde," otherwise known as the **"Mona Lisa"** (see the "Men Have Named You . . ." box, below), now has an entire wall to herself, making it easier to contemplate her enigmatic smile. Another inscrutable female in this wing is the **"Venus de Milo,"** who was found on a Greek island in 1820. Possibly the most photographed woman in the world, this armless marble goddess gives no hint of the original position of her limbs or her exact identity. The **"Winged Victory of Samothrace,"** another magnificent Greek sculpture, is the easiest to locate. Standing at the top of a majestic flight of stairs, her powerful body pushing forward as if about to take flight, it's easy to imagine this headless deity in her original location: overlooking the Sanctuary of the Great Gods on the island of Samothrace.

Because a complete listing of the Louvre's highlights would fill a book, below is a decidedly biased selection of my favorite areas:

13TH- TO 18TH-CENTURY ITALIAN PAINTING   A few standouts in the immense Italian collection include Botticelli's delicate fresco "Venus and the Three Graces Presenting Gifts to a Young Woman," Veronese's enormous "Wedding Feast at Cana," and of course, the "Mona Lisa." The Divine Miss M is in a room packed with wonders, including several Titians and Tintorettos. Once you've digested this rich meal, stroll down the endless Grande Galerie, past more da Vincis ("Saint John the Baptist," "The Virgin of the Rock"), as well as works by Raphael, Caravaggio, and Gentileschi.

GREEK & ROMAN SCULPTURE   While the Winged Victory of Samothrace and the Venus de Milo are not to be missed, the Salle des Caryatides (the room itself is a work of art) boasts marble masterworks like Artemis hunting with her stag and the troubling Sleeping Hermaphrodite, an alluring female figure from behind—and something entirely different from the front.

THE GALERIE D'APOLLON   The gold-encrusted room is an excellent example of the excesses of 17th-century French royalty. Commissioned by Louis XIV, aka "The Sun King," every inch of this gallery is covered with gilt stucco sculptures and

Don't want to wait in line for tickets to the Louvre? Order tickets in advance online (in English) at **www.fnactickets. com** or by calling (℃ **08-92-68-36-22,** .34€/min; you can print out your tickets, get them mailed to you, or you can pick them up at any French branch of the Fnac bookstore chain. If you are of an improvisational bent and prefer to pick up tickets at the entrance, there are ways to avoid the lines that often snake around the glass pyramid entryway:

- Enter directly from the Palais Royal– Musée du Louvre metro stop.
- Take one of the two staircases on either side of the Arc du Carrousel in the Tuileries Gardens that lead directly down to the ticketing area.
- Enter at the Porte des Lions (in the Denon Wing).

Note that the Louvre is open until 9:30pm on Wednesday and Friday—usually a quiet time to visit.

flamboyant murals invoking the journey of the Roman sun god Apollo (ceiling paintings are by Charles Le Brun). The main draw here is the collection of crown jewels. Amongst necklaces bedecked with quarter-sized sapphires and tiaras dripping with diamonds and rubies are the jewel-studded crown of Louis XV and The Regent, a 140-carat diamond that he used to decorate his hat.

THE EGYPTIANS   This is the largest collection outside of Cairo, thanks in large part to Jean-François Champollion, the 19th-century French scientist and scholar who first decoded Egyptian hieroglyphs. Sculptures, figurines, papyrus documents, steles, musical instruments, and of course, mummies, fill numerous rooms in the Sully wing, including the colossal statue of Ramses II, and the strangely moving Seated Scribe. He gazes intently out of intricately crafted inlaid eyes: A combination of copper, magnesite, and polished rock crystal creates a startlingly lifelike stare.

LARGE-FORMAT FRENCH PAINTINGS   Enormous floor to ceiling paintings of monumental moments in history cover the walls in these three rooms. The overcrowded and legendary "Coronation of Napoléon" by Jacques-Louis David depicts the newly minted Emperor crowning Josephine, while the disconcerted pope and a host of notables look on. On the facing wall, "Madame Récamier" (also by David), one of Napoleon's loudest critics, reclines fetchingly on a divan. Farther on are several tumultuous canvases by Eugène Delacroix, including "Liberty Guiding the People," which might just be the ultimate expression of French patriotism. In the painting, which evokes the events of the revolution of 1830, Liberty—breast exposed, a rifle in one hand, the French flag in the other—leads the crowd over a sea of dead bodies. High ideals and gore—sort of sums up the French revolutionary spirit.

Note: When visiting the museum, **watch your wallets and purses**—there has been an unfortunate increase in pickpockets; organized groups even use children to prey on unsuspecting art lovers. On a more positive note, the Louvre has made great strides in improving **accessibility for handicapped visitors** in recent years, including special programs, ramps, and free wheelchairs and folding chairs. For more information, click "accessibility" at the top of the museums website.

Quai du Louvre, 1st arrond. Main entrance in the glass pyramid, cour Napoléon. (℃ **01-40-20-50-50.** www.louvre.fr. Admission 12€, children 17 and younger free. Sat–Mon and Thurs 9am–6pm; Wed and Fri 9am–9:30pm. Métro: Palais-Royal–Musée du Louvre.

EXPLORING PARIS | The Right Bank

Everything about the "Mona Lisa" is mysterious—the identity of the sitter, how long it took to paint, and how it got into the French royal collection, among other things. Most scholars agree that it is a portrait of Lisa Gheradini, the wife of one Francesco del Giocondo, but Ms. Lisa could also be Isabella of Aragon (as suggested by the patterning of her dress) or simply be an embodiment of beauty and happiness (hence the smile), as suggested by the Italian word, *gioconda*.

A few years ago, researchers found evidence of a fine, translucent veil around the subject's shoulders, a garment women in Renaissance Italy wore when they were expecting, provoking an onslaught of speculation that her secret smile had to do with her being pregnant.

What's certain is that the painting created a sensation. The overall harmony of the composition, the use of a distant landscape in the background, the lifelike quality of the subject, had a huge impact on early 16th-century Florentine art. As Giorgio Vasari, a Renaissance painter and biographer lamented, "it may be said that it was painted in such a manner as to make every valiant craftsman, be he who he may, tremble and lose heart."

The painting's history is action packed. One morning in 1911, an artist named Louis Béroud came in to the museum to sketch a copy of the famous portrait, and found a bare spot with four hooks in the wall. After a concerted effort, he convinced the lackadaisical guard to find out what happened. In fact, the "Mona Lisa" had been stolen. The thief had entered the museum posing as a visitor, hid in the building overnight, and in the morning disguised himself as a workman and made off with the painting while the guard went out to smoke a cigarette. Needless to say, panic ensued. There was a nationwide

investigation, and the borders were sealed. What the police didn't realize is that the painting was at first hidden only a mile from the Louvre. Conspiracy theories spread through the newspapers—some thought it was merely a publicity stunt. There was a lot of criticism about the Louvre's lax security, in particular from poet Apollinaire. He soon found himself arrested as a suspect, and his friend Pablo Picasso was also brought in for questioning after they were caught in possession of some other art objects of dubious origins. After they both broke down in tears before the bench, the judge let them go with a slap on the wrist.

After 2 years of false leads and bungled investigations, the "Mona Lisa" was finally found when the thief, Vincenzo Perugia, tried to sell it to an art dealer in Florence. What was the motive for the crime? It seems that Perugia, an Italian patriot who had once worked at the museum, simply felt that the "Mona Lisa" belonged in her country of birth, Italy. During his trial, Perugia claimed to have been bewitched by the painting—and indeed, who hasn't been?

The life of a superstar certainly isn't easy. With millions of admirers around the world, at least a couple are bound to have a few screws loose. Once she was back at the museum (under increased security, of course), things calmed down until 1956, when a deranged visitor threw acid on the painting, severely damaging its lower half (restoration would take several years). A few months later, someone threw a rock at her. The painting is now covered with bulletproof glass, and a full-time guard stands at the ready. So try to be patient with the lines and the velvet ropes—if the "Mona Lisa" gets the kind of security usually reserved for rock stars or heads of state, she has certainly earned it.

Palais Royal ★★ HISTORIC SITE/GARDEN   The gardens and long arcades of the Palais Royal are not only a delight to stroll through, but were also witnesses to one of the most important moments in French history. But first the backstory: Built by Cardinal Richelieu, the lavish palace was left to the King upon his prime minister's death. It was subsequently occupied by a number of royal family members (including Louis XIV as a child) until it came into the hands of a certain Duke Louis Phillippe d'Orleans at the end of the 18th century. An inveterate spendthrift, the young lord soon found himself up to his ears in debt. To earn enough money to pay off his creditors, he came up with the shockingly modern idea of opening the palace gardens to development, building apartments on the grounds. The bottom floor of these lodgings, which make up three sides of the enclosure you see today, were let out as shops, cafes, and boutiques. Though the neighbors screamed, their cries were drowned out by the success of the new project, which made the area into a commercial hub. What's more, since the police had no power over these royal grounds, all sorts of usually illegal activities were given free reign here. Gambling houses and bordellos sprang up between the shops and cafes, and the gardens became the central meeting place for revolutionaries. Things came to a head on July 12, 1789, when Camille Desmoulins stood up on a table in front of the Café de Foy and called the people to arms—two days later, the mob would storm the Bastille, igniting the French Revolution. The glory days of the Palais Royal would come to an abrupt end in 1815, when a new Louis-Philippe showed up, decided this was not the way to treat the home of his ancestors, and kicked everyone out. Once the royals finally left in the 19th century, the palace was taken over by various government ministries, and the apartments in the galleries were let out to artists and writers, including Collette and Jean Cocteau.

Today the shops in the arcades are very subdued, and very expensive—mostly antique toy and stamp dealers, a smattering of high-end designer clothes, and a couple of pricey restaurants, including the legendary Grand Véfour (p. 64). The cour d'honneur on the south end is filled with black and white striped columns by Daniel Buren; though most Parisians have now gotten used to this unusual installation, when it was unveiled in 1987 it caused almost as much of a stir as Camille Desmoulins.

Rue St-Honoré, 1st arrond. Free admission to gardens and arcades, buildings closed to public. Gardens daily 7:30am–dusk. Métro: Palais Royal–Musée du Louvre.

Place Vendôme ★★ SQUARE   In 1686, Louis XIV decided the time had come to design a magnificent square, at the center of which would stand a statue of His Royal Highness. Though the statue is long gone, this is still one of the classiest squares in the city. The work of Jules Hardouin-Mansart, today this über-elegant octagonal ensemble of 17th-century buildings is the home of the original Ritz Hôtel, as well as the world's most glitzy jewelry makers, including Cartier, Van Cleef and Arpels, and Boucheron. The famous statue reigned over the square up until the Revolution, when it was melted down for scrap. When Napoleon took over, he decided it was the perfect place for a huge Roman-style column honoring his glorious army (yes, once again), this time documenting its victory at Austerlitz. A long spiral of bas-reliefs recounting the campaign of 1805, march up the Colonne de la Grande Armée, which was crowned by a statue of the Emperor himself. The original statue did not survive the regime; a few decades later, Napoleon III replaced it with the existing copy.

Enter by rue de Castiglione, 1st arrond. Métro: Tuileries or Concorde.

Sainte-Chapelle ★★★ CHURCH   A wall of color greets visitors who enter this magnificent chapel. Stained-glass windows make up a large part of the walls of the upper level of the church, giving worshippers the impression of standing inside a jewel-encrusted crystal goblet. What isn't glass is elaborately carved and painted in gold leaf and rich colors: vaulting arches, delicate window casings, and an almost oriental wainscoting of arches and medallions. The 15 windows recount the story of the Bible, from Genesis to the Apocalypse, as well as the story of St-Louis, who was responsible for the chapel's construction. Back in the early 13th century, Louis IX (who was later canonized) spent 2 years bargaining with Emperor Badouin II of Constantinople for some of the holiest relics in Christendom: the crown of thorns and a piece of the Holy Cross. The relics were finally purchased for a princely sum, and Louis decided that they should be housed in an appropriately splendid chapel in the royal palace (the relics are now in the treasury of Notre-Dame). The record is not clear, but the architect may have been the illustrious Pierre de Montreuil, who worked on the cathedrals of St-Dennis and Notre-Dame. Whoever it was was a speed-demon; the chapel was built in record time for the Middle Ages, from 1241 to 1248. He was also quite brilliant, as he managed to support the structure with arches and buttresses in such a way that the walls of the upper chapel are almost entirely glass.

The lower chapel, which was meant for the servants, has a low, vaulted ceiling painted in blue and red and gold and covered with fleur-de-lis motifs. Up a small staircase is the upper chapel, clearly meant for the royals. This masterpiece suffered both fire and floods in the 17th century and was pillaged by zealous revolutionaries in the 18th. By the mid–19th century, the chapel was being used to store archives—2m (6½ ft.) of the bottom of each window was removed to install shelves. Fortunately, renewed interest in medieval art staved off plans for Ste-Chapelle's demolition, and eventually led to a conscientious restoration by a team that was advised by master restorer Viollet-le-Duc. The quality of the work on the windows is such that it is almost impossible to detect the difference between the original and the reconstructed stained glass (which makes up about one-third of what you see).

Sainte-Chapelle stages **concerts** from March to November at 7 and 8:30pm; tickets cost 16€ to 40€. You can reserve by phone ✆ **01-44-07-12-38,** or take your chances and buy tickets at the door. Visit www.euromusicproductions.fr for details.

Palais de Justice, 4 bd. du Palais, 1st arrond. ✆ **01-53-40-60-80.** www.monuments-nationaux.fr. 8.50€ adults, 5.50€ ages 18–25, free 17 and younger. Audioguide 4.50€. Mar–Oct daily 9:30am–6pm; Nov–Feb daily 9am–5pm. Métro: Cité, St-Michel, or Châtelet–Les Halles. RER: St-Michel.

St-Eustache ★ CHURCH   A Gothic church with a Renaissance decor, St-Eustache is one of the largest in the city, at over 105m long (344 ft.) and 43m wide (141 ft.). It was built from 1532 to 1640 along the plan of Notre-Dame; the intertwined arches of the ceiling give a similar sense of exalted elevation. These dimensions result in excellent acoustics for the church's huge 8,000-pipe organ, which is considered one of the finest in the city. The church's musical reputation stretches back centuries; Berlioz and Liszt both conducted their works here, among others. Before the Revolution, Saint Eustache was a parish where both the nobility and working class came to worship—Cardinal Richelieu and Madame de Pompadour were both baptized here, as was the playwright Molière. After the Revolution it was turned into a temple to agriculture, and, like many Parisian churches, its interior suffered mightily. It was subsequently restored and is currently undergoing another go-round. Work is progressing slowly and many chapels are gloomy, but you can still admire the soaring nave and the overall effect of this graceful edifice. There are free organ recitals every Sunday at 5:30pm before the 6:00 mass; other concerts are listed on the church's website or at www.fnacspectacles.com.

2 impasse St-Eustache, 1st arrond. ℂ **01-42-36-31-05.** www.st-eustache.org. Free admission. Mon–Fri 9:30am–7pm; Sat–Sun 9am–7pm; Sun organ recitals 5:30pm. Métro: Les Halles.

St-Germain l'Auxerrois ★ CHURCH This is a church with a checkered past. Designated the royal church when the Valois moved in across the street at the Louvre in the 14th century, kings, queens, and their entourages often attended mass here. Many of the artists who worked on the Louvre are buried here, including architects Le Vau and Soufflot. But its most infamous moment came at dawn on August 24, 1572, when the church's bells sounded the signal that began the Saint Bartholomew's Day massacre. Despite her erstwhile tolerance, Catherine de Medicis and her son Charles IX gave their blessing to a plot to slaughter the Huguenot (Protestant) leaders. The crowd murdered every Protestant in sight—between 2,000 and 4,000 were killed over the following 5 days.

The church has been rebuilt several times over the centuries, resulting in a mix of architectural styles. The 12th-century Romanesque tower hovers over a 15th-century Flamboyant Gothic porch embellished with human and animal figures. The vaulted interior is relatively simple and shelters some interesting works of art, amongst which are a monumental **sculpted wooden pew,** designed for the royal family in 1684 by Le Brun, and a 16th-century carved wood **retable** depicting scenes from the life of Christ.

2 place du Louvre, 1st arrond. ℂ **01-42-60-13-96.** www.saintgermainauxerrois.cef.fr. Free admission. Mon–Sat 8am–7pm, Sun 9am–8pm. Métro: Louvre-Rivoli.

Opéra & Grands Boulevards (2nd & 9th Arrondissements)

The grandiose **Opéra Garnier** reigns over this bustling neighborhood, which teems with office workers, tourists, and shoppers scuttling in and around the Grands Magasins (The Big Department Stores) on Boulevard Haussmann. There are more outstanding retail experiences here than for cultural ones.

Musée Grévin ★ MUSEUM This vast cavern of wax figures includes movie stars, historical figures, sports heroes, and rock and rollers, as well as notables from the current political scene. If you're not up on French history or pop culture, you might not recognize some of the faces, but don't worry, Marilyn Monroe, Brad Pitt, George Clooney, and President Obama are here, too. Stars appear in their natural habitats: chic brasseries, cocktail parties, and fashion shows. There are also famous historical tableaus that feature such scenes as Joan of Arc being burned at the stake and Louis XIV holding court at Versailles. If you've had enough wax, take a peek at the light show in the renovated Palais des Mirages, a leftover from the Universal Exposition of 1900.

10 bd. Montmartre, 9th arrond. ℂ **01-47-70-85-05.** www.grevin-paris.com. Admission 24€ adults, 21€ students, 17€ children 6–14, free 5 and under. Daily 10am–6:30pm (hours vary with seasons, check website for exact times). Métro: Grands Boulevards.

With one or two exceptions, all city museums are free (permanent collections only), all the time. That includes the following cultural cornucopias:

- Musée Carnavalet (p. 121)
- Musée d'Art Moderne de la Ville de Paris (p. 127)
- Maison de Balzac (p. 127)
- Musée Bourdelle (p. 151)
- Musée Cognacq-Jay (p. 122)
- Petit Palais (p. 130)
- Maison de Victor Hugo (p. 121)
- Musée Zadkine (p. 144)

You can also get into all national museums free of charge on the first Sunday of every month. Expect even bigger crowds than your usual Sunday. National museums include:

- Musée du Louvre (p. 112)
- Musée National des Arts Asiatique Guimet (p. 129)
- Musée National Eugène Delacroix (p. 144)
- Musée National du Moyen Age/ Thermes et Hôtel de Cluny (p. 141)
- Musée de l'Orangerie (p. 110)
- Musée d'Orsay (p. 148)
- Musée Rodin (p. 149)

Opéra Garnier ★★ OPERA HOUSE   Flamboyant, extravagant, and baroque, this opulent opera house is a splendid example of Second Empire architectural excess. Corinthian columns, loggias, busts, and friezes cover the facade of the building, which is topped by a flattened gold dome. Seventy-three sculptors worked on the decoration, which includes portraits of composers, Greek gods, and symbolic representations of Music, Poetry, Drama, and Dance. The interior of the building is no less dramatic. The vast lobby, built in a spectrum of different colored marble, holds a spectacular double staircase that sweeps up to the different levels of the auditorium, as well as an array of glamorous antechambers, galleries, and ballrooms that make you wonder how the opera scenery could possibly compete. Mosaics, mirrors, gilt, and marble line these grand spaces, whose painted ceilings dance with fauns, gods, and nymphs. The largest room, called the grand foyer, is drenched in gold leaf and hung with gigantic chandeliers, looking something like a real palace, which was in fact, the effect Garnier was going for. The main event, of course, is the auditorium, which might seem a bit small, considering the size of the building. In fact, it holds not even 2,000 seats. The horseshoe shape of the seating area assures that viewers see both the stage and each other—19th century operagoers were equally concerned with what was on the stage and who was in the house. The beautiful ceiling was painted in 1964 with colorful images from various operas and ballets by Marc Chagall.

All of this (with the exception of the Chagall ceiling) sprang from the mind of a young, unknown architect named Charles Garnier, who won a competition launched when Napoleon III decided the time had come to build himself an opera house. Though the first stone was laid in 1862, work was held up by war, civil unrest, and a change in regime; the **Palais Garnier** was not inaugurated until 1875. Some contemporary critics found it a bit much (one called it "an overloaded sideboard"), but today it is generally acknowledged as a masterpiece of the architecture of the epoch.

And what about that phantom? Gaston Leroux's 1911 novel, "The Phantom of the Opera," clearly was inspired by the building's **underground lake,** which was constructed to help stabilize the building.

You can visit the building on your own (for a fee, see ticket prices below), but there's so much history here and so many good stories, you might want to take advantage of the **guided visits in English** (14€ adults, 13€ children under 10; Sept–June Wed, Sat–Sun 11:30am and 2:30pm, July–Aug and French school vacations daily 11:30am and 2:30pm). Either way, your visit will be limited to the lobby, the surrounding foyers, the museum, and if there's not a rehearsal in progress, the auditorium—sorry, you won't get to see the lake. Or simply **buy tickets to a show;** consult the Opéra website to see what's on at the Palais Garnier.

Corner of rue Scribe and rue Auber, 9th arrond. ⓒ **08-92-89-90-90** (.34€ per min.). www.operade paris.fr. Admission 10€ adults, 6€ students, children under 10 enter for free. Oct to mid-July daily 10am–4:30pm, mid-July to Sept 10am–5:30pm. Métro: Opéra.

Le Marais (3rd & 4th Arrondissements)

Home to royalty and aristocracy between the 14th and 17th centuries, the Marais still boasts some remarkable architecture, some of it dating back to the Middle Ages. One of the few neighborhoods that was not knocked down during Baron Haussmann's urban overhaul, its narrow streets are still lined with magnificent *hôtels particuliers* (such as mansions) as well as humbler homes from centuries past. The **Pompidou Center** is probably the biggest and most well-known attraction, but the Marais also harbors a wealth of terrific smaller museums, as well as the delightful **Place des Vosges.** Remnants of the city's **historic Jewish quarter** can be found on rue des Rosiers, which has been invaded by chic clothing shops in recent years. Nowadays, the real Jewish neighborhood is in the 19th arrondissement.

Centre Pompidou ★★ MUSEUM The bizarre architecture of this odd building provokes such strong emotions, it's easy to forget that there is something inside. Believe it or not, President Pompidou searched far and wide to find an architect. In 1971, an international design competition was held with entrants from 49 countries, and the winners were the Italo-British design team of Renzo Piano and Richard Rogers. Their concept was to put the support structure and transport systems on the outside of the building, thereby liberating space on the inside for a museum and cultural center. The result was a gridlike exoskeleton with a tubular escalator inching up one side, and huge multicolored pipes and shafts covering the other. To some, it's a milestone in contemporary architecture; to others, it's simply a horror. Either way, it's one of the most visited structures in France.

For the Pompidou is much more than an art museum. Its over 100,000 sq. m (1,076,390 sq. ft.) of floor space includes a vast **reference library,** a **cinema archive, bookshops,** and a **music institute,** as well as a **performance hall,** a **children's gallery** and areas for educational activities. This might be one of the reasons it feels different from your standard museum and why it draws so many young people.

The actual museum, the **Musée National d'Art Moderne,** is on the fourth and fifth floors. Getting there is half the fun as you glide up the exterior escalators. As the collection is in constant rotation and **temporary exhibitions** are a huge draw, it's impossible to say what you are likely to see on your visit, but the emphasis is generally on works from the second half of the 20th century, with a good dose of surrealism, Dada, and other modern movements from the first half. This is not "pretty" art, but art that is designed to make you think. It might make you think about heading straight for the exit, but if nothing else, there are things here that will surprise you, and get your juices flowing. Works range from relatively tame abstracts by **Picasso** and **Kandinsky** to

Despite its name (*neuf* means "new"), the **Pont Neuf** (Quai du Louvre to Quai de Conti) is the oldest bridge in Paris. The bridge was an instant hit when it was inaugurated by Henri IV in 1607 (its ample sidewalks, combined with the fact that it was the first bridge sans houses, made it a delight for pedestrians), and it still is. For a quiet picnic spot, take the stairs by the statue of Henri IV (in the center of the span) down to the **Square du Vert Galant.**

The **Pont des Arts** (Quai François Mitterrand to Quai de Conti) was originally constructed at the beginning of the 19th century. Delicately arching over the river, the iron pedestrian bridge was actually quite fragile, a fact that was confirmed when it was hit by a barge and collapsed in 1979. Fortunately for us, it was reconstructed. This is probably the most romantic bridge in the city—with its splendid view of the Ile de la Cité and its itinerant artists sketching along the railing—and a must at sunset.

A modern way to get from the Left to the Right bank is via the **Passerelle Simone de Beauvoir** (Quai de Bercy to Quai François Mauriac). A graceful pedestrian passage, the bridge consists of two arching bands of oak and steel, which somehow intertwine and cross the river without the support of a central pillar. The central lens-shaped structure was constructed by the Eiffel factory, which was founded by Gustave.

With its enormous pillars topped by gilded statuary, it's hard to miss the **Pont Alexandre III** (Cours de la Reine to Quai d'Orsay). Linking the vast esplanade of the Invalides with the glass-domed Grand Palais, this elegant bridge fits right in with its grand surroundings. The span was named after Czar Alexander III of Russia, and inaugurated at the opening of the Paris Exposition of 1900.

Incredibly, the small and lovely **Pont Marie** (Quai des Célestins to Quai d'Anjou–Ile St-Louis), composed of three gentle arches, was once loaded down by some 50 houses. The structure could not hold its charge, and during a flood in 1658, the Seine washed away two of its arches and 20 houses fell into the water. The tragedy, which claimed 60 lives, got city officials to thinking, and finally, in 1769, homesteading on bridges was outlawed.

Andy Warhol's multiheaded portrait of Elizabeth Taylor to a felt-wrapped piano by **Joseph Beuys.** Video-installations are often highlighted, as well as new artists.

Just outside of the front of the center is the **Atelier Brancusi,** where the sculptor's workshop has been reconstituted in its entirety; in his will, Brancusi left the workshop's contents to the museum on the condition that every sculpture and object be displayed exactly as it was found in his studio on the day of his death.

There's also a nonstop circus of comics, mimes, and other performances on the vast esplanade outside the building. Take note of the monumental sculpture/mobile by Alexander Calder, and do not miss the delightful **Stravinsky Fountain** around the side of the center; kids love watching its colorful mobile sculptures by Niki de Saint Phalle and Jean Tinguely.

Place Georges-Pompidou, 4th arrond. (✆ **01-44-78-12-33.** www.centrepompidou.fr. Admission 11€–13€ adults, students 9€ 10€ students, free for children 17 and younger; admission varies depending on exhibits. Wed–Mon 11am–10pm. Métro: Hôtel de Ville, RER: Châtelet–Les Halles.

Gaîté Lyrique ★ CULTURAL INSTITUTION   One of the newer additions to the city's cultural scene, this gallery space/concert hall/educational center is devoted to exploring mixed-media and digital art forms. Set in an abandoned 19th-century theater (hence the name), the building has been restored, renewed, and transformed to host rotating exhibits that range from music and multimedia performances to design, fashion, and architecture to new media—there's even an interactive room dedicated to video games.

3 bis rue Papin, 3rd arrond. ℭ **01-53-01-52-00.** www.gaite-lyrique.net. Tues–Sat 2–8pm, Sun noon–6pm. Opening hours and admission prices vary according to the exhibitions and events. Métro: Réaumur-Sébastopol.

Hôtel de Ville ★ HISTORIC SITE   No, it's not a hotel. This enormous Neo-Renaissance wedding cake is Paris's city hall, and the only way to see the inside is to make friends with the mayor. Even if you can't get inside, you can feast on the lavish exterior, which includes 136 statues representing historic VIPs of Parisian history. Since the 14th century, this spot has been an administrative seat for the municipality; the building you see before you dates from 1873, but it is an accurate copy of an earlier Renaissance version that was burned down in 1870 during the Paris Commune. The vast square in front of the building, formerly called the place du Grève, was once used for municipal festivals and executions. It was also the stage for several important moments in the city's history, particularly during the Revolution: Louis XVI was forced to kiss the new French flag here, and Robespierre was shot in the jaw and arrested here during an attempted coup. Today the square is host to more peaceful activities: There's usually a merry-go-round or two to captivate the little ones, and in winter an ice-skating rink is set up.

Periodically, the Hôtel de Ville hosts art exhibits (usually free admission), which can be accessed through the back entrance on rue Lobau.

29 rue de Rivoli, 4th arrond. ℭ **01-42-76-43-43.** www.paris.fr. Free admission to exhibits. Métro: Hôtel-de-Ville.

Maison de Victor Hugo ★ MUSEUM   The life of Victor Hugo was as turbulent as some of his novels. Regularly visited by both tragedy and triumph, the author of The Hunchback of Notre Dame lived in several apartments in Paris, including this one on the second floor of a corner house on the sumptuous place des Vosges. From 1832 to 1848, he lived here with his wife and four children, during which time he wrote "Ruy Blas"; part of "Les Miserables"; met his lifelong mistress and muse, Juliette Drouet; was elected to the Academie Française; lost his 19-year-old daughter in a boating accident on the Seine; and entered the political arena. When Napoleon III seized power in 1851, this passionate advocate of free speech, universal suffrage, and social justice was made distinctly unwelcome, particularly after he declared the new king a traitor of France. Fearing for his life, Hugo left the country and lived in exile until 1870 when he triumphantly returned to France and was elected to the senate. By the time he died in 1885 he was a national hero; his funeral cortege through the streets of Paris is the stuff of legend, and his body was one of the first to be buried in the Panthéon (p. 141). The museum's collection charts this dramatic existence through the author's drawings, original manuscripts, notes, furniture, and personal objects, which are displayed in rooms that recreate the ambiance and the spirit of the original lodgings.

6 place des Vosges, 4th arrond. ℭ **01-42-72-10-16.** www.musee-hugo.paris.fr. Free admission to permanent collection. Tues–Sun 10am–6pm. Métro: St-Paul, Bastille, or Chemin-Vert.

Musée Carnavalet ★★★ MUSEUM   Paris has served as a backdrop to centuries' worth of dramatic events, from Roman takeovers to barbarian invasions, from coronations to decapitations to the birth of the modern French republic. These stories and others are told through objects, paintings, and interiors at this fascinating museum. The collection is displayed in two extraordinary 17th-century mansions—works of art in their own right. Starting with a prehistoric canoe from 4600 BC and continuing into the 20th century, the history of Paris is illustrated with items as diverse as Gallo-Roman figurines, Napoléon's toiletry kit, and an 18th-century portrait of Benjamin Franklin when he was the U.S. ambassador to France.

The main building, the Hôtel de Carnavalet, is a Renaissance mansion that had a make-over by François Mansart (of rooftop fame) in 1660. Finding it much to her liking, the prodigious letter-writer and woman of the world Madame de Sévigné rented the mansion in 1677 and lived there until her death in 1696. The other half of the museum is in the adjoining Hotel Le Peletier de St-Fargeau, built in 1688 for an aristocrat whose claim to fame is that he voted for the execution of Louis XVI and was subsequently assassinated by a royalist. Little of the original interior decoration remains in either building, but this is made up for by the importation of entire rooms, including wall paneling and furniture, from various private mansions of different epochs. Highlights include the Louis XV–style **Salon des Philosophes,** with its beautiful *boiseries* (carved wood paneling); historical objects like the inkwell of Jean-Jacques Rousseau; and the 18th-century **Café Militaire,** a room from an officer's cafe with gilded and sculpted wood paneling representing military motifs like shields, standards, and crowns of laurels.

The luxury and expense of the salons of the aristocracy make a fitting prelude to the excellent section on the French Revolution. Along with portraits of key figures like Marat, Danton, and even Dr. Guillotin (who didn't actually invent the dastardly execution machine but did advocate its use as a means of capital punishment), are several fascinating mementos, such as the keys to the Bastille prison and a copy of the Declaration of the Rights of Man that once hung behind the president of the Convention. Particularly moving are the personal objects of the royal family from their last days in prison—a lock of Marie Antoinette's hair, Louis XVI's razor and water glass, the young Dauphin's writing exercises—reminders that these iconic figures were in fact made of flesh and blood.

All the labels and descriptions are in French, so you may want to invest in an English-language audioguide (5€); even without translations, most of the art and objects speak for themselves.

16 rue des Francs-Bourgeois, 3rd arrond. (℡) **01-44-59-58-58.** www.carnavalet.paris.fr. Free admission for permanent collection. Tues–Sun 10am–6pm. Métro: St-Paul or Chemin Vert.

Musée Cognacq-Jay ★ MUSEUM   This bite-sized museum offers a nice taste of the finer side of 18th-century France. Its founder, Ernest Cognacq, led a rags-to-riches life: At 12 years old, he was selling odds and ends as an itinerant merchant, and by the end of his life he was the owner of a fabulously successful department store (the now-defunct La Samaritaine) with a prodigious private art collection. His rich assortment of 18th-century art and furniture now make up the contents of this small museum, which is housed in a lovely *hôtel particulier* (mansion). The collection leans heavily towards the romantic side of the century, with many lesser works by famous artists like Chardin and Fragonard, but what's most impressive here is the furniture, like the bed *"à la polonaise"* draped in blue damask and framed in gilt or the exquisite Louis XVI-era writing table with its geometric wood inlay.

8 rue Elzévir, 3rd arrond. (℡) **01-40-27-07-21.** www.cognacq-jay.paris.fr. Free admission to permanent collection. Audioguide in English 5€. Tues–Sun 10am–6pm. Métro: St-Paul or Chemin Vert.

Paris is No Longer Picasso-less

As this book was going to press, the **Musée Picasso Paris** (5 rue de Thorigny; ✆ **01-42-71-25-21;** www.museepicasso paris.fr) was about to reopen after several years worth of renovations. Ten additional exposition rooms will be added to house the works of the prolific painter, some 5,000 of which are in the collection. As the museum is being mysterious about when exactly it will open, opening hours and ticket prices, your best bet is to look at the website before you visit.

Musée d'Art et Histoire du Judaïsme ★★ MUSEUM Housed in the magnificent Hôtel de Saint Aignan, one of the many palatial 17th-century mansions that dot the Marais, this museum chronicles the art and history of the Jewish people in France and in Europe. It features a superb collection of objects of both artistic and cultural significance (a splendid Italian Renaissance torah ark, a German gold and silver Hanukkah menorah, a 17th-c. Dutch illustrated Torah scroll, documents from the Dreyfus trial), which is interspersed with texts, drawings, and photos telling the story of the Jews, and explaining the basics of both Ashkenazi and Sephardic traditions. You'll do a lot of reading here; documentation is translated in English, but if you're feeling lazy there's also an informative audioguide. The final rooms include a collection of works by Jewish artists, including Modigliani, Soutine, Lipchitz, and Chagall. Be prepared for airportlike security at the entrance.

71 rue du Temple, 3rd arrond. ✆ **01-53-01-86-60.** www.mahj.org. Admission 8€ adults, 6€ ages 18–25, free 17 and younger. Mon–Fri 11am–6pm; Sun 10am–6pm. Métro: Rambuteau or Hôtel de Ville.

Musée de la Chasse et de la Nature ★ MUSEUM If you can get over the fact that it's a museum dedicated to hunting, this small museum makes for a pleasant outing. You'll find the expected taxidermied animals, but they are discreetly presented among an elegant collection of paintings, tapestries, sculptures, and even contemporary art. Each room has a theme: For example, the blond wood-paneled Salle Cerf et Loup takes on the imagery of the stag and the wolf, illustrated in paintings by artists as disparate as Renaissance-era Lucas Cranach and 20th-century fauvist André Derain. The emphasis is not so much on the kill, as the symbolism behind the images: In the Middle Ages, the stag, which represented Christ, and the wolf, which represented the Devil, could coexist, a theme that is echoed in the 16th- and 17th-century tapestries that cover the walls. Once you've sauntered through rooms dedicated to dogs, birds, horses, and even unicorns, you will walk smack into the trophy room, where discretion is abandoned and hunting is blatantly celebrated in all its gory glory. Intricately inlaid rifles and the heads of various exotic animals bring you back from the celestial spheres of the intellect. Still, there is something intriguing about this place; it reminds you that the relationship between humans and animals dates to way before there were naturalists and environmentalists, and if that relationship was filled with animosity and fear, it was also tinged with a sort of mystical respect.

62 rue des Archives, 3rd arrond. ✆ **01-53-01-92-40.** www.chassenature.org. Admission 8€ adults, 6€ adults with hunting permits, children 17 and under free. Tues, Thurs–Sun 11am–6pm, Wed 11am–9:30pm. Métro: Rambuteau.

Musée des Arts et Métiers ★★ MUSEUM If you've read Umberto Eco's novel, you'll probably want to come here just to see Foucault's original pendulum swing in the church of St-Martin-des-Champs, but there are plenty of other reasons to spend a couple of hours at this temple of technology. The Musée harbors sterling examples of just about every discovery that made the mechanical world possible. True techies will linger over the many displays of gearboxes, steam engines, and other historic gizmos; the less technically inclined (like me) will probably prefer the first versions of telephones, movie cameras, and toasters. There are a lot of "firsts" here, like the first omnibus (a "high-speed" steam vehicle built in 1873), and the Blériot XI (the first plane to cross the English channel), as well as the earliest examples of phonographs, lightbulbs, and tape decks. Those "new" antiques—the typewriters, record players, and VCRs on display in those old wooden cases—drive home the fact that the technological revolution is ongoing, and today's wonders will be tomorrow's curiosities.

60 rue Réaumur, 3rd arrond. ℂ **01-53-01-82-00.** www.arts-et-metiers.net. Admission 6.50€ adults, 4.50€ students, free ages 17 and under. Tues–Wed and Fri–Sun 10am–6pm, Thurs 10am–9:30pm. Métro: Arts et Métiers.

Place des Vosges ★★★ SQUARE Possibly the prettiest square in the city, this beautiful place combines elegance, greenery, and quiet. Nowhere in Paris will you find such a unity of Renaissance-style architecture; the entire square is bordered by 17th-century brick town houses, each conforming to rules set down by Henri IV himself, under which runs arched arcades. In the center is a garden with a geometric arrangement of lush lawns, fountains, and trees. At the epicenter is a huge equestrian statue of Louis XIII, during whose reign (1610–43) the square enjoyed a golden age of festivals and tournaments. But it was a tournament in a previous century that proved pivotal to the creation of this square. In the 16th century, a royal palace called the Hôtel des Tournelles stood on this site. In 1559, an organized combat was held there, during which the current monarch, feisty Henri II, defeated several opponents. Feeling pleased with himself, he decided to fight Montgomery, the captain of his guard. A badly aimed lance resulted in Henri's untimely death; his wife, Catherine de Medicis, was so distraught she decided to have the palace demolished. His descendant, Henri IV, took advantage of the free space to construct a royal square. Over the centuries, a number of celebrities lived in the 36 houses, including Mme. de Sévigny and Victor Hugo (now the Maison de Victor Hugo; see p. 121). Today the homes are for the rich, as are many of the chic boutiques under the arcades, but the park, the fountains, and the children's playground are for everyone.

4th arrond. Métro: St-Paul.

Champs-Élysées, Trocadéro & Western Paris (8th, 16th & 17th Arrondissements)

Decidedly posh, this is one of the wealthiest parts of the city in both per capita earnings and cultural institutions. While the **Champs-Élysées** is more glitz than glory, the surrounding neighborhoods offer high-end shops and restaurants as well as some terrific museums and concert halls. This is also where you will find grand architectural gestures, like the **Arc de Triomphe** and the **Place de la Concorde,** which bookend the Champs and the **Grand Palais** and **Petit Palais,** leftovers from the legendary 1900 Universal Exposition.

Arc de Triomphe ★★★ MONUMENT If there is one monument that symbolizes "La Gloire," or the glory of France, it is this giant triumphal arch. Crowning the Champs-Élysées, this mighty archway both celebrates the military victories of the French army and memorializes the sacrifices of its soldiers. Over time, it has become an icon of the Republic and a setting for some if its most emotional moments: the laying in state of the coffin of Victor Hugo in 1885, the burial in 1921 of the ashes of an unknown soldier who fought in World War I, and General de Gaulle's pregnant pause under the arch before striding down the Champs-Élysées before the cheering crowds after the Liberation in 1944.

It took a certain amount of chutzpah to come up with the idea to build such a shrine, and sure enough, it was Napoleon who instigated it. In 1806, still glowing after his stunning victory at Austerlitz, the Emperor decided to erect a monument to the Imperial Army, along the lines of a Roman triumphal arch. Architects promptly began work on an arch measuring 50m (163 ft.) high and 45m (147 ft.) wide, the largest of its type on the planet. Unfortunately, the defeat at Waterloo put an end to the Empire before the arch was finished and construction came to an abrupt halt. It wasn't until 1823 that building got going again; it was finally finished in 1836 by Louis-Philippe.

The arch is covered with bas-reliefs and sculptures, the most famous of which is the enormous "Depart of the Volunteers" of 1792, better known as the Marseillaise, by François Rude, showing winged, female Liberty leading the charge of Revolutionary soldiers. Just above is one of the many smaller panels detailing Napoleonic battles—in this case, Aboukir—wherein the emperor trods victoriously over the Ottomans. At the base of the arch is the Tomb of the Unknown Soldier, over which a flame is relit every evening. The inscription, which was added after WWI, reads ICI REPOSE UN SOLDAT FRANÇAIS MORT POUR LA PATRIE, 1914–1918 ("Here lies a French soldier who died for his country").

Don't even think about crossing the traffic circle; instead take the underpass near the Champs-Élysées Métro entrance. You can visit the area under the arch free of charge, but if you want to enjoy the view from the rooftop terrace, you have to pay. You also have to climb 284 stairs to get there (only the very young, the very old, and the handicapped get to use the elevator). Though you are not as high up the viewing platforms on the Eiffel Tower, the panorama is quite impressive. Directly below, 12 boulevards radiate from the star-shaped intersection (hence the moniker "Etoile"), and out front is the long sweep of the Champs-Élysées, ending at the obelisk of the place de la Concorde, behind which lurks the Louvre. You can pick out most of the most famous monuments, including Sacre-Coeur and the Eiffel Tower; to the west are the skyscrapers of La Défense, including the huge, hollowed-out Grande Arche, a modern version of the one you are standing on.

Place Charles de Gaulle, 8th arrond. ℂ **01-55-37-73-77.** www.monuments-nationaux.fr. Admission 9.50€ adults, 6€ ages 18–24, free 17 and under. Apr–Sept daily 10am–11pm; Oct–Mar daily 10am–10:30pm. Métro: Charles-de-Gaulle–Etoile.

Grand Palais ★ HISTORIC SITE/MUSEUM Built for the 1900 Universal Exhibition, this giant exhibition hall spans a total area of 72,000 sq. m (775,000 sq. ft.), with the biggest glass roof in Europe—an elegant lighting solution, since the building was constructed prior to electricity. After years of renovations, the Grand Palais is now as gorgeous as it was when it opened, and today it hosts a changing array of sporting and cultural events under the vast "Grand Nef" (or nave), as well as blockbuster temporary art exhibits (Edward Hopper, Chagall, Impressionists, and others). These tend to be mob scenes, so it pays to buy tickets in advance if you are in town during a big show. The entrance to the big exhibits is usually at the side entrance, 3 ave. du Général Eisenhower.

Place Clemenceau, 8th arrond. (☎ **01-44-13-17-17.** www.grandpalais.fr. Opening hours and admission prices vary according to the exhibitions and events. Métro: Champs-Élysées–Clémenceau.

La Cité de l'Architecture et du Patrimoine ★ INSTITUTE/MUSEUM Created to promote French architecture and showcase evolving trends, this vast institution (located in the Palais de Chaillot), includes a museum, a research facility and a top-notch school of architecture. On the ground floor, the enormous Galerie des Moulages, with its vaulting skylights, exhibits casts of the gems of French architecture from the 12th to the 18th centuries. Commissioned starting in the late 19th century as a way of documenting France's architectural heritage, the project turned out to be an invaluable tool when it came to restoring the ravages of two world wars. The cast of the beautiful Queen of Sheba, for example—the original of which graced the face of Reims cathedral—made it possible to create a faithful reproduction after the original was seriously damaged in World War I.

On the 2nd floor, you'll dip into the cool waters of 20th- and 21st-century architecture, represented by intricate architectural models of structures like Piano and Rogers' Centre Pompidou (p. 119) and Rem Koolhaus' Maison Lemoine, a three-layer home built in Floriac, France, for a paralyzed man and his family. Don't miss clambering through a reconstruction of an apartment from Le Corbusier's Cité Radieuse, a shockingly (for the late 1940s) modern approach to urban housing.

1 place du Trocadéro, 16th arrond. (☎ **01-58-51-52-00.** www.citechaillot.fr. Admission 8€ adults, 5€ ages 18–25, free ages 17 and younger. Wed and Fri–Mon 11am–7pm; Thurs 11am–9pm. Métro: Trocadéro.

La Madeleine ★ CHURCH As you peer up the rue Royale from the place de la Concorde, you'll see something that very closely resembles a Roman temple. It is in fact a church that owes its unusual form to its equally singular history. In 1763, architect Pierre Constant d'Ivry laid the first stone of a church that would include a neoclassical facade with multiple columns. He didn't get very far. First the architect died, and then the Revolution broke out, during which construction ground to a halt. No one

A Glass Ship Afloat in the Bois de Boulogne

Move over Bilbao, Paris is the site of the latest Frank Gehry museo-creation: the **Fondation Louis Vuitton.** A stupendous assemblage of glass and steel, the structure seems to hover over the lush greenery of the Bois de Boulogne, a large park on the western edge of the city (p. 155). The main building, snug under the billowing "sails" of glass, is devoted to contemporary art, including the voluminous collection of the foundation's director

Bernard Arnault, a passionate art collector who is also the CEO of the luxury giant LMVH. When Arnault first spoke with Gehry, the famed Canadian-American architect, about a center for contemporary art, the designer scribbled an idea on a piece of paper. A little over a decade later, his scribbles in a design that is at least as intriguing as the art inside. For details check the foundation's website: www.fondationlouisvuitton.fr.

knew what to do with the site until Napoleon finally strode onto the scene and declared that it would become the Temple de La Gloire, to honor the glorious victories of his army. He wanted something "solid" because he was sure that the monument would last "thousands of years." Unfortunately for him, military defeats and mounting debt would again delay construction until Napoleon decided that maybe it wouldn't be such a bad idea to make it a church after all—that way Rome would foot the bill. Once Napoleon was out of the picture for good, inertia took over the project again, and it wasn't until 1842, under the Restoration, that La Madeleine was finally consecrated.

The inside of the church is pretty dark, due to a lack of windows, but there are actually some interesting works of art here, if you can make them out in the gloom. On the left as you enter is François Rude's "Baptism of Christ," further on is James Pradier's sculpture "La Marriage de la Vierge."

Place de la Madeleine, 8th arrond. ☏ **01-44-51-69-00.** www.eglise-lamadeleine.com. Free admission. Daily 9:30am–7pm. Métro: Madeleine.

Galerie–Musée Baccarat ★ MUSEUM The mansion of Marie-Laure de Noailles, an early-20th-century patron of the arts, is an ideal setting for this homage to crystal at its most luxurious. Before you enter the small museum section, take a peek at the Cristal Room, a sumptuous restaurant where Marie-Laure and her friends would feel right at home. While the collection rotates, you can be sure the exposition will include exquisite crystal glasses, vases, plates and other objects made by the house of Baccarat over the last 250 years. When you have finished gaping, have a seat in the lavish ballroom and watch a short film (in English on request) that will make you appreciate the amount of the time, effort and skill that goes into creating these works of art and understand why a simple wine glass starts at over 100€. Speaking of which, when you go back downstairs, check out the boutique, which is almost as impressive as the museum (and doesn't cost 7€ to get into). Be sure to visit the bathrooms; probably the only ones in the city with chandeliers in the stalls.

11 place des États-Unis, 16th arrond. ☏ **01-40-22-11-22.** www.baccarat.com. Museum admission 7€ adults, 5€ students under 25, free for ages 17 and under. Museum open Mon, Wed–Sat 10am–6pm. Métro: Iéna or Boissière.

Maison de Balzac ★ MUSEUM Fleeing his creditors, in 1840, writer Honoré de Balzac rented this small house in what was then the village of Passy, where he lived for 7 years under an assumed name. He also worked like a demon: He was capable of writing for up to 20 hours a day for weeks at a time. The five rooms of Balzac's apartments are hung with paintings and portraits of his family and friends, including several of Madame Hanska, whom he finally married after 18 years of passionate correspondence. There are also a few manuscripts and personal objects, including his turquoise-incrusted cane, which was the talk of Paris, and his monogrammed coffee pot, which kept him going through his marathon work sessions. In his office is the little table where he wrote "The Human Comedy," "a witness," he wrote to Madame Hanska, "to my worries, my miseries, my distress, my joys, everything . . . my arm almost wore out its surface from taking the same path over and over again."

47 rue Raynouard, 16th arrond. ☏ **01-55-74-41-80.** www.balzac.paris.fr. Admission free for permanent collection. Tues–Sun 10am–6pm. Métro: Passy or La Muette.

Musée d'Art Moderne de la Ville de Paris ★ MUSEUM Housed in a wing of the massive Palais de Tokyo, this municipal modern art museum covers ground similar to that of the Pompidou Center but on a smaller scale. Though several big names are represented (Picasso, Rouault, and Picaba, to name a few), in general these are not their best-known works; highlights include a room dedicated to surrealism (the personal collection of André Breton) and a series of paintings by Delaunay and Léger. The contemporary section, from 1960 on, covers seriously abstract movements like Fluxus and Figuration. In recent years, the collection has acquired several new works from the 1980s on, but for the most recent cutting-edge ideas, you are probably better off at the Palais de Tokyo museum (see below) in the wing next door. There's also a huge room covered with brilliant wall murals by Raoul Dufy ("La Fée Electricité"), as well as another huge room with two enormous versions of "La Danse" by Matisse. If the permanent collection isn't particularly exciting, the temporary exhibitions often are so check the website for current listings.

11 ave. du Président-Wilson, 16th arrond. © **01-53-67-40-00.** www.mam.paris.fr. Free admission to permanent collections. Tues–Sun 10am–6pm. Métro: Iéna or Alma-Marceau.

Musée Jacquemart-André ★★★ MUSEUM   The love child of a couple of passionate art collectors, this terrific museum takes the form of a 19th-century mansion filled with fine art and decorative objects. Not only is the collection superb, but it is also of a blissfully reasonable size—you can see a wide range of beautiful things here without wearing yourself to a frazzle.

The house itself is a work of art: At its inauguration in 1875, the marble Winter Garden with its spectacular double staircase was the talk of the town. Nélie Jacquemart and Edouard André devoted their lives to filling this splendid dwelling with primarily 18th-century French art and furniture. The paintings of Fragonard, Boucher, and Chardin are in evidence, as is an impressive assortment of Louis XV- and Louis XVI-era decorative objects. There are many superb portraits, including that of an officious-looking "Comte Français de Nantes" by David. To honor the artists that influenced these French painters, the couple also amassed a number of 17th-century Dutch paintings, including a jaunty "Portrait of a Man" by Frans Hals, and Rembrandt's mysteriously evocative "Pilgrims at Emmaus."

The peripatetic couple, who traveled frequently in search of new items for their collection, also took an interest in Renaissance Italian art; though at the time considered "primitive" by most art fans, that didn't stop Jacquemart and André from snapping up Quattrocento masterpieces like Botticelli's "Virgin and Child." Personally, I think the Italian collection (on the second floor) is the most awe-inspiring part of the museum—not only are there works by masters like Bellini, Uccello, and Mantegna, but they are presented in an intimate space with excellent lighting. You feel like you are walking into a felt-lined jewel-box. Leave time to eat a light lunch or have tea in the Jacquemart-André's lovely dining room, where you can gaze up at a magnificent fresco by Tiepolo on the ceiling (see "Top Tearooms," p. 98).

158 bd. Haussmann, 8th arrond. © **01-45-62-11-59.** www.musee-jacquemart-andre.com. Admission 11€ adults, 9.50€ students and children 7–17, free for children 6 and younger. Daily 10am–6pm. Métro: Miromesnil or St-Philippe-du-Roule.

Musée Marmottan Monet ★★ MUSEUM   Boasting the world's largest collection of Monets, this museum offers an in-depth look at this prolific genius and some of his talented contemporaries. Among the dozens of his canvases is the one that provided name of an entire artistic movement. Pressed to give a name to this misty play of light on the water for the catalogue for the 1874 exposition that included Cézanne, Pissarro, Renoir, and Degas, Monet apparently said, "put 'impression.'" The painting, "Impression, Sunrise," certainly made one, as did the show—thereafter the group was referred to as the Impressionists. Monet never stopped being fascinated with the interaction of light and water, be it in a relatively traditional portrait of his wife and daughter against the stormy sea in "On the Beach at Trouville," or in an almost abstract blend of blues and grays in "Charring Cross Bridge." Monet was also interested in light's transformation; he often painted the same subject at different times of the day. One of his famous series on the Cathedral of Rouen is here: "Effect of the Sun at the End of the Day." Fans of the artist's endless water lily series will not be disappointed; the collection includes dozens of paintings of his beloved garden in Giverny.

Paintings by Renoir, Sisley, Degas, Gauguin and other contemporaries can also be seen in the light-filled rooms of this 19th century mansion, which belonged art collector Paul Marmottan. Upstairs is a new room dedicated to the only female member of the group, Berthe Morisot, known for her intimate portraits and scenes of family life.

2 rue Louis-Boilly, 16th arrond. ℂ **01-44-96-50-33.** www.marmottan.com. Admission 10€ adults, 5€ ages 8–24, free for children 7 and younger. Tues–Wed and Fri–Sun 10am–6pm; Thurs 10am–8pm. Métro: La Muette. RER: Bouilainvilliers.

Musée National des Arts Asiatiques Guimet ★★ MUSEUM   Founded by

in 1889 by collector and industrialist Emile Guimet, today this vast collection of Asian art is one of the largest and most complete in Europe. Here you'll find room after room of exquisite works from Afghanistan, India, Tibet, Nepal, China, Vietnam, Korea, Japan, and other Asian nations. You could spend an entire day here, or you could pick and choose regions of interest (displays are arranged geographically); the free audioguide is a good bet for finding standouts and providing cultural context. Highlights include a marvelous Tibetan bronze sculpture ("Hevajra and Nairât-mya") of a multiheaded god embracing a ferocious goddess with eight faces and 16 arms; a blissfully serene stone figure of a 12th-century Cambodian king ("Jaya-varman VII") who presided over a short-lived Khmer renaissance, and superb Chinese scroll paintings, including a magnificent 17th-century view of the Jingting mountains in autumn.

6 place d'Iéna, 16th arrond. ℂ **01-56-52-53-00.** www.guimet.fr. Admission to permanent collection 7.50€ adults, 5.50€ ages 18–25, free for ages 17 and younger. Wed–Mon 10am–6pm. Métro: Iéna.

Musée Nissim de Camondo ★★ MUSEUM   Having made a fortune in his

business ventures, in 1914 Count Moïse de Camondo built a mansion in the style of the Petit Trianon at Versailles and furnished it with rare examples of 18th-century furniture, paintings, and art objects (like a series of six Aubusson tapestries illustrating the fables of La Fontaine and a pair of bronze vases covered with petrified wood that once belonged to Marie Antoinette). After the count's death in 1935, the house and everything in it was left to the state as a museum, named after the count's son, who was killed fighting in World War I. The family's troubles did not stop there—in 1945, the count's daughter and her family were deported and died at Auschwitz. This little-visited museum is a delight—the count's will stipulated that the house be left exactly "as is" when it was transformed into a museum, as a result you can wander through salons filled with gilded mirrors, inlaid tables, and Beauvais tapestries; a fully equipped kitchen; and a gigantic tiled bathroom—all in the same configuration as when Camondo and his family lived there. Be sure to pick up a free English audioguide.

63 rue de Monceau, 8th arrond. ℂ **01-53-89-06-40.** www.lesartsdecoratifs.fr. Admission 7.50€ adults, 5.50€ ages 18–25, free for children 17 and younger. Wed–Sun 10am–5:30pm. Métro: Villiers.

Palais de Tokyo ★★ MUSEUM/PERFORMANCE SPACE   If you're traveling with cranky teenagers who've had enough of La Vieille France, or if you're also sick of endless rendezvous with history, this is the place to come for a blast of contemporary madness. This vast art space not only offers a rotating bundle of expositions, events, and other happenings but is also one of the only museums in Paris that stays open until midnight. While some might quibble about whether or not the works on display are really art, there's no denying that this place is a lot more fun than its stodgy neighbor across the terrace (see above). You'll find a completely different crowd here, who are generally young and intense. There's no permanent collection, just continuous temporary exhibits, installations, and events, which include live performances and film screenings. The center, whose mission includes nurturing, promoting, and providing studio space for emerging artists, underwent a major expansion in 2012 that almost tripled its size—it is now one of the largest sites devoted to contemporary creativity in Europe. Check the informative website for what's on during your visit. In warm weather, you can eat on the splendid terrace or in its arty-cool restaurant, Tokyo Eat.

13 ave. du Président-Wilson, 16th arrond. (✆ **01-81-97-35-88.** www.palaisdetokyo.com. Admission 10€ adults, 8€ ages 18–25, free for ages 17 and younger. Wed–Mon noon–midnight. Métro: léna.

Parc Monceau ★★ PARK/GARDENS   Located in a posh residential neighborhood and ringed by stately mansions, this small park is the brainchild of the duke of Chartres (the future Philippe Egalité), who commissioned a fanciful garden in 1769 filled with **"folies,"** faux romantic ruins, temples, and antiquities inspired by exotic far-away places. Don't be surprised to stumble upon a minaret, a windmill, or a mini-Egyptian pyramid here; the most famous *folie* is the **Naumachie,** a large oval pond surrounded in part by Corinthian columns. The park has had several makeovers over the centuries, but it is still essentially an English-style garden, complete with wooded glens and hillocks. There is a sizeable **playground** in the southwest corner, as well as a **merry-go-round** near the north entrance, where there is a **round pavilion** surrounded by columns; the Duke of Chartres used to keep a small apartment on the second floor from which he could see the entire park. Today the pavilion serves a more practical purpose: Inside you'll find clean public toilets.

35 bd. de Courcelles, 8th arrond. Free admission. 8am–sundown. Métro: Monceau or Villiers.

Petit Palais ★★ MUSEUM   The collection may not be exhaustive, and you may not see any world-famous works, but you will enjoy a wonderful mix of periods and artists at this small-ish municipal fine arts museum, whose chronology stretches from the ancient Greeks to World War I. The paintings of masters like Monet, Ingres, and Rubens are displayed here, as well as the Art Nouveau dining room of Hector Guimard, and the exquisite multilayered glass vases of Emile Gallé. Those interested in earlier works will find Greek vases, Italian Renaissance majolica, and a small collection of 16th-century astrolabes and gold-and-crystal traveling clocks. Intricately carved ivory panels and delicately sculpted wood sculptures (including a grinning, long-locked Saint Barbara who looks like she is about to burst out in a fit of the giggles) stand out in the small Medieval section, and a series of rooms dedicated to 17th-century Dutch painters like Steen and Van Ostade is considered one of the best collections of its kind in France (after the Louvre). Refresh yourself after your visit at the cafe in the gorgeous inner courtyard.

Avenue Winston Churchill, 8th arrond. (✆ **01-53-43-40-00.** www.petitpalais.paris.fr. Free admission to permanent collection. Tues–Sun 10am–6pm. Métro: Champs-Élysées–Clémenceau.

Place de la Concorde ★★★ SQUARE   Like an exclamation point at the end of the Champs-Élysées, the place de la Concorde is a magnificent arrangement of fountains and statues, held together in the center by a 3,000 year-old Egyptian obelisk (a gift to France from Egypt in 1829). When it was inaugurated in 1763 during the reign of Louis XV, this vast plaza was on the outer edges of the city; today, though part of an urban landscape, it still gives the impression of open space. If it weren't for the cars hurtling around the obelisk like racers in the Grand Prix, this would be a delightful spot for a breath of fresh air (if you feel compelled to cross to the obelisk and you value your life, find the stoplight and cross there).

It's hard to believe that this magnificent square was once bathed in blood, but during the Revolution, it was a grisly stage for public executions: King Louis XVI and his wife, Marie-Antoinette, both bowed down to the guillotine here, as did many prominent figures of the Revolution, including Danton, Camille Desmoulins, and Robespierre. Once the monarchy was back in place, the plaza hosted less lethal public events like festivals and trade expositions. In 1835 the *place* was given its current look: Two immense fountains, copies of those in St-Peter's Square in Rome, play on either side of the obelisk; 18 sumptuous columns decorated with shells, mermaids, sea horses, and other sea creatures each hold two lamps; and eight statues representing the country's largest cities survey the scene from the edges of the action. On the west side are the famous **Marly Horses,** actually copies of the originals, which were suffering from erosion and have since been restored and housed in the Louvre. On the north side of the square are two palatial buildings that date from the square's 18th-century origins: On the east side is the **Hôtel de la Marine,** and on the west side is the **Hôtel Crillon,** where on February 6, 1778, a treaty was signed by Louis XVI and Benjamin Franklin, among others, wherein France officially recognized the United States as an independent country and became its ally.

8th arrond. Métro: Concorde.

Montmartre (18th Arrondissement)

There are few places in this city that will fill you with the urge to belt out sappy show tunes like the *butte* (hill) of Montmartre. Admiring the view from the esplanade in front of the oddly Byzantine **Basilique du Sacré-Coeur,** you'll feel like you have finally arrived in Paris, and that you now understand what all the fuss is about. Try to ignore the tour buses and crowds mobbing the church and the hideously touristy **place du Tertre** behind you and wander off into the warren of streets towards the **place des Abbesses,** or up **rue Lepic** where you'll eventually stumble across the **Moulin de la Galette** and **Moulin du Radet,** the two surviving windmills (there were once 30 on this hill).

Basilique du Sacré-Coeur ★★ CHURCH   Poised at the apex of the hill like a *grande dame* in crinolines, this odd-looking 19th-century basilica has become one of the city's most famous landmarks. After France's defeat in the Franco-Prussian War, prominent Catholics vowed to build a church consecrated to the Sacred Heart of Christ as a way of making up for whatever sins the French may have committed that had made God so angry at them. Since 1885, prayers for humanity have been continually chanted here (the church is a pilgrimage site, so dress and behave accordingly). Inspired by the Byzantine churches of Turkey and Italy, construction of this multi-domed confection began in 1875. It was completed in 1914, though it wasn't consecrated until 1919 due to World War I. The white stone was chosen for its self-cleaning capabilities: When it rains, it secretes a chalky substance that acts as a fresh coat of paint. The interior of the church includes a somewhat garish mosaic ceiling, installed in the 1920s. Most visitors climb the 237 stairs to the dome, where the splendid view of the city extends over 48km (30 miles).

35 rue Chevalier de la Barre, 18th arrond. ⓒ **01-53-41-89-00.** www.sacre-coeur-montmartre.com. Free admission to basilica, joint ticket to dome and crypt 8€ adults, 5€ ages 4–16, free under 4. Basilica daily 6am–10:30pm; dome and crypt daily 8:30am–8pm May–Sept, 9am–5pm Oct–Apr. Métro: Abbesses; take elevator to surface and follow signs to funicular.

Musée de Montmartre ★★ MUSEUM   The main reason to visit this small museum is to get an inkling of what Montmartre really was like back in the days when Picasso, Toulouse-Lautrec, Van Gogh, et al. were painting and cavorting up here on the *Butte* (as opposed to the hideously commercial version up the hill on Place du Tertre). While there are few examples of the artists' works here, there are plenty of photos, posters, and even films documenting the neighborhood's famous history, from the days when its importance was mainly religious, to the gory days of the Paris Commune, and finally to the artistic boom in the 19th and 20th centuries. Next to an original poster of Jane Avril by Toulouse-Lautrec, for example, you'll see a photo of the real Jane Avril, as well as other Montmartre cabaret legends like Aristide Bruant and La Goulue. The few paintings and drawings by famed painters like Utrillo and Modigliani are supplemented by works by lesser-known Montmartrois, like Steinlen, Léandre, and de Belay. The 17th-century house that shelters the museum was at various times the studio and home of Auguste Renoir, Raoul Dufy, Susan Valadon, and Maurice Utrillo. Surrounded by gardens and greenery it offers a lovely view of the last scrap of the Montmartre vineyard. English-language audio-guides are a big help here.

12 rue Cortot, 18th arrond. ⓒ **01-49-25-89-37.** www.museedemontmartre.fr. Admission 9€ adults, 7€ ages 18–25, 5€ ages 10–17, free under 10. Daily 10am–6pm. Métro: Lamarck-Caulaincourt.

Musée de l'Erotisme ★ MUSEUM   Just down the street from Place Pigalle, the city's historic red light district, this sex museum attempts to take a serious look at erotic art, from Peruvian pottery to R. Crumb. The visit starts with traditional art from around the world—Japanese prints, Persian miniatures, and Indian statues depicting bodies in a multitude of gymnastic poses. Further on, you'll see antique naughty postcards, modern art, and temporary exhibits. Many of the works, particularly in the contemporary art segment, seem designed more to provoke than to excite, but the exhibit on the *maisons closes,* or bordellos, is actually interesting. Covering the period from the end of the 19th century to 1946 (when bordellos were declared illegal and closed down in France), these poignant photos and prints document a hazy subculture that, for better or worse, has ceased to exist. There's no English language text, but this is one place where the subject matter is pretty universal.

72 bd. de Clichy, 18th. ⓒ **01-42-58-28-73.** www.musee-erotisme.com. Admission 10€ adults, children 17 and younger not permitted. Daily 10am–2am. Métro: Blanche.

République, Bastille & Eastern Paris (11th & 12th Arrondissements)

While you can't really point to any major tourist attractions in this area, this part of town has great nightlife and clothing stores for the young crowd. There are also some important historical sites: The French Revolution was brewed in the workshops of the **Faubourg St-Antoine,** and was ignited at the **Place de la Bastille.** The former stomping grounds of the medieval Knights Templar, the recently remodeled **Place de la République** is a potent symbol of the French Republic.

Parc Zoologique de Paris ★★ ZOO   After 6 years of reconstruction, the Paris Zoo finally reopened in April 2014, to the delight of children and parents of all stripes. Little remains of the old-fashioned zoo that once was; today a lush, ecologically correct animal reserve invites visitors to five regions of the world, from the plains of Sudan to Europe, via Guyana, Patagonia and Madagascar. Going for quality, instead of quantity, the new zoo may not have room for elephants and bears, but it does introduce visitors to animals they might not be familiar with, like the fossa, a catlike carnivore from Madagascar, or the capybara, a giant South American rodent. There is still a good sampling of zoo favorites like lions, baboons, penguins and a troupe of giraffes—if you are lucky you can get an up close look while the latter get lunch in the giraffe house. The enclosures are well adapted to their inhabitants, so much so that at times it's hard to see them. But if you are patient you'll see wolves peeking out of the foliage, or a bright red tomato frog griping a vine. There are over 1,000 animals in all, yet the zoo is human-sized—you can see the whole thing in a couple of hours. Don't miss the huge aviaries, one of which is home to a huge flock of flamingos.

Parc de Vincennes, 12th arrond. (𝒞 **01-44-75-20-10.** www.parczoologiquedeparis.fr. 22€ adults, 17€ students 12–25, 14€ children 3–11, free ages 2 and under. Mid-Oct to mid-Mar daily 10am–5pm, mid-Mar to mid-Oct Mon–Fri 10am–6pm, Sat–Sun and school holidays 9:30am–7:30pm.

Place de la Bastille ★ SQUARE   The most notable thing about this giant plaza is the building that's no longer there: the Bastille prison. Now an enormous traffic circle where cars careen around at warp speed, this was once the site of an ancient stone fortress that became a symbol for all that was wrong with the French monarchy. Over the centuries, kings and queens condemned rebellious citizens to stay inside these cold walls, sometimes with good reason, other times on a mere whim. By the time the Revolution started to boil, though, the prison was barely in use; when the angry mobs stormed the walls on July 14, 1789, there were only seven prisoners left to set free. Be that as it may, the destruction of the Bastille came to be seen as the ultimate revolutionary moment; July 14 is still celebrated as the birth of the Republic. Surprisingly, the giant bronze column in the center honors the victims of a different revolution, that of 1830.

12th arrond. Métro: Bastille.

La Promenade Plantée ★ WALKING TRAIL   Transformed from an unused train viaduct, this beautiful aerial garden walkway runs from the place de la Bastille to the Bois de Vincennes. The 4.5km (2.8-mile) pedestrian path runs along flower gardens, tree bowers, rose trellises, and fountains and takes you over the 12th-arrondissement, past the Gare de Lyon, and through the Reuilly Gardens. At ground level along Ave. Daumesnil, the brick archways now shelter the **Viaduct des Arts,** a series of galleries and workshops that show off the work of highly skilled artisans.

Enter by the staircase on Avenue Daumesnil just past the Opéra Bastille, 12th arrond.

Belleville, Canal St-Martin & La Villette (10th, 19th & 20th Arrondissements)

One of the most picturesque attractions in this area is the **Canal St-Martin** itself, which extends up to **La Villette,** a former industrial area that has been transformed into a gigantic park and cultural compound. Other intriguing outdoor attractions include the romantic **Père-Lachaise cemetery,** the resting place of France's most noteworthy

The Canal St-Martin is a pretty waterway that connects the river Seine, near Bastille, to the Canal de l'Ourcq, near the Villette in the 19th arrondissement. When Parisians talk about *le canal*, they are usually referring to the popular stretch of the quays Jemmapes and Valmy, which begins just above République and runs up by the Gare de l'Est. Inaugurated in 1825 with the aim of bringing fresh drinking water to the heart of the city, it narrowly escaped being entirely paved over in the 1970s. Finally listed a historic monument in 1993, today its tree lined banks and high arched bridges make it a delightful place to stroll, especially on Sundays, when the east side is closed to cars. You can take a boat tour with **Paris Canal** (𝄐 **01-42-40-96-97;** www.pariscanal.com) or **Canauxrama** (𝄐 **01-42-39-15-00;** www.canauxrama.com).

notables, and the verdant **Buttes Chaumont park.** The Belleville neighborhood is home to one of the city's bustling Chinatowns, as well as many artists' studios.

Cimetière du Père-Lachaise ★★★ CEMETERY   It's hard believe that a cemetery could be a top tourist attraction, but this is no ordinary cemetery. Romantic and rambling as a 19th-century English garden, this hillside resting-place is wonderfully green, with huge leafy trees and narrow paths winding around the graves, which include just about every French literary or artistic giant you can imagine, plus several international stars. Proust, Apollinaire, Collette, Delacroix, Seurat, Modigliani, Bizet, Rossini, are all here, as well as Sarah Bernhardt, Isadora Duncan, Simone Signoret and Yves Montand (buried side by side, of course). Though some are simple tombstones, many are miniature architectural marvels, embellished with exquisite marble and stone figures, or even phone-booth-size chapels, complete with stain glass windows. Some of the standouts include:

Héloïse and Abélard: These two legendary lovers actually existed, and their 12th-century remains were brought here in 1817, when the city built them this monument, which is covered by an openwork chapel taken from an abbey in southwestern France.

Molière and La Fontaine: Though there was no romantic link, the celebrated playwright and noted fable writer were also brought here in 1817 and placed in nearby sarcophagi, both of which stand appropriately high on pillars. If the authenticity of the remains is in doubt, they still make a fitting memorial to these two brilliant talents.

Oscar Wilde: Usually covered with lipstick kisses, this huge stone monument is topped with a winged figure that resembles an Aztec deity. An elegant homage to this brilliant writer, who died a pauper in Paris in 1900.

Celebrity graves can be hard to find, so a map is essential. You can find one at the newsstand across from the main entrance or use the one in this book (p. 135). There are also good maps on the website, as well as the Paris municipal site: www.paris.fr (search for "Père Lachaise").

16 rue de Repos, 20th arrond. No telephone number. www.pere-lachaise.com. Admission free. Mon–Fri 8am–6pm; Sat–Sun 8:30am–6pm (closes at 5pm Nov to early Mar). Métro: Père-Lachaise or Philippe Auguste.

Cité des Sciences et de l'Industrie ★★ MUSEUM   This gigantic science and industry museum began life as an immense slaughterhouse. During construction the 1960s, it was touted as the most modern of its kind. It turned out to be the center of a

Père-Lachaise Cemetery

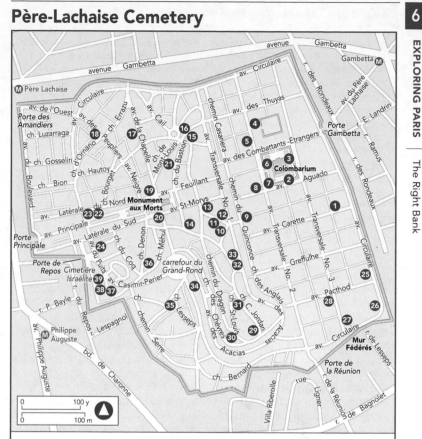

Abélard & Héloïse **37**	Honoré de Balzac **16**	Alfred de Musset **21**
Guillaume Apollinaire **5**	Eugène Delacroix **15**	Edith Piaf **27**
Pierre-Auguste Beaumarchais **30**	Gustave Doré **14**	Camille Pissarro **38**
Hans Bellmer **24**	Isadora Duncan **6**	Marcel Proust **4**
Sarah Bernhardt **9**	Paul Eluard **26**	Gioacchio Antonio Rossini **22**
Georges Bizet **17**	Max Ernst **2**	
Maria Callas **3**	Théodore Géricault **20**	Rothschild family plot **39**
Frédéric Chopin **36**	Jean-Auguste-Dominique Ingres **13**	Henri de Saint-Simon **31**
Colette **23**	Jean La Fontaine **33**	Georges Seurat **18**
Auguste Comte **34**	René Lalique **12**	Simone Signoret & Yves Montand **8**
Jean Baptiste Camille Corot **11**	Lefebvre Masséna **29**	Gertrude Stein & Alice B. Toklas **25**
Honoré Daumier **10**	Amedeo Modigliani **28**	Oscar Wilde **1**
Jacques-Louis David **19**	Molière **32**	Richard Wright **7**
	Jim Morrison **35**	

Though the grave itself is unexceptional, the tomb of '60s rock star **Jim Morrison** is possibly the most visited, or at least the most hyped, in the cemetery. For years, fans made pilgrimages, leaving behind so much graffiti, litter, and mind-altering substances that families of those buried nearby began to complain, and the tomb was surrounded by a fence. Still, nothing can dispel the enduring attraction of the Morrison legend. In 1971, battling a variety of drug, alcohol, and legal problems, the singer/musician came to Paris, ostensibly with the goal of taking a break from performing and getting his life back on track. Four months later, he was found dead in a Parisian bathtub, at age 27. Since no autopsy was performed, the exact cause of his death was never known (though there was good reason to suspect a drug overdose), which has lead to wild speculation on the part of his fans. Rumors still circulate that he was a target of the CIA, murdered by a witch, committed suicide, or that he faked his own death and is currently residing in India, Africa, or New Jersey under the name "Mr. Mojo Risin'."

corruption scandal and was quickly abandoned when the city's abattoirs were transferred elsewhere. After years of head-scratching, the building was finally turned into this terrific museum, which includes a planetarium, a 3-D movie theater, and a multimedia library, not to mention a real live submarine. The heart of the museum is Explora, two huge floors of interactive exhibits and displays, as well as excellent temporary exhibits. On the ground floor, parents will be delighted to find the Cité des Enfants (separate admission, 9€ adults, 6€ under 25 for a 1½-hr. session; see website for hours, reservations essential, particularly during French school vacations), which has separate programs for 2- to 7-year-olds and 7- to 12-year-olds. Kids get to explore their own sensations and the world around them in a series of hands-on activities and displays. If all this isn't enough, outside you can clamber into the Argonaut (3€, free under 7), a real submarine that was one of the stars of the French navy in the 1950s, or dip inside the gigantic metal sphere, called the Geode (adults 12€, under 25 9€), an IMAX-type movie theater showing large screen films.

Parc de La Villette, 30 ave. Corentine-Cariou, 19th arrond. ✆ **01-40-05-70-00.** www.cite-sciences.fr. Varied ticket packages 12€–20€ adults, 6€–15€ under 25, free ages 2 and under. Tues–Sat 10am–6pm; Sun 10am–7pm. Métro: Porte de La Villette.

Musée de la Musique ★ MUSEUM Located on the north end of the Parc de la Villette, this museum has a permanent collection of over a thousand instruments, sculptures, paintings, and other objects that recount the history of music in Europe from the 16th to 20th centuries. Pore over a beautiful and rare 17th-century guitar with ivory inlay, a clutch of Stradivarius violins, or a concert piano that Franz Liszt once played on. A separate section on music from around the world includes another 700 objects, mostly from Africa and Asia. As you wander about, you can listen to the instruments you look at on headphones, and you will probably come across live demonstrations by local musicians as well. The museum is housed in the **Cité de la Musique,** which includes a library, concert hall and educational facilities.

In the Cité de la Musique, 221 ave. Jean-Jaurès, 19th arrond. ✆ **01-44-84-44-84.** www.cite-musique.fr. Admission 7€ adults, 5.60€ ages 26–28, free for under 26. Tues–Sat noon–6pm; Sun 10am–6pm. Métro: Porte de Pantin.

Parc de la Villette ★★ PARK   This vast complex, which includes a park, museums, concert halls, and other cultural institutions (see above), was built on the site of the city's slaughterhouses, abandoned since the mid-1970s. Construction began in 1980, when Bernard Tschumi, a French-Swiss architect, was chosen to create an urban cultural park accessible to one and all. The park is certainly a success on the cultural end: It harbors **Cité de la Musique** and **Cité des Sciences et de l'Industrie**— two excellent museums, as well as the **Zénith** and **Cabaret Sauvage** concert halls, and other assorted theaters and cultural spaces. As far as the green spaces—well, let me put it this way: If it is possible for a park to have a sense of humor, this one definitely has one. There are 11 themed gardens, around which are dotted 25 red "folies"—oddball contemporary structures that sometimes house a drink stand or an information booth, and sometimes are just there for the heck of it. The gardens range from the sublime to the silly; a few are strictly reserved for children (who can bring along their parents).

From mid-July to mid-August the **Cinéma en Plein Air** takes place Tues–Sun at sundown, presenting classic movies for free.

19th arrond. ⓒ **01-40-03-75-75.** www.villette.com. Daily 6am–1am. Métro: Porte de Pantin or Porte de la Villette.

Parc des Buttes Chaumont ★ PARK   Up until 1860, this area was home to a deep limestone quarry, but thanks to Napoleon III, the gaping hole was turned into an unusual park, full of hills and dales, rocky bluffs and cliffs. It took 3 years to make this romantic garden; over a thousand workers and a hundred horses dug, heaped, and blasted through the walls of the quarry to create green lawns, a cool grotto, cascades, streams, and even a small lake. By the opening of the 1867 World's Fair, the garden was ready for visitors. The surrounding area was, and still is, working-class; the Emperor built it to give this industrious neighborhood a green haven and a bit of fresh air. There are **pony rides** for the kids on weekends and Wednesdays, plus a **puppet theater,** a **carousel,** and **two playgrounds.**

Rue Botzaris, 19th arrond. Open 7am–dusk. Métro: Botzaris or Buttes Chaumont.

THE LEFT BANK
Latin Quarter (5th & 13th Arrondissements)

For several hundred years, the students that flocked to this quarter spoke Latin in their classes at the **Sorbonne** (founded in the 13th c.). Today students still abound around the Sorbonne, and even though classes are taught in French, the name stuck. Intellectual pursuits aside, this youth-filled neighborhood is a lively one, with lots of cinemas and cafes. History is readily visible here, dating back to the Roman occupation: The **rue St-Jacques** and **boulevard Saint-Michel** mark the former Roman cardo, and you can explore the remains of the **Roman baths** at the **Cluny Museum.**

Jardin des Plantes ★★ GARDEN   This delightful botanical garden, tucked between the Muséum National d'Histoire Naturelle (see below) and the Seine, is one of my favorite picnic spots. Created in 1626 as a medicinal plant garden for King Louis XIII, in the 18th century it became an internationally famed scientific institution thanks to naturalist, mathematician, and biologist Georges-Louis Leclerc, Count of Buffon, with the help of fellow-naturalist Louis-Jean-Marie Daubenton. Today the museums are still part academic institutions, but you certainly don't need to be a student to appreciate these lush grounds.

Left Bank Attractions

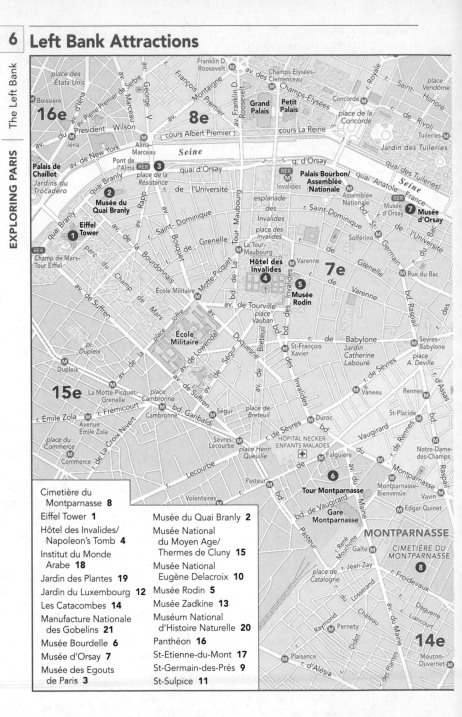

Cimetière du
   Montparnasse **8**
Eiffel Tower **1**
Hôtel des Invalides/
   Napoleon's Tomb **4**
Institut du Monde
   Arabe **18**
Jardin des Plantes **19**
Jardin du Luxembourg **12**
Les Catacombes **14**
Manufacture Nationale
   des Gobelins **21**
Musée Bourdelle **6**
Musée d'Orsay **7**
Musée des Egouts
   de Paris **3**

Musée du Quai Branly **2**
Musée National
   du Moyen Age/
   Thermes de Cluny **15**
Musée National
   Eugène Delacroix **10**
Musée Rodin **5**
Musée Zadkine **13**
Muséum National
   d'Histoire Naturelle **20**
Panthéon **16**
St-Etienne-du-Mont **17**
St-Germain-des-Prés **9**
St-Sulpice **11**

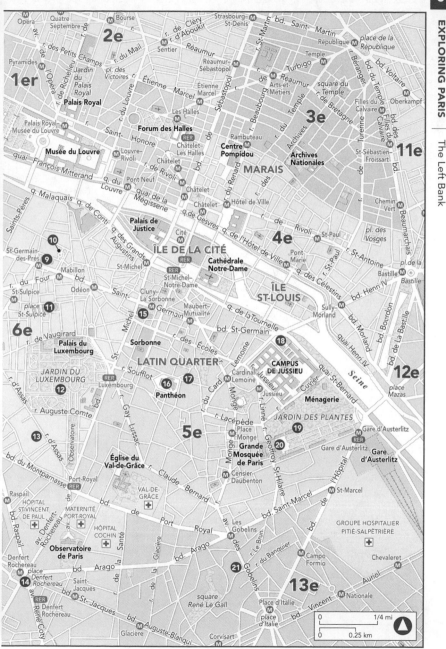

The garden also harbors a small, but well-kept zoo, the **Ménagerie du Jardin des Plants** (© **01-40-79-56-01;** 11€ adults, 9€ students 18–26 and children 4–16, free under 4; daily 9am–6pm). Created in 1794, this is the oldest zoo in the world. Due to its size, the zoo showcases mostly smaller species, in particular birds and reptiles. But there's also a healthy selection of mammals (240 to be exact), including rare species like red pandas, Przewalski horses, and even Florida pumas. After years of renovations, the **Grandes Serres** (© **01-40-79-56-01;** 6€ adults, 4€ children and students from 4 to 25, free 3 and under) a series of magnificent 19th-century greenhouses filled with lush plantlife from warmer climes, have been reopened to the public (a good bet on a cold day).

Rue Geoffroy-St-Hilaire, 5th arrond. © **01-40-79-56-01.** www.jardindesplantes.net. Free admission to gardens; 8am–dusk; Métro: Gare d'Austerlitz.

Manufacture Nationale des Gobelins ★ FACTORY TOUR   Back in the 17th century, Louis XIV purchased this famed tapestry factory with the aim of furnishing his new chateau (Versailles) with the most splendid tapestries around. France's most skilled workers created sumptuous carpets and wall-coverings using designs sketched by the top artists of the era (Le Brun and Boucher, to name just two). The workshop's reputation has survived the centuries, and the factory is still active, using the same materials used in the time of Louis XIV (wool, cotton, silk). Still state-owned, today the factory operates under the auspices of the French Ministry of Culture, and produces modern tapestries to hang in some of France's most grand public spaces. This is definitely not a mass-market operation—these tapestries take several years to finish. Highly skilled workers (they study for 4 years at the on-site school) work from paintings by contemporary artists to create enormous works of art; during the tour you'll see the weavers in action at their giant looms. It is humbling to see how carefully and patiently the weavers work, tying tiny individual knots and/or passing shuttles of wool through a forest of warp and weft, all the while following an intricate design scheme. To visit the ateliers, you must take a guided, 1½-hour tour (in French, Tues–Thurs at 1pm); there is also an exposition space that offers temporary shows on design themes.

42 ave. des Gobelins, 13th arrond. © **01-44-08-53-49.** www.mobiliernational.culture.gouv.fr. Admission to the Galerie des Gobelins (open only for temporary exhibits) 6€ adults, 4€ students. Tues–Sun 11am–6pm. Tours: 9€ adults, 7€ students. Tues–Thurs at 1pm. Métro: Gobelins.

Musée de l'Institut du Monde Arabe ★ MUSEUM   While it harbors an substantial collection, one of the biggest draws to this museum-library-research center is the building itself. Designed by architect Jean Nouvel in 1987, the south facade is covered by a metallic latticework echoing traditional Arab designs, with 30,000 light-sensitive diaphragms that open and close according to how bright it is outside. The airy museum space presents a collection that emphasizes the diversity of peoples and cultures in the Middle East, reminding us, among other things, that it was the birthplace of all three major Western religions. While intellectually stimulating, if art is what you are after, the Islamic Art section of the Louvre will be more satisfying. There's a terrific view of the Seine and Notre-Dame from the rooftop restaurant, Le Zyriab.

1 rue des Fossés St-Bernard, 5th arrond. © **01-40-51-38-38.** www.imarabe.org. Admission 8€, 4€ under 26. Tues–Thurs 10am–6:30pm, Fri 10am–9:30pm, Sat–Sun 10am–7pm. Métro: Jussieu, Cardinal Lemoine, Sully-Morland.

Muséum National d'Histoire Naturelle ★★ MUSEUM   This natural history museum was established in 1793, under the supervision of two celebrated naturalists,

George Louis Lerclerc, Count of Buffon, and Louis Jean-Marie Daubenton. Originally (and still) an academic research institution, this temple to the natural sciences contains a series of separate museums, each with a different specialty. The biggest draw is no doubt the **Grande Galerie de l'Evolution,** where a sort of Noah's ark of animals snakes its way around a huge hall filled with displays that trace the evolution of life and man's relationship with nature. Another interesting hall, the just renovated **Galerie de Minérologie et de Géologie,** includes a room full of giant crystals, and another with eye-popping precious stones from the Royal Treasury, as well as various minerals and even meteorites. For dinosaurs, saber-toothed tigers, ancient humans, and thousands of other fossilized skeletons, repair to the **Galeries de Paléontologie et d'Anatomie Comparée.** The Muséum recently opened a new **Galerie des Enfants,** with hands on interactive displays for the little tykes. Except for the Grande Galerie, which has a joint ticket deal with the Galerie des Enfants, you'll have to pay for each Galerie separately.

36 rue Geoffrey, 5th arrond. ⓒ **01-40-79-54-79.** www.mnhn.fr. Admission to each galerie 5€–9€ adults; 4€–7€ students, seniors 60 and older, and children 4–13, free 3 and under. Wed–Mon 10am–6pm. Métro: Jussieu or Gare d'Austerlitz.

Musée National du Moyen Age/Thermes de Cluny (Musée de Cluny)

★★ MUSEUM Ancient Roman baths and a 15th-century mansion set the stage for a terrific collection of Medieval art and objects at this museum. Built somewhere between the 1st and 3rd centuries, the baths (visible from bd. St-Michel) are some of the best existing examples of Gallo-Roman architecture. They are attached to what was once the palatial home of a 15th-century abbot, whose last owner, a certain Alexandre du Sommerard, amassed a vast array of Medieval masterworks. When he died in 1842, his home was turned into a museum and his collection put on display. Sculptures, textiles, furniture, and ceramics are shown, as well as gold, ivory, and enamel work. There are several magnificent tapestries, but the biggest draw is the **"Lady and the Unicorn"** series, one of only two sets of complete unicorn tapestries in the world (the other is in New York City). In five of these late-15th-century tapestries, the lady, her unicorn, a lion, and various other symbolic representations of the animal and vegetable kingdoms illustrate the five senses, while in the sixth she stands before a tent bearing the inscription "To My Only Desire" while placing a necklace in a case held by her servant. The meaning of this last tapestry remains an enigma—but the mystery merely adds to its beauty.

Among the many sculptures displayed are the famous severed heads from the facade of Notre-Dame. Knocked off of their bodies during the furor of the Revolution, 21 of the heads of the Kings of Judah were found by chance in 1977 during repair work in the basement of a bank. Other treasures include Flemish retables, Visigoth crowns, bejeweled chalices, woodcarvings, stained glass windows, and beautiful objects from daily life, like hair combs and game boards.

6 place Paul Painlevé, 5th arrond. ⓒ **01-53-73-78-00.** www.musee-moyenage.fr. Admission 8€ adults, 6€ ages 18–26, free 17 and under. Wed–Mon 9:15am–5:45pm. Métro/RER: Cluny–La Sorbonne or St-Michel.

Panthéon ★ CHURCH/MAUSOLEUM

High atop the "montagne" (actually a medium-sized hill) of St-Geneviève, the dome of the Panthéon is one of the city's most visible landmarks. This erstwhile royal church has been transformed into a sort of national mausoleum—the final resting place of luminaries such as Voltaire, Rousseau,

Hugo, and Zola. Initially dedicated to St-Geneviève, the church was commissioned by a grateful Louis XV, who attributed his recovery from a serious illness to the saint. The work of architect Jacques-Germain Soufflot, who took his inspiration from the Pantheon in Rome, it must have been magnificent—the vast interior was clearly created with a higher power in mind. However, during the Revolution its sacred mission was diverted towards a new god—the Nation—and it was converted into a memorial and burial ground for Great Men of the Republic. This meant taking down the bells, walling up most of the windows, doing away with religious statuary and replacing it with works promoting patriotic virtues. The desired effect was achieved—the enormous empty space, lined with huge paintings of great moments in French history, resembles a cavernous tomb. Though the building is of architectural interest, unless you're a fan of one of the men (or women) who are buried under the building (a staircase leads down to the actual crypt), it's probably best admired from the outside. *Note:* The building is undergoing a major restoration, so don't be alarmed to see the dome swathed in a white covering. At press time it looked like a giant upside down paper cup was sitting on the dome; soon it will be plastered with anonymous portraits as part of a photo project by the artist JR (see www.au-pantheon.fr for more info).

Place du Panthéon, 5th arrond. ℰ **01-44-32-18-00.** www.monuments-nationaux.fr. Admission 7.50€ adults, 4.50€ ages 18–25, free for children 17 and younger. Apr–Sept daily 10am–6:30pm; Oct–Mar daily 10am–6pm. Métro: Cardinal Lemoine, RER: Luxembourg.

St-Etienne-du-Mont ★★ CHURCH   One of the city's prettiest churches, this gem is a joyous mix of late Gothic and Renaissance styles. The 17th-century facade combines Gothic tradition with a dash of classical Rome; inside, the 16th-century chancel sports a magnificent **rood screen** (an intricately carved partition separating the nave from the chancel) with decorations inspired by the Italian Renaissance. Book-ended by twin spiraling marble staircases, this rood screen is the only one left in the city. The entire church has been cleaned, making it easy to appreciate its riches, which include 16th- and 17th-century stained glass. A pilgrimage site, this church was once part of an abbey dedicated to St-Geneviève (the city's patron saint), and stones from her original sarcophagus lie in an ornate shrine here. That's about all that is left of her—the saint's bones were burned during the Revolution, and their ashes were thrown in the Seine. The remains of two other great minds, Racine and Pascal, are buried here.

1 place St-Geneviève, 5th arrond. ℰ **01-43-54-11-79.** www.saintetiennedumont.fr. Free admission. Tues–Sat 8:45am–7:45pm, Sat–Sun 8:45am–noon and 2–7:45pm. Métro: Cardinal Lemoine or Luxembourg.

St-Germain-des-Prés & Luxembourg (6th Arrondissement)

In the 20th century, the St-Germain-des-Prés neighborhood became associated with writers like Jean-Paul Sartre, Simone de Beauvoir, Albert Camus, and the rest of the intellectual bohemian crowd that gathered at **Café de Flore** or **Les Deux Magots** (p. 101). But back in the 6th century, a mighty abbey was founded here that ruled over a big chunk of the left bank for almost 1,000 years. The French Revolution put a stop to that, and most of the original buildings were pulled down. You can still find remains of both epochs in this neighborhood, notably at the 10th-century church **St-Germain-des-Prés** and the surviving bookstores and publishing houses that surround it. After your tour, relax at the delightful and nearby **Jardin du Luxembourg.**

Jardin du Luxembourg ★★★ GARDEN   Out of the many parks and gardens in Paris, this a personal favorite. Rolling out like an exotic oriental carpet before the Italianate Palais du Luxembourg (the seat of the French Senate since 1958, not open to the public), this vast expanse of fountains, flowers, lush lawns, and shaded glens is the perfect setting for a leisurely stroll, a relaxed picnic, or a serious make-out session, depending on who you're with. At the center of everything is a fountain with a huge basin, where kids can sail toy wooden sailboats (2€ for a half-hour) and adults can sun themselves in the green metal chairs at the pond's edge. Sculptures abound: At every turn there is a god, goddess, artist, or monarch peering down at you from his or her pedestal—Vulcan, Venus, George Sand, or Anne de Bretagne, to name but a few. The most splendid waterworks is probably the Medici Fountain (most easily reached via the entrance at place Paul Claudel behind the Odéon), draped with lithe Roman gods sculptured by Auguste Ottin, and topped with the Medici coat of arms, in honor of the palace's first resident, Marie de Medicis.

In 1621, the Italian-born French queen, homesick for the Pitti Palace of her youth, bought up the grounds and existing buildings and had a Pitti-inspired palace built for herself as well as a smaller version of the sumptuous gardens. She moved in in 1625, only to be banished in 1630 for taking the wrong side against powerful Cardinal Riche-lieu. The palace passed on to various royals until the Revolution, when it was turned into a prison. American writer Thomas Paine was incarcerated there in 1793 after he fell out of favor with Robespierre; he narrowly escaped execution. On the plus side, the Revolutionaries increased the size of the garden and made it a public institution. The orchards of the neighboring charterhouse were annexed, the remnants of which can still be visited at the southwest corner of the gardens. There, visitors can see a horticulture school where pear trees have been trained into formal, geometric shapes, as well as beehives that are maintained by a local apiculture association. After the Revolution, the palace and grounds stayed in government hands up until today (the palace houses the French senate), with the exception of the Orangerie, which now houses the **Musée du Luxembourg** (19 rue de Vaugirard, 6th arrond.; ℂ **01-40-13-62-00;** www.museeduluxembourg.fr; admission varies with exhibits; Tues–Thurs and Sat–Sun 10am–7:30pm, Mon and Fri 10am–10pm; Métro: Odéon, RER: Luxem-bourg), which is only open for its excellent temporary exhibits.

Entry at Place Edmond Rostand, place André Honnorat, rue Guynemer, or rue de Vaugirard, 6th arrond. ℂ **01-42-34-20-00.** www.senat.fr/visite/jardin. 8am–dusk. Métro: Odéon; RER: Luxembourg.

Attention Bored Kids & Tired Parents

Frazzled parents take note: There are lots of activities in the Jardin de Luxembourg for kids who need to blow off steam. First off, there is the extra-large **playground** (1.20€ adults, 2.50€ under 12) filled with all kinds of things to climb on and play in. Then there are the wonderful wooden **sailboats** (2.50€ per half-hour) to float in the main fountain, as well as an ancient **carousel** (1.50€, next to the playground). At the **marionette theater** (4.70€ each for par-ents and children; Wed, Sat, Sun, and school vacation days; shows usually start after 3pm, Sat–Sun additional shows at 11am), you can see Guignol himself (the French version of Punch) in a variety of puppet shows.

Musée National Eugène Delacroix ★ MUSEUM   Housed in what was once the painter's apartment and studio, this small museum is dedicated to Eugène Delacroix, one of the greatest artists of the Romantic period. Old and sick, Delacroix moved here in 1857 to be closer to the church of St-Sulpice, where he was decorating a chapel. He managed to finish the paintings, 3 years before he died here, in 1863. "It takes great fortitude to be yourself," he once said, and he certainly had it: At his death he left behind some 8,000 paintings, drawings, and pastels. Though none of his major works are in the museum, several of his smaller paintings decorate the walls, including the mysterious Mary Magdalene in the Wilderness. Furniture, mementos, and other personal items are on display, including the artist's palate and paint box. The museum is located on the exquisitely beautiful place de Furstenberg, a small and leafy square.

6 place de Furstenberg, 6th arrond. ✆ **01-44-41-86-50.** www.musee-delacroix.fr. Admission 6€ adults, free for children 17 and younger. Wed–Mon 9:30am–5pm. Métro: St-Germain-des-Prés or Mabillon.

Musée Zadkine ★★ MUSEUM   You could easily miss the alleyway that leads to this tiny museum in the small but luminous house where Ossip Zadkine lived and worked from 1928 to his death in 1967. A contemporary and neighbor of artists such as Brancusi, Lipchitz, Modigliani, and Picasso, this Russian-born sculptor is closely associated with the Cubist movement; his sober, elegant, "primitive" sculptures combine abstract geometry with deep humanity. Dozens of examples of his best works, like a superb 9-ft plaster sculpture of biblical Rebecca carrying a water pitcher, or a vaguely African head of a woman in limestone are displayed in small, light-filled rooms. Be sure to visit artist's workshop, tucked behind the tranquil garden. *Note:* Due to the museum's small size, during temporary exhibits you'll have to pay to enter even the permanent collection (which is usually free).

100 bis rue d'Assas, 6th arrond. ✆ **01-55-42-77-20.** www.zadkine.paris.fr. Free admission to permanent collections. Tues–Sun 10am–6pm. Métro: Notre-Dame des Champs or Vavin.

St-Germain-des-Prés ★★ CHURCH   The origins of this church stretch back over a millennium. First established by King Childebert in 543, who constructed a basilica and monastery on the site, it was built, destroyed, and rebuilt several times over the centuries. Nothing remains of the original buildings, but the bell tower dates from the 10th century and is one of the oldest in France. Most of the rest of the church was built in the 11th and 12th centuries and is Romanesque in style. The church and its abbey became a major center of learning and power during the Middle Ages, remaining a force to be reckoned with up until the eve of the French Revolution. Once the monarchy toppled, however, all hell broke loose: The abbey was destroyed, the famous library burned, and the church vandalized. Restored in the 19th century, the buildings have regained some of their former glory, though the complex is a fraction of its original size.

The first thing you'll notice on entering is that much of the interior is painted in a range of greens, and golds—one of the few Parisian churches to retain a sense of its original decor. The paint, however, is in a sorry state; the interior is scheduled to be restored during 2015. There are several murals by 19th-century artist Hippolyte Flandrin over the archways in the nave. The heart of King Jean Casimir of Poland is buried here, as are the ashes of the body of René Descartes (his skull is in the collections of the Musée de l'Homme). On the left as you exit you can peek inside the **chapel of**

St-Symphorien, where during the Revolution over 100 clergymen were imprisoned before being executed on the square in front of the church. The chapel was restored in the 1970s and decorated by contemporary artist Pierre Buraglio in 1992.

Classical music concerts are regularly held in the church on Thursday and Friday evenings. (Tickets and information are at www.fnacspectacles.com.)

3 place St-Germain-des-Prés, 6th arrond. $\mathcal{C}$ **01-55-42-81-10.** www.eglise-sgp.org. Free admission. Mon–Sat 8am–7:45pm; Sun 9am–8pm. Métro: St-Germain-des-Prés.

St-Sulpice ★★ CHURCH   The majestic facade of this enormous edifice looms over an entire neighborhood. Construction started in the 17th century over the remains of a medieval church; it took over a hundred years to build, and one of the towers was never finished. Inside, the cavernous interior seems to command you to be silent; several important works of art are tucked into the chapels that line the church. The most famous of them are **three masterpieces by Eugène Delacroix:** "Jacob Wrestling with the Angel," "Heliodorus Driven from the Temple," and "St-Michael Vanquishing the Devil" (on the right just after you enter the church). Jean-Baptiste Pigalle's statue of the "Virgin and Child" lights up the Chapelle de la Vierge at the farthest most point from the entrance. A bronze line runs north–south along the floor; this is part of a **gnomon,** an astronomical device set up in the 17th century to calculate the position of the sun in the sky. A small hole in one of the stained-glass windows creates a spot of light on the floor; every day at noon it hits the line in a different spot, climbing up to the top of an obelisk and lighting a gold disk at the winter equinox. Because of their size, churches were an ideal spot for this type of measurement, making for a rare collaboration between science and religion.

Place St-Sulpice, 6th arrond. $\mathcal{C}$ **01-42-34-59-98.** Free admission. Daily 7:30am–7:30pm. Métro: St-Sulpice.

Eiffel Tower & Les Invalides (7th Arrondissement)

The Iron Lady towers above this stately neighborhood, where the very buildings seem to insist that you stand up straight and pay attention. Stuffed with embassies and ministries, you'll see lots of elegant black cars with smoked glass cruising the streets, as well as many a tourist eyeing the **Eiffel Tower** or the golden dome of **Les Invalides,** and scurrying in and out of some of the city's best museums, like the **Musée du Quai Branly, Musée d'Orsay,** and **Musée Rodin.**

Eiffel Tower ★★★ MONUMENT   In his wildest dreams, Gustave Eiffel probably never imagined that the tower he built for the 1889 World's fair would become the ultimate symbol of Paris, and for many, of France. Originally slated for demolition after its first 20 years, the Eiffel Tower has survived over a century and is one of the most-visited sites in the nation. No less than 50 engineers and designers worked on the plans, which resulted in a remarkably solid structure that despite its height (324m/1,063 ft., including the antenna) does not sway in the wind.

But while the engineers rejoiced, others howled. When the project for the tower was announced, a group of artists and writers, including Guy de Maupassant and Alexandre Dumas *fils,* published a manifesto that referred to it as an "odious column of bolted metal." Others were less diplomatic: Novelist Joris-Karl Huysmans called it a "hole-riddled suppository." Despite the objections, the tower was built—over 18,000 pieces of iron, held together with some 2.5 million rivets. In this low-tech era, building

No need to go to the gym after marching up the 704 steps that lead you to the second floor of the Eiffel Tower. Not only will you burn calories, but you'll save money: At 5€ for adults, 4€ ages 12 to 24, and 3€ ages 4 to 11, this is the least expensive way to visit. Extra perks include an up-close view of the amazing metal structure and avoiding the long lines for the elevator.

techniques involved a lot of elbow grease: The foundations, for example, were dug entirely by shovel, and the debris was hauled away in horse-drawn carts. Construction dragged on for 2 years, but finally, on March 31, 1889, Gustave Eiffel proudly led a group of dignitaries up the 1,710 steps to the top, where he unfurled the French flag for the inauguration.

Over 100 years later, the tower has become such an integral piece of the Parisian landscape that it's impossible to think of the city without it. Over time, even the artists came around—the tower's silhouette can be found in the paintings of Seurat, Bonnard, Duffy, Chagall, and especially those of Robert Delaunay, who devoted an entire series of canvases to the subject. It has also inspired a whole range of stunts, from Pierre Labric riding a bicycle down the stairs from the first level in 1923, to Philippe Petit walking a 700m-long (2,296-ft.) tightrope from the Palais de Chaillot to the tower during the centennial celebration in 1989. Eiffel performed his own "stunts" towards the end of his career, using the tower as a laboratory for scientific experiments. By convincing the authorities of the tower's usefulness in studying meteorology, aerodynamics, and other subjects, Eiffel saved it from being torn down.

The most dramatic view of the tower itself is from the wide esplanade at the Palais de Chaillot (Métro: Trocadéro) across the Seine. From there it's a short walk down through the gardens and across the Pont d'Alma to the base. Though several elevators whisk visitors skyward, they do take time to come back down, so be prepared for a wait. The first floor boasts new chic pavilions and displays and part of the floor is now glassed over so that visitors can literally "walk on air". Personally, I think the view from the second level is the best; you're far enough up to see the entire city, yet still close enough to clearly pick out the various monuments. But if you are aching to get to the top, an airplanelike view awaits. The third level is, mercifully, enclosed, but thrill-seekers can climb up a few more stairs to the outside balcony (entirely protected with a grill).

Champ de Mars, 7th arrond. ⓒ **01-44-11-23-23.** www.tour-eiffel.fr. Lift to 2nd floor 9€ adults, 7.50€ ages 12–24, 4.50€ ages 4–11; Lift to 2nd and 3rd floors 15€ adults, 14€ ages 12–24, 11€ ages 4–11; stairs to 2nd floor 5€ adults, 4€ ages 12–24, 3€ ages 4–11. Free admission for children 3 and under. Mid-June to Aug daily 9am–midnight, Sept to mid-June daily 9:30am–11pm; Sept to mid-June stairs open only to 6pm. Métro: Trocadéro or Bir Hakeim. RER: Champ de Mars–Tour Eiffel.

Hôtel des Invalides/Napoleon's Tomb ★★ MUSEUM Military history rules at this grandiose complex, which houses a military museum, church, tomb, hospital, and military ministries, among other things. Over the entryway, LUDOVICUS MAGNUS is inscribed in huge letters, in homage to the builder of this vast edifice, otherwise known as Louis XIV. Determined to create a home for soldiers wounded in the line of duty, Louis commissioned architect Libéral Bruant to design a monumental structure with formal gardens on what was then the outskirts of the city. The first war veterans arrived in 1674—between 4,000 and 5,000 soldiers would eventually move in, creating a minicity with its own governor. An on-site hospital was constructed for the severely wounded, which is still in service today.

As you cross the main gate, you'll find yourself in a huge courtyard (102×207m, 335×207 ft.), the *cour d'honneur,* which was once the site of military parades. At the far end on the second story is a statue of "The Little Corporal" (Napoleon I) that once stood on top of the column in place Vendôme. The surrounding buildings house military administration offices and the recently renovated **Musée de l'Armée,** one of the world's largest military museums, with a vast collection of objects testifying to man's capacity for self-destruction. The most impressive section is **Arms and Armor,** a panoply of 13th- to 17th-century weaponry. Viking swords, Burgundian battle axes, 14th-century blunderbusses, Balkan *khandjars,* Browning machine guns, engraved Renaissance serpentines, musketoons, grenadiers—if it can kill, it's enshrined here. And that's just the beginning. There is also a huge wing covering the exploits everyone from **Louis XIV to Napoleon III,** another on the two **World Wars,** and a shrine to **Charles de Gaulle.** Also onsite is the **Musée des Plans et Reliefs,** a somewhat dusty collection of scale models of fortresses and battlefields.

The **Eglise des Soldats** is actually the front half of the **Eglise du Dôme,** which was split in two when Napoleon's tomb was installed under the dome. The "Soldier's Church" is lovely and light-filled, decorated with magnificent chandeliers and a collection of flags of defeated enemies.

On the other side of the glass partition rests the Little Corporal himself. The **Tomb of Napoléon** lies under one of the most splendid domes in France. Designed by Hardouin-Mansart and constructed from 1679 to 1706 the interior soars 107m (351 ft.) up to a skylight, which illuminates a brilliantly colored cupola fresco by Charles de la Fosse. Ethereal light filters down to an opening in the center of the room, where you can look down on the huge porphyry sarcophagus, which holds the emperor's remains, encased in five successive coffins (one tin, one mahogany, two lead, and one ebony). Surrounding the sarcophagus are the tombs of two of Napoleon's brothers, his son, and several French military heroes. Don't blame the over-the-top setting on Napoleon; the decision to transfer his remains to Paris was made in 1840, almost 20 years after his death. Tens of thousands of people crowded the streets to pay their respects as the coffin was carried under the Arc de Triomphe and down the Champs-Élysées to Les Invalides, where it waited another 20 years until the spectacular tomb was finished.

Place des Invalides, 7th arrond. ℭ **01-44-42-37-72.** www.invalides.org. Admission to all the museums, the church, and Napoleon's Tomb: 9.50€ adults, free for 17 and younger. Apr–Oct 10am–6pm, Nov–Mar 10am–5pm. Métro: Latour-Maubourg, Varenne, Invalides; RER: Invalides.

Musée des Egouts de Paris ★ MUSEUM   If you want to get a better idea of Jean Valjean's underground ordeal in "Les Miserables," take a trip through Paris's sewer museum. Though you won't actually get on a boat, you will be able to walk through a short stretch of the city's 2,400 km (1,490 miles) of sewers (don't worry, you'll be on a raised sidewalk on the side of the, uh, water), which should give you a pretty good idea of the different types of passageways and equipment that exist in this underground domain. There's also a film and a circuit of displays that explain the history of the city's water supply and waste disposal issues (this was no joke, for centuries the lack of a proper sewage system helped spread diseases like the Black Plague), as well as technical aspects of this stinky world. Because it is indeed stinky—delicate noses should think twice before entering.

Pont de l'Alma, in front of 93 quai d'Orsay, 7th arrond. (✆ **01-53-68-27-81.** www.paris.fr. Admission 4.40€ adults; 3.60€ students, and children 6–16; free for children 5 and younger. May–Sept Sat–Wed 11am–5pm; Oct–Apr Sat–Wed 11am–4pm. Métro: Alma-Marceau. RER: Pont de l'Alma.

Musée d'Orsay ★★★ MUSEUM   What better setting for a world-class museum of 19th-century art than a beautiful example of Belle Époque architecture? The magnificent Gare d'Orsay train station, built to coincide with the 1900 World's Fair, has been brilliantly transformed into an exposition space. The huge, airy central hall lets in lots of natural light, which has been artfully combined with artificial lighting to illuminate a collection of treasures that were once scattered among the Louvre and the Musée National d'Art Moderne.

The collection spans the years 1848 to 1914, a period that saw the birth of many artistic movements, such as the Barbizon School and Symbolism, but today it is best known for the emergence of Impressionism. Seeing them all together in one place makes it instantly obvious what a fertile time this was. All the superstars of the epoch are here, including Monet, Manet, Degas, Renoir, Cézanne, and Van Gogh.

The top floor is the home of the most famous Impressionist paintings, like Edouard Manet's masterpiece, "Le Déjeuner sur l'Herbe." Though Manet's composition of bathers and friends picnicking on the grass draws freely from those of Italian Renaissance masters, the painting shocked its 19th-century audience, which was horrified to see a naked lady lunching with two fully clothed men. Manet got into trouble again with his magnificent "Olympia," a seductive odalisque stretched out on a divan. There was nothing new about the subject; viewers were rattled by the unapologetic look in her eye—this is not an idealized nude, but a real woman, and a tough cookie, to boot.

The middle level is devoted to the post-Impressionists with works by artists like Gauguin, Seurat, Rousseau, and Van Gogh, like the latter's "Church at Auvers-sur-Oise," an ominous version of the church in a small town north of Paris where he moved after spending time in an asylum in Provence. This was one of some 70 paintings he produced in the 2 months leading up to his suicide.

A few other standouts:

o Renoir's "Dance at Le Moulin de la Galette, Montmartre"—the dappled light and the movement of the crowd in this joyous painting are such that you wonder if it's not going to suddenly waltz out of its frame. The blurred brushstrokes that created this effect rankled contemporary critics.

o Monet's "La Gare St-Lazare"—here is another train station when steam engines were still pulling in on a regular basis. The metallic roof of the station frames an almost abstract mix of clouds and smoke; rather than a description of machines and mechanics, this painting is a modern study of light and color.

o Gauguin's "The White Horse"—the horse isn't even really white, but you don't care when you gaze at Gauguin's Tahitian version of paradise. Not everyone was charmed by the artist's use of vibrant color: The pharmacist who commissioned the painting refused it because the horse was too green.

There are also sculptures and decorative arts on display here, including a remarkable collection of Art Nouveau furniture and objects. Photo fans will appreciate the fine examples of early photography, including Félix Nadar's portrait of Charles Baudelaire; there are also some interesting works by nonphotographers like Edward Dégas and Emile Zola.

1 rue de la Légion d'Honneur, 7th arrond. ℭ **01-40-49-48-14.** www.musee-orsay.fr. Admission 11€ adults, 8.50€ ages 18–25, free ages 17 and younger. Tues–Wed and Fri–Sun 9:30am–6pm; Thurs 9:30am–9:45pm. Métro: Solférino. RER: Musée d'Orsay.

Musée du Quai Branly ★★★ MUSEUM Just a few blocks from the Eiffel Tower, this museum's wildly contemporary design has forever changed the architectural landscape of this rigidly elegant neighborhood. Its enormous central structure floats on a series of pillars, under which lays a lush garden, which is separated from the noisy boulevard out front by a huge glass wall. Looking up from the garden level, the museum looks a little like the hull of a container ship, with its rust colored body and oddly stacked "boxes" sticking out from its sides. However you feel about the outside, you cannot help but be impressed by the inside: a vast space filled with exquisite examples of the traditional arts of Africa, the Pacific Islands, Asia, and the Americas. Designed by architect Jean Nouvel, this intriguing space makes an ideal showcase for a category of artwork that has too often been relegated to the sidelines of the museum world.

This magnificent collection is displayed in a way that invites you to admire the skill and artistry that went into the creation of these diverse objects. Delicately carved head rests from Papua New Guinea in the form of birds and crocodiles vie for your attention with intricately painted masks from Indonesia. There's a selection of giant wooden flutes from Papua New Guinea, "magic stones" from the island nation of Vanuatu, Australian aboriginal paintings, an extensive Asian art section, and an African collection, which includes embroidered silks from Morocco, geometric marriage cloths from Mali, and wooden masks from the Ivory Coast. The Americas collection includes rare Nazca pottery and Inca textiles, as well as an intriguing assortment of North American works, like Haitian voodoo objects, Sioux beaded tunics, and a huge totem pole from British Columbia. Though some documentation is translated in English, **audioguides** (5€) are a big help for non-French speakers.

37 quai Branly and 206 and 218 rue de Université, 7th arrond. ℭ **01-56-61-70-00.** www.quaibranly.fr. Admission 9€ adults, free for children 17 and younger. Tues–Wed and Sun 11am–7pm; Thurs–Sat 11am–9pm. Métro: Alma-Marceau. RER: Pont d'Alma.

Musée Rodin ★★★ MUSEUM There are not many museums that draw visitors who never even go inside. The grounds of this splendid place are so lovely that many are willing to pay 2€ just to stroll around. Behind the Hôtel Biron, which houses the museum, is a formal garden with benches, fountains and even a little cafe (no picnics allowed, unfortunately). Of course, it would be foolish not to go inside and drink in the some of the 6,600 sculptures of this excellent collection (don't worry, not all are on display), but it would be equally silly not to take the time to admire the large bronzes in the garden, which include some of Rodin's most famous works. Take for example, "The Thinker." Erected in front of the Panthéon in 1906 during an intense political crisis, Rodin's first public sculpture soon became a Socialist symbol and was quickly transferred to the Hôtel Biron by the authorities, under the pretense that it blocked pedestrian traffic. Other important sculptures in the garden include the "Burghers of Calais," "Balzac," and the "Gates of Hell," a monumental composition that the sculptor worked on throughout his career.

Indoors, marble compositions prevail, although there are also works in terracotta, plaster, and bronze, as well as sketches and paintings on display. The most famous of the marble works is "The Kiss," which was originally meant to appear in the "Gates of Hell." In time, Rodin decided that the lovers were too happy for this grim composition, and he explored it as an independent work. The sculpture was inspired by the tragic story of Paolo and Francesca, in which a young woman falls in love with her husband's brother. Upon their first kiss, the husband discovers them and stabs them both. As usual with Rodin's works, the critics were shocked by the couple's overt sensuality, but not as shocked as they were by the large, impressionistic rendition of "Balzac," exhibited at the same salon, which critic Georges Rodenbach described as "less a statue than a strange monolith, a thousand-year-old menhir." There are hundreds of works here, many of them legendary, so don't be surprised if after a while your vision starts to blur. That'll be your cue to head outside and enjoy the garden. Note: The Hôtel Biron has been undergoing major renovations that are scheduled to be finished by 2015, but don't be surprised if parts of the building are still closed during your visit. The most famous pieces should still be on display (though in less than optimal viewing conditions), and the statues in the garden will all be present and accounted for.

79 rue de Varenne, 7th arrond. (© **01-44-18-61-10.** www.musee-rodin.fr. Admission 9€ adults, 7€ ages 18–25, free for children 17 and younger. Tues and Thurs–Sun 10am–5:30pm, Wed 10am–8:30pm. Métro: Varenne or St-Francois-Xavier.

Montparnasse (14th & 15th Arrondissements)

Even though its heart was ripped out of it in the early 1970s, when the original 19th century train station was torn down and the Tour Montparnasse, an ugly skyscraper, was erected, this neighborhood still retains a redolent whiff of its artistic past. Back in the day, artists such as Picasso, Modigliani, and Man Ray hung out in cafes like **Le Dôme, La Coupole, La Rotonde,** and **Le Sélect,** as did a "Lost Generation" of English-speaking writers like Hemmingway, Fitzgerald, Faulkner, and James Joyce. Today the cafes are mostly filled with rich tourists, but there are still quiet corners and even artists' studios.

Cimetière du Montparnasse ★ CEMETERY   This quiet cemetery is the final resting place of many French celebrities. A map to the left of the main gateway will direct you to the gravesite of its most famous couple, Simone de Beauvoir and Jean-Paul Sartre. Others resting here include Samuel Beckett, Guy de Maupassant, Pierre Larousse (famous for his dictionary), Capt. Alfred Dreyfus, auto tycoon André Citroën; sculptors Ossip Zadkine and Constantin Brancusi, actress Jean Seberg, composer Camille Saint-Saëns, photographer Man Ray, poet Charles Baudelaire, and American intellectual and activist Susan Sontag, who was interred here in 2005. You can download a map on the municipal website, www.paris.fr.

3 bd. Edgar-Quinet, 14th arrond. (© **01-44-10-86-50.** www.paris.fr. Mon–Fri 8am–6pm; Sat 8:30am–6pm; Sun 9am–6pm. Métro: Edgar-Quinet.

Les Catacombes ★ CEMETERY/HISTORIC SITE   Definitely not for the faint of heart, the city's catacombs are filled with the remains of millions of ex-Parisians, whose bones line the narrow passages of this mazelike series of tunnels. In the 18th century, the Cimetière des Innocents, a centuries-old, overpacked cemetery near Les Halles, had become so foul and disease-ridden that it was finally declared a health hazard and closed. The bones of its occupants were transferred to this former quarry, which were later joined by those of other similarly pestilential Parisian cemeteries. In 1814, the quarry stopped accepting new lodgers, and the quarry inspector had a novel idea. Rather than leaving just a hodgepodge of random bones, he organized them in neat stacks and geometric designs, punctuating the 2 kilometers (1¼ miles) with sculptures and pithy sayings carved into the rock. The one at the entrance sets the tone: STOP—HERE IS THE EMPIRE OF DEATH. The visit will be fascinating for some, terrifying for others; not a good idea for claustrophobics or small children. The lighting is appropriately eerie, so you should bring a flashlight if you really want to see. Explanations are in English, French, and Spanish. The ceiling drips, so a hooded jacket or sweatshirt and rubber-soled shoes are indispensable. You'll want to bring a sweater of some sort anyway, as it's cool down here (around 54°F/12°C).

1 avenue du Colonel Henri Rol-Tanguy, 14th arrond. (☏ **01-43-22-47-63.** www.catacombes.paris.fr. Admission 8€ adults, 6€ seniors, 4€ ages 14–26, free for children 13 and younger. Tues–Sun 10am–5pm (last entry at 4pm). Métro: Denfert-Rochereau.

Musée Bourdelle ★ MUSEUM This museum is a testament to the sculptor Antoine Bourdelle, whose work went far beyond the 10 years he spent as Rodin's assistant. A renowned teacher who influenced an entire generation of sculptors, including Alberto Giacometti and Aristide Maillol, Bourdelle was one of the pioneers of 20th-century monumental sculpture. Proud, muscular centaurs, gods, and goddesses stride across these rooms, as well as monuments to famous people. You can also visit the sculptor's studio. Audioguides in English (5€) are a big help here.

18 rue Antoine-Bourdelle, 15th arrond. (☏ **01-49-54-73-73.** www.bourdelle.paris.fr. Free admission to the permanent collection. Tues–Sun 10am–6pm. Métro: Montparnasse-Bienvenüe.

ORGANIZED TOURS & CLASSES

If you've only got a couple of days and you just don't have the stamina to do the research, an organized tour can provide good background information on the city and help you get your bearings. Here are a few ideas for getting to know Paris in an easy and different way.

Boat Tours

The famed **Bateaux-Mouches** (☏ **01-42-25-96-10;** www.bateaux-mouches.fr; Métro: Alma-Marceau) cruises leave from Pont de l'Alma on the Right Bank of the Seine, and last for a little over 1 hour; though they tend to be crowded and touristy, it still can be a worthwhile way to enjoy the beauty of the sites alone the Seine. Tickets cost 13€ for adults, 5.50€ for kids 4 to 11, free 3 and under; the recorded commentary is in French, English and up to 3 other languages.

On the other side of the river, in front of the Eiffel Tower, the **Bateaux Parisiens** (☏ **01-76-64-14-45;** www.bateauxparisiens.com; Métro: Bir Hakeim; RER: Champ de Mars Tour Eiffel) offers similar 1-hour tours, but in smaller boats. The recorded commentary is available in 13 languages, and tickets cost 13€ for adults, 5€ children 3 to 12, free 2 and under. Bateaux Parisiens also runs a tour departing from Notre-Dame but the service is a lot less regular.

A little less touristy, the **Vedettes du Pont Neuf** (☎ **01-46-33-98-38;** www.vedettes dupontneuf.com; Métro: Pont Neuf) runs hour-long cruises with live guides in French and English from the Square du Vert Galant at the tip of the Ile de la Cité. Tickets cost 14€ for adults, 7€ children 4 to 12, free 3 and under; cheaper tickets can be bought on the Internet.

Canauxrama (☎ **01-42-39-15-00;** www.canauxrama.com; Métro: Jaurés or Bastille) tours the picturesque Canal St-Martin. Boats leave from either the Bassin de la Villette or the Bassin de l'Arsenal (near the place de la Bastille) and tickets cost 16€ for adults, 8.50€ children 4 to 12, free 3 and under. The cruise takes about 2½ hours. The first part, which runs under the place de la Bastille, is a little gloomy, but after you'll enjoy a lovely ride through locks and under pretty arched bridges. Tours daily from May to September; less frequent service the rest of the year.

Bus Tours

If you can stand the kitschy atmosphere, the hop-on, hop off buses are not a bad way to go if you want to see the city in a hurry. **L'Open Tour** (☎ **01-42-66-56-56;** www.parislopentour.com) offers four routes, which run from around 9am to 7pm. A 1-day adult pass costs 31€, and a 2-day pass 36€; either pass is 16€ for children 4 to 11. **Big Bus Paris** (formerly "Les Cars Rouges"; ☎ **01-53-95-39-53;** www.cars rouges.com) offers a hop-on, hop-off trip that stops at nine top sites from around 9:30am to 7:30pm. There's multilingual commentary available. A 2-day adult ticket costs 31€, 13€ for children 4 to 12.

Cycling Tours

Fat Tire Bike Tours (☎ **01-56-58-10-54;** www.fattirebiketours.com/paris; Métro: Dupleix) offers a 4-hour day- or night-tour of Paris by bike in English; adult tickets cost 30€, 28€ students and children 4 to 12. Kid-sized bikes and toddler trailers available. They also offer tours of Versailles and Giverny.

Paris à Vélo, C'est Sympa (22 rue Alphonse Baudin, 11th arrond.; ☎ **01-48-87-60-01;** www.parisvelosympa.com; Métro: Richard Lenoir) offers 3 themed 3-hour bike tours in French and English: Heart of Paris, Unusual Paris, and Paris Contrasts. Adult tickets cost 34€, 28€ ages 12 to 25, 18€ 11 and under. They also rent bikes.

Bike About Tours (☎ **06-18-80-84-92;** www.bikeabouttours.com) offers 3½ hour tours in small groups, led by friendly, knowledgeable, fluent-English speakers for 30€ per person (28€ students). All tours leave from the statue of Charlemagne in front of Notre-Dame at 10am (and 3pm during the summer) and focus on back streets and neighborhoods (you'll see major monuments too). Bike rentals here too.

Other Guided Tours

4 Roues Sous 1 Parapluie (☎ **08-00-80-06-31;** www.4roues-sous-1parapluie.com) offers chauffeur-driven themed rides around Paris in its colorful fleet of Citroën 2CV, the tiny, low-cost and now classic French car that was jokingly referred to as "4 wheels under an umbrella." If there are three people in the car, prices start at 10€ per person for a 15-minute tour and 60€ per person for a 1½ hour tour. The fewer people in the car, the more expensive the tour.

Paris is a dream-come-true for shopaholics. **Chic Shopping Paris** (☎ **09-77-19-77-85;** www.chicshoppingparis.com) offers tours in English designed to give visitors a behind-the-scenes shopping experience. Themed tours include a Chic and Cheap tour, a Sunday Shopping tour, and an Arts and Antiques tour of a flea market. Tours last 4 to 4½ hours and start at 100€ per person; custom tours are available.

Hot Air Balloon Tours

A unique way to see the city from above is by a hot air balloon. Located in the Parc André Citroën in the 15th arrondissement, **Ballon de Paris** (✆ **01-44-26-20-00;** www.ballondeparis.com; Métro Javel or Balard) has a hot air balloon that reaches an altitude of 150m (492 ft.) but remains tethered to the ground. Tickets cost 12€ adults, 6€ ages 3 to 11, free 2 and under. Tours can be cancelled due to weather conditions; check website or call ahead to make sure the balloon is flying.

Walking Tours

Sight Seeker's Delight (✆ **07-63-07-09-68;** www.sightseekersdelight.com) offers a range of walking tours in English, including Paris along the Seine, Père Lachaise Cemetery, and a night tour. Tours last from 2½ to 4 hours and prices vary between 25€ and 40€ per person (ages 4 to 10 half price, 3 and under free).

Paris Walks (✆ **01-48-09-21-40;** www.paris-walks.com) organizes 2-hour walks of the city, based on either a theme or a neighborhood. Most of the walks cost 12€ for adults (10€ ages 15–20, and 8€ 14 and under) and do not require reservations, but some, such as the Chocolate Tour, need to be booked in advance.

Paris Greeters (www.parisgreeters.fr) arranges free tours for 1 to 6 people with local volunteers. There's no catalogue of specific tours; your walk is pretty much up to the greeter, who will choose a neighborhood. You register online and request a specific day and language, you'll then be contacted with the details of your tour.

Cooking Classes

There are several cooking schools in Paris that offer short term or 1-day courses. The most famous is **Le Cordon Bleu** (✆ **01-53-68-22-50;** www.cordonbleu.edu; Métro: Vaugirard)—this is where Julia Child mastered the art of French cooking. Well known for its professional cooking courses, it also offers short courses for lay food enthusiasts, with prices starting at 45€ for a 2-hour demonstration and 105€ for a 3-hour hands-on lesson. Classes are translated into English and fill up fast; reserve ahead.

Less formal but equally enjoyable are the cooking classes offered by **La Cuisine Paris** (✆ **01-40-51-78-18;** www.lacuisineparis.com; Métro: Hôtel de Ville), a friendly school set up by a Franco-American team. They offer small classes by professional chefs in both French and English, including the popular French Macaron Class. Prices range from 65€ for 2 hours to 150€ for 4 hours.

Similarly, **Cook'n with Class** (✆ **01-42-57-22-84;** www.cooknwithclass.com; Métro: Simplon or Jules Joffrin) offers a range of individual and small-group classes, the most popular of which is the Morning Market Class; it includes a walk to a local market. Set up by a French chef, all classes are taught in English by professionals and prices range from 125€ for 3-hour classes to 185€ for 5-hour classes.

Language Classes

The **Alliance Française** (✆ **01-42-84-90-00;** www.alliancefr.org) has been offering quality French classes for almost a century. Depending on how many hours and what kind of course you take, courses cost 100€–250€ per week for 1–3 weeks; rates go down when you attend more than 3 weeks.

OUTDOOR ACTIVITIES

"Working out" is still a somewhat foreign concept in France, but that doesn't mean that you can't exercise. Though gyms are few and far between, pools are everywhere, and any enterprising sports enthusiast can easily find places to bike, rollerblade, or run.

Public Pools

There are 38 public pools (*piscines,* pronounced "pee-*seen*") in Paris, and they are accessible to everyone. They are generally quite clean and always have lockers and dressing areas. The size of the pools varies—most are 25m (82 ft.), and a few, like the one at Les Halles, are 50m (164 ft.). The most unusual is the **Piscine Josephine Baker** (② 01-56-61-96-50; Métro: Quai de la Gare), a floating swimming pool docked on quai François Mauriac in the Seine (don't worry, the water is not from the river). The best way to find addresses and hours is to visit www.paris.fr and click on the blue "piscine" icon on the upper right-hand corner. Entry to almost all municipal pools is 3€; you can buy a card for 10 entries for 24€.

Ice-Skating Rinks

There are **two indoor municipal ice-skating rinks** open year round: Patinoire Pailleron (32 rue E. Pailleron, 19th arrond.; ② 01-40-40-27-70; www.pailleron19.com; Métro: Bolivar) and Patinoire Sonja Henie (8 bd. Bercy, 12th arrond.; ② 01-40-02-60-60; Métro: Bercy). The latter has DJ-hosted soirees until midnight Fridays and Saturdays. In addition, every year, **two large outdoor rinks** are set up from December through February in front of the **Hôtel de Ville** and the **Gare Montparnasse.** Both are free—you'll just have to pay a small fee for skate rental. For more information all of these rinks, visit www.sport.paris.fr and search for "patinoire."

Cycling

You can **rent a bike** by the hour in the **Bois de Vincennes** at Lac Daumesnil or Lac des Minimes and in the **Bois de Boulogne** (in front of the Jardin d'Acclimatation or next to the Lac Inferieur [lower lake]). If you are up to the challenge of Parisian traffic and want to cycle around the city, you can try **Velib',** the city's wildly popular rent-a-bike program—just be sure you are armed with the right kind of credit card or have picked up an internet subscription for your stay (for details on how the system works, visit www.velib.fr and/or see p. 226). For longer-term rentals, try **Paris à Vélo, C'est Sympa** (www.parisvelosympa.com) or **Bike About Tours** (www.bikeabouttours.com).

Running

Today, *le footing,* as running is called, is considered pretty commonplace, though nowhere near as omnipresent as in London or New York. You can run anywhere, of course, but a few favored places are around the lakes in the **Bois de Boulogne** and the **Bois de Vincennes** (see below), the **Promenade Plantée** (p. 133), along the quays of the Seine, and the Jardin du Luxembourg.

Tennis

The French are huge tennis fans, and Parisians are no exception. There are **43 public tennis courts** in the city, all of which can be reserved online at the city's website (www.paris.fr/tennis). The courts in the **Jardin de Luxembourg** are particularly nice, as are those in the **Marais** (5–7 rue Neuve-Saint-Pierre, 4th arrond.; Métro: Saint Paul). The fee for an hour of play is 7.50€ in an open court, and 14€ for covered courts. *Note:* You will need to bring your own tennis equipment.

Parks

There are two huge parks on the outskirts of Paris where you can bike, run and even watch horse races.

Bois de Boulogne ★★ PARK   In the 7th century, Dagobert, King of the Francs, used to go hunting in the woods that we now know as the Bois de Boulogne; it remained a hunting domain for the kings of France up until Louis XVI, who finally opened it up to the public. That was mighty grand of him, and we thank him for it—this lovely natural haven is just what stressed-out Parisians need. Thick stands of trees, broken up by grassy knolls, manicured gardens, and even a lake or two plus several posh restaurants are tucked into this verdant spread. There is even a nice spot for tiny urbanites to unwind: The **Jardin d'Acclimatation** (see below), a large children's garden/amusement park, is a delight for kids of all ages.

What you see today, however, is not what Dagobert saw. Once Louis XVI was beheaded, and the Revolution got underway, the park was ravaged. What was left of it was completely demolished during subsequent military campaigns: In 1814 it was occupied and pillaged by some 40,000 English and Russian soldiers. It wasn't until Napoleon III decided to remodel the entire city in the mid-1800s that the Bois de Boulogne was attended to. Inspired by the English public parks that he had visited during his years of exile, the Emperor gave the command to rebuild the park. Over 400,000 trees were planted, and dozens of chalets, pavilions, snack stands, and restaurants were built. A network of roads and trails was laid down totaling 95km (59

The New Banks of the Seine & Paris Plage

Over the last couple of years, portions of the Seine's banks have had a pedestrian-friendly overhaul, most impressively along the stretch between the Musée d'Orsay to the Pont d'Alma (known as **Les Berges,** or "the embankments"). Not only have cars been banished, but the quays have been embellished with promenades, gardens, cultural spaces, cafes, sports facilities, and picnic areas. You can eat, drink, flirt at one of the bars, walk, or even take a tai chi class at various points along the route. There are kids' activities too. For details and schedules visit www.lesberges.paris.fr.

Meanwhile, another hugely successful riverside event is now into its second decade: **Paris Plage.** Every year, from mid-July to mid-August, tons of sand are shipped in and dumped on the riverbanks to create a fun and funky "beach," complete with beach volleyball, tea dances, concerts, drink stands, and all sorts of excellent silliness. Success has been such that the beach can be found on the Voie Georges Pompidou (near the Hôtel de Ville, 4th arrond.) but also along edges of the Bassin de la Villette (19th arrond.), where you can rent paddleboats and canoes. The number of activities and events swells every season, for a complete rundown visit the city website (www.paris.fr) and search "Paris Plage English."

miles). Finally, the park was ready for the public, and the public was definitely ready for the park. Here are a few of its most popular areas:

○ The **Parc de Bagatelle** is a park-within-a-park, a lush **garden,** a small **château** (where in the summer there are concerts, check listing magazines for details), and a **rose garden** with over 1,000 varieties. New varieties are introduced every year in June, during an international rose competition. The version of the garden you see today was designed by Forestier, a friend of Monet, who was inspired by Impressionism, which is evident in the artfully placed clusters of flowers and plants.

○ The **Pré Catelan** is most famous for its elegant and extremely pricey restaurant, but there are plenty of other reasons to come here. This green enclave includes lush lawns, playgrounds, and flowerbeds, as well as the **Jardin Shakespeare,** which attempts to re-create settings from the Bard's plays. Here you'll find the heaths of Macbeth, the Forest of Arden, and the pond where Ophelia meets her watery death.

○ The **Jardin d'Acclimatation** is an old-fashioned amusement park, with lots of grassy areas and nifty playgrounds (see "Especially for Kids," below)

In addition to walking, rollerblading, and cycling (**bike rentals** at the edge of the Lac Inferieur and at the Jardin d'Acclimatation), you can **rent a boat** on the lake or even **go fishing** in some of the ponds.

16th arrond. www.paris.fr. Métro: Porte d'Auteuil, Les Sablons, Porte Maillot, or Porte Dauphine.

Bois de Vincennes ★★ PARK   There aren't as many gardens and restaurants here as in its western counterpart, but there is more of a sense of wilderness in this vast patch of greenery on the eastern end of Paris. Endless paths and alleys wind through woods and open fields; this is a great place for a long bike ride or a hike. Not that there are just trees here—if rambling isn't your game, there are plenty of other things to do as well. For starters, there is the newly reopened **Parc Zoologique de Paris** (p. 133), a state-of-the-art zoo. Then there are the remains of a medieval castle and a large garden in the park, as well as theaters and a hippodrome for those who prefer to sit back and watch the action. In short, there are almost as many pleasures here as in the Bois de Boulogne, if not as much elegance.

Like the Bois de Boulogne, the Bois de Vincennes was once a royal hunting ground with a lodge built by Louis VII back in the 12th century. By the 13th century, it had grown into a castle, which Louis IX (St-Louis) became very fond of; it is said that he dispensed justice under one of the nearby oak trees. It wasn't until the 18th century, under Louis XV, that these woods were turned into a public park; unfortunately, after the Revolution, the army decided to use it as a training ground, and the castle became a prison (some of its more famous lodgers included the Marquis de Sade and the philosopher Denis Diderot). Needless to say, this did not do wonders for the landscaping. Finally, in the 19th century, Napoleon III made the park part of his urban renewal scheme, and it got the same thorough makeover as the Bois de Boulogne. Its troubles were not completely over however. In 1944, the retreating German army left the château in ruins, but it has since been almost completely restored.

A few of the park's high points:

○ The **Parc Zoologique de Paris** (aka the Paris Zoo), see p. 133.

○ The **Parc Floral**—created in 1969, this modern mix of **flowerbeds, ponds, picnic areas,** and **playgrounds** (including a few rides) is a very pleasant place to spend the afternoon, particularly between May and September when there are free music and theater performances at the open-air theater. In July, the Paris Jazz

Festival takes off for 3 weeks, and in most of August and September, the Festival Classique au Vert cooks up a great program of classical music. For the kids, **Guignol puppet shows** (www.guignolparcfloral.com; 2.80€ adults and children) play most Wednesdays, Saturdays, and Sundays at 3pm and 4pm, and every day during school holidays.

○ The **Château de Vincennes**—I'll bet you didn't know there was a medieval castle in Paris. Well, there is, and after 12 years of restoration, you can visit the imposing **castle keep,** a **gothic chapel** with 16th century stained glass windows, and the multi-turreted **ramparts,** on top of which you can take a stroll and pretend you are a knight on the lookout for enemy invaders (ave. de Paris, 12th arrond.; www.chateau-vincennes.fr; ℂ **01-48-08-31-20; 8.50€** adults, 5.50€ 18–25, free 17 and under; mid-Sept to mid-May 10am–5pm, mid-May to mid-Sept 10am–6pm; Métro: Château de Vincennes).

Like the Bois de Boulogne, there are plenty of other outdoor activities here. You can **rent bikes** in front of either of the two large lakes, or on the esplanade by the château, or **boats** for rowing around the lake. There are several **playgrounds,** as well as a **farm** (La Ferme de Paris) where children can watch cows being milked and sheep being shorn. There is also a **hippodrome** here for thoroughbred racing fans.

Bois de Vincennes, 12th arrond. www.paris.fr. Admission free to main park. Parc Floral admission: Oct–May free, June–Sept Wed, Sat–Sun 5.5€ adults, 2.75€ ages 7 to 25, free ages 6 and under, Mon–Tues and Thurs–Fri free. Metro: Porte Dorée or Château de Vincennes.

ESPECIALLY FOR KIDS

Paris is not an especially kid-friendly city, but it's not kid-unfriendly either. For one, Parisians generally like kids, as long as they are not running wild. If you visit in the summer, in addition to the suggestions below, just about any age child (including grown-up ones) will have a blast at **Paris Plage** or along the **newly reopened banks of the Seine** between Musée d'Orsay and Pont d'Alma (see box, above). Here are some attractions that children may enjoy:

Bois de Boulogne (p. 155)
Bois de Vincennes (p. 156)
Centre Pompidou (p. 119)
Château de Vincennes (p. 157)
Cité des Sciences et de l'Industrie (p. 134)
Gaîté Lyrique (p. 120)
Grévin (p. 117)
Jardin d'Acclimatation (p. 158)
Jardin des Plantes (p. 137)
Jardin des Tuileries (p. 109)
Jardin du Luxembourg (p. 143)
La Promenade Plantée (p. 133)
Les Dimanches du Galop (p. 204)
Musée des Arts et Métiers (p. 124)
Musée des Egouts de Paris (p. 147)
Muséum National d'Histoire Naturelle (p. 140)
Palais de Tokyo (p. 130)
Parc de la Villette (p. 137)

Created by an itinerant merchant and tooth-puller in Lyon about 200 years ago, **Guignol,** the sly hero of traditional French puppet shows, is still packing houses all over the country. This valiant valet, who often finds himself in difficult situations due to his master's mischief, has an amazing way with children, who scream, hoot, and holler according to how Guignol's adventures unfold. There's lots of audience participation: The wide-eyed puppet will ask the children to help him find the robber/wolf/bad guy, and then will promptly head in the wrong direction as the kids desperately try to get him back on track. It's noisy, but good fun—even if you don't understand French, the stories are pretty easy to fig-ure out. This is a great way to take part in an authentically French experience—though it might be a little overwhelming for sensitive souls under 3. Guignol puppet theaters can be found in the Jardin d'Acclimation, the Jardin du Luxembourg, the Parc Floral, Parc des Buttes-Chaumont, and on the Champs-Élysées. For listings and links, visit www.paris.fr and search for "guignol."

Parc des Buttes Chaumont (p. 137)
Parc Zoologique de Paris (p. 133)
Parc Floral (p. 156)
Eiffel Tower (p. 145)

And here are some more ideas for kid entertainment, according to age group:

FOR TINY TOTS (0–5 YEARS OLD): There are nice **playgrounds** with safe equip-ment all over the city. For precise locations, visit www.jardins.paris.fr (search "aires de jeux"), ask at your hotel, or just follow the strollers. The Tuileries Gardens and the Luxembourg Gardens both have a large fountain where you can **rent wooden toy sailboats** (for around 2€) and push them around with a long stick (a big hit with my son when he was 3-ish). Most large gardens or parks in this book have a **merry-go-round.** Kids will also love the activities in the Luxembourg gardens (see box, p. 143).

FOR THE MIDDLE YEARS (6–9 YEARS OLD): This is when it's time to turn to attractions like **Grévin** (p. 117), the **Cité des Enfants** (p. 136) the **Jardin d'Acclimatation** (p. 158), and if you are really desperate, there's always **Disneyland Paris** (p. 218). The newly reopened **Parc Zoologique de Paris** (p. 133) is a good bet; there another, smaller, **zoo** at the Jardin des Plantes (the Ménagerie, p. 140). You might also consider going to one of the nice **municipal pools** (p. 154), which usually include a kiddie pool.

FOR THE TWEENS (10–13 YEARS OLD): At this age the scale can tip both ways, between "not another museum!" and actually getting interested in some of the cultural offerings. A few museums are particularly suited to this age, like the **Musée des Arts et Metiers** (p. 124), the **Gaîté Lyrique** (p. 120), and in particular, the **Cité des Sci-ences et de l'Industrie. Boat** or **bike tours** (p. 151 and 152) also work for this crew.

Paris has one old-fashioned amusement park just off the Porte Maillot in the Bois de Boulogne:

Jardin d'Acclimatation ★ AMUSEMENT PARK/GARDEN   You'll see plenty of grandmothers in fur coats at this elegant amusement park, which is adjacent to the swank suburb of Neuilly. There's a farm with some animals, but the main attraction here are the rides, which include bumper cars, merry-go-rounds, and small roller coasters. As the rides *(manèges)* quickly add up (you pay as you go), you may want to point your offspring in the direction of the huge playground, which includes an area where kids can run around under giant sprinklers in the hot weather. In the same area, you'll find a puppet theater (www.guignol.fr; Wed, Sat–Sun, and school holidays 3 and 4pm); Guignol's adventures are presented free of charge. To reach the park from Porte Maillot, take the *Petit Train* (little train) from Allée de Longchamp just at the entrance to the Bois de Boulogne.

Bois de Boulogne. *C* **01-40-67-90-85.** www.jardindacclimatation.fr. Admission 3€ adults and children over 2 years old, 1.50€ seniors, free children 2 and younger; attractions 2.90€ per ticket, 35€ a book of 15 tickets. Apr–Sept 10am–7pm, Oct–Mar 10am–6pm. Métro: Sablons or Porte Maillot.

WALKING
TOURS OF PARIS

7

aris is a walking city. You simply won't be able to fully appreciate the flavor of the place if you don't get out, stroll through the streets and absorb the sights, sounds, and even smells that make up its sensory identity. A mere city block can encompass several centuries' worth of history and happenings. Below are walking tours of two of the city's best areas for ambling about.

WALKING TOUR 1: MONTMARTRE

START:	**Place des Abbesses (Métro: Abbesses).**
FINISH:	**Sacré Coeur (Métro: Abbesses).**
TIME:	**About 1½ hours.**
BEST TIME:	**Weekdays, when there are less crowds and stores are open.**
WORST TIME:	**Weekends, when the area around Sacré Cour looks like the Métro at rush hour.**

Montmartre has become forever linked with a certain mythic image of Paris: quaint cobblestone streets, accordion serenades, and the Sacré-Coeur hovering in the background. Or maybe it's the Moulin Rouge and cancan girls whooping it up on the place Blanche. Although the area just around the Sacré-Coeur is probably the most tourist-clogged in the capital and the Moulin Rouge is a tour-bus trap, there's still magic on the Butte, and it's not hard to find. If legendary artists like Picasso and Utrillo are gone, new ones have taken their place, and they aren't the ones hawking portraits in the place du Tertre. In fact, within a couple blocks from the mobs on the *place,* there actually *are* quiet cobbled streets, lined with lovely vine-trimmed houses, and punctuated by cute cafes and shops.

---

1 Place des Abbesses

The first thing you'll notice when you are coming out of the Métro is the exit itself: This lovely Art Nouveau confection of smoked glass and metal is one of two surviving Métro entrances by Hector Guimard with a glass roof. Now, look around the leafy plaza. Back in 1134, King Louis *Le Gros* (the Fat, otherwise known as Louis VI) founded an abbey up here, and this square is named after the various abbesses who ran it. As most of them came from wealthy,

Montmartre Walking Tour

1 Place des Abbesses
2 Bateau Lavoir
3 Moulin de la Galette and the Moulin du Radet
4 Allée des Brouillards
5 Place Dalida
6 Clos Montmartre Vineyard
7 Au Lapin Agile
8 Musée de Montmartre
9 Rue St-Rustique
10 Place du Tertre
11 Sacré Coeur

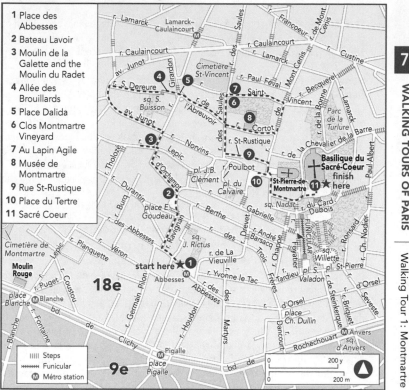

Montmartre for the Weary: Montmartrobus

The actual distance on the walk described below is not long, but the terrain will make it seem a lot longer. Montmartre is up on a high hill (a *butte*) overlooking the city, so be prepared for some steep ups and downs. Visitors with reduced mobility (or who are simply tired) might replace parts of this walk with the **Montmartrobus,** a bus that is part of the city bus system and makes a circuit of the Butte. The bus, which costs a regular Métro ticket, leaves place Pigalle every 15 minutes. For information and a map, visit www.ratp.fr.

aristocratic families, they did not fare well during the French Revolution. In 1794, the 43rd abbess, Louise de Montmorency-Laval, who was 71 years old and both blind and deaf, was guillotined and the abbey was pillaged. Her crime? She was found guilty of "blindly and deafly plotting against the revolution."

Walk west on rue des Abbesses to rue Ravignan, where you will make a right uphill. At the top of the short street is place Emile Goudeau. At no. 11bis–no. 13 is the:

2 Bateau-Lavoir

This building started out as a piano factory but later was home to a virtual hall of fame of artists, actors, and poets, when they were all young and struggling. In 1889, this odd edifice—constructed on different levels to accommodate the steep slope it was built on—was split up into artists' studios. By 1904, a young man named Pablo Picasso was living and working there, as well as Kees Van Dongen, Juan Gris, and Amadeo Modigliani, not to mention the poets Max Jacob and Guillaume Apollinaire, among others. It was here that Picasso painted "Les Demoiselles d'Avignon" (even though he was nowhere near Provence), a painting that signaled the birth of Cubism. Unfortunately, this fertile artistic breeding ground, which was dubbed the **Bateau Lavoir,** or the Floating Laundry, by Jacob, burned down in 1970. All that's left of the original structure is one facade on the small plaza. The rest was rebuilt in 1978 and today still houses artists' studios. You can see a few vine-covered studios here.

Turn left on tiny rue d'Orchampt, a quiet cobbled street, which curves up to an intersection with rue Lepic. Take a short detour left down rue Lepic to the:

3 Moulin de la Galette & Moulin du Radet

There were once over 30 windmills on Montmartre's slopes, which were covered in vineyards. Here are the last two that still exist, the **Moulin du Radet,** which is now a swank restaurant called the Moulin de la Galette. What is even more confusing is that the "real" **Moulin de la Galette,** of Renoir painting fame, is down the street at No. 75, and is also known as the Moulin Blute-Fin. Whatever its name, this old mill, which was owned by the same family of millers since the 17th century, was a witness to tragedy. In 1814, it had the misfortune of being attacked by a garrison of Cossacks, who were in town because the Allies (Germany, Prussia, and Russia, among a host of others) had come to Paris to stop French attacks on the rest of Europe and put Napoleon in his place. The miller tried valiantly to defend his property but ended up hacked to pieces and nailed to the blades of his windmill. Years later, the miller's son turned the farm into an outdoor music hall, the famous Moulin de la Galette depicted in a legendary painting by Renoir (you can see the painting at the Musée d'Orsay, p. 148). Other painters that frequented these bucolic dance parties included Toulouse-Lautrec, Van Gogh, and Utrillo. Today you won't get to dance here—the mill is private property and a prim little sign outside informs you that it is under electronic surveillance and protected by radars and guard dogs.

Return to rue Giradon and turn left, then left again on ave. Junot, walking past some of Montmartre's most elegant homes. Follow ave. Junot as it curves to the right, making a sharp right on rue Simon Dereure. The street ends at place Casadesus; climb the stairs to the footpath called:

4 Allée des Brouillards

This tranquil path leads past a number of massive houses, set back in large gardens, most of which are at least partially shielded from prying eyes by tall fences. The largest garden surrounds a white country manor known as the **Château des Brouillards,** or Fog Castle. Built in 1772 for a lawyer in the Parisian Parliament, this romantic dwelling most likely got its name from the mist that crept up from a nearby spring when the water contacted the cold morning air (real fog is a rare thing up here). Gérard de Nerval lived here in 1854, and surely this was the ideal writer's haven for this quintessential Romantic-era poet. Painter Pierre-Auguste Renoir lived and worked in one of the houses behind the Château; his son, filmmaker Jean Renoir, was born there.

Continue down the path to its end, at:

5 Place Dalida

This small crossroads is graced with a bust of one of Montmartre's most beloved residents, Yolanda Gigliotti, aka Dalida. This Egyptian-born singer, of Italian ancestry, was one of France's biggest stars, recording hundreds of hits and winning 70 gold records. The blond bombshell moved to the Butte in 1962, where she lived out the rest of her stormy life in a four-story mansion that her fans dubbed "Sleeping Beauty's Castle." After a series of unfortunate love affairs, two of which ended with her partners' suicides, she took her own life in 1987. Her **statue** looks out on one of the most prototypical views of Montmartre, down rue de l'Abreuvoir: a cobbled lane leading up a hill with the Sacré-Coeur in the background.

Walk up rue de l'Abreuvoir and turn left on rue des Saules:

6 Clos Montmartre Vineyard

As you make your way down rue des Saules, you will notice an unlikely vineyard on the right-hand side of the street. This is in fact the last of Montmartre's vineyards—for centuries the Butte was covered with them. Back in the 16th century, winemaking was the primary industry in the area—though nobody ever bragged about the high quality of the product, which was mainly known for its diuretic virtues. A ditty about Montmartre's wine went thus: "The wine of Montmartre—whoever drinks a pint, pisses a quarte." By the way, in those days, a "quarte" equaled 67 liters (70 quarts). Whatever its merits, this tiny vineyard still produces. Rare bottles of Clos Montmartre are auctioned off every year by the district and the proceeds benefit local public projects.

Continue down rue des Saules to the intersection with rue St-Vincent:

7 Au Lapin Agile

The story goes that a habitué of this rowdy corner cabaret—which was then called the Cabaret des Assassins—a certain André Gill, painted a sign for the place showing a rabbit *(lapin)* jumping out of a stock pot. The cabaret became known as the Lapin à Gill (Gill's rabbit), which in time mutated into Au Lapin Agile (the Agile Rabbit). The singer Aristide Bruant (immortalized in a poster by Toulouse-Lautrec) bought the inn in 1902, and asked Frédé, a local guitar legend, to run it. Under Frédé's guidance, the cabaret thrived, and the best and the brightest of the Montmartre scene was drawn to its doors, including Picasso, Verlaine, Renoir, Utrillo, and Apollinaire. Not everyone who came was a fan of modern art, however. The writer Roland Dorgelès had had enough of "Picasso's band" from the Bateau Lavoir and decided to play a trick on them: He tied a paintbrush to the end of Frédé's donkey, Lolo, and let him slop paint over a canvas. Dorgelès then entered the painting, which he titled "And the Sun Set Over the Adriatic," in the Salon des Independants, a major art show in Paris. The critics loved it—until they found out who really painted it and a scandal ensued. Today Au Lapin Agile is still a cabaret, though a much calmer one, showcasing traditional French *chanson* (see box on p. 194). The shows are heavy on nostalgia and sing-alongs, but they can be good fun.

Turn left on rue St-Vincent, then right on rue Mont Cenis. Climb the stairs and turn right on rue Cortot:

8 Musée de Montmartre

At No. 12 rue Cortot lies the recently overhauled **Musée de Montmartre** (*©* **01-49-25-89-37;** www.museedemontmartre.fr; p. 132), which offers an overview of the history of the neighborhood and is housed in the former residence of Rosimond, a famous 17th-century actor who was in Molière's troupe. In another century, Renoir painted here (this is where he created the "Bal du Moulin de la Galette"), as did Utrillo, who lived here with his mother, the model and painter Susan Valadon, and her lover André Utter.

Continue to the end of rue Cortot and turn left on rue des Saules; walk up to rue St-Rustique and turn left:

9 Rue St-Rustique

By now you'll have noticed the crowds thickening, and a change in the atmosphere towards the Disneyesque. Trinket shops appear on every corner, and "artists" badger you to draw your portrait. Dive quickly into rue St-Rustique, a narrow channel of calm. Not only does the noise die down, but you'll be rewarded with an excellent photo-op of the bulblike tops of Sacré Coeur sprouting above the end of the street. This is one of the oldest streets in Montmartre, with no sidewalks and a medieval-style gutter in its center.

Walk to the end of rue St-Rustique and turn right. On your right is the entrance to:

10 Place du Tertre

Now there's no avoiding it: the most tourist-drenched, mob-swamped spot in Paris. If you squint hard enough and use a tremendous amount of imagination, you'll see the lovely village square as it once was—but most likely you'll just be trampled by the crowds who are wandering around trying to figure out what all the fuss is about. Do not eat here, even if you are starving—you will be taken for a ride. A quick walk down the hill towards the place des Abbesses will lead you to plenty of nice restaurants and cafes. You will probably be approached by people begging to do your portrait—these "artists" may do nice caricatures, but if you think you're looking at the next Picasso, you're kidding yourself.

Duck back out of place du Tertre and continue down rue du Mont Cenis until it curls around to the left and becomes rue Azaïs. Keep walking until you're in front of:

11 Sacré Coeur

After you've looked up at the gleaming white basilica and its odd, pseudo-Byzantine domes, turn around and admire the stunning view from the esplanade, or parvis, in front of the church; on a clear day you can see as far as 50km (31 miles). No matter how many people are standing around snapping pictures, it just won't ruin the beauty of this sight. Though you won't be able to see the Eiffel Tower (it's too far over on the right, though you can see it if you climb up the dome) you will take in a majestic panorama that includes the Pompidou Centre, St-Eustache, the Opéra, and the Louvre, not to mention distant hills and vales

Cinemacity—A Walking Tour App for Film Buffs

If you get misty-eyed watching Paris on the big screen, this is the app for you. Created by the Franco-German TV channel **Arte**, known for its cultural programming, this app offers walking tours to locations where movies were filmed, and even lets you watch the clip. You can also follow a "fictionalized" route, where you walk from one point to another to follow a story line. You can get the app in French, English, or German, and what's more, it's free. For more info and links to downloads, visit http://cinemacity.arte.tv.

beyond the city. What you are mainly looking at here is eastern Paris, the more plebian side—an entirely appropriate view from this historically working-class, low-rent neighborhood. The view actually gets better as you walk down to the bottom-most level of the esplanade; from here you can also take in the lovely gardens below, which had a starring role in the ultimate Montmartre movie, "Amélie," by Jean-Pierre Jeunet.

WALKING TOUR 2: **THE MARAIS**

START:	**Village St-Paul (23–27 rue St-Paul, Métro: St-Paul).**
FINISH:	**Place des Vosges**
TIME:	**1½ hours, not including time spent in shops, restaurants, or museums.**
BEST TIME:	**During the week, when the streets are full of life, and Sundays, when unlike other parts of the city, many shops and restaurants are open.**
WORST TIME:	**Saturdays, when most of the neighborhood is flooded with shoppers, and the Jewish quarter is completely shut down.**

The Marais is one of the few areas that Baron Haussmann largely ignored when he was tearing up the rest of the city; for that reason it still retains a medieval feel. Though very few buildings actually date from the Middle Ages, this warren of narrow streets and picturesque squares is layered with a rich history, which is apparent in the pleasing hodgepodge of architectural styles. The neighborhood's glory days date from the 16th and 17th centuries when anyone who was anyone simply had to build a mansion or a palace here. Though the area fell from grace in the 18th and 19th, many of the grand *hôtels particuliers* (private mansions) survived the slings and arrows of time and were reborn as museums and public archives when the neighborhood was restored in the later half of the 20th century. Today, the Marais is a fascinating mix of hip gentrification and the remnants of a working class neighborhood. It is at once the center of the city's gay life, as well as the historic Jewish quarter, even if a much larger community lives in the 19th. Some of the city's best museums and boutiques are here, so you could easily spend an entire day here.

1 Village St-Paul

Many centuries ago, when the area was still mostly marshland (*marais* means "swamp"), there was a small hamlet on this spot. While the neighborhood has been transformed many times since, a small reminder of this village lives on, hidden behind an ordinary row of buildings on rue St-Paul. Pass through the entryway and you'll come into a kind of large interior courtyard that dates from the 14th century, when it was part of the gardens of Charles V's royal residence. At one point the houses and buildings that were built over and around the gardens were slated for demolition; a neighborhood committee saved them and in the 1970s the village was restored and turned into a sort of antiques center, with dozens of stores (see "Shopping," p. 172). The village hosts seasonal *déballages,* or outdoor arts and antiques fairs. Today the commercial emphasis has shifted from antiquities to design.

Exit the village on rue des Jardins St-Paul. On one side of this street is a playground that runs along a huge stone wall, the:

2 Rampart of Philippe Auguste

Before you is the best-preserved stretch of the city walls built by Philippe Auguste. Before leaving town on a crusade in 1190, Philippe decided the time had come to beef up security. The result was a mighty rampart that defined what was then the city limits. The wall in front of you once ran in a semicircle from the Seine, up to around rue Etienne Marcel and curved over to protect the Louvre and back down to the Seine (a similar semicircle was built 20 years later on the Left Bank). Aside from this stretch, there are only small fragments here and there on both banks so you'll have to imagine the rest; you'll also have to imagine the towers and the six massive portals that once were the only land access into the city.

Turn left down rue des Jardins St-Paul and right on rue de l'Avé Maria. Just where it branches off to the right on rue du Figuier is:

3 Hôtel de Sens

Built between 1475 and 1519, this splendid fortress/mansion is a rare example of medieval urban architecture. When Paris came under the jurisdiction of the Bishop of Sens back in the 15th century, he promptly built himself a suitably fabulous home in the city. Later, Henri IV briefly used it to house his strong-minded wife, Queen Margot, whose many love affairs were causing him no end of headaches. The bishops stopped coming to the Hôtel de Sens altogether in 1622, preferring to rent it out. After the Revolution it served as a laundry operation, a jam factory, and a glass warehouse. By the time it was bought by the city in 1911 it was in a pitiful state; the building's restoration—which started in 1929—wouldn't be completed until 1961. The Hôtel now houses the Bibliothèque Forney, a library dedicated to the decorative arts. Take a minute to admire the turrets and towers in the courtyard (visible from the street).

Follow the side of the building down rue du Figuier and turn left onto the path that leads around to the back of the hôtel, where there are pretty French gardens. The path leads to rue des Nonnains d'Hyères, where you'll turn right, then walk left on rue de Jouey to where it intersects with:

4 Rue François Miron

Walk down rue François Miron to the corner of rue Cloche Perce. You will notice two multistoried half-timbered houses: the **Maison à l'Enseigne du Faucheur** (No. 11) and the **Maison à l'Enseigne du Mouton** (No. 13). Pre-Haussmann, there were houses like these all over the city; now they are extremely rare. These two date from the 14th century, though after 1607 the crisscrossed wood facades

The Marais Walking Tour

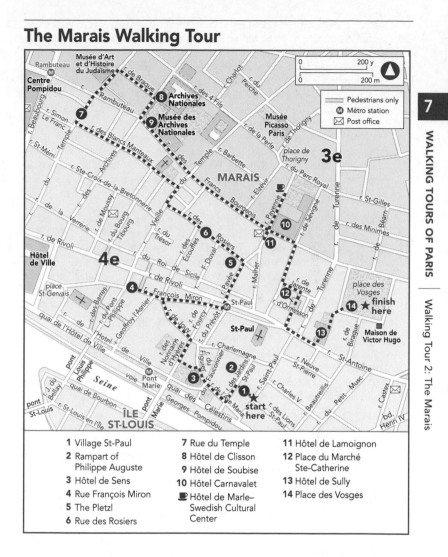

1 Village St-Paul
2 Rampart of Philippe Auguste
3 Hôtel de Sens
4 Rue François Miron
5 The Pletzl
6 Rue des Rosiers

7 Rue du Temple
8 Hôtel de Clisson
9 Hôtel de Soubise
10 Hôtel Carnavalet
Hôtel de Marle–Swedish Cultural Center

11 Hôtel de Lamoignon
12 Place du Marché Ste-Catherine
13 Hôtel de Sully
14 Place des Vosges

of all such houses were covered with a layer of plaster in accordance with a law that aimed to reduce the risk of fire. When these houses were restored in the 1960s, the plaster was removed, and the wood was once again revealed.

Double back and continue down rue François Miron until it ends at the St-Paul Métro station. Cross the rue de Rivoli and continue up rue Pavée to:

5 The Pletzl

You are now entering the city's oldest Jewish quarter, once called the *Pletzl* ("little place" in Yiddish), where there has been a Jewish presence since the 13th century. This community swelled and shrank over the centuries, in line with various edicts and expulsions, but the largest influx was in the 1880s, when tens of thousands of Eastern European Jews, fleeing poverty and persecution back home, settled in France. The Pletzl was hit hard during the infamous roundups of 1942, when police came and emptied apartment buildings and even schools of their Jewish occupants and sent them off to Nazi concentration camps. Though the neighborhood is slowly being eaten up by the advancing gentrification in the area, and chic shops butt up against kosher butchers, there's still a small community here, and a fairly traditional one at that. At No. 10, you'll see an unusual synagogue, known as the **Synagogue de la rue Pavée** which was designed by Hector Guimard, the Art Nouveau master who created the famous Métro entrances. This is the only existing religious edifice by Guimard, whose wife was Jewish (they fled to the U.S. during World War II). In 1940, on Yom Kippur, the Germans dynamited the synagogue; it was eventually restored and is now a national monument (open for religious services only).

Continue up rue Pavée to where it crosses:

6 Rue des Rosiers

Rumor has it that this street got its name from the rose bushes that once lined its edges, back in the days when it ran along the exterior of the city walls. Up until recently, it was the main artery of the Jewish quarter; today all that's left are a few kosher restaurants and a bookstore or two. There's still great falafel to be found here (see L'As du Fallafel, p. 72); if you happen to be in the area around lunchtime, you might get handed a free sample from one of the competing restaurants.

Turn left on rue des Rosiers and continue to the end, where you'll turn right on rue Vieille du Temple. You are now in the thick of the trendier (and gay) part of the neighborhood, which is filled with fun restaurants and boutiques. Take the first left at rue des Blancs Manteaux and follow this pretty street all the way to where it ends at:

7 Rue du Temple

By the time you hit this street you'll notice that the neighborhood has changed from trendy to workaday; rue du Temple is lined with jewelry and clothing wholesalers. But this street—which back in medieval times led to the stalwart fortress of the Knights Templar—also harbors some lovely examples of 17th-century *hôtels particuliers* (private mansions). Turn right and walk to No. 71, the **Hôtel de St-Aignan,** otherwise known as the **Musée d'Art et d'Histoire du Judaïsme** (p. 123). Even if you don't visit the museum, you can peek into the courtyard during opening hours. This exercise in 17th-century grandeur includes a sneaky architectural lie: One of the three facades facing the courtyard, which seems to be the front of an enormous building, is really just a facade. Despite the presence of carefully curtained windows, on the other side of the wall is merely another wall, yet another chunk of Philippe Auguste's ramparts.

Continue up to rue de Braque and turn right. Walk to the end where the street intersects with rue des Archives.

8 Hôtel de Clisson

The vaulted archway across the street is what is left of the **Hôtel de Clisson,** a magnificent mansion that was built in 1380 and for centuries housed some of the grandest of the grand, including dukes of Guise, who hung out there for 135 years. Well, it may have been good enough for them, but by 1700, when the

François de Rohan, the Prince of Soubise got his hands on it, he decided the time had come for a change.

Turn right and walk down rue des Archives to rue des Francs Bourgeois and turn left. First thing you'll see on your left is the sumptuous gateway to the:

9 Hôtel de Soubise

The enormous *cour d'honneur,* a huge horseshoe-shaped courtyard, is edged with open galleries holding 56 pairs of double columns. These lead to a largely 17th-century palace, which now holds the National Archives. This jaw-dropping sight was the creation of architect Pierre Alexis Delamair, who was hired by the Prince of Soubise to build to the courtyard and overhaul the building. Later the prince's son, the future Cardinal de Rohan, asked Delamair to build him his own palace next door, the adjoining **Hôtel de Rohan-Strasbourg** (more archives are stashed here, not open to the public). A part of the Hôtel de Soubise houses the **Musée des Archives Nationale** (60 rue des Francs-Bourgeois, 3rd arrond.; ✆ **01-40-27-60-96;** admission to permanent collection 6€ adults, 4€ over 60, free under 26; Mon and Wed–Fri 10am–5:30pm, Sat–Sun 2–5:30pm), which displays tantalizing items from the vast National Archives, as well as temporary expositions. For example, you can see the **Serment de Jeu de Paume,** a document that signaled the birth of the French republic, and **Marie Antoinette's last letter.** You can also visit the **apartments of the Prince and Princess of Soubise.** Though just a few rooms, they retain the sumptuous decor of the period and give a sense of how the other half lived in the 18th century. You will most likely have the rooms to yourself, giving the odd impression that you have somehow stumbled into a private château.

Continue down rue des Francs Bourgeois and window shop (or just plain shop) in the stylish boutiques that line this street. On the corner of rue de Sévigné, look up and see the:

10 Hôtel Carnavalet

One of the great things about the **Musée Carnavalet** (p. 121) is that it's free, so even if you don't feel like doing the museum, you can lounge in its beautiful gardens and admire the exterior of this magnificent mansion, which dates from the Renaissance. Originally built in 1548, the *hôtel* got its name from its second owner, the widow of a Breton nobleman named François Kernevenoy, whose surname no one could pronounce. The mangled Parisian pronunciation, "Carnavalet," stuck. In 1660, a new owner gave François Mansart the job of enlarging and modernizing his lodgings—the result was so pleasing that in 1677, Madame de Sévigné, famed letter-writer and woman of the world, rented the building and lived there until her death. When it was made into a museum, in 1866, more improvements and enlargements were made, including the creation of two garden courtyards, the **Cour de la Victoire** (which you can enter directly from rue des Francs Bourgeois in good weather), and the **Cour Henri IV.** There are superb sculptures in the various courtyards, including a **bronze statue of Louis XIV** in the **Cour d'Honneur** at the main entrance. This last, by Coysevox, once stood in the courtyard of the Hôtel de Ville and is one of the rare surviving bronzes of a French king—almost all the others were melted down during the Revolution.

From rue des Francs Bourgeois, backtrack to the intersection with rue Payenne and take a short detour to the right, about a half a block down:

Take a Break ☕

The Hôtel de Marle is the home of the Swedish Cultural Center (11 rue Payenne, 3rd arrond.; © 01-44-78-80-20; Tues–Sun noon–6pm), which has a lovely cafe with tables in the courtyard in the summer. Nibble a vanilla-scented *kanelbulle* while you take in the exterior of this 16th-century mansion, which at one point was the home of Yolande de Polastron, a close friend of Marie Antoinette. If you still need a rest, sprawl out on a bench in the Square Georges Cain, a small, but leafy park just across the street.

Walk back down rue Payenne, cross rue des Francs Bourgeois and walk another half block down rue Pavée (the extention of rue Payenne) to:

11 Hôtel de Lamoignon

Built in 1584 for Diane de France, the legitimized daughter of one of Henri II's extramarital encounters, this massive mansion was acquired by a famous family of magistrates (the Lamoignons) in the 17th century. You'll have no problem getting into the courtyard here (the building now houses the **Library of the History of the City of Paris**), where you can get a good look at the facade. The dog's heads, arrows, quivers and other hunting imagery carved into the stonework are references to the first owner's namesake, Diana, goddess of the hunt. A later Lamoignon, Guillaume, who was the first president of the Parisian Parliament, turned his home into a meeting place for the leading lights of the epoch—Madame de Sévigné, Racine, and Bourdaloue were regulars at his parties. The building became a library in the 1960s.

Go back up to rue des Francs Bourgeois and turn right. Turn right again on rue de Sévigné and left on rue de Jarente to:

12 Place du Marché Ste-Catherine

Though there's no longer an open-air market here, as the name suggests, this shaded plaza is still a lovely oasis of green and quiet in this busy neighborhood. There are no cars allowed on the square, and the cafes on its edges all have outdoor seating in nice weather.

Continue to rue St-Antoine and turn left without crossing the street to No. 62:

13 Hôtel de Sully

The most splendiferous of the many splendiferous mansions in the Marais, the **Hôtel de Sully** was built by a rich 17th-century businessman, a certain Mesme-Gallet. While his version was quite sumptuous, the mansion really came to life when it was bought by the Duc de Sully, who hired architect François Le Vau to give it a makeover. After his death, like so many mansions in the Marais, the palacelike edifice was sold, divided, and built upon; in 1827 it was a boarding house for young girls, and up until the end of World War II it was still disfigured by shops and outbuildings. Using the original plans and contemporary drawings and etchings, the building was completely restored in the 1970s to Le Vau's version; you can now stroll through the courtyard and admire the sculpted exterior in its virtually pristine state. Though the building is closed to the public, you can traipse through the front courtyard to a second one, where there is a peaceful **garden** and *orangerie* (a hothouse for orange trees).

Go through the archway in the back of the garden to the:

14 Place des Vosges

Officially inaugurated in 1612, this exquisite **Renaissance square,** bordered by 36 virtually identical stone and brick town houses, was the idea of King Henri IV, who unfortunately didn't live to see it finished. After a stroll under the arcades, which run below the town houses, have a seat on a bench in the square and admire the tall trees and the elegant symmetry of the landscaping, as well as the huge **statue** in the middle of Louis XIII astride his horse. This statue is a 19th-century replacement for the original, which was melted down during the Revolution. The square has seen a number of illustrious tenants over the centuries: Madame de Sévigné was born at No. 1 *bis,* the 19th-century actress Rachel lived at No. 9, poet Théophile Gautier and novelist Alphonse Daudet both lived at No. 10. The most famous inhabitant, no doubt, was Victor Hugo, who lived at No. 6 from 1832 to 1848; his house is now the **Maison de Victor Hugo** (p. 121).

SHOPPING

Vuitton, Chanel, Baccarat—the names of famous French luxury brands slide around your tongue like rich chocolate. But while it's fun to window shop at Cartier, few of us can actually afford to buy anything there. Guess what? Neither can most Parisians. And yet they manage to look terrifically put together. What's their secret? I'll attempt to shed some light on this puzzling mystery; the shops below will give you a point of departure for your Parisian shopping adventure.

8

Paris has always been the capital of *luxe*. As early as the 16th century, the city was known as the place to go for luxury goods, and over the centuries an entire industry grew up around the whims and whimsies of the French aristocracy. To keep up appearances, nobles spent outrageous amounts of money on sumptuous clothing, opulent homes, and lavish dinner parties for dozens of similarly well-heeled aristocrats. By the 18th century, thousands of merchants and artisans were working full-time to fill the voluminous orders of some 150 grand families, not to mention Louis XIV and his court in Versailles. So it's no wonder that even today, the high and mighty, or just plain rich, come here to deck themselves out in the best of the best.

Yet there is so much more shopping to explore than those big box luxury stores on the Champs-Élysées. There are small boutiques by up-and-coming designers, lesser-known but fantastic chocolate stores, and hip yet inexpensive French chain stores where you can throw together a look in a matter of minutes. Paris can be a shopaholic heaven, if you know where to go to find your *bonheur* (happiness).

SHOPPING BY AREA

In Paris, each neighborhood has its own personality, and each personality imposes itself on one or two main shopping streets. To preserve your sanity, and shoe leather, aim for the areas with the highest concentration of your kind of store.

The Right Bank
LOUVRE & ILE DE LA CITÉ (1ST ARRONDISSEMENT)

The east side of this arrondissement includes the subterranean shopping mall **Forum des Halles** (still open despite the massive renovation project going on upstairs), which is a short stroll from a major shopping strip on the **rue de Rivoli.** Both feature a wide range of affordable international clothing chains. As you move west, the atmosphere shifts dramatically. The arcades of the **Palais Royal** have recently been taken over by fashionable labels like Marc Jacobs and Stella McCartney. Further on, chic **rue**

St-Honoré is lined with pricey, sophisticated stores. As you head further west, the prices go through the roof at **Place Vendôme,** which probably has the city's highest density of gemstones per square meter. Even if you are too shy to enter Chaumet or Boucheron, you can happily drool over the window displays.

OPÉRA & GRAND BOULEVARDS (2ND & 9TH ARRONDISSEMENTS)

Boulevard Haussmann cuts through this neighborhood like a steamship's wake, drawing hoards of shoppers towards the city's two most famous department stores, **Galeries Lafayette** and **Printemps.** These two behemoths have spawned an entire neighborhood full of inexpensive shops just north of the boulevard on **rue de Provence, rue de Mogador,** and **rue Caumartin.** To the south and east of the boulevard lies a maze of **19th-century covered shopping arcades** (see "Arcadia" box, below), as well as a **market street** lined with enticing **food stores,** rue de Montorgueil.

THE MARAIS (3RD & 4TH ARRONDISSEMENTS)

The success of the hip boutiques on the **rue des Francs-Bourgeois** has been such that stylish clothing stores have been cropping up on all the streets around it, even crowding

Arcadia

Paris is filled with covered arcades, primarily in the 2nd arrondissement. These lovely iron and glass galleries are 19th-century antecedents of today's shopping malls—each one is lined with shops, tearooms, and even the occasional hotel—and range in ambiance from slightly seedy to ultra hip.

Built in 1825, the city's longest arcade, **Passage Choiseul** (40 rue des Petits Champs, 2nd arrond.; Métro: Pyramides), runs from rue des Petits Champs to rue de Saint Augustin and shelters everything from bargain shoe shops and used book stores to art galleries and an organic hamburger joint. The **Passage des Panoramas** (11 bd. Montmartre, 2nd arrond.; www.passagedespanoramas.fr; Métro: Grands Boulevards) intersects with several other short arcades (**Feydeau, Montmartre, Saint-Marc,** and **Variétés**), making an interesting warren of bookshops, collectors' shops (stamps, coins, postcards, engravings), and increasingly, trendy restaurants. Across the street is the entrance to **Passage Jouffroy** (10 bd. Montmartre, 9th arrond;

www.passagejouffroy.com; Métro: Grands Boulevards), which is lined with collectors' shops featuring figurines, dollhouses, and cinema memorabilia. Pricier gifts are to be found at **Passage Verdeau** (across the street from the back end of Jouffroy, 31 bis rue du Faubourg Montmartre, 9th arrond.; Métro: Grands Boulevards), a particularly atmospheric arcade with stores selling rare books, antique engravings, and vintage photos.

Farther south, near the Palais Royal, is the chic **Galerie Vivienne** (4 rue des Petits Champs, 2nd arrond.; www.galerie-vivienne.com; Métro: Bourse), a beautifully restored arcade with a mosaic tile floor and neo-classical arches. Stores here sell high-end clothes, handbags, textiles and objets d'art. Legrand Filles et Fils (p. 185) has tons of fine bottles of wine, as well as a wine school and cafe. Toward Les Halles is the very stylish **Passage du Grand Cerf** (10 rue Dussoubs, 2nd arrond.; Métro: Etienne Marcel), which is filled with flashy designer jewelry, clothing stores, and interior design agencies.

out the kosher restaurants on **rue des Rosiers,** the historic Jewish quarter. Not as pricey as the luxury boutiques to the west, these stores have stylish duds at vaguely attainable prices (and they are open on Sun, a rarity in this city). **Rue de Bretagne** in the northern Marais is a hotbed of independent French designers.

CHAMPS-ÉLYSÉES, TROCADÉRO & WESTERN PARIS (8TH, 16TH & 17TH ARRONDISSEMENTS)

Rue du Faubourg St-Honoré is dotted with dozens of chic boutiques, but it pales in comparison to ultra-exclusive **avenue Montaigne.** Paris's most glamorous shopping street is lined with unspeakably fancy shops, where you float from Dior to Chanel, and everything in between. Teens, tourists, and other young things flock to the neighboring **Champs-Élysées** to crowd into hot mass-market flagships. High-end food shops (Hédiard, Fauchon) live in the area around the **Madeleine.**

MONTMARTRE (18TH ARRONDISSEMENT)

The winding streets that fan out around Montmartre's **place des Abbesses** are filled with small, fairly affordable design, fashion, jewelry, and food shops. Wander along **rue des Abbesses,** down **rue Houdon,** and up **rue des Martyrs** and discover hidden treasures. If you are looking for adventure and serious bargains, head east to the working-class Barbès neighborhood, where on **Boulevard Rochechouart** you'll find Tati, a huge discount department store.

RÉPUBLIQUE, BASTILLE & EASTERN PARIS (11TH & 12TH ARRONDISSEMENTS)

As **rue du Faubourg St-Antoine** heads east from the place de la Bastille, you'll find a number of chains stores. The choices get more interesting in and around **rue de Charonne,** home to off-beat, youth-oriented clothing and goodies. A great place to window shop and wander is the **Viaduc des Arts,** which runs along avenue Daumesnil: a collection of about 30 specialist craft stores occupying a series of vaulted arches under the **Promenade Plantée** (p. 133).

Taxes, Detaxe & Refunds

Most items purchased in stores (aside from certain categories like food and tickets to performances) are subject to a 20% Value Added Tax (VAT) which is included in the price you pay (and not tacked on at the end like in the U.S.). The good news is that non-European Union residents who are over 15 and stay in France less than 6 months can get a refund of VAT (TVA in French) if they spend over 175€ in a single shop on the same day. Ask the retailer for a *bordereau de vente à l'exportation* (export sales invoice), which will have a bar code. Both you and the shopkeeper sign the slip, and you then choose how you will be reimbursed (credit on card, bank transfer, or cash). Once you get to the airport, scan the code in one of the new "Pablo" terminals (if your airport doesn't have one, just go to the "detaxe" counter). If you chose to be reimbursed by credit to your bank account or credit card, that will happen automatically once you scan the slip. If you chose cash, you'll need to go to the "detaxe" counter, where you'll be refunded on the spot. For more info visit Rendezvous en France (www.rendezvous enfrance.com). Search for "French Shopping Tips" for a complete rundown on tax-free shopping.

BELLEVILLE, CANAL ST-MARTIN & LA VILLETTE (10TH, 19TH & 20TH ARRONDISSEMENTS)

Not a major shopping zone, this a place to come and explore specialty shops from the city's various immigrant communities. The **Canal St-Martin** is a bastion of local bohemian charm, and you can find interesting shops along neighboring streets like **rue de Marseille, rue Beaurepaire,** the **quai de Valmy,** and **quai de Jemmapes.**

The Left Bank

LATIN QUARTER (5TH & 13TH ARRONDISSEMENTS)

Chain stores have taken over a large chunk of the **Boulevard St-Michel,** which used to be known for its cafes and bookstores. There are a few survivors though, like the massive Gibert Joseph, which has several outposts on the Boul' Miche selling books, films, stationary, and more. Food enthusiasts will enjoy the delicious goodies on sale in the shops at the southern end of **rue Mouffetard.**

ST-GERMAIN-DES-PRÉS & LUXEMBOURG (6TH ARRONDISSEMENT)

Even if it's technically in the 7th arrondissement, the shopping nerve center of this smart neighborhood is **Le Bon Marché,** the city's most stylish department store. Radiating eastward is a network of streets with oodles of delightful shops, ranging from bargain-oriented **rue St-Placide** to chain stores and shoe heaven on **rue de Rennes** to designer labels and cute boutiques on **rue St Sulpice, rue du Cherche Midi,** and **rue du Vieux Colombier.** Down towards the Seine, **rue Bonaparte** and **rue Jacob** tempt with classy, if pricey, offerings, and you can stop in at the legendary La Hune bookstore just off **Boulevard St-Germain,** for a taste of the neighborhood's intellectual past.

EIFFEL TOWER & NEARBY (7TH ARRONDISSEMENT)

Most of this area is more focused on culture and architecture than fashion, but along its eastern edge, around the **rue du Bac** and **rue du Grenelle,** you'll find hopelessly expensive designer shops. The market street of **rue Cler** has dozens of charming bakeries, charcuteries, and fruit sellers.

Shopping Hours

For shoppers, Paris is most definitely not a 24-hour city. In general, shops are open from 9 or 10am to 7pm. Many larger stores and most department stores stay open late (that is, 9pm) 1 night during the week (called a nocturne) and most supermarkets are open until at least 8pm, often 9 or even 10pm. Many shops are closed on Monday, and most are closed on Sunday, which is still considered a day of rest in this country. This is great for family get-togethers, but hard on working shoppers, who have only Saturday to get to the stores. Don't shop on Saturday if you can avoid it; the crowds are annoying, to say the least.

The French tradition of closing for lunch is quickly vanishing in Paris (though it is still very common elsewhere in France). However, smaller, family-run operations sometimes still close between noon and 2pm.

Final note: Many shops close down for 2 or 3 weeks during July or August, when a mass vacation exodus empties out major portions of the city.

MONTPARNASSE & NEARBY (14TH & 15TH ARRONDISSEMENTS)

There's an ugly shopping center in the Tour Montparnasse complex filled with the usual chain stores, but the more interesting shopping draw here is farther south on **rue d'Alesia,** which is lined with outlet stores *(déstock)* selling surplus and discounted wares, including designer labels like Sonia Rykiel. **Rue Daguerre** is a lovely market street filled with food shops that is as cute as rue Cler, but less famous (you'll hear a lot more French here). Further south in the 15th, **rue de Commerce** buzzes with shops and restaurants.

8 DEPARTMENT STORES

Les Grands Magasins

Known as the *grands magasins* ("big stores"), the great Parisian department stores were born in the late 19th century and have become landmarks in their own right.

BHV ★★   Here's a department store that even men will love. Sure, it has acres of clothes and perfumes, but it's mostly known for what it has in its basement: **hardware, electronics, gadgets,** and other items for *bricoleurs* (do-it-yourselfers) of all nationalities. There are also terrific **kitchen, hobby,** and **decoration** sections upstairs. The practical side of this store has been such a success that it has spawned several ministores, all on streets surrounding the mother ship. There's **BHV Homme** (36 rue de la Verrerie) for men's clothing, **BHV Vélo** (40 rue de la Verrerie) for cyclists, **BHV Moto** (14 rue du Temple) for motorcyclists, and **BHV La Niche** (42 rue de la Verrerie) for pets. 52 rue de Rivoli, 4th arrond. ℰ **09-77-40-14-00.** www.bhv.fr. Métro: Hôtel de Ville.

Galeries Lafayette ★★   This grandest of the *grand magasins* was a humble haberdasher shop when it was opened in 1895. Success inspired architectural excess, like the sumptuous Belle Epoque dome under which fashionable goodies are displayed. I prefer Galeries Lafayette to its more glamorous rival next door (see Printemps). It's a bit less expensive and so huge you can usually find just what you're looking for. There's everything from luxury labels to kids' stuff, even stationary, wine and a gourmet shop. A separate building's just for men **(Lafayette Homme)** and another across the street has housewares **(Lafayette Maison).** 40 bd. Haussmann, 9th arrond. ℰ **01-42-82-34-56.** www.galerieslafayette.com. Métro: Chausée d'Antin-Lafayette.

Le Bon Marché ★★★   Founded by an enterprising milliner in the mid-1800s, this was the one of the world's first department stores. Despite its name (*bon marché* means "affordable"), this is the most expensive of Paris' grand magasins. It is also the most stylish, with beautiful displays and fabulous clothes of every imaginable designer label, both upscale and mid-range. Right next door is their humongous designer supermarket, **La Grande Epicerie** (see "Specialty Groceries," below). 24 rue de Sèvres, 7th arrond. ℰ **01-44-39-80-00.** www.lebonmarche.com. Métro: Sèvres–Babylone.

Printemps ★★   The glistening domes of this 19th-century building bring to mind a grand hotel on the French Riviera. *Printemps* means "spring," which is certainly eternal in this elegant store. Split into four sections (women's fashions, menswear, housewares, and beauty), four of the seven floors of women's fashion are devoted to designer labels. If you can't handle the crowds inside, you can always enjoy the famed *vitrines,* or **window displays,** which are usually very creative and original. Better yet, ride to the top of Printemps Beauté/Maison and enjoy the splendid

Sale Mania

In the name of fair competition, the French government has strict controls on sales. Two times a year, around the second week in January and the second week in July (official dates are pasted a couple of weeks in advance on advertisements all over the city), retailers are allowed to go hog wild and slash prices as far as they want. (The rest of the year sale prices don't usually dip down below 30%.) Though recent changes in the law have made it easier for stores to have sales when they want, old habits die hard. Everyone still breathlessly awaits the two big seasonal sales, and when the opening day finally arrives, chaos ensues. Don't feel you have to get there the first day—not only are the crowds horrific, but many stores are coy about their initial reductions. Personally, I think the best time to go is the second or third week, when the crowds have thinned and the stores start really cutting their prices (sales go on for at least 5 weeks). Unless you're a dedicated masochist, don't try to shop on a weekend during sale season; you'll be trampled on, and sneered at. If you must shop on the weekend, go early in the morning when the stores open.

panoramic view; there's even a cafe for lunch. 64 bd. Haussmann, 9th arrond. (℃) **01-42-82-50-00.** www.printemps.com. Métro: Havre-Caumartin or St-Lazare.

MARKETS: FOOD & FLEA
Food Markets

Marchés (open-air or covered markets) are small universes unto themselves where nothing substantial has changed for centuries. The fishmonger trumpeting the wonders of this morning's catch probably doesn't sound a whole lot different than his ancestor in the Middle Ages (though their dress has changed), and I'm sure housewives assessed the goods in the stalls with the same pitiless stares that they do today. Certainly the hygiene and organization have improved and there are no more jugglers or bear baiters to entertain the crowds, but the essence of the experience remains the same—a noisy, bustling, joyous chaos where you can buy fresh, honest food.

Even if you don't have access to cooking facilities, *marchés* are great places to pick up picnic goodies or just a mid-morning nosh; along with fruit and vegetable vendors, you'll find bakeries, *charcuteries* (sort of like a deli, but better), and other small stands selling homemade jams, honey, or desserts. Some of the covered markets have small cafes inside—these are ideal for sitting down and soaking up the atmosphere.

A few marché rules: Unless you see evidence to the contrary, don't pick up your own fruits and vegetables with your hands. Wait until the vendor serves you and point. Also, don't be surprised if the line in front of the stand is an amorphous blob of people; this is the French way. Surprisingly, fist-fights are rare; somehow everyone seems to be aware of who came before them, and if they aren't, no one seems to care.

There are *marchés* in every arrondissement in the city. Below is a selective list; you can find hours and locations of all on the municipal website (www.paris.fr, search for "marché"), or just ask at your hotel for the one closest to where you're staying.

o **Marché d'Aligre:** One of the city's largest; aka Marché Beauvau (place d'Aligre, 12th arrond.; outdoor market Tues–Sun 9am–1pm, covered market Tues–Sat 9am–1pm and 4–7:30pm, Sun 9am–1:30pm; Métro: Ledru Rollin or Gare de Lyon)

o **Marché Barbès** (bd. de la Chapelle in front of Hospital Lariboisière, 18th arrond; Wed 8am–1pm and Sat 7am–3pm; Métro: Barbès-Rochechouart)

o **Marché Bastille** (bd. Richard Lenoir between rue Amelot and rue St-Sabin, 11th arrond.; Thurs and Sun 7am–2:30pm; Métro: Bastille)

o **Marché Batignolles** Organic (bd. Batignolles between rue de Rome and Place Clichy, 17th arrond.; Sat 9am–3pm; Métro: Rome)

o **Marché Edgar Quinet** (bd. Edgar Quinet, near Gare Montparnasse, 14th around. Wed and Sat 7am–2:30pm; Métro: Edgar Quinet)

o **Marché Grenelle** (bd. Grenelle, between rue Lourmel and rue du Commerce, 15th arrond.; Wed and Sun 7am–2:30pm; Métro: Dupleix)

o **Marché Monge** (place Monge, 5th arrond; Wed, Fri, and Sun 7am–2:30pm; Métro: place Monge)

o **Marché Raspail** (bd. Raspail between rue de Cherche-Midi and rue de Rennes, 6th arrond.; Tues and Fri, 7am–2:30pm; **organic** Sun 9am–3pm) Métro: Rennes)

o **Marché Saxe-Breteuil** (ave. du Saxe near place de Breteuil, 7th arrond.; Thurs and Sat 7am–2:30pm; Métro: Ségur)

Antiques Fairs & Brocantes

You've probably heard of the famous *marché aux puces,* or **flea market** at Clignancourt (see below), and if you're an inveterate browser, it's probably worth the visit. But the better deals are to be had at the *brocantes,* antiques or jumble sales, held periodically around the city. Though most of what you will find at these sales is sold by professional *brocanteurs* who scout estate sales and other insider sources, your selection will be much wider and the chances of your finding a post-war ceramic pastis pitcher, or heirloom lace curtains at affordable prices are much higher than at some of the more overpopulated flea markets. To find out where and when the *brocantes* are happening, visit www.quefaire.paris.fr/brocantes or look in the **special supplements** of "Le Parisien" (Sun) or "Le Figaro" (Wed, the supplement is called "Figaroscope").

Flea Markets

Marché aux Puces de la Porte de Vanves ★★ This weekend event sprawls along two streets and is the best flea market in Paris—dealers swear by it. There's little in terms of formal antiques and furniture. It's better for old linens, vintage Hermès scarves, toys, ephemera, costume jewelry, perfume bottles, and bad art. Asking prices tend to be high, as dealers prefer to sell to locals. Get there early—the best stuff goes fast. Open Saturday and Sunday, 7am to 2pm. Ave. Georges-Lafenestre, 14th arrond. No phone. www.pucesdevanves.typepad.com. Métro: Porte de Vanves.

Marché aux Puces de Paris St-Ouen–Clignancourt ★ Engulfing the Porte de Clignancourt at the northern edge of the city, this claims to be the largest antiques market in the world. Split into 15 specialty markets, thousands of visitors descend on this sprawling mini-city each weekend (also open Mon). Once a bargain-hunter's dream, prices now often rival those of regular antiques dealers. Still, hard-core browsers will get a kick wandering through the serpentine alleyways of this Parisian medina, and may turn up a treasure. *Note:* Beware of pickpockets. Porte de Clignancourt, 18th arrond. ✆ **01-40-11-77-36.** www.marcheauxpuces-saintouen.com. Sat 9am–6pm; Sun 10am–6pm; Mon 11am–5pm. Métro: Porte de Clignancourt.

RECOMMENDED STORES
Antiques & Collectibles

Le Louvre des Antiquaires ★   Across from the Louvre, this giant antiques market includes 250 vendors spread over three levels. If you are in the market for an Art Deco diamond brooch, an 18th-century carved tobacco box, or a medieval iron key, this is the place to go. It won't be a bargain, but it could be the keepsake of a lifetime. Pick up a free map and brochure from the information desk. 2 place du Palais Royal, 1st arrond. ℰ **01-42-97-27-27.** www.louvre-antiquaires.com. Métro: Palais-Royal.

L'Objet qui Parle ★★   This delightful and quirky shop sells a jumble of vintage finds, including framed butterflies, teapots, furniture, chandeliers, crockery, hunting trophies, religious paraphernalia, and old lace. Great for souvenir shopping. 86 rue des Martyrs, 18th arrond. ℰ **06-09-67-05-30.** Métro: Abbesses.

Village St-Paul ★★   When you pass through an archway on rue St-Paul, you come upon a lovely villagelike enclosure, the remnant of a centuries old-hamlet that was swallowed up by the city. Today, it is a village of antiques dealers and design shops, selling everything from old bistro chairs and vintage lingerie to Brazilian eco-furniture and Iranian kilim rugs. Check their website for their periodic *brocantes,* or antiques fairs. No phone. www.levillagesaintpaul.com. Métro: St-Paul.

Beauty & Perfume

At the airport, you'll be assaulted with **duty-free shops** carrying loads of tax-free perfume, and another colony of similar shops is near the Opéra. But don't be afraid to go elsewhere because you will most likely get the same tax rebate no matter where you go (as long as you spend more than 175€; see box on taxes, p. 174). Discounts can also be found at two huge perfume chains: the ubiquitous **Marionnaud** (www.marionnaud.fr) and the user-friendly **Sephora** (www.sephora.fr). If you would like to bring home something more original, try one of the shops listed below.

The Different Company ★★   There is indeed something different about this perfume company. For one, this is an independent operation, founded in 2000, that makes its own unique fragrances with mostly natural materials. Signature scents include Osmanthus, Sel de Vétiver, and Rose Poivrée. 10 rue Ferdinand Duval, 4th arrond. ℰ **01-42-78-19-34.** www.thedifferentcompany.com. Métro: St-Paul.

Detaille 1905 ★   Founded by the Countess of Presle in 1905, this beautiful old store offers its own elegant line of eau de toilette and other beauty products for both men and women, such as its signature *Baume Automobile,* developed by the Countess when she realized (even back then) what pollution can do to your skin. These unique products can only be purchased at the wood-paneled boutique or ordered by phone or online through the shop's website. 10 rue St-Lazare, 9th arrond. ℰ **01-48-78-68-50.** www.detaille.com. Métro: Notre Dame de Lorette.

Editions de Parfums Fréderic Malle ★★   A superb range of original fragrances have been developed in this chic temple to the nose, which was established by master perfumer Fréderic Malle in 2000. Sample his wares in special "smelling columns," round, phone-booth-like tubes where you can experience aromas like Noir Epice and Lipstick Rose. There are two other stores at 140 avenue Victor Hugo in the 16th arrondissement, and 21 rue du Mont Thabor in the 1st. 37 rue de Grenelle, 7th arrond. ℰ **01-42-22-76-40.** www.fredericmalle.com. Métro: Rue du Bac.

Make Up Forever ★ Why not come back from Paris with a whole new look? This French cosmetics company, which trains professional makeup artists, also runs a boutique in the Marais where you can not only buy products but also have a **makeup lesson** (25 min. for 25€, 60 min. for 60€; call to reserve ahead). There is a second location at 5 rue de la Boétie in the 8th arrondissement. 5 rue des Francs Bourgeois, 4th arrond. ✆ **01-42-71-23-19.** www.makeupforever.fr. Métro: St-Paul.

Books

ENGLISH BOOKSTORES

Several of Paris' English language bookshops have shut down in the last couple of years—a real blow to the expat community since they tend to double as cultural meeting places. Those that have survived are good places to pick up English language newsletters, chat in English, and attend readings (sometimes by famous authors).

The Abbey Bookshop ★ Canadians will be happy to find a cozy store that specializes in Canadian authors, as well as other English-language literature. You'll have to squeeze in between the piles of books, but this is a relaxed, welcoming place with good events and readings. 29 rue de la Parcheminerie, 5th arrond. ✆ **01-46-33-16-24.** www.abbeybookshop.wordpress.com. Métro: St-Michel.

Galignani ★★ The oldest English-language bookstore in Paris, this old-fashioned shop has thrived since 1810. Owned by the literary Gagliani family, whose ancestor used one of the first printing presses back in 1520, the store is filled with a terrific range of both French and English books, with a special emphasis on French classics, modern fiction, sociology, and fine arts. 224 rue de Rivoli, 1st arrond. ✆ **01-42-60-76-07.** www.galignani.com. Métro: Tuileries.

San Francisco Book Company ★★ This centrally located shop has a good stock of used books, including hardback classics, paperback airplane reading, and rare and out of print editions. They also sell a few new books, particularly Lost Generation authors. 17 rue Monsieur Le Prince, 6th arrond. ✆ **01-43-29-15-70.** www.sanfrancisco booksparis.com. Métro: Odéon.

Shakespeare & Company ★★★ This venerable shrine is a must on any Parisian literary tour. Run by George Whitman for some 60 years before he passed away in 2011 at 98, today it is helmed by his daughter, Sylvia, who was named after Sylvia Beach (who founded the original bookshop in 1919). Many legendary writers (Allen Ginsberg, Henry Miller, to name a couple) have stopped in over the decades for a cup of tea; many an aspiring author has camped out in one of the back rooms. Today, Whitman's presence is still felt at this historic bookshop, which sells used and new books. Check the website for ongoing readings and other events. 37 rue de la Bûcherie, 5th arrond. ✆ **01-43-25-40-93.** www.shakespeareandcompany.com. Métro/RER: St-Michel–Notre-Dame.

WH Smith ★ If a big bookstore is what you're after, a visit to the Paris branch of this English chain might be in order. They have the largest selection of English-language books in the city, as well as a huge range of magazines. 248 rue de Rivoli, 1st arrond. ✆ **01-44-77-88-99.** www.whsmith.fr. Métro: Concorde.

FRENCH BOOKSTORES

Gibert Joseph ★★ Wander the endless aisles of this book-lover's haven, which sells both French and English books, as well as French comics ("BDs"), maps, and just about anything else on the printed page. There are six stores to choose from (all right next to each other), selling used books, new books, DVDs, art supplies, and stationery. 26–34 bd. St-Michel, 6th arrond. ℂ **01-44-41-88-88.** www.gibertjoseph.com. Métro: Cluny–La Sorbonne.

Librarie La Hune ★ This mythic bookstore has been catering to existentialists and other intellectuals since 1945. Excellent selection, mostly in French. 18 rue de l'Abbaye, 6th arrond. ℂ **01-45-48-35-85.** www.groupe-flammarion.com. Métro: St-Germain-des-Prés.

Les Mots à la Bouche ★ This is Paris's largest, best-stocked gay bookstore. You can find French- and English-language books as well as gay-info magazines such as "Têtu" and "Muse." 6 rue Ste-Croix-la-Bretonnerie, 4th arrond. ℂ **01-42-78-88-30.** www.mots bouche.com. Métro: Hôtel-de-Ville.

Clothing & Shoes

agnès b ★ This designer's relaxed but elegant urban fashion has been winning over Parisians, and the rest of the planet, since the '70s. Guys can wander over to see her menswear collection around the corner at **agnès b. homme** (1 rue Dieu, 10th arrond.). There a dozen other locations scattered around the city (including in the Galeries Lafayette) see website for addresses. 13 rue de Marseille, 10th arrond. ℂ **01-42-06-66-58.** www.agnesb.com. Métro: Jacques Bonsergent.

Antoine & Lili ★ Hot pink is the signature color at this wacky store, where the gaily painted walls are hung with colorful objects from around the world. Clothes are

Sylvia Beach—Mother of the Lost Generation

Born in Baltimore in 1887, **Sylvia Beach** fell in love with Paris early in life and moved there for good at the end of World War I. A few years later, with the encouragement of her companion, bookshop owner Adrienne Monier, Beach opened **Shakespeare & Company,** a bookstore and lending library specializing in English and American books. For the next 20 years, the shop at 8 rue Dupuytren served as an unofficial welcome center for American and English visitors, particularly literary ones, and specifically those who would later come to be known as members of **"The Lost Generation":** T. S. Eliot, Ezra Pound, F. Scott Fitzgerald, Gertrude Stein, and Ernest Hemingway. But the one who made the biggest impression, literally, was James Joyce. After his novel "Ulysses" was banned in both the U.S. and England and no publisher would touch the manuscript, Beach courageously published it herself. In February 1922, after endless proofs and corrections by the author, the 1,000 copies arrived in the store, all of which were snapped up instantaneously. Later, the book became a modern classic, making a mint for its publisher, Random House. Beach never saw a penny but claimed that she didn't mind because she'd have done anything for Joyce and his art. In 1941, during the Nazi occupation of Paris, the contents of the entire bookstore "vanished" overnight (hidden in a vacant apartment in the same building) to avoid confiscation by the Germans. The books were saved, but Beach spent 6 months in an internment camp. After the war, she returned to Paris, but the bookshop's doors never reopened. The store's memory lives on, however, in its more recent incarnation at 37 rue de la Bûcherie (see Shakespeare & Company, above).

innovative and fresh, yet wearable, and come in a range of bright colors. There are five Parisian branches, check the website for addresses. 95 quai de Valmy, 10th arrond. ☎ **01-40-37-41-55.** www.antoineetlili.com. Métro: Jacques Bonsergent.

Azzedine Alaïa ★★ Alaïa, who became the darling of French fashion in the 1970s, designs beautiful body-hugging clothing. If you can't afford the current collection, try the **stock shop** around the corner at 18 rue de la Verrerie (☎ **01-42-72-83-19;** closed at lunchtime), where last season's leftovers are sold at serious discounts. There's a second (full price) boutique at 5 rue de Marignan in the 8th arrond. 7 rue Moussy, 4th arrond. ☎ **01-42-72-19-19.** www.alaia.fr. Métro: Hôtel-de-Ville.

Comptoir des Cotonniers ★ Yes, it's a chain, but it's an elegant one, with streamlined clothing that works well both in the office and on casual outings. There are dozens of locations all over town. 12 place St-Sulpice, 6th arrond. ☎ **01-56-81-00-20.** www.comptoirdescotonniers.com. Métro: St-Sulpice.

Des Filles à la Vanille ★★ A store that smells as good as it looks, this place has a great selection of big, fuzzy, funky sweaters, unusual long slit skirts, and gauzy dresses, as well as its own line of perfumes. There is another branch at 150 bd. St-Germain in the 6th. 56 rue St-Antoine, 4th arrond. ☎ **01-48-87-90-02.** Métro: St-Paul.

French Trotters ★ Airy and spacious, this Marais emporium is the new flagship store for this temple of urban chic. While the original store (which is still open, 30 rue de Charonne, 11th arrond.) featured both hot local French labels and the store's own brand of relaxed *branchitude* (hipness), this one sells all that plus housewares, books, and stationary. Terrific styles for men, women, and children (there's a separate store for tykes next to the original at 28 rue de Charonne) alike. 128 rue Vieille du Temple, 3rd arrond. ☎ **01-44-61-00-14.** www.frenchtrotters.fr. Métro: Saint Sébastien-Froissart or Files du Calvaire.

Uniqlo ★★ It's hard not to like this Japanese outfit that sells colorful, upbeat clothing for both men and women at low cost, like offbeat T-shirts, bright basics,

---

Affordable Fashion—A Quick Guide to the Chains

Several European chain stores sell fashionable clothing at remarkably low prices. Fresh and fun, these stores have loads of colorful, mod clothing—but don't expect high quality. The following stores have branches throughout the city:

Alain Manoukian Distinctive design at moderate prices. Colors tend towards the bright and punchy. They have men's clothing too. www.groupe-manoukian.com.

Caroll A little more upscale and conservative, with a good selection of moderately priced clothing for working women who want something more feminine than a power suit. www.caroll.com.

H&M Everything from evening wear to bare-bones basics; from time to time they collaborate with high-end design houses. www.hm.com.

Mango Colors at this Spanish chain tend to favor a Mediterranean complexion, a nice change from the Nordic hues at other stores. www.mango.com.

Promod A French chain with great clothes in wearable colors. The look is young, but not adolescent. www.promod.com.

Zara Another Spanish outfit, Zara stocks both work and play clothes for the young and trendy. Great for basics like T-shirts and turtlenecks. www.zara.com.

sherbet-colored jeans, and fluffy fleeces. If the main offerings are too youthfully perky for you, try the upscale section with comfortable office clothes by name designers. There are two other Paris locations: 39 rue des Francs Bourgeois in the Marais, and in the Beaugrenelle shopping center, 12 rue Linois, in the 15th. 17 rue Scribe, 9th. ⓒ **01-58-18-30-55.** www.uniqlo.com. Métro: Havre-Caumartin or Chaussée d'Antin-La Fayette.

Vicxite.A ★ You'll find fun, contemporary clothing by young designers here in bright patterns and unusual combinations at accessible prices. 47 rue des Abbesses, 18th arrond. ⓒ **01-42-55-31-68.** Métro: Abbesses.

Zadig & Voltaire I don't know what the philosopher would make of this trendy young French brand, but Voltaire might have appreciated its rock 'n' roll spirit. Perfectly worn jeans, comfortable cashmeres, biker boots, and more, for men, women, and children. There are dozens of branches around the city. 3 rue du Vieux Colombier, 6th arrond. ⓒ **01-45-48-39-37.** www.zadig-et-voltaire.com. Métro: St-Sulpice.

LINGERIE

Judging from the sheer number of lingerie stores in even the smallest towns in France, French women must put aside a large portion of their budgets for underwear purchases. And for good reason—French lingerie is exquisite and worth the splurge.

Orcanta ★★ This is a chain with a great selection of name brands (such as Lise Charmel, Chantal Thomas, and Huit), and there are usually at least a rack or two of discounted items. More locations on the website. 60 rue St-Placide, 6th arrond. ⓒ **01-45-44-94-44.** www.orcanta.fr. Métro: St-Placide.

Princesse Tam Tam ★ This chain store has its own stylish line of young and sexy bathing suits and underthings. 109 ave. Victor Hugo. ⓒ **01-47-27-77-53.** www.princesse tamtam.com. Métro: Victor Hugo.

Tab Lingerie ★★ Deep discounts on major brands (Léjaby, Simone Pérèle) can be found at this cramped treasure trove, which tempts passersby with a rack stuffed with lacy things at 30 to 70% off. The store entrance is at the end of the narrow corridor. 52 rue de la Chausée d'Antin. ⓒ **01-48-74-41-11.** Métro: Chausée d'Antin–Lafayette.

CHILDREN'S CLOTHING

Du Pareil au Même ★ Covering everything from baby needs to early adolescence, the style at this inexpensive chain store (found all over the city) is fun and original, with lots of bright colors, cute logos, and appliqués. 1 rue St-Denis, 1st arrond. ⓒ **01-42-36-07-57.** www.dpam.com. Métro/RER: Chatelet-Les Halles.

Lilli Bulle ★★ If you're looking for something a little different and original, this is a good place to start. These cool and colorful clothes will make your kids look like they live in this fun and funky neighborhood. 3 rue de la Forge Royale, 11th arrond. ⓒ **01-43-73-71-63.** www.lillibulle.com. Métro: Faidherbe-Chaligny.

Marie Puce ★★ A little softer and gentler than Lilli, Marie offers easy elegance for tots who need to dress up (at least a little) but can't stand frills. Most of the clothing here is 100% Made in France. 60 rue du Cherche Midi, 6th arrond. ⓒ **01-45-48-30-09.** www.mariepuce.com. Métro: Sèvres-Babylone or St-Placide.

VINTAGE CLOTHING

Most Parisian vintage shops sell designer clothing. You may find treasures, but you'll pay for them. For the truly cheap, try the *brocantes* and flea markets.

Chine Machine ★   Terrific finds are in the offing for vintage hunters at this trendy store in the heart of Montmartre, which specializes in hot fashions from yesteryear. 100 rue des Martyrs, 18th arrond. ℰ **01-80-50-27-66.** Métro: Abbesses.

Didier Ludot ★   This isn't just clothing, it's history. Fancy frocks created between 1900 and 1980 line this swank boutique, which is almost more of an antiques shop than a clothing store. 24 galerie de Montpensier, in the arcades of the Palais Royal, 1st arrond. ℰ **01-42-96-06-56.** www.didierludot.fr. Métro: Palais-Royal–Musée du Louvre.

Kiliwatch ★★   This hip emporium is a true vintage store, featuring everything from torn jeans and dayglo dresses to leather jackets and high-fashion. There are books and knickknacks, too. 64 rue Tiquetonne, 1st arrond. ℰ **01-42-21-17-37.** http://espace kiliwatch.fr. Métro: Etienne-Marcel.

Concept Stores

Over the last few years, these hard-to-categorize stores with eclectic collections of stuff have popped up in several parts of the city. These are good places to hunt for that atypical gift you've been seeking.

Bü ★   A cross between Colette (see below), Ikea, and an upscale hardware store, Bü has reasonably priced housewares, stationery, leather handbags, luggage, and toys, as well as quality cleaning supplies and brushes, and gardening tools. A small *epicerie* section features gourmet cooking oils and regional products. 45 rue Jussieu, 5th arrond. ℰ **01-40-56-33-22.** www.bu-store.com. Métro: Jussieu or Cardinal-Lemoine.

Colette ★★   What can you say about a store that sells both Hermès scarves and knitted hot dogs? This shopping phenomenon offers both high style and high concept—basically, if it's utterly cool and happening, they sell it. Karl Lagerfeld jeans, heart-shaped sunglasses, psychedelic nail polish, artsy toilet brushes. 213 rue St-Honoré, 1st arrond. ℰ **01-55-35-33-90.** www.colette.fr. Métro: Tuileries.

Food & Drink
CHOCOLATE
A La Mère de Famille ★   Founded in 1761, this piece of Parisian history (rumor has it the original owner hid the mother superior of the nearby convent from raging revolutionaries during the Terror) has committed its soul to candies and chocolates *à l'ancienne.* You'll find classic chocolates as well as old-fashioned bonbons like *berlingots,* lemon drops, caramels, and jellied fruits. There are five other locations. 35 rue du Faubourg Montmartre, 9th arrond. ℰ **01-47-70-83-69.** www.lameredefamille.com. Métro: Grands Boulevards.

La Maison du Chocolat ★★   With eight shops in Paris, and a few others in London, New York, Tokyo, and Hong Kong, I guess you could call it a chain, but this is still one of the better places to buy chocolate. You'll find everything here, from exquisite basics to modern fantasies, like cognac truffles or chocolates scented with fennel or tea. They also do amazing things with éclairs and *macarons.* 225 rue du Faubourg St-Honoré, 8th arrond. ℰ **01-42-27-39-44.** www.lamaisonduchocolat.com. Métro: Ternes.

Michel Chaudun ★★★   This shop gets my vote for the chocolatier with the best sense of humor. Where else would you find a chocolate cell phone or chocolate Ping-Pong paddles? Chaudun is renowned for his skills as a chocolate sculptor and for the exquisite taste of his masterworks. Be sure to try the *pavés*—melt-in-your-mouth little squares of chocolate ganache made to resemble cobblestones. 149 rue de l'Université, 7th arrond. ℂ **01-47-53-74-40.** Métro: Invalides.

Patrick Roger ★★ This cutting-edge chocolate boutique could easily be mistaken for a jewelry shop. Here you can sample chocolates with names like "Insolence" (almond and chestnut) and "Zanzibar" (thyme and lemon), as well as candied fruits, nougat, and other delicacies. Five other locations in Paris. 108 bd. St-Germain, 6th arrond. ℂ **01-43-29-38-42.** www.patrickroger.com. Métro: Odéon.

SPECIALTY GROCERIES

Fauchon ★ Some (like me) find it over-hyped and over-priced, but others think it's heaven on Earth. Founded in 1886, this tearoom-cum-luxury food emporium has been wowing the crowds for over a century, and the crowds are certainly still coming. Today you can find Fauchon everywhere from Hamburg to Ho Chi Min City. At the original store there are two restaurants, a *pâtissier, boulangerie,* and a gourmet delicatessen, while in a nearby second store (30 place de la Madeleine), you'll find even more specialty items like jams, pastas, and chocolates, as well as a wine cellar. 26 and 30 place de la Madeleine, 8th arrond. ℂ **01-70-39-38-00.** www.fauchon.com. Métro: Madeleine.

La Grande Epicerie Paris ★★ This huge gourmet grocery Mecca, an outgrowth of Le Bon Marché department store (see above), stocks every gourmet substance you could possibly imagine, and many that you couldn't. Sculpted sugar cubes, designer mineral waters, truffled balsamic vinegar, pink salt from the Himalayas—need I go on? There is also an excellent (if expensive) take-out department if you are looking for picnic items. 38 rue de Sèvres, 7th arrond. ℂ **01-44-39-81-00.** www.lagrandeepicerie.fr. Métro: Sèvres-Babylone.

WINES

Wine in France is stunningly cheap. In Paris you can buy a bottle of something extremely pleasant for as little as 5€ or 6€. But before you start planning to stock your wine cellar back home, consider this sad truth: Most non-E.U. countries won't let you bring back much more than a bottle or two. Wine stores abound, and even the most humble of them are generally staffed by knowledgeable wine-lovers who will be glad to help you find the perfect bottle to celebrate your Parisian adventure.

Cave des Abbesses ★ This small wine shop/wine bar has been serving knowing residents of Montmartre for 15 years. Not only will the staff help you muddle through the excellent vintages, but you can sample a few while you're there and nibble on cheese and *charcuterie.* 43 rue des Abbesses, 18th arrond. ℂ **01-42-52-81-54.** www.caves bourdin.fr. Métro: Abbesses

La Cave des Papilles ★★ This wine shop specializes in natural wines from small artisanal vineyards. "Natural" is not the same thing as organic (they sell those, too), but it's close. Basically, it means wines that are carefully raised and processed, using traditional methods. You can pick up some of these beauties for a mere 10€; the knowing staff will help you choose. 35 rue Daguerre, 14th arrond. ℂ **01-43-20-05-74.** www.lacavedespapilles.com. Métro: Denfert Rochereau.

Legrand Filles et Fils ★★ More than just a wine store, this is a place where you can learn everything there is to know about the sacred grape. Not only does this store have a dedicated, knowledgeable staff and a huge stock of wines, but they also host wine tastings, wine classes, and sell wine books, paraphernalia, and glasses. Located in the glamorous Passage Vivienne (see "Arcadia," above). 1 rue de la Banque, 2nd arrond. (C) **01-42-60-07-12**. www.caves-legrand.com. Métro: Bourse.

Les Domaines Qui Montent ★★   French wine-drinkers know that you'll get the best prices when you buy direct at a vineyard. In an attempt to make these prices available to urbanites, this association of some 150 wine producers offers a vast selection of *vins du producteur,* wines that come from small, independent vineyards where the emphasis is on quality and *terroir,* not quantity. Prices are very good. They have two other locations: 136 bd. Voltaire in the 11th, and 2 place Lili Boulanger in the 9th. 22 rue Cardinet, 17th arrond. (C) **01-42-27-63-96**. www.lesdomainesquimontent.com. Métro: Courcelles or Wagram.

Gifts & Souvenirs

Cire Trudon ★★   Founded in 1643, this historic shop once made candles for kings. Today, the charming, old-fashioned store still manufactures magnificent candles out of traditional materials. 78 rue de Seine, 6th arrond. (C) **01-43-26-46-50**. www.ciretrudon.com. Métro: Odéon.

La Plaque Emaillée Jacquin ★   Established in 1908, this shop manufactures cast-iron enameled plaques, like the famous street signs you see all over Paris. You can pick up reproduction advertisements (absinthe, body shop, and such), Parisian street signs, or custom order one to commemorate virtually any event, person, or piece of real estate that appeals to you. They make engraved brass or Plexiglas plaques as well. *Note:* Custom orders take 3 or 4 weeks to fill before they are shipped. 18 bd. des Filles-du-Calvaire, 11th arrond. (C) **01-47-00-50-95**. www.la-plaque-emaillee.com. Métro: St-Sébastien.

La Tuile à Loup ★★   Dedicated to promoting (and selling) authentic handicrafts from the provinces of France, this cozy shop has a stock that includes handwoven baskets, cutlery, woodcarvings, and pottery. They have a particularly good collection of ceramics, in both traditional styles and works by contemporary artists. 35 rue Daubenton, 5th arrond. (C) **01-47-07-28-90**. www.latuilealoup.com. Métro: Censier-Daubenton.

Housewares, Kitchen & Decoration

Dehillerin ★   A culinary presence for some 200 years, this place has a phenomenal range of cooking equipment in every size, shape, and material. If you are looking for some arcane cooking instrument, this is the place to find it. This store is geared towards professionals who come from city restaurants to stock up, so it's kind of hard to just browse around. 18–20 rue Coquillière, 1st arrond. (C) **01-42-36-53-13**. www.e-dehillerin.fr. Métro or RER: Les Halles.

La Maison Ivre ★★   This shop carries a great assortment of table linens, kitchen accessories, and beautiful handmade pottery from all over France, especially Provençal ceramics, including ovenware, bowls, platters, plates, pitchers, mugs, and vases. The beautiful tea towels, placemats, and tablecloths here make great gifts and pack easily. 38 rue Jacob, 6th arrond. (C) **01-42-60-01-85**. www.maison-ivre.com. Métro: St-Germain-des-Prés.

La Vaissellerie ★   With five locations in the city center, this is the most convenient choice for discount china and ceramics. These small stores are so chock-full of cute gift items that their wares generally spill out onto the sidewalk. In addition to china, they have piles of salt shakers, cheese knives, and all sorts of utensils you never knew you needed (like champagne corks) as well as kitchen magnets, shopping bags, cookie boxes, and so on. Other locations are listed on the website. 85 rue de Rennes, 6th arrond. © **01-42-22-61-49.** www.lavaissellerie.fr. Métro: St-Sulpice.

Plastiques ★★ Who knew plastic could be so much fun? This colorful shop is loaded with plastic dishes, lampshades, toothbrush holders, and all sorts of other gift ideas in all the colors of the rainbow. A couple doors down, on the corner of rue d'Assas, is their second shop, which has a fabulous range of designer plasticized table cloths and *toile ciré* (oilcloth), which come in various table sizes or by the meter. 103 rue de Rennes, 6th arrond. © **01-45-48-75-88.** www.plastiques-paris.fr. Métro: St-Sulpice or Rennes.

Jewelry & Accessories

Bijoux Blues ★★ Hand-crafted, unique jewelry at reasonable prices made in an atelier in the Marais—who could ask for more? Made of Austrian and bohemian crystals, natural and semiprecious stones, pearls, and coral, the designs are fun and funky, yet elegant. Pieces can be custom-designed. 30 rue St-Paul, 4th arrond. © **01-48-04-00-64.** www.bijouxblues.com. Métro: St-Paul.

Bijoux Burma ★ Pretend you are a princess with these excellent copies of the kind of spectacular pieces you could never afford. These are some of the best fakes around. This quality costume jewelry is the secret weapon of many a Parisian woman. You can even pretend you are really going into one of Paris's finest jewelry shops as all six branches are strategically placed in the fanciest shopping neighborhoods. 50 rue François-Premier, 8th arrond. © **01-47-23-70-93.** www.bijouxburma.com. Métro: Franklin-D-Roosevelt.

White Bird ★★ If you are looking for a unique engagement ring or present for your sweetheart, this is a good bet. This low-key store offers a terrific selection of jewelry made by talented, independent craftspeople, and designers. That means you can find something beautifully different here. 38 rue du Mont Thabor, 1st arrond. © **01-58-62-25-86.** www.whitebirdjewellery.com. Métro: Concorde.

Music & Electronics

Fnac ★ A huge chain that sells a compelling combination of books, music, and electronics, Fnac (pronounced "fnack") has branches all over the city. Since electronics stores are few and far between in Paris, this is an ideal spot to drop in if you need something for your computer, iPod, or digital camera. There's also a ticket office *(billeterie)* that covers just about every museum, concert, and event in town. 136 rue de Rennes, 6th arrond. © **09-69-32-43-34.** www.fnac.com. Métro: St-Placide.

Stationery

Gibert Joseph ★ One of the largest selections of everything from elegant fountain pens to creamy pastels can be found at this multi-leveled store. Mostly geared toward student needs, this is a good place to find both the practical and the pretty at reasonable prices. 26–34 bd. St-Michel, 6th arrond. © **01-44-41-88-88.** www.gibertjoseph.com. Métro: Cluny–La Sorbonne.

L'Art du Papier ★★ This delightful stationery store has a fabulous selection of colored papers and envelopes, as well as ink-stamps, sealing wax, and the essentials for hobbies like calligraphy and "le scrapbooking." There are three other locations: 16 rue Daunou in the 2nd, 197 bd. Voltaire in the 11th, and 17 ave. de Villiers in the 17th. 48 rue Vavin, 6th arrond. © **01-43-26-10-12.** www.art-du-papier.fr. Métro: Vavin.

Toys & Games

Au Nain Bleu ★   It's worth coming to Au Nain Bleu, the oldest and fanciest toy store in Paris, just to see a place that still makes custom-ordered toys. They also have teepees to play in, electric cars to drive, and imperial costumes that will allow your little darlings to dress up like Napoleon and Empress Josephine. In other words, this is not your average toy store. 252 bd. St-Germain, 7th arrond. ℂ **01-42-65-20-00.** www.aunain bleu.com. Métro: Solferino.

Le Bonhomme de Bois ★   Wooden toys are the order of the day at this shop. There's also puzzles, mobiles, stuffed animals, and mini-knights in shining armor. There are four other branches in Paris: 13 rue Maubeuge in the 9th; 19 rue de la Roquette in the 11th; 141 rue d'Alésia in the 14th; and 46 ave. Niel in the 17th. 43 bd. Malesherbes, 8th arrond. ℂ **01-40-17-03-33.** www.bonhommedebois.com. Métro: St-Augustin.

ENTERTAINMENT & NIGHTLIFE

P aris blooms at night. Its magnificent monuments and build-ings become even more beautiful when they're cloaked in their evening illuminations. The already glowing Eiffel Tower bursts out in twinkling lights for the first 10 minutes of every hour. While simply walking around town can be an excellent night out, the city is also a treasure trove of rich evening offerings. There are bars and clubs from chic to shaggy, sublime theater and dance perfor-mances, top-class orchestras, and scores of cinemas and art-film houses.

While Paris isn't a 24-hour town like some international capitals, and many neighborhoods may seem pretty quiet after sundown, there are still plenty of places to go if you are ready for a night out. So whether you're determined to spend the bucks to go to the Moulin Rouge or happy with a 3€ beer in a student bar in the Latin Quarter, I'm here to help you find your way. Below is a biased selection of some of the better ways to spend your Parisian evenings; the end of the chapter is dedicated to sport fans in search of a game/race/match.

GETTING TICKETS Many hotels will help you get tickets and most venues have a reservation link on their websites, but the easiest way to get tickets is at **Fnac,** the giant bookstore/music chain that has one of the most comprehensive box offices in the city (follow the signs to the "Billeterie"). You can also **order your tickets online** in English at www.fnactickets.com, or by phone at ✆ **08-92-68-36-22** (.34€ per min.). **Ticketnet.fr** offers a similar service.

Discount hunters can stand in line at one of the city's three **half-price ticket booths,** both run by **Le Kiosque Théâtre** (www.kiosquetheatre.com; Tues–Sat 12:30–8pm, Sun 12:30–4pm). There's one in front of the Mont-parnasse train station, the other is on the west side of the Madeleine (facing 15 place de la Madeleine, exit rue Tronchet from the Madeleine Métro stop), and a third in the center of Place des Ternes (17th arrond.). Half-price tickets for same-day performances go on sale here at 12:30pm. Don't dawdle—by noon the line is usually already long. Not up to the challenge? There are plenty of ticket discounts at **BilletRéduc,** www.billetreduc.com (in French).

THEATER

There are hundreds of theaters in Paris, most of which have something going on almost every night. The obvious catch here is, almost all of it is in French. Even if you can't spit out much more than *bonjour* and *merci,*

For up-to-the-minute dates and schedules for what's happening in music, theater, dance, and film, pick up the weekly listing magazines **"Pariscope"** or **"l'Officiel des Spectacles"** (both .50€), the Parisian bibles for weekly events. **"Télérama"** also has a weekly pull out listings guide, complete with reviews. All of the above come out on Wednesdays and are available at any newsstand.

Online, **Télérama's website** has good listings (www.telerama.fr, click on "sortir") as does **"l'Officiel des Spectacles"** (www.offi.fr). Both sites are in French only. For reviews and listings in English, try the **"Paris Voice"** (www.parisvoice.com), an English-language online magazine that regularly reviews shows around town. By the way, if you see a sign at a theater or on an events website that says *location*, that means "box office," not location.

fear not, there are options. There are a few English language shows like the hit "How To Become a Parisian in One Hour" (see "Belly Laughs in English," below) or you can opt for one of the many avant-garde offerings at theaters like Théâtre de Chaillot or Théâtre de la Ville, where shows that combine dance, theater and images don't really need translation. Ticket prices, particularly for the large, state-funded theaters, are remarkably low. For example, the most expensive seats are 36€ at the Odéon and 41€ at the Comédie-Française.

Comédie-Française ★★ In 1680, Louis XIV announced the birth of a company of actors, chosen by Himself, with the aim of "making theater productions more perfect." Some 300 years later, it is still considered by many the crème de la crème of the French theater scene. In addition to the gorgeous just-restored main theater **(Salle Richelieu)**, the company presents its offerings in its two other theaters: the medium-size **Théâtre du Vieux Colombier** (21 rue du Vieux Colombier, 6th arrond.; Métro: St-Sulpice or Sèvres–Babylone) and the smaller **Studio-Théâtre** (Galerie du Carrousel du Louvre, under the Pyramid, 99 rue de Rivoli, 1st arrond.; Métro: Palais Royal–Musée du Louvre). Place Colette, 1st arrond. ℂ **01-44-58-15-15.** www.comedie-francaise.fr. Métro: Palais-Royal–Musée du Louvre.

Odéon, Théâtre de l'Europe ★ Less venerable and more modern, this grand theater presents both new plays and old classics, but even the classics usually get a modern twist. There are lots of cutting edge, contemporary pieces here, including several from other European countries (hence the moniker "Théâtre de l'Europe"). Foreign productions are supertitled, which can be a plus if you can read French. The Odéon's second space, **Ateliers Berthier** (1 rue André Suarès, 17th arrond.; Métro: Porte de Clichy) presents smaller scale productions, as well as theater for young actors. Place de l'Odéon, 6th arrond. ℂ **01-44-85-40-40.** www.theatre-odeon.fr. Métro: Odéon.

LANDMARK MULTIUSE VENUES

Théâtre de la Ville ★★ It's hard to say which lineup is the most impressive here: theater (new and recent authors), dance (modern dance companies, such as Anne Teresa De Keersmaeker and Pina Bausch), or music (mostly young stars of the classical music scene). A lot of international productions stop by here on tour, so if you

English-language shows are rare, and comics are even more so, but there are a couple of long-standing gigs in town that are worth a detour. At press time, the best place to go for a good giggle was **How to Become a Parisian in One Hour** (playing at Théâtre des Nouvautés, info and reservations at www.oliviergiraud.com), a one-person show written by Olivier Giraud, a Frenchman who spent several years in the U.S. More humor is on tap at **SoGymnase,** Paris' only English-language comedy club, on the fourth floor of the Théâtre du Gymnase Marie Bell (38 ave. Bonne Nouvelle, 10th arrond.; ℂ **01-42-46-79-79;** www.sogymnase.com). Along with stand-up and one-person shows by local expat comics, they also invite visiting talent from the US and the UK.

Paris is the nation's dance capital, and most of the country's best companies are based here, including the phenomenal **Ballet de l'Opéra de Paris** (see "Opéra de Paris," below). Top French choreographers like Angelin Preljoçaj, Blanca Li, and José Montalvo produce here, as well as other European stars like Sidi Larbi Cherkaoui and Mats Ek. Two of the biggest dance venues are **Théâtre de Chaillot** or **Théâtre de la Ville** (see above). For some reason, dance is often grouped with classical music in listings magazines and websites.

missed it at home you might catch it be here. There's also a separate World Music series featuring groups from all over Europe, Asia, and Africa. 2 place du Châtelet. 4th arrond. ℂ **01-42-74-22-77.** www.theatredelaville-paris.com. Métro: Châtelet.

Théâtre du Châtelet ★ Specializing in all that is big and splashy, this lovely 19th-century theater hosts visiting international orchestras, divas, and ballet companies, as well as excellent revivals of musical theater classics like "West Side Story" and "Sweeney Todd." Musicals generally come with a full orchestra and are often in v.o. (*version originale,* or original language), but reserve early as they sell out way in advance. 1 place du Châtelet, 1st arrond. ℂ **01-40-28-28-40.** www.chatelet-theatre.com. Métro: Châtelet.

Théâtre National de Chaillot ★★ Dance and theater are on equal footing at this beautiful Art Deco theater in the Palais de Chaillot, where contemporary choreographers and theater directors share a jam-packed program. There is a lot of blurring of lines here between the two disciplines; dance programs often include video and text, and theater productions often incorporate the abstract. *Tip:* One of the best views of the Eiffel Tower can be seen from the theater's lobby, which has a bar and restaurant where you can eat before the show. 1 place du Trocadéro, 16th arrond. ℂ **01-53-65-30-00.** www.theatre-chaillot.fr. Métro: Trocadéro.

OPERA & CLASSICAL MUSIC

Cité de la Musique ★★ This modern complex offers a wide range of music options, from classical to contemporary to jazz. Along with impressive classical

With few exceptions, the major concert halls and theaters are in action between September and June, taking off the summer months. Not only that, but since the city virtually empties out as Parisians storm the beaches during the annual vacation exodus, many smaller venues and dance clubs also close their doors. On the upside, there are several wonderful summer music festivals, including the Festival Chopin and Jazz à La Villette (p. 192), many of which take place in Paris's lovely parks and gardens. But if you have your heart set on opera or theater, you're better off visiting during the colder weather.

offerings by visiting orchestras and soloists, there's also a good dose of the offbeat and unexpected, like a flamenco Scarlatti program or The Bryan Ferry Orchestra. Young musicians and rising stars are highlighted; small orchestras and chamber musicians also show up on the program. The **Jazz à La Villette** festival in August/September is not to be missed. Ticket prices are very democratic: Top names rarely run over 45€, and many concerts have a one-price ticket for around 15€ to 20€. 221 ave. Jean-Jaurès, 19th arrond.© **01-44-84-44-84.** www.cite-musique.fr. Métro: Porte de Pantin.

Opéra Comique/Salle Favart ★ For a lighter take on opera, try this architectural puff pastry filled with light operas and (French) musicals. Created in 1714 for theatrical performances that included songs, the Opéra Comique endured several fires before finally settling down in a beautiful 19th-century theater complete with huge chandeliers and endless gold curlicues. In 2014-15, the theater celebrates its 300th birthday with a varied season that includes an 18th-century opera-ballet ("Les Fêtes Vénitiennes"), a Strauss operetta ("La Chauve Souris"), and a 21st-century opera ("Au Monde"). 5 rue Favart, 2nd arrond.© **08-25-01-01-23** (.15€ per min.). www.opera-comique.com. Métro: Richelieu–Drouot or Quatre-Septembre.

Opéra de Paris ★★★ This mighty operation includes both the **Palais Garnier** (place de l'Opéra, 9th arrond., an attraction in itself; p. 118) and the **Opéra Bastille** (2 place de la Bastille, 12th arrond.), a slate-colored behemoth that has loomed over the place de la Bastille since 1989, when the national opera company decided it needed a new home. Not wanting to abandon the Palais Garnier, the company decided to split its energies between the two venues. In theory, more operas are performed at the Bastille, which has more space and top-notch acoustics, and the Garnier, home of the **Ballet de l'Opèra de Paris,** focuses more on dance, but the reality is you can see either at both. The opera program sticks pretty much to the classics (though the productions themselves can be cutting-edge), while the ballet offerings are more adventurous, and probably will become more so now that Benjamin Millepied has taken the reins. © **08-92-89-90-90** (.34€ per min.); from outside France © (0)1-71-25-24-23. www.operade paris.fr.

Salle Pleyel ★★★ The Paris equivalent of Carnegie Hall, this mythic concert hall has hosted the likes of Otto Klemperer, Daniel Barenboïm, Louis Armstrong, and Ravi Shankar. The Orchestre de Paris, directed by Christoph Eschenbach, makes its home here, and the Radio France Philharmonic also makes numerous appearances. You'll also find jazz and high-brow pop on the agenda. 252 rue du Faubourg-St-Honoré, 8th arrond. © **01-42-56-13-13.** www.sallepleyel.fr. Métro: Ternes or Charles de Gaulle–Etoile.

Many of Paris's most beautiful churches and cathedrals, including Notre Dame, St-Eustache, and Sainte-Chapelle, host organ and other classical music concerts. Not only is the setting delightful, but the acoustics are generally otherworldly as well. While there is no ticket central for these artistic houses of God, concerts are usually listed in the weekly listings magazines ("Pariscope," "l'Officiel des Spectacles") under classical music. The churches generally print monthly music schedules, which they display near the entrance to the sanctuary (and sometimes post on their websites). Ticket prices are reasonable; you shouldn't pay more than 25€.

Philharmonie de Paris ★★★   Hovering over La Villette like a visiting spaceship, this spanking new mega-venue (scheduled to open in Jan 2015) will seat 2,400 spectators and will serve as the new home of the Orchestre de Paris. Yet another creation of über-architect Jean Nouvel (this time in partnership with Harold Marshall and with input from Yasuhisa Toyota), this silvery apparition also includes an institute, an exposition space, and of course, a nifty cafe and restaurant. In keeping with La Villette's policy of making culture accessible to one and all, the season will include concerts specially designed for young people, families, and audiences that don't usually find themselves in concert halls. 221 ave. Jean-Jaurès, 19th arrond. ☎ **01-44-84-44-84.** www.philharmoniedeparis.com.

CABARET

At the end of the 19th century, cabarets and music halls opened in Montmartre, frequented by oddballs and artists, as well as bourgeois, aristocrats and demi-mondaines looking for a good time. At the time, these nightclubs offered an offbeat reflection of the times, where singers like Aristide Bruand would sing about the life of the destitute and sharp political satire would share the stage with cheeky dancing girls dancing that new step, the cancan. Those days are long gone. Although some visitors feel they simply haven't enjoyed the true Paris experience without seeing a show at the Moulin Rouge or the Lido, these days there is nothing particularly Parisian, or even French about them. Today's audiences are more likely to arrive in tour buses than touring cars, and today's shows are more Vegas than Paris. What you will see here is a lot of scenic razzmatazz and many sublime female bodies, mostly *torse nue* (topless). If you still want to see one of these shows, do yourself a favor and have dinner somewhere else. The food in these establishments is generally mediocre at best. (The following theaters have strict dress codes, so be sure to inquire about them when making reservations.)

Chez Michou ★★   If you are looking for an alternative to the standard girls-with-feathers cabaret show, this might just be the place to go. There are girls here, of a sort—this is Paris' most famous drag show. Michou, the venerable master of ceremonies, presents a bevy of cross-dressed beauties who lip-sync in a range of terrific costumes; some imitate celebrities ranging from Céline Dion to Whoopi Goldberg. 80 rue des Martyrs, 18th arrond. ☎ **01-46-06-16-04.** www.michou.com. 32€–40€ show only at bar, 55€–65€ show only seated; 110€–140€ dinner package. Métro: Pigalle.

9

ENTERTAINMENT & NIGHTLIFE — Cabaret

The Crazy Horse ★★ Don't come here expecting to see cancan. This temple to "The Art of the Nude" presents an erotic dance show with artistic aspirations. Since 2006, when burlesque star Dita Von Teese guest starred here, sexy celebrities have made the occasional on-stage appearance. Be advised that unlike the other shows, this one is known for what the girls aren't wearing. Lighting effects are plentiful, music is mostly modern, and the performers, who slither, swagger, and lip-synch with panache, have names like Zula Zazou and Nooka Karamel. Note that there is no dining onsite; there are dinner-show packages with nearby restaurants. 12 ave. George V, 8th arrond. ℂ 01-47-23-32-32. www.lecrazyhorseparis.com. 65€ show only with seats at the bar; 105€ show only seated; from 125€ for the show and champagne; show plus dinner packages 184€–215€. Métro: George V or Alma Marceau.

Lido de Paris ★ For the full-on glamour gala, head for the Lido. Headdresses and high heels are of such dimensions that the dancers can't really do much dancing, but you're probably not coming here for prima ballerina turns. The current show, "Bonheur," includes 600 costumes, an Indian temple, and circus acts. Unlike some of the other cabarets, the music is live here. There are a few lunch time shows. 16 ave. des Champs-Élysées, 8th arrond. ℂ 01-40-76-56-10. www.lido.fr. 90€–110€ show only; 160€–300€ show with dinner. Métro: George V.

Moulin Rouge ★ When it opened in 1889, the Moulin Rouge was the talk of the town, and its huge dance floor, multiple mirrors, and floral garden inspired painters like Toulouse-Lautrec. In 1907, Mistinguett made her debut here; in later decades legendary French singers like Charles Trenet and Charles Aznavour regularly wowed the crowds. Times have changed—today's Moulin Rouge relies heavily on

Chanson—The Next Generation

You've all heard it, the tremulous voice, the monotonous tunes, the intense sincerity of it all—yes, I'm talking about chanson, those peculiarly melody-challenged songs that Edith Piaf sang. If you don't understand the words, it's hard to understand why so many French people get all misty-eyed when they listen to it. But that's just it, with chanson, it's the words that count. Each song is a poem set to music, in fact some lyrics are the works of famous French authors. In recent years, a new generation of young singers/writers have been coming up with their own poetic versions of the trials and tribulations of life, and their heroes are not so much Piaf and Aznavour as Leonard Cohen and Bob Dylan. The biggest venue for chanson these days is the newly reborn **Les Trois Baudets** (64 bd. de Clichy, 18th arrond.;

ℂ 01-42-62-33-33; www.lestrois baudets.com), but here are two other venues that specialize in this quintessentially French style:

o **Théâtre des 2 Anes** (100 bd. de Clichy, 18th arrond.; ℂ 01-46-06-10-64; www.2anes.com; Métro: Blanche). Depending on the night, it could be humor or singing here, but it will always be with an ironic edge.

o **Au Lapin Agile** (48 bis rue Custine, 18th arrond.; ℂ 01-46-06-85-87; www.au-lapin-agile.com; Métro: Lamarck-Caulaincourt). This legendary spot was once the hangout of then unknown artists and poets like Picasso, Utrillo, and Apollonaire. Despite being a tourist destination, the shows here are nostalgic and heartfelt, with the audience often joining in.

lip-synching and prerecorded music, backed up by dozens of be-feathered Doriss Girls, long-legged ladies that prance about the stage. Be prepared for lots of glitz and not a whole lot else. 82 bd. Clichy, place Blanche, 18th arrond. ℂ **01-53-09-82-82.** www.moulinrouge.fr. 99€ show alone; 109€ show with ½ bottle of champagne; 180€–210€ show with dinner. Métro: Blanche.

Paradis Latin ★ This cabaret may be a bit less glitzy than the others, but it makes more of an attempt to harken back to the cabarets of yesteryear, which featured live and sometimes talented performers. You'll see a variety of acts here, as well as the obligatory topless beauties in feathered costumes and a rollicking cancan. There is a fair amount of interaction with the audience, and a good portion of the show is translated in English. The metallic armature holding up the roof here was designed by Gustave Eiffel. 28 rue du Cardinal Lemoine, 5th arrond. ℂ **01-43-25-28-28.** www.paradislatin.com. 65€–90€ show only; 130€–190€ dinner and show; Métro: Cardinal Lemoine.

MOVIES

With 376 movie theaters and between 450 and 500 films on offer every week, Paris merits its title as cinephile capital of the world. Close to 90 of its theaters have been officially dubbed "Arts et Essai," or art house cinemas, which specialize in rare films and old classics, as well as new independent works. These theaters often host film series on a particular auteur (Woody Allen, John Huston, and others), and they always show films in v.o. *(version originale),* the original, nondubbed version. Many of the mainstream movies shown in the big chain movie theaters dubbed in French (v.f., or *version française*); if you want to see a mainstream English-language film, make sure you find one in v.o. You can find listings of both mainstream and art house theaters in "Pariscope" and "l'Officiel du Spectacle," or on the Internet at Allocine (www.allocine.fr).

Some of the most famous art houses include **Le Champo, Reflet Medecis, Action Ecoles,** and **Accatone,** all in the Latin Quarter. One of the prettiest is **La Pagode** (57 bis rue de Babylone, 7th arrond.; ℂ **01-45-55-48-48;** Métro: St-François-Xavier). This incredible oriental pagoda has exquisite sculpted woodwork, brocaded fabrics, and lacquered tiles. The newest addition to the art house scene is the recently reborn **Louxor** (170 bd. Magenta, 10th arrond.; ℂ **01-44-63-96-96;** www.cinemalouxor.fr; Métro: Barbès-Rochechouart), a gorgeous neo-Egyptian 1920s movie palace that had been abused and abandoned until the city finally took it over and restored it. Today, it is once again a film fan heaven, now with three screens of movie pleasure.

In addition to regular movie theatres, there are three giant cinema archives that have their own theaters and programs:

Designed by Frank Gehry, the wacky building that is the **Cinémathèque Française** (51 rue de Bercy, 12th arrond.; ℂ **01-71-19-33-33;** www.cinematheque.fr; Métro: Bercy) is home to a cinema, library, museum, and research center. The entire history of film can be found between these walls, and programming includes comprehensive retrospectives of great cineastes and themed series on the evolution of film.

In the mighty monster that is the **Centre Pompidou** (Place Georges Pompidou, 4th arrond.; ℂ **01-44-78-12-33;** www.centrepompidou.fr; Métro: Rambuteau, RER: Châtelet–Les Halles), there is a huge collection of films, which are on view in their movie theaters (see website for calendar). Funded by the City of Paris, the **Forum des Images** (Forum des Halles, Porte St-Eustache, 1st arrond; ℂ **01-44-76-63-00;** www.forumdesimages.fr; Métro: Châtelet–Les Halles) has a bank over 7,500 films, including thousands that feature Paris as either the subject or the setting. The agenda is not limited to the French capital; features and documentaries from all over the world are shown here.

LIVE ROCK, JAZZ & MORE

There's a wide range of places to go to hear live music in Paris, ranging from tiny medieval basements to huge, modern concert venues. Wherever your musical tastes lead you, you are bound to enjoy your outing: Not only do many of the world's greatest musicians swing through the city on a regular basis, but you can't beat the walk to the nightclub/bar/theater with the lights of Paris twinkling in the background.

Live Music

JAZZ CLUBS

Paris has been a fan of jazz from its beginnings, and many legendary performers like Sidney Bechet and Kenny Clark made the city their home. Still a haven for jazz musicians and fans of all stripes, there are dozens of places around town to duck in and listen to a good set or two. Here are a few of the best:

Baiser Salé ★★ On a street lined with famous jazz clubs, this one holds its own with a lineup that shows off jazz in all its diversity. Some of the biggest Franco-African jazz stars, like Richard Bona and Angelique Kidjo, got their start here, and the program still highlights the best in African, Caribbean, and Asian, as well as French jazz. There are regular jam sessions on Sundays and Mondays. 58 rue des Lombards, 1st arrond. ✆ **01-42-33-37-71.** www.lebaisersale.com. Cover free to 22€ depending on the act. Métro: Châtelet.

Caveau de la Huchette ★ Since 1946, this place has been a temple of swing. Count Basie and Lionel Hampton once played here. Though today's program is considerably less illustrious, some excellent jazz musicians still play here, setting the groove for the dance floor. The first part of the evening (starting at 10pm), is for enjoying the music. After that there's Swing and Lindy Hop. 5 rue de la Huchette, 5th arrond. ✆ **01-43-26-65-05.** www.caveaudelahuchette.fr. Cover 13€ Sun–Thurs; 15€ Fri–Sat; students 24 and younger 10€. Métro/RER: St-Michel.

Caveau des Oubliettes ★ There are not too many jazz clubs in the world where you can both listen to music and admire an authentic, French Revolution-era guillotine. Located in the Latin Quarter, just across the river from Notre-Dame, this underground nightspot was once a medieval prison, complete with dungeons and spine-tingling passages, where prisoners were tortured. Today patrons laugh, drink, talk, and flirt in the narrow passageways and listen to jazz in the lounge. 52 rue Galande, 5th arrond. ✆ **01-46-34-23-09.** www.caveaudesoubliettes.fr. Free cover, 1 drink min. (from 5.50€). Métro: St-Michel.

Le Duc des Lombards ★★ This is one of the most famous jazz clubs in Paris, where famous names come to play in a small, intimate space. That said, it's a relatively low-key place and tickets aren't too hard to get—but good seats are (they are not numbered) so get here early if you want to sit up front. Free jam sessions on Fridays and Saturdays after midnight. 42 rue des Lombards, 1st arrond. ✆ **01-42-33-22-88.** www.ducdeslombards.com. Cover free–30€. Métro: Châtelet.

Le Sunset/Le Sunside ★★ Yet another famous jazz club on the rue des Lombards, what sets this one off is its split personality. Le Sunset Jazz, created in 1983, is dedicated to electric jazz and international music, whereas le Sunside, launched in

2001, is devoted to acoustic jazz for the most part. Some of the hottest names in French jazz appear here regularly (Jacky Terrasson, Didier Lockwood, to name a couple) along with a new crop of international stars. 60 rue des Lombards, 1st arrond. ✆ **01-40-26-46-60.** www.sunset-sunside.com. Tickets 15€–30€. Métro: Châtelet.

New Morning ★★★ If you are looking for big names and hot acts, look no further. This place has terrific lineups, including jazz masters like Ravi Coltrane and Terrance Blanchard, pop legends Martha Reeves and the Vandellas, as well as a long list of young upstarts and world music stars. This relatively large club (the room holds 300), fills up quick and it's no wonder: This truly is one of the best jazz venues in town, and the top ticket price is only around 30€. 7 rue des Petites-Ecuries, 10th arrond. ✆ **01-45-23-51-41.** www.newmorning.com. Cover 18€–28€. Métro: Château-d'Eau.

CONCERT VENUES

Cabaret Sauvage ★★ Is it a cool club or a circus tent? The answer is not clear at this unusual space where you are just as likely to encounter Brazilian samba, electro funk, or trapeze artists. Blues bands from the Balkans and Vietnamese jazz musicians share the calendar with avant-garde circus acts and Algerian acrobats. Although this big-top cabaret is essentially a performance space with an accent on world music and dance, it also hosts themed dance parties, where you can boogie to jungle and techno, as well as raï, mambo, samba, and so forth. Parc de la Villette, entrance at 59 bd. Mac Donald, 19th arrond. ✆ **01-42-09-03-09.** www.cabaretsauvage.com. Métro: Porte de la Villette.

La Cigale ★★ This 19th-century music hall draws some of the biggest artists working in music today—everything from indie rock to hip-hop and jazz. Balcony seating is available for those who arrive early, and there's plenty of open floor space for those who want to dance. 120 boulevard de Rochechouart, 18th arrond. ✆ **01-49-25-89-99.** www.lacigale.fr. Métro: Pigalle or Anvers.

Le Bataclan ★ This former music hall opened in 1864 with a wild "Chinese Cafe" architecture that brought in the crowds. All that remains is the funky facade, but the stage inside still draws full houses (and this is a big place) for a wide range of concerts, from indie-rock to Argentine tango. 50 bd. Voltaire, 11e. ✆ **01-49-23-96-33.** www.bataclan.fr. Métro: Oberkampf.

Olympia ★★★ For French musicians, playing the Olympia is a little like reaching the golden heaven of the Greek gods. Legends like Georges Brassens, Edith Piaf, Louis Armstrong, and Aretha Franklin have all appeared at this cavernous hall, which draws French and international pop, rock, and jazz stars like Juliette Greco, Herbie Hancock, and Elvis Costello. 28 bd. des Capucines, 9th arrond. ✆ **08-92-68-33-68** (.34€ per min). www.olympiahall.com. Métro: Opéra or Madeleine.

LIVE MUSIC BARS

L'Alimentation Générale ★★ The ambiance is comfortable and slightly kitsch; this bar/restaurant/music space was created in the spirit of an *alimentation génerale,* a little corner grocery store that stays open late and sells a little bit of everything. Thus the programming is eclectic, including a good dose of world music. DJs or live bands play here practically every night, and the cover charge ranges from nothing to 10€ (drink included). Happy hour Wednesday to Saturday from 7–9pm. 64 rue Jean-Pierre Timbaud, 11th arrond. ✆ **01-43-55-42-50.** www.alimentation-generale.net. Métro: Parmentier.

L'International ★ Here's a no-brainer for a fun night out that won't hurt your pocketbook: two to three bands and a DJ set in a relaxed setting for free. On the eclectic agenda is a string of folk, rock, electro, you-name-it bands playing to hip indie crowds. Beer is cheap and there are periodic after-show parties until 4am. 5/7 rue Moret, 11th arrond. ⓒ **01-49-29-76-45**. www.linternational.fr. Métro: Ménilmontant.

OPA ★   A temple to the independent spirit, OPA is free and promotes unknown stars of tomorrow. There's an industrial ambiance here; this is not the place to wear those new boots you just bought in the Marais. There are live bands Wednesday through Saturday, and dance parties 'til dawn on Friday and Saturday nights (after the bands). 9 rue Biscornet, 12th arrond. ⓒ **01-46-28-12-90**. www.opa-paris.com. Métro: Bastille.

CATEGORY-DEFYING VENUES

There are an increasing number of venues that are so multifunctional they defy any attempt to fit them under the usual headings. Sure, you can enjoy music and dance in these places, but you can also go to a screening, check out a poetry lounge, visit an art expo, happen in on a lecture/demonstration, and of course, eat, drink and be merry. Many are all-day affairs, where the activities change as the sun goes down, others are purely for night owls. With so many variables, checking the venue's program online is the best way to find out what's on during your stay.

La Bellevilloise ★★   This 19th-century building was the home of the city's first workers' cooperative, offering cultural activities and meeting spaces to the down-trodden. Today, the structure has been transformed, but the mission is still a cultural one. Dedicated to "light, night, and creativity" this lofty space has been divvied up into art galleries, performance spaces, a concert hall, a club, and a restaurant with a lovely outdoor terrace where you can have a drink. The program ranges from film festivals to fashion shows, with a good dose of contemporary music. On the weekends there are daytime activities, like workshops, specialty markets, and dance classes. 19–21 rue Boyer, 20th arrond. ⓒ **01-46-36-07-07**. www.labellevilloise.com. Métro: Gambetta.

Le Carreau du Temple ★★   The latest addition to the growing list of multi-tasking cultural centers rising from the ashes of neglected historic architecture, this former covered market spent several sorry decades as a used clothing bazaar. Today, after a several-million-euro facelift, this city-owned and operated venue features sports facilities, rehearsal rooms, concert halls, and other spaces where artists, musicians, actors, and fashion mavens can strut their stuff. This means you can see theater or dance, watch fashion shows, work out, or enjoy one of the concerts or dance parties on their eclectic program. 4 rue Eugène Spuller, 3rd arrond. ⓒ **01-83-81-93-30**. www.carreaudu temple.eu. Métro: Temple or République.

Le Centquatre ★★★   What was once the municipal morgue is now a vast space dedicated to all things artistic and fun. There is food for both the spirit and the stomach here: theater, dance, music, visual arts, as well as a gourmet grocery, cafes and restaurants. Along with concerts and dance parties for grown-ups, there are activities for families and little ones (musical events, art workshops, and so forth). If that's not enough, you can also shop for bargains in the Emmaüs shop (a charitable organization that sells wonderful used things) or browse at the bookstore. In short, there's something for everyone to do at most times of the day or night. 5 rue Curial, 19th arrond. ⓒ **01-53-35-50-00**. www.104.fr. Métro: Riquet.

Point Ephemere ★   Describing itself as a "center for artistic dynamics," this converted warehouse on the banks of the Canal St-Martin prides itself on nurturing up-and-coming artists, musicians, dancers, and filmmakers, and offers residencies to a chosen few who work in studios on the premises. The packed program includes lots of *soirées*, or dance parties, with an emphasis on electronic music, though plain old experimental rock is represented as well. Dance concerts, art expositions, and discussion forums are also on the agenda. Tickets for most events are in the 12€ to 20€ range. There is a suitably downscale-hip quay-side bar and restaurant, with an outdoor terrace in nice weather. 200 quai Valmy, 10th arrond. ℂ **01-40-34-02-48.** www.pointephemere.org. Métro: Jean Jaurès.

THE BAR SCENE

There is an astounding assortment of bars in Paris, a city which does not seem to have a particularly feisty nightlife at first sight. There are cafes galore, of course, but a cafe is not necessarily a bar. Though both serve alcoholic beverages, cafes offer a laid-back place to sip at any time of day or night, whereas anything that calls itself a bar usually has an edgier feel and gets going after dark. Two recent developments may be responsible for the per-capital barstool increase: First, France has finally discovered cocktails and is putting its culinary talent to work behind the bar. Second, there is a new fondness for beer, a beverage that has often been treated with scorn and dismay in this wine-drinking country. Artisanal brewpubs are cropping up all around town. Bars, be they beer, wine or cocktail oriented, generally stay open until around 2am.

Bars & Cafes

Andy Wahloo ★★ This is a tiny temple to 1970s North African culture and kitsch. Sip your drink beneath a silk-screened Moroccan coffee and listen to some of the best Algerian raï around. Come early, before the crowds snatch up all the upturned paint cans that serve as seating. 69 rue des Gravilliers, 3rd arrond. ℂ **01-42-71-20-38.** www.andywahloo-bar.com. Métro: Arts et Métiers.

Café Charbon ★★ This turn-of-the-20th-century beauty (it was once a dance hall) welcomes hoards of happy night-birds under its arched ceilings; the door in the back leads to the nightclub, La Nouvelle Casino, where live bands and DJs shake it up until the wee hours. You can come here any time of day, for coffee, a drink, or a good meal. 109 rue Oberkampf, 11th arrond. ℂ **01-43-57-55-13.** Métro: Parmentier or Ménilmontant.

Chez Jeannette ★ This old bar was revamped by a young hip bunch, who had the good sense to preserve its old, kitschy decor. Located on a somewhat scruffy stretch of rue du Faubourg St-Dennis, it seems out of place on its block, but that's part of what makes the place cool. Hot meals also served here. 47 rue du Faubourg Saint-Denis, 10th arrond. ℂ **01-47-70-30-89.** www.chezjeannette.com. Metro: Château d'Eau.

Dédé La Frite ★ Here's the gimmick at Dédé's: Instead of a boring bowl of peanuts, you can get a dish of French fries with your drink. This is a cute and hip corner bar where you have a choice of two sidewalks terraces. 135 rue de Montmartre, 2nd arrond. ℂ **01-40-41-99-90.** Metro: Bourse.

Where's the Party Tonight?

Sponsored by the city's tourist office and the Paris city hall, **Paris Nightlife** (www.parisnightlife.fr) offers a calendar with a hefty dose of listings for what's on after dark each night. It might not list absolutely everything, but it's pretty comprehensive, from clubbing, to jazz dens, to tea dances.

Experimental Cocktail Club ★ If you are looking for a sophisticated spot to spot stars, you've come to the right place. Known, not surprisingly, for its gourmet cocktails, this cosmopolitan lounge has the feel of a retro speakeasy. 37 rue St-Sauveur, 2nd arrond. ℰ **01-45-08-88-09.** www.experimentalcocktailclub.com. Métro: Sentier.

La Rotonde ★★ Not to be confused with the historic but stuffy Rotonde in Montparnasse, this huge, round 18th-century pavilion sits at the southern end of the Bassin de La Villette on place Stalingrad. It originally served as a sort of giant toll-booth (a *barrière d'octroi*), when "foreign" merchants were obliged to pay a tax to sell their goods in Paris. Today, it houses a restaurant, a wine bar/beer garden/tearoom (Le Refuge), and on warm days, a delightful terrace where you can sip in the sun. 6–8 place de la Bataille de Stalingrad, 19th arrond. ℰ **01-80-48-33-40.** www.larotonde.com. Métro: Stalingrad or Jaurès.

Le Bar du Plaza Athénée ★★ Knock yourself out and order a shockingly expensive drink at this classy, historic joint, which simply drips with glamour and fabulousness. At press time, the hotel was closed for an in-depth makeover, but rest assured, the bar will be as fabulous as it ever was when it reopens in June 2014. Hotel Plaza-Athénée, 25 ave. Montaigne, 8th arrond. ℰ **01-53-67-66-00.** www.plaza-athenee-paris.fr. Métro: Alma-Marceau.

Le China ★ This sleek bar and restaurant evokes 1930s Shanghai with its dim lighting, red walls, and deep leather Chesterfield couches. The restaurant serves pricey gourmet Chinese cuisine, while the long zinc bar (the longest in Paris) on the ground floor invites you to order a cocktail. Downstairs is another bar, with live jazz and pop music. 50 rue de Charenton, 12th arrond. ℰ **01-43-46-08-09.** www.lechina.eu. Métro: Ledru Rollin.

Le Merle Moqueur ★ What people love about this place is that it hasn't changed a bit since their student days. There are still dozens of *rhum arrangés* (flavored rums)

Irish Bars—Drinking in English

Had enough of trying to speak French? Looking for a place to unwind in semi-familiar surroundings? There are a few dozen Irish bars in Paris, where you can appreciate the joys of a good pint of Guinness.

○**Carr's Restaurant & Pub** This roomy bar caters to the drinking and eating needs of expats, tourists, and a varied assortment of Parisians. Known for its live music, Celtic and otherwise, as well as its Irish stew. 1 rue du Mont-Thabor, 1st arrond. ℰ **01-42-60-60-26.** www.carrsparis.com. Métro: Tuileries.

○**Galway's** Tucked into an ancient building on the quai des Grands

Augustins (shouting distance from place St-Michel), this place might be a little dark and a little cramped, but it's almost always filled to the brim with happy customers sipping a pint. 13 quai des Grands Augustins. ℰ **01-43-29-64-50.** Métro: St-Michel.

○**The Quiet Man** Named after a famous John Wayne movie set in Ireland, this cozy spot is one of the better Irish pubs in Paris, though the owner is actually French. 5 rue des Haudriettes, 3rd arrond. ℰ **01-48-04-02-77.** www.thequietman.eu. Métro: Rambuteau.

to choose from and the bar is still packed. Best after 10pm, when the crowds get animated. 11 rue de la Butte aux Cailles, 13th arrond. No phone. Métro: Place d'Italie.

Wine Bars

Wine fans can lose their heads in this city, not because they drink too much, but because there are so many tempting wine bars out there to choose from. Not only can you sample all sorts of delightful fruits of the vine at a *bar à vin*, but you can usually nibble something salty and delicious (generally cheese or charcuterie) to complement what's in the glass.

5e Cru ★ Offering a multitude of the best and the brightest French wines, this trendy spot also tickles the taste buds with a terrific lunch menu. At night, there are cheese and charcuterie platters as well as frequent themed wine tastings. 7 rue du Cardinal Lemoine, 5th arrond. ✆ **01-40-46-86-34.** www.5ecru.com. Métro: Jussieu.

Le Baron Rouge ★★ This neighborhood institution spills out on a corner that it shares with the sprawling Marché d'Aligre. There are only a few tables, so most people stand at the counter or outside, glass in hand, especially during market hours. Huge vats of wine are stacked up inside, and you can fill up if you bring a bottle. In season, platters of oysters are served to accompany your wine. Otherwise, there is only cheese and charcuterie. It's a little rough and tumble getting your drink order in at the bar. 1 rue Théophile Roussel, 12th arrond. ✆ **01-43-43-14-32.** Metro: Ledru-Rollin.

Les Caves Populaires ★★ This is a neighborhood wine bar where locals come to shoot the breeze. The waiters are friendly, the decor low key, and the wine and cheese and sausage platters are cheap. A good excuse to explore the offbeat Batignolles neighborhood, a mix of artsy types, old timers and students. 22 rue des Dames, 17th arrond. ✆ **01-53-04-08-32.** Metro: Place de Clichy.

Rouge Passion ★ Here's a mellow wine bar for the young and in love, or just those who are in love with wine. Run by a friendly young couple from Nice, this popular spot also serves great food. 14 rue Jean-Baptiste Pigalle, 9th arrond. ✆ **01-42-85-07-62.** www.rouge-passion.fr. Metro: Pigalle.

DANCE CLUBS

Like in any big city, Parisian clubs are divided into different scenes: Some places are more "see and be seen," while others tend to focus less on what you're wearing and more on the music being played. Certain locations stay popular for years, but most will wax and wane in their level of "coolness." Also, the French love their fashion, so dressing to impress is obligatory—sneakers will rarely get you past the line outside. Most clubs don't really get going until at least 11pm, if not later.

Batofar ★★ For over 15 years, this bright red boat has been the site of music, dancing, and general good times. Docked on the quai François Mauriac, just in front of the imposing François Mitterand National Library, this multifunctional floating venue includes a dance club, bar, restaurant, and a terrace for cocktails hour and low-key soirees. From May to September there is even a "beach" set up on the riverbank, where you can eat, drink, and continue to be merry. The main event here is the dance club though, and on good nights you'll see hundreds of gyrating dancers moving in rhythm to house, garage, techno, and live jazz music. Facing 11 quai François Mauriac, 13th arrond. ✆ **01-53-60-17-00.** www.batofar.org. Métro: Quai de la Gare.

Chez Moune ★ If you want to stomp around in your best dancing shoes while pumping your fist in the air, Chez Moune is the place to do it. A former lesbian cabaret that dates from the 1930s, this fun club is filled with young *branché* (hip) Parisians dancing their hearts out. What's more, there is often no cover. The music pounds (mostly electro and house), the walls glitter (mirror tiles everywhere), and the beat goes on and on. 54 rue Jean-Baptiste Pigalle, 9th arrond. © **01-45-26-64-64.** Métro: Pigalle.

Favela Chic ★★ It's always Rio here at this Brazilian hotspot where you can dance to bossa jazz, samba rap, and tropical electro into the wee hours of the night. The dance floor may be crowded, and the conditions may get saunalike, but the music is great and they make some of the best mojitos in town. There are plenty of themed party nights here with guest DJ's. There's a restaurant here, too. 18 rue du Faubourg du Temple, 11th arrond. © **01-40-21-38-14.** www.favelachic.com. Métro: République.

Machine du Moulin Rouge ★★ A heck of a lot more hip than its historic next door neighbor, this three-story club has dance floors, concert space, and bars—basically, everything you need for a rollicking night out. The music savvy crowds come for electronic everything: rock, funk, pop, dubstep, glitch, drum'n'bass, house—not to mention live music by rising stars. If that's not enough for you, there are themed soiree nights, hosted by various labels and radio stations. 90 bd. de Clichy, 18th arrond. © **01-53-41-88-89.** www.lamachinedumoulinrouge.com. Métro: Blanche.

Nouveau Casino ★★ The cool big brother of Café Charbon (see "Bars" above), this former movie theater is now a giant dance club with live music, a huge bar that vaguely resembles an iceberg, hanging chandeliers, and a terrific program that includes all sorts of avant-garde dance music and bands with names like Flatbush Zombies and Moon Safari Club. 109 rue Oberkampf, 9th arrond. © **01-43-57-57-40.** www.nouveaucasino.net. Métro: St-Maur, Parmentier, or Ménilmontant.

Rex Club ★ Set in the bowels of the huge movie theater of the same name, this is one of the old stalwarts of the Parisian rock and roll scene. There's a high-tech industrial theme to the decor, but it's the live music and DJs that people come for, and come they do. This space recalls the big techno-grunge clubs of London, complete with an international mood-altered crowd. The music here is usually deep and dark, bass-heavy house, and other electronica. 5 bd. Poissonnière, 2nd arrond. © **01-42-36-10-96.** www.rexclub.com. Métro: Bonne Nouvelle.

Showcase ★ This unusual club is actually under a bridge. Seriously. Set in an old boat hangar beneath the Pont Alexandre III, it has incredible views of the Seine. The club had a major makeover in 2014 and now focuses on high-quality electro, techno and house. Port des Champs-Élysées under the Pont Alexandre III. © **01-49-97-08-77.** www.showcase.fr. Métro: Invalides.

Social Club ★★ This club is so hip that you actually don't dress up (or rather, you try to make it look like you are not dressing up); the vibe is alternative and the mood is chill. You can pick from live hip-hop, jazz, funk, drum'n' bass, and all-night electro parties. 142 rue de Montmartre, 2nd arrond. © **01-40-28-05-55.** www.parissocialclub.com. Métro: Bourse, or Grands Boulevards.

THE GAY & LESBIAN SCENE

Paris has a vibrant gay nightlife scene, primarily centered around the Marais. Gay dance clubs come and go so fast that even the magazines devoted to them, like

"Qweek" (www.qweek.fr)—distributed free in the gay bars and bookstores—have a hard time keeping up. **"Têtu"** magazine, sold at most newsstands, has special nightlife inserts for gay bars and clubs.

Gay & Lesbian Bars & Clubs

Banana Café ★ This popular night spot is known for its party hardy atmosphere as well as its go-go boys, who do their go-go thing every night of the week. In addition to the usual nightly frolicking, there are themed parties, tea dances, and drag nights. 13 rue de la Ferronnerie, 1st arrond. ℰ **01-42-33-35-31.** www.bananacafeparis.com. Métro/RER: Châtelet.

La Bôite à Frissons–Tango ★ An old classic, this is a kinder, gentler atmosphere with an emphasis on ballroom dancing. Later in the night, the music gets more lively, but you won't find any techno here. There are special nights for boys, nights for girls, and nights for a little bit of everything—check the website for details. 13 rue au Maire, 4th arrond. ℰ **01-42-72-17-78.** www.boite-a-frissons.fr. Métro: Arts et Métiers.

Le Cox ★ Even though it's been a fixture on the gay scene for years, Le Cox still draws big crowds for its cool bar and great DJs. The clientele is a pleasant mix—everything from hunky American tourists to sexy Parisians. 15 rue des Archives, 4th arrond. ℰ **01-42-72-08-00.** www.cox.fr. Métro: Hôtel de Ville.

Le Raidd ★ This wild place offers hunky bartenders, a spacious dance floor, go-go dancers, and male strippers who take it all off under an open shower. Very trendy, on weekends you'll have to get past the *selectionneur* at the door who decides who's cool enough to enter. 23 rue du Temple, 4th arrond. ℰ **01-42-77-04-88.** www.raiddbar.com. Métro: Hôtel-de-Ville or Rambuteau.

Le Rive Gauche ★ Low key and stylish, this swanky joint hosts a regular lesbian party on Saturday nights for a young, hip crowd. Men are welcome when accompanied by women. 1 rue du Sabot, 6th arrond. ℰ **01-40-20-43-23.** www.lerivegauche.com. Métro: St-Germain-des-Prés.

Le 3w Kafe ★ The most popular lesbian bar in the Marais, this is a good place to come to find company. Downstairs, a DJ spins on weekends, when there's dancing. Men can only enter the premises if accompanied by a woman. 8 rue des Ecouffes, 4th arrond. ℰ **01-48-87-39-26.** Métro: St. Paul.

Open Café ★ More relaxed, more diverse than neighboring Le Cox, this cafe-bar has a busy sidewalk terrace that is usually full both day and night. Everyone from humble tourists to sharp-looking businessmen to TV stars hangs out here. 17 rue des Archives, 4th arrond. ℰ **01-42-72-26-18.** www.opencafe.fr. Métro: Hôtel-de-Ville.

SPECTATOR SPORTS

For inveterate sports fans who need a good dose of athletic adrenaline, Paris can supply an ample fix. The French go crazy for soccer, rugby, tennis, and horse racing, among other things.

Horse Racing

Paris boasts an army of avid horse-racing fans who get to the city's eight racetracks whenever possible. Information on current races is available in newspapers like **"L'Equipe,"** sold at kiosks throughout the city, and online at www.france-galop.com.

The epicenter of Paris horse racing is the **Hippodrome de Longchamp,** in the Bois de Boulogne, 16e (✆ **01-44-30-75-00;** RER or Métro: Porte Maillot and then a free shuttle bus on race days, otherwise bus 244). Established in 1855, during the autocratic and pleasure-loving reign of Napoleon III, it's the most prestigious track, boasts the greatest number of promising thoroughbreds, and awards the largest purse in France. The most important events at Longchamp are the **Grand Prix de Paris** in July and the **Qatar Prix de l'Arc de Triomphe** in early October.

Another racing venue is the **Hippodrome d'Auteuil,** also in the Bois de Boulogne (✆ **01-40-71-47-47;** Métro: Porte Auteuil), known for its steeplechases and obstacle courses. You wouldn't necessarily think of a hippodrome for a family outing, but on Sundays in April and May, both host **Les Dimanches au Galop,** a day-long racing fiesta that includes races by both professionals and amateurs, shows, games, and of course pony-rides, all free of charge. Visit www.dimanchesaugalop.com for details.

Rugby

Rugby is very popular in France, especially in the southwest, but Parisians will come out for matches as well. The high-profile matches are played at the **Stade de France** (✆ **08-92-70-09-00,** .34€ per min.; www.stadefrance.com), the 81,000-person-capacity stadium in St-Denis, Paris's northern suburb. The rugby season generally runs from August to April.

Soccer (Football)

Known throughout France as *le football,* or just *le foot,* soccer is one of France's most popular national sports. The Paris team is *Paris Saint-Germain,* also known as *PSG.* They play their home matches at the **Parc des Princes,** 24 rue du Commandant Guilbaud, 16e (✆ **32-75,** .34€ per min.; www.leparcdesprinces.fr; Métro: Porte de Saint-Cloud), a stadium with a capacity of almost 49,000 spectators. Their season runs September to May; tickets start at 12€ and go through the roof. *Note:* A small, but nasty segment of PSG fans can get violent at games, particularly when the match is against a rival team like Marseille. National games, played at the **Stade de France** (see above) that pit the French national team (not PSG) against another country's national team, are generally much calmer.

Tennis

France's version of Wimbledon, the **French Open** (or as it's known here, **Roland Garros;** www.rolandgarros.com), takes place over 2 weeks between late May and early June in the Roland Garros Stadium in the 16th arrond. (Métro: Porte d'Auteuil). Tickets should be purchased well in advance, as this is a world-scale tennis event; tickets can be purchased online.

DAY TRIPS FROM PARIS

Parisians generally feel that their capital is the center of the universe. They may be correct, if only geographically speaking. Paris is at the heart of the region of *Ile-de-France* (the Island of France) and is encircled by seven suburban *départements* commonly and regally referred to as the *petite* and *grande couronnes*. These "crowns" are dotted with cultural and historic treasures, from majestic palaces to picturesque artistic villages, and are only a short journey from the city center.

Paris has no lack of interesting day-trip destinations. Your main problem will be deciding which one(s) to go to. If you've never been there, your first choice should probably be the château and gardens of **Versailles.** They're close by, easily accessible by train, and truly not to be missed. **Chartres** would be my second choice, for its breathtaking Gothic cathedral its winding streets and half-timbered houses, which will give you a taste of something completely different from Paris. After that, it's a toss-up. If castles are your game, **Fontainebleau** should be high on your list. Fans of Claude Monet will love exploring the gardens at **Giverny,** and families with kids in tow will **Disneyland Paris,** a European version of the American theme park.

All of these destinations are reachable by train from Paris. Train tickets do not require reservations and can be bought the day of an excursion at the departing train or subway station. You can find more information about the train schedule of suburban trains at www.transilien.com. For Chartres and Vernon/Giverny, you can also check www.voyages-sncf.com.

VERSAILLES ★★★
21km (13 miles) SW of Paris, 71km (44 miles) NE of Chartres

The grandeur of the Château of Versailles is hard to imagine until you are standing in front of it. Immediately, you start to get an idea of the power (and ego) of the man who was behind it, King Louis XIV. One of the largest castles in Europe, it is also forever associated with another, less fortunate king, Louis XVI and his wife Queen Marie Antoinette, who were both forced to flee when the French Revolution arrived at their sumptuous doorstep. The palace's extraordinary gardens, designed by the legendary landscape architect André Le Nôtre, are almost worth the visit on their own.

Don't feel you have to see everything—for many, a visit to the palace is enough culture, and a nice relaxing stroll/picnic/nap in the park is a great way to finish off the day. If you can't handle crowds but you still want to

Ile de France

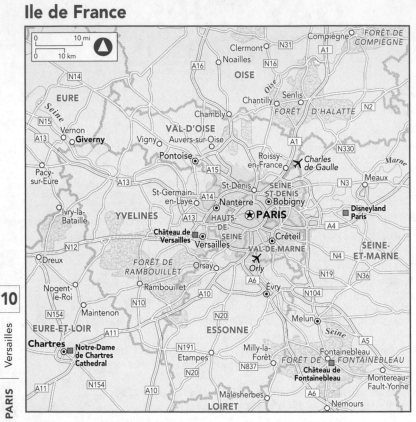

get a taste of life during the Ancien Régime, you could just visit Marie Antoinette's Estate—you'll miss the palace, but you'll get to revel in a beautiful garden and see the pretty Trianons, hamlet, and other small buildings.

Essentials

GETTING THERE   Take the **RER C** (www.transilien.fr; 30 min. from the Champs de Mars station) to **Versailles Rive Gauche–Château de Versailles.** Make sure the final destination for your train is Versailles Rive Gauche–Château de Versailles and *not* Versailles Chantier, which will leave you on the other end of town, a long walk from the Château. Even worse, the Versailles Chantier trains actually run in the opposite direction, touring all around Paris before arriving at Versailles, which will add an hour or so to your journey. Assuming you've taken the right train, it's about a 5-minute walk from the Versailles Rive Gauche train station to the château—don't worry, you can't miss it. For a little more (4.20€ adults), you can also take the **SNCF** Transilien suburban train (www.transilien.fr; 45 min.) from the Gare St-Lazare station to **Versailles-Rive Droite,** and then walk about 10 minutes to the Chateau (around 45 min. total).

Versailles

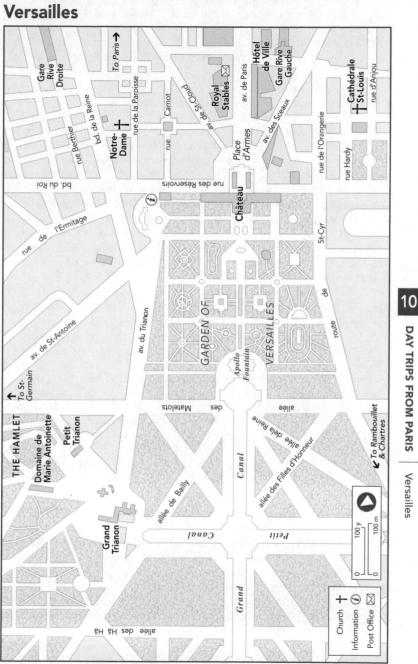

Unless you have a **Paris Visite** or other pass that includes zones 1–4, you will need to buy a special ticket (one-way fare 3.45€ adults; 1.70€ 4–10; free under 4); a regular Métro ticket will not suffice. Another option is to buy a 1-day **Mobilis** pass for zones 1–4 (11€), which gives you unlimited travel in those zones for the day. You can buy a ticket from any Métro or RER station; the fare includes a free transfer to the Métro.

TICKETS   If you are made of tough stuff and want to see everything, you can buy the all-inclusive **Château Passeport,** which grants you access to the main chateau, the gardens, the Trianon Palaces, and the Marie Antoinette Estate (Nov–Mar 18€ adults; April–Oct 25€ includes Les Grandes Eaux; free 17 and under). If you are merely human, you can buy a **ticket to just the Palace** (15€; free 17 and under) or **just the Trianons and Marie Antoinette's Estate** (10€). The under 18 crowd (who get in free), may have to buy a ticket to get into the gardens (9€) from Apr–Oct. You can avoid some of the long lines at the entrance by purchasing your tickets online. A **Paris Museum Pass** (p. 106) will get you into everything except Les Grandes Eaux musicales (Apr–Oct), so you'll have to buy a separate ticket to get into the gardens (9€).

VISITOR INFORMATION   Château de Versailles, ℂ **01-30-83-78-00,** www.chateauversailles.fr. Palace: Apr–Oct Tues–Sun 9am–6:30pm; Nov–Mar 9am–5:30pm. Marie Antoinette's Estate: Apr–Oct Tues–Sun noon–6:30pm; Nov–Mar Tues–Sun noon–5:30pm. Garden and park: Apr–Oct daily 8am–8:30pm; Nov–Mar daily 8am–6pm. **Versailles Tourist Office,** 2 bis ave. de Paris, ℂ **01-39-24-88-88,** www.versailles-tourisme.com.

EVENING SHOWS   From mid-June to mid-September, there are spectacular **fountain night shows** (24€ adults; 20€ 6–17 years old) where you stroll around the gardens and enjoy illuminated fountains, music, and fireworks. During the same period, you can walk through the Hall of Mirrors and the royal apartments accompanied by musicians and dancers in Baroque period costumes in the **Royal Serenade** (17€ adults, 10€ 6–17 years old). There are **combination tickets** for the two events (39€ adults, 28€ 6–17 years old).

Since it reopened after an extensive restoration, big names in classical music, theater, and dance are filling the stage at the magnificent **Opéra Royal;** reserve well in advance and expect royal ticket prices (45€–100€).

DAYTIME SHOWS   From April to October on weekends and Tuesdays, **"Les Grandes Eaux Musicales"** (depending on your ticket, this could be included, otherwise 9€ adults; 7€ ages 6–17) play throughout the gardens closest to the castle. This consists of fountains playing to Baroque music. While pleasant, you won't miss anything essential if your ticket does not offer you entrance to this part of the gardens (the rest of the park is accessible from side entrances and is free of charge).

TICKETS   You can purchase tickets to all shows mentioned above at the chateau, online at www.chateauversailles-spectacles.fr, or from any Fnac store (ℂ **08-92-68-36-22,** .34€ per min; www.fnacspectacles.com).

LES GRANDES ECURIES   The **Académie de Spectacle Equestre** is housed in the **royal stables,** situated immediately opposite château. Both the school and its shows are directed by Bartabas, whose equestrian theater company, Zingaro, has garnered world fame. Visitors can watch hour-long riding demonstrations by the students and their mounts on the weekends and sometimes Thursdays at 11:15am; tickets cost 6.50€ to 12€. On some weekend afternoons, a more elaborate "equestrian ballet" is on offer; tickets to those shows are 16€–25€. After the shows, visitors can tour the stables. For additional information and schedule see www.bartabas.fr.

Versailles

The Chateau of Versailles

Back in the 17th century, after having been badly burned by a nasty uprising called Le Fronde, Louis XIV decided to move his court from Paris to Versailles, a safe distance from the intrigues of the capital. He also decided to have the court move in with him, where he could keep a close eye on them and nip any new plots or conspiracies in the bud. This required a new abode that was not only big enough to house his court (anywhere from 3,000 to 10,000 people would be palace guests on any given day), but also one that would be grand enough to let the world know who was in charge.

There was already a château on the site when Louis came to town; his father, Louis XIII, had built a small castle, "a hunting lodge," there in 1623. This humble dwelling simply would not do for the so-called "Sun King," who brought in a flotilla of architects, artists, and gardeners to enlarge the castle and give it a new look. In 1668, the King's architect, Louis Le Vau, began work on the enormous "envelope," which literally wrapped the old castle in a second building. From the front, you can see the remnants of the old castle; the buildings that surround the recessed central courtyard (called the **Marble Court**) are what's left of that structure.

Meanwhile, legendary garden designer André Le Notre was carving out formal gardens and a huge park out of what had been marshy countryside. Thousands of trees were planted, and harmonious geometric designs were achieved with flower beds, hedges, canals, and pebbled pathways dotted with sculptures and fountains.

Construction, which involved as many as 36,000 workers, ground on for years; in 1682 the King and his court moved in, but construction went on right through the rest of his reign and into that of Louis XV. Louis XVI and his wife, Marie Antoinette, made few changes, but history made a gigantic one for them: On October 6, 1789, an angry mob of hungry Parisians marched on the palace and the royal couple was eventually forced to return to Paris. Versailles would never again be a royal residence.

The palace was ransacked during the Revolution, and in the years after it fell far from its original state of grace. Napoleon and Louis XVIII did what they could to bring the sleeping giant back to life, but by the early 1800s, during the reign of Louis-Philippe, the castle was slated for demolition. Fortunately for us, this forward-thinking king decided to invest his own money to save Versailles for future generations, and in 1837 the vast structure was made into a national museum. Little by little, precious furniture and art objects were retrieved or re-created; paintings, wall decorations, and ceilings were restored. Not surprisingly, restoration is ongoing, so be prepared for the unexpected when you arrive. Even if a few areas are closed, the place is so huge that should you feel so inclined, you can still tour yourself into a 17th-century stupor.

Touring the Palace

The rooms in the "envelope," or the newer part of the building, were designed to impress, which they do. They include a series of rooms called the **Grand Apartments,** used primarily for ceremonial events (a daily occurrence), the **Queen's Apartments,** and the **Galerie des Glaces.** These, along with the **King's Apartments,** and the **Chapel,** are the must-sees of the palace. If you have time and fortitude, you can take a **guided visit** to the royal family's private apartments (16€, some in English, check website for schedule) to see a more intimate look at castle life.

Each room in the **Grand Apartments ★★★** is dedicated to a different planet (that circles around the sun, as in Sun King), and each has a fabulous painting on the ceiling depicting the god or goddess associated with said heavenly sphere. The first and probably the most staggering, painting-wise, is in the **Salon d'Hercule ★★**. It holds an enormous canvas by Paolo Veronese, "Christ at Supper with Simon," as well as a splendid, divinity-bedecked ceiling portraying Hercules being welcomed by the gods of Olympus by Antoine Lemoyne. At 480 sq. m (5,166 sq. ft.), it is one of the largest paintings in France. The **Salon d'Apollon ★**, not surprisingly, was the throne room, where the Sun-King would receive ambassadors and other heads of state.

The ornate **Salon de Guerre ★** and **Salon de Paix ★** bookend the most famous room in the place, the recently restored **Galerie des Glaces (the Hall of Mirrors) ★★★**. Louis XIV commanded his painter-in-chief, Charles Le Brun, to paint the 12m-high (40-ft.) ceiling of this 73m-long (240-ft.) gallery with representations of his accomplishments. This masterwork is illuminated by light from the 17 windows that overlook the garden, which are matched on the opposite wall by 17 mirrored panels. Add to that a few enormous crystal chandeliers, and the effect is dazzling. This splendid setting was the scene of a historic event in a more recent century: In 1919, World War I officially ended when the Treaty of Versailles was signed here.

The **Queen's Apartments ★★** include a gorgeous bedroom with silk hangings printed with lilacs and peacock feathers, which looks exactly as it did in 1789, when the Queen, Marie Antoinette, was forced to flee revolutionary mobs through a secret door (barely visible in the wall near her bed). The **King's Apartments ★★★** are even more splendiferous, though in a very different style: Here the ceilings have been left blank white, which brings out the elaborate white and gold decoration on the walls. The **King's Bedroom ★★★**, hung from top to bottom with gold brocade, is fitted with a banister that separated the King from the 100 or so people who would watch him wake up in the morning.

You should also make sure to see the **Chapel ★★★**, a masterpiece of light and harmony by Jules Hardouin Mansart, where the kings attended mass. This lofty space (the ceiling is more than 25m/82 ft. high) reflects both Gothic and Baroque styles, combining a vaulted roof, stained glass, and gargoyles with columns and balustrades typical of the early 18th century.

Touring the Domaine de Marie Antoinette

Northwest of the fountain lies the **Domaine de Marie Antoinette ★★★** (if you don't have a Château passport or museum pass you'll pay a separate ticket to get in). It was here that the young queen sought refuge from the strict protocol and infighting at the castle. Her husband gave her the **Petit Trianon ★★**, a small manor that Louis XV used for his trysts, which she transformed into a stylish haven. When the queen had finished decorating the manor in the latest fashions, she set to work creating an entire world around it, including a splendid **English garden ★**, several lovely pavilions, a jewel-like **theater ★★**, and even a small **hamlet ★**, complete with a working farm and a dairy, where she and her friends would play cards and gossip, or just go for a stroll in the "country." Although the **Grand Trianon ★** is not really linked to the story of Marie Antoinette, it is worth a brief visit. Built by Louis XIV as a retreat for him and his family, this small marble palace consists of two large wings connected by an open columned terrace from which there is a delightful **view ★** of the gardens. The furniture and decor dates from the Napoleonic era.

Touring the Gardens & Park

The entire 800-hectare (2,000-acre) park is laid out according to a precise, symmetrical plan. From the terrace behind the castle, there is an astounding **view ★★★** that runs past two parterres, down a central lawn (the Tapis Vert), down the **Grand Canal ★★**

and seemingly on into infinity. Le Nôtre's masterpiece is the ultimate example of French-style gardens; geometric, logical, and in perfect harmony—a reflection of the divine order of the cosmos. Given that the Sun King was the star of this particular cosmos, a solar theme is reflected in the statues and fountains along the main axis of the perspective; the most magnificent of these is the **Apollo Fountain ★★★** where the sun god emerges from the waves at dawn on his chariot. On the sides of the main axis, near the castle, are a set of six groves, or **bosquets ★**, leafy mini-gardens that are hidden by walls of shrubbery; some were used as small outdoor ballrooms for festivities, others for intimate rendezvous out of reach of the prying eyes of the court. Today, you can **picnic, bike ride** (bikes can be rented next to the restaurant), or even **row a boat** on a sunny day.

Place d'Armes. ✆ **01-30-83-78-00.** www.chateauversailles.fr. Palace 15€ adults, free for 18 and under. Marie Antoinette's Estate 10€ adults, everything free for children 17 and younger. Palace Apr–Oct Tues–Sun 9am–6:30pm; Nov–Mar Tues–Sun 9am–5:30pm. Marie Antoinette's Estate Apr—Oct Tues–Sun noon–6:30pm; Nov–Mar Tues–Sun noon–5:30. Garden and park: Apr–Oct daily 8am–8:30pm; Nov–Mar daily 8am–6pm.

CHARTRES ★★★

97km (58 miles) SW of Paris, 76km (47 miles) NW of Orléans

You'll see it long before you see the actual town: the spire of the cathedral of Chartres rising above a sea of wheat fields. About an hour from Paris, you can easily visit this stunning church and its inspiring stain-glassed windows and still have enough time to wander through the narrow streets of the ancient (and beautiful) town.

Essentials

GETTING THERE From Paris's Gare Montparnasse, **trains** run directly to Chartres, taking about an hour. Tickets cost 16€ one-way; for more information and reservations, see www.voyages-sncf.com or call ✆ **36-35.** If **driving,** take A10/A11 southwest and follow signs to Le Mans and Chartres. (The Chartres exit is marked.)

VISITOR INFORMATION The **Office de Tourisme** in the Maison du Saumon, 8 rue de la Poissonerie (✆ **02-37-18-26-26;** www.chartres-tourisme.com).

Exploring the Cathedral

This magnificent Gothic cathedral, with its carved portals and three-tiered flying buttresses, would be a stunning sight even without its legendary **stained-glass windows**—though the world would be a drearier place. For these ancient glass panels are truly glorious: a kaleidoscope of colors so deep, so rich, and so bright, it's hard to believe they are some 700 years old. Meant as teaching devices more than artwork, the windows functioned as a sort of enormous cartoon, telling the story of Christ through pictures to a mostly illiterate populace. From its beginnings, pilgrims came from far and near to see a piece of cloth that believers say was worn by the Virgin Mary during Christ's birth. The **relic** is still here, but these days it's primarily a different sort of pilgrim that is drawn to Chartres: More than 1.5 million tourists come here every year to admire the magnificent edifice.

A Romanesque church stood on this spot until 1194, when a fire burnt it virtually to the ground. All that remained were the towers, the Royal Portal, and a few remnants of stained glass. The locals were so horrified that they sprung to action; in a matter of only 3 decades a new cathedral was erected, which accounts for its remarkably unified

Chartres Cathedral

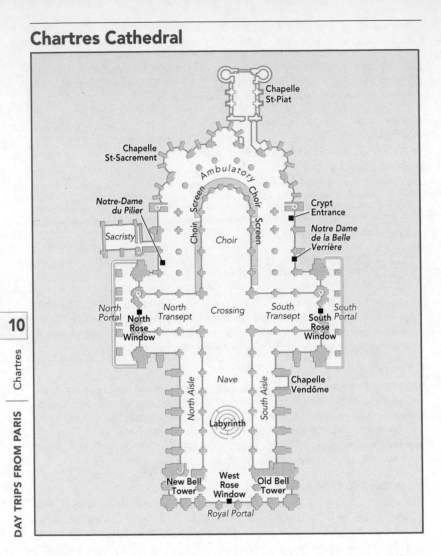

Chapelle
St-Piat

Chapelle
St-Sacrement

Ambulatory

Choir Screen

Notre-Dame
du Pilier

Crypt
Entrance

Sacristy

Notre Dame
de la Belle
Verrière

Choir Screen

Choir

*North
Portal* **North
Rose
Window** *North
Transept* *Crossing* *South
Transept* **South
Rose
Window** *South
Portal*

North Aisle *Nave* *South Aisle*

**Chapelle
Vendôme**

Labyrinth

**New Bell
Tower** **West
Rose
Window** **Old Bell
Tower**

Royal Portal

Gothic architecture. This was one of the first churches to use buttresses as a building support, allowing the architect (whose name has been lost) to build its walls at twice the height of the standard Romanesque cathedrals and make space for its famous windows. The new cathedral was dedicated in 1260 and has miraculously survived the centuries with relatively little damage. The French Revolution somehow spared the cathedral. During World War I and World War II, the precious windows were carefully dismounted piece by piece and stored in a safe place in the countryside.

Before you enter the church, take in the **facade ★★**, which is a remarkable assemblage of religious art and architecture. The base of the two towers dates from the early 12th century (before the fire). The tower to your right (the **Old Tower,** or South Tower) is topped by its original sober Romanesque spire; that on your left (**New Tower,** or

For over 3 decades, Malcolm Miller has been studying the cathedral and giving **guided tours in English.** His rare blend of scholarship, enthusiasm, and humor will help you understand and appreciate what you are looking at. The 75-minute tour usually begins at noon and some-times also at 2:45pm Monday through Saturday (10€ adults; 5€ students). No need to reserve; a sign at the meeting point inside at the entrance to the cathedral's gift shop indicates that day's tour schedule. You can also rent an **audioguide** (in English) for 6.20€.

North Tower) was blessed with an elaborate Gothic spire by Jehan de Beauce in the early 1500s, when the original burned down. Below is the **Royal Portal ★★★**, a masterpiece of Romanesque art. Swarming with kings, queens, prophets, and priests, this sculpted entryway tells the story of the life of Christ. The rigid bodies of the figures contrast with their lifelike faces; it is said that Rodin spent hours here contemplating this stonework spectacle. You can **climb to the top of the New Tower** to take in the **view ★**; just remember to wear rubber-soled shoes, as the 300 steps are a little slippery after all these centuries.

Once inside the cathedral, you'll really understand what all the fuss is about. The dimness is pierced by the radiant colors of the **stained-glass windows ★★★**, which shine down from all sides. Three windows on the west side of the building, as well as the beautiful rose window to the south called **Notre Dame de la Belle Verière ★** date from the earlier 12th-century structure; the rest, with the exception of a few modern panels, are of 13th-century origins. The scenes depicted in glass, read from bottom to top and recount stories from the Bible as well as the lives of the saints. You will soon find yourself wondering how in the world medieval artists, with such low-tech materials, managed to create such vivid colors. The blues, in particular, seem to be divinely inspired. In fact, scientists have finally pierced at least part of the mystery: The blue was made with sodium and silica compounds that made the color stand up to the centuries better than glass made with other colors.

Another indoor marvel is the **chancel enclosure ★★★**, which separates the chancel (the area behind the altar) from the ambulatory (the walkway that runs around the outer chapels). Started in 1514 by Jehan de Beauce, this intricately sculpted wall depicts dozens of saints and other religious superstars in yet another recounting of the lives of the Virgin and Christ. Back in the ambulatory is the Chapel of the Martyrs, where the cathedral's cherished **relic** resides: a piece of cloth that the Virgin Mary apparently wore at the birth of Christ, which was a gift of Charles the Bald in 876.

Chartres also harbors a rare **labyrinth ★**, which is traced on the floor of the cathedral near the nave. A large circle, divided into four parts, is entirely filled by a winding path that leads to the center. In the Middle Ages, these labyrinths represented the symbolic path that one must follow to get from Earth to God; pilgrims would follow the path while praying, as if they were making a pilgrimage to Jerusalem. *Note:* The cathedral asks that visitors not talk or wander around during mass, which is generally held in the late morning and early evening. You are welcome to sit in on services, of course.

16 Cloître Notre-Dame. ℂ **02-37-21-22-07.** www.cathedrale-chartres.monuments-nationaux.fr. General admission to the cathedral is free, admission to the towers 7.50€ adults, 4.50€ adults 18–25, free for children 17 and under. Cathedral open daily 8:30am–7:30pm.

Exploring the Old Town

Give yourself a little time to explore the medieval cobbled streets of the **Vieux Quartier (Old Town)** ★. There are several gabled houses in the narrow lanes near the cathedral, including the colorful facades of **rue Chantault,** one of which is 8 centuries old. Seek out rue du Bourg, where you'll find the famous **Salmon House** (which houses the tourist office) and some lovely sculptures (including a certain fish). In the lower town, you can stroll along the picturesque **Eure River** with its stone bridges and ancient wash-houses. If you go on a Saturday or Wednesday morning there is a covered farmers market in **place Billard** (until 1pm), the perfect place to grab some supplies for a casual lunch in the park behind the cathedral or along the river.

Musée des Beaux-Arts de Chartres ★   Housed in an impressive former Episcopal palace, this museum of fine arts boasts a collection covering the 16th to the 20th centuries, including the work of masters such as Zurbarán, Watteau, and Soutine.

29 Cloître Notre-Dame. (✆ **02-37-90-45-80.** www.chartres-toursime.com. May–Oct Mon, Wed and Sat 10am–noon and 2–6pm Sun 2–6pm; the rest of the year, until 5pm. Admission 3.40€ adults, 1.70€ students, free 17 and under.

GIVERNY ★★

74km (46 miles) NW of Paris

For this trip, a lot depends on the weather. If you luck out and the sun is shining, it's worth the shlep by train or car to bask in the glory of this stunning garden, which bears the artistic stamp of its genius creator, Claude Monet. The painter and his family moved to this tiny town in 1883, and Monet liked it so much he spent the rest of his life here, painting views of the dreamlike garden that he created out of the grassy slope behind his house. Today, the **Fondation Claude Monet à Giverny** (84 rue Claude Monet, Giverny; ✆ **02-32-51-28-21;** www.fondation-monet.com) is open to the public, and for a small fee, you too can wander in and out of the brilliant flower beds, lush bowers, and water-lily ponds that inspired this impressionist master. Once you are done with the garden, you can sample the bucolic joys of the village, which manages to stay charming despite the seasonal tourist infestation. You can also take in one of the excellent temporary exhibits at the **Musée des Impressionismes** (see below). On the other hand, if it is raining or truly dreary out, you'll be better off staying in town and getting your Monet fix at the **Musée Marmottan Monet** (p. 128) and/or visit the water-lilies at the **Orangerie** (p. 110).

Essentials

GETTING THERE   **Trains** (SNCF, for schedules visit www.voyages-sncf.com) leave every hour or two from the Gare St-Lazare train station to Vernon, the closest stop to Giverny, which is about 7km (4.5 miles) away. The trip takes around 45 minutes and costs 14€ one-way. From Vernon you can either take a shuttle bus (8€ round-trip) or rent a bike at the station (L'Arrivé de Giverny, ✆ **02-32-21-16-01;** 14€ for the day) and pedal there on the marked bike path.

If you're **driving,** take the Autoroute A14 to the A13 toward Rouen. Take exit 16 for Vernon and follow the D181 across the Seine into the town. From Vernon take the D5 to Giverny. Expect it to take about an hour; try to avoid weekends.

Where to See Impressionist Paintings in Giverny

While you won't see any original paintings at the Fondation Monet, you will see plenty of Impressionist art at the **Musée des Impressionismes** (99 rue Claude Monet; © **02-32-51-94-65**; www.mdig.fr; 7€ adults, 4.5€ students, 3€ 7–12 years old, free 6 and under; Apr–Oct 10am–6pm). Housed in a sleek modern building with yet another lovely garden, this airy museum offers temporary exhibits that explore the high points of the movement, both in France and abroad.

TICKETS   By all means, try to buy your tickets to the gardens in advance. Not only will you avoid standing in the extremely slow-moving line at the ticket booth, but you will have the right to use the special entrance for the *billet coupe-file* (cut in front of the line ticket) and walk right in. You can buy your tickets online at the Fondation Claude Monet site (see above), at a Fnac ticket office, or on the Fnac site (in English, www.fnactickets.com). Tickets cost 9.50€ for adults, 5€ for students, and children 6 and under can visit for free.

VISITOR INFORMATION   The **Office de Tourisme des Portes de l'Eure** is located close to the Fondation Monet at 80 rue Claude Monet (© **02-32-51-39-60**; www.cape-tourisme.fr).

Exploring Giverny

When you enter this kingdom of color, you'll quickly realize that Monet wasn't just a brilliant painter, he was also a gifted gardener. His dual talents complemented each other completely; by the end of his life, the garden was just as much a work of art as the paintings, or perhaps they *were* the paintings. If you have already visited the Orangerie in Paris, and seen his magical "Nympheas," or water lilies, spread across huge canvases in two oval-shaped rooms, in a way, you have already visited this garden; they were painted here, with the aim of faithfully re-creating the feeling you would have if you were looking at the same flowers at Giverny.

There are actually two gardens here: The first and closest to the house is the **Clos Normand ★★**, an ostensibly French-style garden that is a glorious riot of color. Gladioli, larkspur, phlox, daisies, and asters, among other flowers, clamor for your attention; irises brighten the small lawn. In the midst of it all is **Monet's house ★**, where you can see where he lived and admire his **Japanese print collection.**

The painter's most famous works, the endless water lily series, were born in the **Water Garden ★★★**, farther down the slope. Here, Monet's intention was to build a garden that resembled those in the Japanese prints he collected, including a **Japanese bridge ★** that figures prominently in several of his canvases. Today the garden looks much as it did when Monet was immortalizing it. Willows weep quietly into the ponds, heather, ferns, azaleas, and rhododendrons carpet the banks, and frogs croak amongst the water lilies. This garden was a sanctuary for the painter, who came here to explore one of his favorite subjects: the complex interplay of water and light.

Be advised that it will be virtually impossible to experience the gardens as Monet did—more or less alone. This is an extremely popular outing for both individuals and tour groups, so your best bet is to come on a slow day like Monday or Wednesday, and/or to arrive after 3pm, when the groups have left. You can't picnic in the gardens, but you can lunch at the **Restaurant Baudy** in the village, an old inn where many an Impressionist used to stay when they would come to visit Claude (81 rue Claude Monet; ℂ **02-32-21-10-03;** www. restaurantbaudy.com).

84 rue Claude-Monet. ℂ **02-32-51-28-21.** www.fondation-monet.com. Admission 9.50€ adults, 5€ students, free for children 6 and under. Apr–Oct daily 9:30am–6pm. Closed Nov–Mar.

FONTAINEBLEAU ★★★

60km (37 miles) S of Paris, 74km (46 miles) NE of Orléans

Napoleon called it "the house of the centuries; the true home of kings," and he had a point: Fontainebleau was a royal residence for over 700 years. Elegant and dignified, this grand chateau carries the architectural imprint of many a monarch, in particular, Francis I, Henri IV, and Napoleon himself. Surrounded by a dense forest and verdant countryside, a trip out here is a relaxing green interlude to your Parisian trip.

GETTING THERE Trains to Fontainebleau leave from the Gare de Lyon (for schedules and info visit www.transilien.fr). The trip takes 40 minutes and costs 8.75€ for adults and 4.35€ for ages 4–10 one-way. Get off the train at Fontainebleau–Avon and take the local bus (line 1) direction Lilas, to the Chateau stop; the fare is 1.90€ one-way. The buses come frequently and are timed to arrive at the arrival of the train from Paris. If you're **driving,** take A6 south from Paris, exit Fontainbleau.

VISITOR INFORMATION The **Office de Tourisme** is at 4 rue Royale, Fontaine-bleau (ℂ **01-60-74-99-99;** www.fontainebleau-tourisme.com), opposite the main entrance to the château.

Exploring Fontainebleau

Though kings were already living here by the 12th century (Philippe August and Saint Louis both spent a good deal of time at the castle), it was during the Renaissance that Fontainebleau really took on its regal allure. In 1528, inveterate castle-builder King François I decided to completely rebuild Fontainebleau and make it into a palace that would rival the marvels of Rome. He tore down everything but the core of the medieval castle, and hired an army of architects and artisans to construct a new one around it. He also brought in two renowned Italian artists, Il Rosso and Primaticcio, to decorate his new home. Their style of work came to be known as the School of Fontainebleau, which was characterized by the use of stucco (moldings and picture frames) and frescos that depicted various allegories and myths. This school was highly influenced by the Mannerist style of Michelangelo, Raphael, and Parmigianino.

François I was also an art collector: His vast accumulation of Renaissance treasures included Da Vinci's "Mona Lisa" and "The Virgin of the Rock," both of which once hung here. After François' death, his descendants continued work on the castle, but it wasn't until the 17th century and the arrival of Henri IV on the scene that there were any major transformations. Henri added several wings and a courtyard (the **Cour des Offices ★★**), and also made major changes to the decor, inviting a new clutch of artists, who established a second School of Fontainebleau. This time, the artists were of French and Flemish origins (Ambrose Dubois, Martin Fréminet, and others), and used oil paint and canvas instead of frescos. Louis XIV, preferring Versailles, didn't bother much with Fontainebleau, but Louis XV and Louis XVI found the palace very much to their liking and added their own decorative and architectural flourishes. Napoleon was also very fond of this palace and made a lasting imprint on the castle's interior. No doubt, Fontainebleau made an imprint on the Emperor as well: On April 20, 1814, he abdicated here, before being sent off to exile on the island of Elba.

Touring the Chateau

Most of what you'll want to see (and what I describe below) is in the **Grands Appartements.** The **Petits Appartements,** a series of rooms that were Napoleon's private residence, requires an additional ticket.

Your first encounter with the château will take place in the **Cour du Cheval Blanc ★★★** at the entrance to the palace. It was in this grand square, which is surrounded by wings of the castle on three sides, that Napoleon said adieu to his faithful imperial guards. "Continue to serve France," he pleaded, "Her welfare was my only concern." The main building before you dates from François I's era; the sumptuous **horseshoe staircase ★★** was added by Henri II. On the left, as you enter, is the **Chapelle de la Trinité ★**. When he was 7, Louis XIII climbed up the scaffolding to watch Martin Fréminet, his art instructor, paint the glorious ceiling. This is where Louis XV married Polish princess Marie Leczinska and where the future Napoleon III was baptized. Linking the chapel with the royal apartments is the **Gallery of François I ★★★**, a stunning example of Renaissance art and decoration. Overseen by Il Rossi, a team of highly skilled artists covered the walls with exceptional frescos, moldings, and boisseries (carved woodwork). The paintings, which are full of mythological figures, pay tribute to the glory of the monarchy and the wisdom of the King's rule. Throughout the gallery (and elsewhere in the castle) you will see the salamander, François' official symbol.

The other major must-see is the **Salle de Bal ★★★**. This 30m (98-ft.) long ballroom is a feast of light and color; the frescos by Primaticcio and Nicolo dell'Abate have been completely restored, and their rich hues radiate like they were painted yesterday. Huge windows let in light from both sides of this long room; the monumental fireplace at the far end was designed by 16th-century architect Philibert Delorme.

The **Royal Apartments ★★** have been decorated and redecorated by successive monarchs. Louis XIII was born in the **Salon Louis XIII ★**, a fact that is symbolized in the ceiling mural showing Love riding a dolphin. Though several different queens slept in the **Chambre de l'Impératrice ★★**, its current set-up reflects the epoch of Empress Josephine (Napoleon's first wife). The sumptuous bed, crowned in gilded walnut and covered in embroidered silk, was made for Marie Antoinette in 1787. The queen would never see it; the Revolution exploded before she could arrange a royal visit to the château. Napoleon transformed the Kings' bedroom into the **Salle du Trône ★**, or Throne Room. Since several centuries worth of kings, from Henri IV to Louis XVI slept here, the decor is a mix of styles: The throne and other furnishings are Empire, the folding chairs are Louis XVI, and the ceiling murals date from the 17th and 18th centuries.

You can learn more about the Emperor at the **Musée Napoléon 1er ★**, located in the Louis XV wing, where you'll see historic memorabilia and artwork relating to his reign, like the tent he slept in during military campaigns, and a remarkable mechanical desk. Separate from the Musée Napoléon, and at the price of an additional ticket, you can visit the **Petits Appartements,** which date from Louis XV, but were redecorated in Empire style for Napoleon and his Empress (first Josephine, then Marie-Louise).

The Forest of Fontainebleau is riddled with *sentiers* (hiking trails) made by French kings and their entourages who went hunting in the forest. A "Guide des Sentiers" is available at the tourist information center (see above, you can also download trail maps from their website).

Bike paths also cut through the forest. You can rent bikes at **A La Petite Reine,** 14 rue de la Paroisse, in the center of town, a few blocks from the chateau (ⓒ **01-60-74-57-57;** www.alapetitereine. com). The cost of a bike is 8€ per hour, 15€ for a full day.

Touring the Gardens

The formal gardens must have been beautiful when André Le Nôtre put his hand to them in the 17th century, but today, though well-kept, they look a little arid. More lush is the **Garden of Diane ★**, a quiet spot of green on the north side of the castle created during the time of François I, which centers around a statue of the goddess surrounded by four dogs. The **English Garden ★**, complete with an artificial stream and lush groves of tall trees, was added by Napoleon. The vast **Carp Pond ★** , which extends directly from the south side of the **Cour de la Fontaine,** has a small island in the center with a small pavilion where an afternoon snack would be served to the royal residents. Surrounding the gardens and its park is the enormous **Fontainebleau Forest ★★**, which, if you have the time, is definitely worth the visit (see box, below).

Place du Général-de-Gaulle. ⓒ **01-60-71-50-70.** www.musee-chateau-fontainebleau.fr. *Grands appartements* 11€ adults, 9€ students 18–25; ticket to *petits appartements* 6.50€ adults, 5€ students 18–25; all admissions free 17 and under. Apr–Sept Wed–Mon 9:30am–6pm; Oct–Mar Wed–Mon 9:30am–5pm.

DISNEYLAND PARIS ★

41km (25 miles) E of Paris

It might not be particularly French, but there's no denying that this is a fun place to visit—especially if you're traveling with kids. Once there, even curmudgeons like myself cannot resist getting swept up in the fun rides and the good cheer. There are two parks here, **Disneyland Paris** and **Disney Studios;** depending on your stamina, you can do them both in a day.

Essentials

GETTING THERE   You could arrive by **TGV** (the French railway's high-speed train), but a less spectacular and less complicated option is to simply climb on the **RER A** (Transilien; www.transilien.fr; 40 min.; 7.50€ adults, 3.75€ ages 4–10 one-way) and take it all the way to its terminus at Marne-la-Vallée–Chessy (just make sure that this is the terminus—the RER A has multiple destinations). When you get out, you'll be about a 5-minute walk from the entrance. By **car,** head east on the A4 and take the Parcs Disney exit.

VISITOR INFORMATION   **Disneyland Paris Guest Relations Office,** located in City Hall on Main Street, U.S.A. (ⓒ **08-25-30-05-00,** .15€ per min; www.disneylandparis.com). For general tourist information for the region, visit the **Espace**

Fast Pass Those Long Lines

Disneyland Paris has instituted a program that's done well at the other parks. With the **Fast Pass** system, visitors reserve a 1-hour time block at various rides, by printing a fast pass from the machine at the entrance to the attraction. Within that block, the wait is usually no more than 8 minutes. See the website for details.

Tourisme, between the train station and Disney Village (*✆* **01-60-43-33-33;** www.tourisme77.fr).

ADMISSION   Admission varies depending on the season. In peak season, a 1-day park ticket (for either the main park or Walt Disney Studios) costs 64€ for adults, 58€ for children 3 to 12, and is free for children 2 and younger; a 2-day park-hopper ticket is 139€ for adults, 126€ for kids; and a 3-day park-hopper ticket is 169€ for adults, 156€ for kids. There are oodles of special offers throughout the year, some that include transportation to and from Paris; check the website for details.

HOURS   Hours vary throughout the year, but most frequently they are 10am to 7pm. Check the website for exact hours during your stay.

Exploring Disney

In the U.S., there is Disneyland and Disney World; in France, you could call it Disney Universe. There are two parks in this giant resort, the classic Disneyland, complete with the Matterhorn and Space Mountain, and Disney Studios, where you can try your hand at cinematography or delve into the world of cartoons. But the parks are just the beginning of your excellent adventure in Marne-la-Vallée: There are also seven hotels, a golf course, spa, tennis courts, and an ice skating rink, not to mention Disney Village, with its boutiques, restaurants, discotheque, cinema, and IMAX theater. For the purposes of this guide, we'll just stick with parks. In general, Disneyland is a better choice for the under-7 crowd; though even the little ones will still get a kick out of the cartoon attractions at Disney Studios.

Disneyland Park

Isn't it comforting that some things never change? Here you are in France, and yet there is Frontierland, Adventureland, and Fantasyland, just the way you remember them back home. Okay, not exactly. For one thing, everyone's speaking French. And Japanese. And Bulgarian, Hindi, and Farsi. The success of this resort is its international appeal. When you enter the park, you'll step right into **Main Street USA,** that utopian rendition of early-20th-century America, complete with horse and buggies and barber-shop quartets. Here you'll find the **information center** as well as a train, which leaves from Main Street Station. The train, which does a circuit around the park, will whisk you off to **Frontierland,** where you'll find a paddle-wheel steamboat, a petting zoo, and the Lucky Nugget saloon, among other things. Next, you'll chug through **Adventureland,** with old favorites like the Swiss Family Robinson treehouse and the Pirates of the Caribbean, as well as newer attractions like Aladdin's Oriental Palace. Onward towards **Fantasyland** with Sleeping Beauty's Castle (Le Château de Belle au Bois Dormant), whizzing teacups, flying Dumbos, and "It's a Small World." Last stop is **Discoveryland,** home of Space Mountain and the submarine Nautilus, as well as "Buzz Lightyear's Lazer Blast." There are parades every afternoon on Main Street, and a spectacular light and fountain show, Disney Dreams, around closing time.

Disney Studios

Though the primary draw here, of course, is Disneyland Park, Disney Studios makes an interesting alternative for older kids who have already done Disney and are up for something different. Along with films, stunt shows, and parades, the park offers an introduction to the wonders of movie making at **Disney Animation Studios** and the **Back Lot,** with its special effects and stunt shows.

Naturally, there are fun rides here too, like the **Tower of Terror** (based on the "Twilight Zone" TV show), **Crush's Coaster** and the **Rock 'n Rollercoaster** (featuring Aerosmith tunes). Smaller visitors will appreciate **Toy Story Playland,** where they can speed around on the **RC Racer** or try the **Toy Soldiers Parachute Drop.**

PLANNING YOUR TRIP TO PARIS

Even if all roads do not lead to it, getting to Paris is a pretty straightforward affair. But once you arrive, you'll need to know how to get around and how to take care of practical matters. Below I supply all the nitty-gritty details you need to have a comfortable, safe, and affordable stay in Paris.

A good place to start your information quest is at the Paris Tourist Office (25 rue des Pyramides, 1st arrond.; ✆ **01-49-52-42-63**; www.paris info.com; Métro: Pyramides). The Tourist Office has several branches sprinkled around the city; check the website for addresses and hours.

GETTING THERE

By Plane

Paris has two international airports: **Aéroport d'Orly,** 18km (11 miles) south of the city (mostly European flights), and **Aéroport Roissy-Charles-de-Gaulle** (mostly long haul carriers, also known as CDG), 30km (19 miles) northeast (for both airports: www.aeroportsdeparis.fr; ✆ **00-33-1-70-36-39-50** from abroad, or **39-50** from France). If you are taking Ryanair or another discount airline that arrives at **Beauvais,** be advised that that airport is located about 80km (50 miles) from Paris.

ROISSY-CHARLES-DE-GAULLE AIRPORT There are three terminals at CDG which are some distance apart from each other. A free train called the CDGVAL connects all three of them to the two train stations.

The quickest way into central Paris is the fast **RER B** (www.ratp.fr), suburban trains that leave every 10 to 15 minutes between 5am and 10pm (midnight on weekends). It takes about 40 minutes to get to Paris, and RER B stops at several central Métro stations including Châtelet-Les-Halles and Saint-Michel–Notre-Dame. A single ticket, which can be bought at the machines in the stations at the terminals, costs 9.50€.

Air France operates two buses from the airport to the center of Paris (**Les Cars Air France;** ✆ **08-92-35-08-20;** www.lescarsairfrance.com). There are two routes, one stopping at Port Maillot with a terminus at Charles de Gaulle–Etoile, and one stopping at Gare de Lyon with a terminus at Gare Montparnasse. There are good Métro connections from all stops. Depending on the route, a one-way trip costs 15€ to 16€ adults and 7.50€ to 8€ children 2 to 11; both trips take about an hour, depending on traffic. Buses leave every 30 minutes between 6am and 9:30pm. The

Roissybus (*C* **32-46** from France only; www.ratp.fr) departs from the airport daily from 6am to 11pm and costs 11€ for the 60-minute ride. The bus leaves you in the center of Paris, at the corner of rue Scribe and rue Auber, near the Opéra.

A **taxi** from Roissy into the city will cost at least 50€, not including 1€ per item of luggage, and the fare is 15% higher from 5pm to 10am, as well as on Sundays and Bank Holidays. Long, orderly lines for taxis form outside each of the airport's terminals.

ORLY AIRPORT   Orly has two terminals—Orly Sud and Orly Ouest. To get to the center of Paris, take the 8-minute monorail **OrlyVal** to the RER station "Anthony" to get **RER B** into the center. Combined travel time is about 45 to 55 minutes. Trains run between 6am and 11pm and the one-way fare for the OrlyVal plus the RER B is 11€ adults and 5.70€ children under 10. Alternatively, you can take the **"Paris par le Train" bus** (www.parisparletrain.fr) to the Pont de Rungis station and then get **RER C** to Paris. Buses leave every 15 minutes between 4:40am and 1am. Combined travel time is about 30 minutes, and the one-way fare for the Paris par le Train bus and the RER C is 6.60€.

The **Air France bus** (**Les Cars Air France;** *C* **08-92-35-08-20;** www.cars airfrance.com) leaves from Orly Sud and Orly Ouest every 20 minutes between 6am and 11:40pm, stopping at Gare Montparnasse, Invalides, and Charles de Gaulle–Etoile. The fare is 13€ one-way, 21€ round-trip, and 6.50€ for children ages 2 to 11. Depending on the traffic, the journey takes about an hour.

A **taxi** from Orly to central Paris will cost at least 50€, not including 1€ per item of luggage, and the fare is 15% higher from 5pm to 10am, as well as on Sundays and Bank Holidays.

BEAUVAIS AIRPORT   Beauvais airport (*C* **08-92-68-20-66,** .34€ per min.; www.aeroportbeauvais.com) is located around 80km (50 miles) from Paris and is served by budget airlines such as Ryanair and Wizz Air. Buses leave about 20 minutes after each flight has landed, and, depending on the traffic, takes about 1 hour and 15 minutes to get to Paris. The bus drops you at Porte Maillot. To return to Beauvais, you need to be at the bus station at least 3 hours before the departure of your flight. A one-way ticket costs 16€.

By Train

One of best ways to get around France and Europe is by train. The French railway agency (the SNCF, Societé Nationale des Chemins de Fer Français) has a vast network that connects most major cities and quite a few smaller towns, though you will often have to pass through Paris to get from one place to another. For reservations and information visit the SNCF website (www.voyages-sncf.com).

The SNCF connects to railways in neighboring countries, including the U.K. The **Eurostar** (www.eurostar.com), which passes under the channel for a nerve-wracking 20 minutes, will get you from Paris's Gare du Nord to Saint Pancras Station, London in just 2½ hours. If London is your destination, know that even though the regular ticket price is high (310€ one-way!), there are scads of discounts available on the website, especially if you purchase in advance. Brussels is only an hour and a quarter away by high-speed train, and discounts go down to 22€. Visit the **Thalys** site (www.thalys.com) for high-speed trains to Brussels, Amsterdam, and Cologne. For rail passes that you can use throughout Europe, visit **Rail Europe** (www.raileurope.com).

Paris has six major train stations: **Gare d'Austerlitz** (13th arrond), **Gare de Lyon** (12th arrond.), **Gare Montparnasse** (14th arrond.), **Gare St-Lazare** (8th arrond.), **Gare de l'Est** (10th arrond.), and **Gare du Nord** (10th arrond.). Stations can be reached by bus or Métro; For details on a specific station visit the **SNCF** station site (www.gares-connexions.com/en). *Warning:* As in many cities, stations and surrounding areas are rather seedy and frequented by pickpockets. Be alert, especially at night.

By Bus

Cheapest of all, and the most time consuming, is the bus. For travel within Europe, contact **Eurolines** (from France ℂ **08-92-89-90-91,** .34€ per min.; international ℂ 33-1-41-86-24-21; www.eurolines.com), a consortium of dozens of different bus lines with routes that span the continent and then some (Casablanca to Moscow, anyone?). Most long-haul buses arrive at the **Eurolines France** station on the eastern edge of the city, 23 ave. du Général-de-Gaulle, Bagnolet, Métro: Gallieni.

By Car

I wouldn't recommend driving in Paris to my worst enemy, but renting a car and driving around France can be a lovely way to see the country. All of the major car-rental companies have offices here (see below), but you'll often get better deals if you reserve before you leave home. **AutoEurope** (www.autoeurope.com) is an excellent source for discounted rentals. Check its prices against:

Avis: ℂ 08-21-23-07-60 (.12€ per min); www.avis.com
Budget: ℂ 08-25-00-35-64; www.budget.com
Europcar: ℂ 08-25-358-358; www.europcar.com
Hertz: ℂ 08-25-861-861; www.hertz.com
Rent-a-Car: ℂ 08-91-700-200; www.rentacar.fr
Thrifty: ℂ 01-82-88-16-77; www.thrifty.com

Before you step on the gas, at the very least, try to get a list of international road signs; your car rental agency should have one. Driving in France is not substantially different from driving in most English-speaking countries (though British travelers will have to get used to driving on the "wrong" side of the road). However, you'll have to get used to French drivers, who tend to zoom around with what the more timid among us would call reckless abandon. Truthfully, since the installation of radars a few years ago, drivers have become much more well-behaved; you too should pay attention to speed limits or risk a steep fine. The two biggest driving differences: *priorité à droite,* which means priority is always given to vehicles approaching from the right at intersections, unless otherwise indicated; and the fondness for roundabouts. Rule number one: The person getting into the roundabout does *not* have priority. Rule number two: Be sure to take a look at the sign posted before the roundabout that indicates which exit goes in what direction so that you'll be prepared when it's time to get off. The good news is that if you miss your turnoff, you can just circle around until you figure out where it is.

By Ferry from England or Ireland

Ferry travel to France appears to be in its waning days, since more and more travelers are opting for low-cost flights or a much speedier passage through the Channel Tunnel. In England the two leading operators of ferries are **P&O Ferries** (ℂ **08-25-12-01-56,** .15€ per min.; www.poferries.com), which runs ferries from Dover to Calais, and

Brittany Ferries (*℃* 08-25-828-828, .15€ per min.; www.brittanyferries.com), which runs ferries from Portsmouth to Caen, Cherbourg, or Le Havre. **Irish Ferries** (*℃* 01-70-72-03-26;** www.irishferries.com) operates an overnight ferry from Cherbourg to Rosslare or Dublin. Call or check websites for times, prices, and points of departure/arrival.

GETTING AROUND

Finding an Address

The river Seine divides Paris into the **Rive Droite (Right Bank)** to the north and the **Rive Gauche (Left Bank)** to the south. You can figure out which is which if you face west. (Figuring out which way is west is another problem.) Paris is divided into 20 municipal districts called **arrondissements,** which spiral out clockwise starting with the 1st, which is the geographical center of the city. Not easy to figure out without a map, so I heartily suggest that you invest in some version of "Paris par Arrondissement," a small book of maps showing the streets, Métro and bus routes that costs around 8€. My personal favorite is "Paris Pratique par Arrondissment," which has a bus and metro map for each arrondissement, and shows where the Velib' stands are.

By Public Transport

For everything you ever wanted to know about the city's public transport, visit the **RATP** (*℃* 32-46 in France; www.ratp.fr). Paris and its suburbs are divided into six travel zones, but you'll probably only be concerned with zones 1 and 2, which covers the city itself.

RATP tickets are valid on the Métro, bus, and RER. You can buy tickets at the window (if you are lucky—ticket booths are an endangered species) or from machines at most Métro entrances. You can also buy them from cafes that have a TABAC sign outside. A **single ticket** costs 1.70€ and a *carnet* of 10 tickets costs 14€. Children 4 to 10 years old pay half price; under 4 rides free. Tourists can benefit from a **Paris Visite** pass, which offers unlimited travel in zones on bus, Métro, and RER, and discounts on some attractions. Think hard about how much you are going to use your pass however, as you'll probably end up walking a lot, and in the end a cheaper *carnet* of 10 tickets might do the trick. A 1-day adult pass for zones 1 to 3 costs 11€, a 2-day pass 18€, a 3-day pass 24€, and a 5-day pass 35€. It is also possible to buy more expensive passes for zones 1 to 5, which will also get you to the airport. Slightly cheaper is the 1-day **Mobilis** ticket, which offers unlimited travel in zones 1 zones 1 up to 5; a pass for zones 1 and 2 costs 6.80€. For travelers under 26, look out for the **Ticket Jeunes,** a 1-day ticket which can be used on a Saturday, Sunday, or bank holiday, and provides unlimited travel in zones 1 to 3 for 3.75€, or zones 1 to 5 for 8.10€.

If you're staying for a while, may be worth getting the **Navigo Découverte** (www.navigo.fr), a swipe card that you can buy at certain Métro or train stations for 5€. You must provide a passport photo, but once you have the card it offers unlimited travel in the relevant zones. The weekly tariff (which runs Mon–Sun) for zones 1 and 2 is 20€, and the monthly tariff (which runs from the first to the last day of the month) is 67€.

BY MÉTRO (SUBWAY)

The city's first Métro, or subway, was at the apex of high-tech when it was inaugurated on July 19, 1900, and over a century later, it still functions very well. Its biggest problem is not actually technical but political: Subway workers are fond of strikes *(grèves)* and periodically instigate slowdowns or complete shutdowns of a few lines. Usually, strikes are merely annoying and most of the time your route will not be affected, though your trip might take a little longer than normal. If you see the euphemism "Movement Social" on the TV monitor as you enter the station, read the message carefully to see if your line is involved (low groans and cursing by ticket holders is also a good indicator of strike activity).

Strikes aside, the Métro is usually efficient and civilized, especially if you avoid rush hour (7:30–9:30am and 6–8pm). It's generally safe at night (although you might want to think twice about using it to get to more isolated parts of the city), and you don't need to worry about taking it at 3am because you can't. Alas, when people dolefully talk about "The Last Métro," they're usually not discussing a movie by François Truffaut. Instead, they're referring to a fact of Parisian life: Your evening out must be carefully timed so that you can run to the station before the trains shut down between midnight and 1am. To ease your pain, the transit authority has recently added an extra hour on weekends, so now the Métro closes around 2am on Friday, Saturday, and pre-holiday evenings. The suburban trains (the RER, see below) close down around the same time (without the weekend bonus hour).

Most Métro lines ramble across the city in anything but a straight line, connecting at strategic points where you can transfer from one to the other. A map is essential (pick one up at any ticket window). The key is to know both the number of the line and its final destination. So if you are on the no. 1 line (direction La Défense) and you want to transfer at the enormous Châtelet station to get to St-Michel, at Châtelet you'll need to doggedly follow the signs to the no. 4, direction Mairie de Montrouge.

BY RER

Your only underground express choice is the **RER** (pronounced "ehr-euh-ehr"), the suburban trains that dash through the city making limited stops. The down sides are: (a) they don't run as often as the Métro, (b) they're a lot less pleasant, and (c) they're hard to figure out since they run on a different track system and the same lines can have multiple final destinations. *Important:* Make sure to hold on to your ticket as you'll need it to get out of the turnstile on the way out.

BY BUS

Thanks to a rash of new dedicated bus lanes, buses can be an efficient way to get around town, and you'll get a scenic tour to boot. The majority run from 6:30am to 9:30pm (a few operate until 12:30am) and service is reduced on Sundays and holidays. You can use Métro tickets on the buses or you can buy tickets directly from the driver (2€). Tickets need to be validated in the machine next to the driver's cabin.

Inside the bus, the next stop is usually written on an electronic panel on the ceiling of the bus. Press the red button when you want to get off. Your regular Métro ticket gives you a free transfer, to be used within 1½ hours; if you buy your ticket on the bus there is no transfer included.

After the bus and Métro services stop running, head for the **Noctilien** night bus (www.transilien.com/static/noctilien). The 47 lines crisscross the city and head out to the suburbs every half-hour or so from 12:30am to 5:30am. Tickets cost the same as for the regular bus (see above).

BY TRAM

Over the past few years, Paris has added three new tramway lines, with extensions and new lines in progress. They connect Paris with its suburbs; within Paris they run along the outer circle of boulevards that trace the city limits. Tickets are the same price as the Métro.

"Ride a bike around Paris," you ask, "Are you nuts?" Yes and no. True, you have to have a bit of the daredevil in you to take to the streets on a bicycle in this traffic-crazed city, but since July 2007, when the City of Paris inaugurated a wildly successful system of low-cost bike rentals called Velib' (vel-*leeb*), it's really hard to resist the temptation to do so. Quite simply it's fun to check out these high-tech, sexy looking bikes and take them for a spin, dropping them off at bike stands with no fuss and no muss.

Here's how it works: You buy a 1- or 7-day subscription (1.70€ or 8€, respectively) from the machine at one of the futuristic-looking bike stands, which gives you the right to as many half-hour rides as you'd like for 1 or 7 days. If you want to go over a half-hour, you can either check in your bike, wait 5 minutes, and check it out again, or you can pay 1€ for your extra half-hour, 2€ for the half-hour after that one and 4€ for the third half-

hour on. Everything is meticulously explained in English on the website, www.velib.fr, and there's even a number you can call for English-speaking assistance (℡ **01-30-79-79-30**). There's one big catch, however—to use the machines you must have a credit or debit card with a chip in it. This can be a problem for North American tourists, so I advise either getting a TravelEx "cash passport" with money on it (www.travelex.com) or just **buy your subscription online ahead of time** (make sure you have your secret code to punch in on the stand). Helmets are not provided, so if you're feeling queasy about launching into traffic, bring one along. There are few bike lanes so far, but success has been such that new ones are being added, and cyclists have the right to ride in the bus lanes. *One more tip:* Before you ride, get a map of the city that shows where the bike stands are so you don't waste precious time looking for a place to check in or check out.

By Bicycle

Cycling in Paris has been revolutionized by the hugely successful **Velib'** bike rental scheme launched in 2007 (the name comes from *vélo,* meaning "bicycle," and *liberté,* meaning "freedom"). It takes a little effort for a tourist to sign up, but it's worth it to see Paris from two-wheels (see box, below).

Alternatively, you can rent a bike from **Paris à vélo, c'est sympa!,** 22 rue Alphonse Baudin (℡ **01-48-87-60-01;** www.parisvelosympa.com; Métro: St-Sébastien-Froissart or Richard Lenoir). Rentals cost 12€ for half a day and 15€ for a full day, but they do require 250€ or a passport as a deposit. Vespas are available for rent from **Left Bank Scooters** (℡ **06-78-12-04-24;** www.leftbankscooters.com) from 70€ per day (55€ if you rent 4 or more days), and the company will deliver the scooters to your hotel or apartment. A credit card deposit of 1,200€ is required, but this can be reduced to 500€ for an additional fee. This amount is held rather than charged on a credit card.

A Word About Driving in Paris

Don't. Even if you are a Formula 1 racecar driver with years of experience, you'll be alternately outraged and infuriated by the aggressive tactics of your fellow drivers and the inevitable *bouchons* (literally, a bottle stopper or cork), or jams that tie up traffic and turn a simple jaunt into a harrowing nightmare. To make matters worse, it's easy to believe that the street and direction signs were cunningly placed by a sadistic

First there was the highly successful Velib' bike-rental system, and now it has a four-wheeled cousin: **Autolib'** (© **08-00-94-20-00;** www.autolib.eu). The concept is the same: a short-term self-service rental, but this time, you get to tool around in a spiffy electric car. There are hundreds of rental stations in Paris and the surrounding area, but more are being added. To register you can go to one of the Autolib' subscription kiosks or to the Autolib' information center (5 rue Edouard, 5th arrond.) with your driving license, a valid form of ID, and a credit card, or you can simply **register online.** A 1-day subscription is free, but you pay 9€ per half hour. A 7-day subscription is 10€ plus 7€ per half hour, a month is 25€ plus 6.50€ per half-hour, and a year is 120€ plus 5.5€ per half hour. You are given a badge that you then pass over the sensor at a rental station to unlock the car. Unplug it from the charger and drive away. To return it, use the GPS to find an Autolib' station and plug in the Bluecar. For information about other car rental companies, please refer to the "By Car" section of "Getting There," earlier in this chapter.

madman who gets kicks out of watching hapless drivers take wrong turns. No matter how carefully you try to follow the signs pointing toward, say, Trocadéro, you'll suddenly find yourself on an outer boulevard headed for Versailles.

Your troubles are not over once you get to your destination because then you will have to park, which is a whole other trauma. Spots are elusive, to say the least, and you'll probably find yourself touring the neighborhood for at least 20 minutes until you find one. By then you'll have figured out why it is that Parisians park on the sidewalks: Often, there's nowhere else to park.

One final hurdle: feeding the **parking meter.** All parking is *payant*—that is, you must pay. And you can't use coins in the *horodateur* (parking meter) anymore—you must buy either pay with a credit card or buy a "Paris Carte" parking card at a *tabac,* or smoke shop. This card is inserted directly into the meter, which will print out a ticket that you must put on your dashboard; parking costs from 1.20€ to 3.60€ per hour, and you can't stay in the same spot for more than 2 hours. Mercifully, on Sundays and after 7pm the rest of the week, all street parking is free. If you are not up to the challenge, try one of the many **underground parking lots,** indicated by a sign with a white "P" on a blue background; parking in one of these is between 3€–4€ per hour, and you can stay all day (you don't need a card here).

If, despite my ranting, you still feel compelled to rent a car and drive around the city, or are forced to do so due to extenuating circumstances, at the very least, get your hands on a basic explanation of international street signs (this should be available at your car-rental agency), and a good street map. Try to do your driving on a Sunday, when most Parisians head for the country (but forget about Sat, when they all do their shopping). Finally, try to keep your cool, because no matter how sure you are that you are following the rules of the road, at some point, someone in another car will curse you. Good luck—you're going to need it.

By Boat

The **Batobus** (© **08-25-05-01-01;** www.batobus.com) is a fleet of boats that operates along the Seine, stopping at such points of interest as the Eiffel Tower, Musée d'Orsay, the Louvre, Notre-Dame, and the Hôtel de Ville. Unlike the Bateaux-Mouches (p. 151), the Batobus does not provide a recorded commentary. The only fare option available is a day pass valid for either 1 or 2 days, each allowing as many entrances and exits as you want, a sort of hop-on, hop-off on water. A 1-day pass costs 15€ for adults, and 7€ for children 16 and under. From September to April boats operate daily every 25 minutes between 10am and 7pm; April to September boats operate daily every 20 minutes between 10am and 9:30pm. The timetable changes slightly every year so it's always worth double-checking on the website.

By Taxi

This is the most expensive way to get around and not necessarily the most efficient. Merely hailing a cab can be an ordeal, since you'll have to find a taxi stand (in practice, you can hail them in the street, but not all will stop). Taxi stands resemble bus stops and sport a blue "TAXI" sign. You can also call the dispatcher at ℂ 01-45-30-30-30. Once you get inside, you'll have to pray that your driver is skilled in dodging through Parisian traffic, which is horrendous. Sooner or later you'll find yourself stuck in a jam, watching the meter tick and cursing yourself for not having taken the Métro.

Calculating fares is a complicated business. When you get in, the meter should read 2.50€. Then, the basic rates for Paris *intramuros* ranges from 1€–1.50€ per kilometer, depending on the day of the week and the hour. There's a minimum fare of 6.86€; if you have more than three people in your party, you'll also be charged 3€ for each additional passenger. You'll also be charged 1€ for each suitcase you put in the trunk. Unless you're a math whiz, it's near impossible to calculate exactly what your fare should be, but if you feel you've been seriously overcharged, you can contact the **Préfecture de Police** (ℂ 08-91-01-22-22; www.prefecture-police-paris.interieur.gouv.fr). The saving grace here is that the distances are usually not huge, and barring excessive traffic, your average cross-town fare should fall between 15€ and 20€ for two without baggage. Tipping is not obligatory, but a .50€ to 1€ tip is customary for short trips; for longer hauls a 5 to 10% tip should do.

It's often easier to call a cab then to hail one on the street: Contact **Les Taxis Bleus** (ℂ **36-09,** .15€ per min; www.taxis-bleus.com) or **Taxi G7** (ℂ **36-07,** .15€ per min; www.taxisg7.fr). Avoid minicabs or unlicensed taxis.

On Foot

If you have the time and the energy, the best mode of transport in this small and walkable city is your own two feet. You can cross the center of town (say from the Place St-Michel to Les Halles) in about 20 minutes. This is the best way to see and experience the city, and take in all the little details that make it all so wonderful. You could spend an afternoon exploring one small neighborhood, or try one of the walking tours in Chapter 7.

FAST FACTS: PARIS

Area Codes The country code for France is 33 and the area code for Paris is 01. See "Telephones," later in this section, for further information.

Business Hours Opening hours in Paris are erratic. Most museums close 1 day a week (usually Mon or Tues) and some national holidays. Museum hours tend to be from 9:30am to 6pm. Generally, **offices** are open Monday to Friday from 9am to 6pm, but don't count on it—always call first. **Banks** tend to be open from 9am to 5pm Monday to Friday, but some branches are also open on Saturday. **Large stores** are open from around 10am to 6 or 7pm. Some **small stores** have a lunch break that can last for up to 2 hours, from noon onward, but this is becoming increasingly rare. Most shops, except those in the Marais or on the Champs-Élysées, are closed on Sunday. Restaurants are typically closed on Sundays and/or Mondays and many businesses across the city are closed in August.

Car Rental See "By Car" under "Getting There" and "By Car" under "Getting Around," earlier in this chapter.

Cellphones See "Mobile Phones," later in this section.

Crime See "Safety," later in this section.

Customs What you can bring into France: Citizens of E.U. countries can bring in any amount of goods as long as the goods are intended for their personal use and not for resale. Non-E.U. citizens are entitled to 200 cigarettes, 100 small cigars, 50 cigars, or 250g of tobacco duty-free. You can also bring in 2 liters of alcoholic beverages less than 22% alcohol, and 1 liter of spirits (more than 22% alcohol). In addition, you can bring in 50g (1.76 oz.) of perfume.

Disabled Travelers I suppose you could blame it on its centuries-old streets,

but Paris has only recently started making a concerted effort make itself accessible to disabled travelers (and citizens). While the city still won't win any prizes for accessibility (tortuous sidewalks, few ramps at public facilities, endless stairways in Métro stations), there has been slow and steady progress in the right direction. There are now over 60 wheelchair accessible bus lines, several RER stations, and stations on the Métro line 14. To find the closest accessible stations, maps and more, visit www.info-mobi.com (in English) or call ℂ **09-70-81-83-85.** Many museums are now accessible; visit their websites for details. Several art museums offer tactile visits for the blind. Any hotel that has three or more stars (under the French national rating system, not ours) must have at least one handicap-accessible room. Hotels that are particularly sensitive to the subject may bear the "Tourisme & Handicaps" label. The Paris Tourist Office (www.parisinfo.com) has a good listing of accessible hotels on their site, as well as plenty of other info and links for disabled travelers. Click on "Practical Paris" and then "Leisure and Disability," where you'll find information on everything from cinemas and shopping to public pools.

Dentists & Doctors
Doctors are listed in the **Pages Jaunes** (French equivalent of the Yellow Pages, www.pagesjaunes.fr)

under "Médecins." The standard fee for a consultation with a general practitioner (*médecin generaliste*) is about 23€. **SOS Médecins** (ℂ **36-24** or 01-47-07-77-77) makes house calls that cost around 50€–70€ (prices quoted are for people without French social security). To download a list of English-speaking dentists and doctors in Paris, visit the U.S. Citizens Services page on the US embassy website (http://france.usembassy. gov) and click on "Resources for US Citizens." You can also reach U.S. Citizens Services by phone at ℂ **01-43-12-22-22.** See also "Emergencies" and "Health," below in this section.

Drinking Laws Supermarkets, grocery stores, and cafes sell alcoholic beverages. The legal drinking age is 18, but persons under that age can be served alcohol in a bar or restaurant if accompanied by a parent or legal guardian. Wine and liquor are sold every day of the week, year-round. Cafes generally open around 6am and serve until closing (midnight–2am). Bars and nightclubs usually stay open until 2am, but they must stop serving alcohol 1½ hours before closing.

The law regarding drunk driving is tough. A motorist is considered "legally intoxicated" if his or her blood-alcohol limit exceeds .05%. If it is under .08% the driver faces a fine of 135€.

WHAT YOU CAN take out OF FRANCE

Australian Citizens A helpful brochure is available from the Australian Customs and Border Protection Service "Know Before You Go," online under "Guide for Travelers." For more information, call the **Australian Customs Service** (② **1300/363-263** in Australia, or 612/9313-3010 if you're abroad; www.customs.gov.au). The duty-free allowance in Australia is A$900 or, for those 17 or younger, A$450. Those over 18 can bring home up to 2 liters of alcoholic beverages.

Canadian Citizens For a clear summary of Canadian rules, ask for the booklet "I Declare" issued by the **Canada Border Services Agency** (② **800/461-9999** in Canada, or 204/983-3500 from abroad, under "Travel Tips"; www.cbsa-asfc.gc.ca). Canada allows its citizens a C$800 exemption. You can also bring back either up to 1.5 liters of wine, 1.14 liters of other alcoholic beverage, or up to 8.5 liters of beer.

New Zealand Citizens The answers to most questions regarding customs can be found on the website of the **New Zealand Customs Service** under "Customs charges, duties and allowances" (② **0800/4-CUSTOMS,** 0800/428-786, or 649/927-8036 from outside New Zealand; www.customs.govt.nz).The

duty-free allowance for New Zealand is NZ$700. You are allowed to bring back 4.5 liters of wine or beer, and not more than 1.25 liters of spirits.

U.K. Citizens When returning to the U.K. from an E.U. country such as France, you can bring in an unlimited amount of most goods. There is no limit on what you can bring back from an E.U. country, as long as the items are for personal use (this includes gifts) and you have already paid the duty and tax. However, you may be asked to prove that the goods are for your own use. For information, contact **HM Revenue Customs** (② **44/0300-200-3700;** www.hmrc.gov.uk).

U.S. Citizens For specifics on what you can bring back and the corresponding fees, download the invaluable free pamphlet "Know Before You Go" online at **www.cbp.gov**. Or, contact the **U.S. Customs & Border Protection (CBP;** ② **877/227-5511** in the U.S. or 202/325-8000 from outside the U.S). Returning U.S. citizens who have been away for 48 hours or more are allowed to bring back, once every 30 days, $800 worth of merchandise duty-free. Included in your allowance is 1 duty-free liter of alcoholic beverage, after that it depends what state you live in, so check with your state customs office for amounts.

Over .08% and it could cost 4,500€ or up to 2 years in jail.

Driving Rules The French drive on the right side of the road. At junctions where there are no signposts indicating the right of way, cars coming from the right have priority. When entering a roundabout (rond point), you do not have priority; once you are on be sure to

signal when you are about to turn off.

Electricity Electricity in France runs on 220 volts AC (60 cycles). Adapters or transformers are needed to fit sockets, which you can buy in branches of Darty, FNAC, or BHV. Make sure your appliance can handle 220 volts, otherwise you risk frying it. If it can't, be sure to use a transformer.

Embassies & Consulates If you have a passport, immigration, legal, or other problem, contact your consulate. Call before you go—they often keep odd hours and observe both French and home-country holidays.

   The Embassy of **Australia** is at 4 rue Jean-Rey, 15e (② **01-40-59-33-00;** www.france.embassy.gov.au;

Métro: Bir Hakeim), open Monday to Friday 9am to 5pm except public holidays. The Consular section is open Monday to Friday from 9am to noon and 2 to 4pm.

The Embassy of **Canada** is at 35 ave. Montaigne, 8e (℡ **01-44-43-29-00;** www.amb-canada.fr; Métro: Franklin-D-Roosevelt or Alma-Marceau), open Monday to Friday 9am to noon and 2–5pm.

The Embassy of **Ireland** is at 4 rue Rude, 16e (℡ **01-44-17-67-00;** www.embassyofireland.fr; Métro: Argentine), open Monday to Friday 9:30am to noon.

The Embassy of **New Zealand** is at 7ter rue Léonard-de-Vinci, 16e (℡ **01-45-01-43-43;** www.nzembassy.com/france; Métro: Victor Hugo), open Monday to Friday 9am to 1pm.

The Embassy of the **United Kingdom** is at 35 rue du Faubourg St-Honoré, 8e (℡ **01-44-51-31-00;** http://ukinfrance.fco.gov.uk; Métro: Concorde or Madeleine), open Monday to Friday 9:30am to 1pm and 2:30 to 6pm.

The Embassy of the **United States,** 2 ave. Gabriel, 8e (℡ **01-43-12-22-22;** http://france.usembassy.gov; Métro: Concorde), is open Monday to Friday 9am to 6pm.

Emergencies In an emergency, call ℡ **112,** or the fire brigade (*Sapeurs-Pompiers;* ℡ **18**), who are trained to deal with all kinds of medical emergencies, not just fires. For a medical emergency and/or ambulance, call ℡ **15.** For the police, call ℡ **17.**

Etiquette & Customs Parisians like pleasantries and take manners seriously: Say *bonjour, madame/monsieur,* when entering an establishment and *au revoir* when you depart. Always say *pardon* when you accidentally bump into someone. With strangers, people who are older than you, and professional contacts, use *vous* rather than *tu* (*vous* is the polite form of the pronoun you).

Health For travel abroad, non-E.U. nationals should consider buying medical travel insurance. For U.S. citizens, Medicare and Medicaid do not provide coverage for medical costs incurred abroad, so check what medical services your health insurance covers before leaving home. That said, medical costs are a fraction of what they cost in the U.S. (for example, a visit to a GP costs 23€), so you may even decide to do a little medical tourism (be sure to bring your prescriptions). U.K. nationals will need a **European Health Insurance Card (EHIC)** to receive free or reduced-cost medical care during a visit to a European Union (E.U.) country, Iceland, Liechtenstein, Norway, or Switzerland (go to www.nhs.uk/ehic for further information).

If you suffer from a chronic illness, consult your doctor before your departure. Pack prescription medications in your carry-on luggage and carry them in their original containers, with pharmacy labels—otherwise they won't make it through airport security. Carry the generic name of prescription medicines, in case a local pharmacist is unfamiliar with the brand name.

For further tips on travel and health concerns, and a list of local English-speaking doctors, contact the **International Association for Medical Assistance to Travelers (IAMAT;** ℡ **716/754-4883** in the U.S., or 416/652-0137 in Canada; www.iamat.org). You can also download a list of English-speaking dentists and doctors in Paris, at the U.S. Citizens Services page on the US embassy website (http://france.usembassy.gov) and click on "Resources for US Citizens." See also "Doctors," "Pharmacies," "Emergencies," and "Hospitals."

Holidays Major holidays are New Year's Day (Jan 1), Easter Sunday and Monday (late Mar/Apr), May Day (May 1), VE Day (May 8), Ascension Thursday (40 days after Easter), Pentecost/Whit Sunday and Whit Monday (7th Sun and Mon after Easter), Bastille Day (July 14), Assumption Day (Aug 15), All Saints Day (Nov 1), Armistice Day (Nov 11), and Christmas Day (Dec 25).

Hospitals In my experience, French public

hospitals are very good. Most Parisian hospitals have 24-hour emergency rooms, some have a specialty (Hôpital Necker is the best children's hospital, for example). For addresses and information on all Paris' public hospitals, visit www. aphp.fr.

There are two private hospitals in nearby suburbs with English-speaking staff that operate 24 hours daily (and cost much more than the public ones): the **American Hospital of Paris** (63 bd. Victor Hugo, 92200 Neuilly-sur-Seine; ℂ **01-46-41-25-25;** www. american-hospital.org; Métro: Pont de Levallois (15 min. walk from station); bus: 43, 82, 93, 163, 164, and 174) and **Hertford British Hospital, Hôpital Franco-Britannique** (3 rue Barbès or 4 rue Kleber, Levallois; ℂ **01-47-59-59-59;** www.ihfb.org/en; Métro: Anatole-France).

Hot Lines S.O.S. Help is a hot line for English-speaking callers in crisis at ℂ **01-46-21-46-46;** www. soshelpline.org. Open daily 3 to 11pm.

Internet & Wi-Fi Many Parisian hotels and cafes have Internet access, and Wi-Fi (pronounced *wee-fee*) is becoming increasingly common in cafes and public spaces. Cybercafes open and close so quickly it is hard to list them, but the three huge **Milk** locations seem to be reliably open 24/7 (www.milklub.com).

Language English is increasingly common in Paris, particularly in tourist areas, but you'll get much better service (or at least a shadow of a smile) if you at least attempt to use a few French words like "bonjour" and "merci." For handy French words and phrases, as well as food and menu terms, refer to chapter 12, "Useful Terms & Phrases."

Legal Aid In an emergency, especially if you get into trouble with the law, your country's embassy or consulate will provide legal advice. See "Embassies & Consulates," above.

LGBT Travelers France is known for being a particularly tolerant country when it comes to gays and lesbians, which made the acrimonious blather surrounding the legalization of same-sex marriage in 2013 all the more upsetting. "Gay Paree" boasts a large gay population, and for the last decade, an openly gay mayor, Bertrand Delanoë. The center of gay and lesbian life is in the Marais. The annual Gay Pride March takes place on the last Sunday in June. Information and resources can be found in Paris's largest, best-stocked gay bookstore, **Les Mots à la Bouche,** 6 rue Ste-Croix de la Bretonnerie, 4th arrond. (ℂ **01-42-78-88-30;** www.motsbouche.com; Métro: Hôtel-de-Ville), which carries publications in both French and English. "Têtu" (www.tetu.com) is a national magazine dedicated to gay life; to find listings and events, try Qweek (www.qweek.fr), a website focused on Paris. The Paris Tourist Office website (www. paris-info.com) has an entire section devoted to Gay Paris (under "Practical Paris") listing clubs, events, gay-friendly hotels and restaurants, associations, and more.

Lost & Found All lost objects—except those found in train stations or on trains—are taken to the **Bureau des Objets Trouvés** (36 rue des Morillons, 15e; ℂ **08-21-00-25-25**). It's better to visit in person than to call, but be warned that there are huge delays in processing claims. Objects lost on the Métro are held by the station agents before being sent onto the Bureau des Objets Trouvés.

Mail There are post offices (**La Poste;** ℂ **36-31;** www.laposte.fr) in every arrondissement. Most are open Mon–Fri 8:30am–8pm, Sat 8am–1pm; the main post office (52 rue du Louvre; Métro: Louvre-Rivoli) is open Mon–Sat 7:30am–6am and Sunday 10am–6am. Stamps are also sold in *tabacs* (tobacconists).

Medical Requirements Unless you are arriving from an area of the world known to be suffering from an epidemic, especially cholera or yellow fever, inoculations or vaccinations are not required for entry in France.

Mobile Phones The three letters that define much of the world's wireless capabilities are **GSM** (Global System for Mobile Communications), a big, seamless network that makes for easy cross-border mobile phone use throughout Europe and dozens of other countries worldwide. You can use your mobile phone in France provided it is GSM and tri-band or quad-band; just confirm this with your operator before you leave.

Using your phone abroad can be expensive, and you usually have to pay to receive calls, so it's a good idea to get it "unlocked" before you leave. This means you can buy a SIM card from one of the three main French providers: **Bouygues Télécom** (www.bouyguestelecom.fr), **Orange** (www.orange.fr), or **SFR** (www.sfr.fr). A SIM card with a 5€ call credit costs about 10€. Alternatively, if your phone isn't unlocked, you could buy a cheap

mobile phone. To top-up your phone credit, buy a Mobicarte from *tabacs*, supermarkets, and mobile phone outlets. Prices range from 5€ to 100€.

Money & Costs Frommer's lists exact prices in the local currency. The currency conversions quoted above were correct at press time. However, rates fluctuate, so before departing consult a currency exchange website such as www.oanda.com to check up-to-the-minute rates.

For decades Paris was known as one of the most expensive cities on earth. It still is a pricey destination, but it's not as expensive as Tokyo or Oslo. However, it's increasingly difficult to find even an average hotel for less than 150€.

ATMs are widely available in Paris, but if you're

venturing into rural France, it's always good to have cash in your pocket. Be sure you know your personal identification number (PIN) and daily withdrawal limit before you depart. Many banks impose a fee when you withdraw money abroad, and that fee can be higher for international transactions than for domestic ones. In addition, the bank from which you withdraw cash may charge its own fee. For currency exchange, look for **Travelex** (www.travelex.fr) counters at Paris airports and train stations, or try one of the few remaining private operations on the Champs-Élysées. They charge a small commission.

Visa is the most common credit card in France but international credit cards are widely accepted. Foreign

THE VALUE OF THE EURO VS. OTHER POPULAR CURRENCIES

Euro (€)	US$	C$	UK£	A$	NZ$
1	1.38	1.52	0.83	1.47	1.60

WHAT THINGS COST IN PARIS

	EURO€
Taxi from the airport to downtown Paris (Orly or CDG)	50.00–70.00
Métro ticket	1.70
Double room, expensive	350.00–800.00
Double room, moderate	150.00–350.00
Double room, inexpensive	100.00–150.00
Three-course dinner for one without wine, moderate	25.00–30.00
Bottle of beer	3.00–6.00
Espresso	1.00–2.50
1 liter of premium gas	1.50–1.75
Admission to most museums	8.00–13.00

credit cards, particularly those without an embedded chip, do not always work in machines. Check for hidden fees when using your card abroad—some bank charges can be up to 3% of the purchase price. The following number can be used to report any lost or stolen credit card: **08-92-70-57-05**. **American Express** (📞 **01-47-77-72-00**; www.americanexpress.com) and **MasterCard** (📞 **08-00-90-13-87**; www.mastercard.com) have their own emergency numbers. **Visa** 📞 **08-00-90-11-79**; www.visaeurope.com) lists the standard one for all cards. There are still shops, restaurants, and bars, often family run, that don't accept credit or debit cards, so it's always good to both check in advance and have cash on you.

Travelers' checks are no longer accepted in many stores and restaurants, and not even American Express sells them anymore at their Paris office (though they do cash them at their Kanoo Change, 11 rue Scribe). If you are determined to use them, you can still buy them through American Express (in the U.S., www.americanexpress.com), but a better solution would be to buy a **MasterCard Cash Passport** (www.cashpassport.com), a pre-paid, reloadable currency card with a chip and a PIN number that works like a debit card.

For help with currency conversions, tip calculations, and more, download Frommer's convenient Travel Tools app for your mobile device. Go to www.frommers.com/go/mobile and click on the "Travel Tools" icon.

Newspapers & Magazines The most serious and intellectual national daily is **Le Monde** (www.lemonde.fr), which is strong on both politics and economic issues. **Le Figaro** (www.lefigaro.fr) leans more to the right, **Libération** (www.liberation.fr), tilts to the left. For more local news, try **Le Parisien** (www.leparisien.fr).

English-language newspapers are available at kiosks across the city; the most widely available is the "International New York Times" (www.inyt.com), the former "International Herald-Tribune." Nostalgics can still find the Herald-Tribune online at www.iht.com. **WH Smith** (248 rue de Rivoli; 📞 **01-44-77-88-99**; www.whsmith.fr;) has a good selection of English-language press.

Passports Citizens of the U.K., New Zealand, Australia, Canada, and the United States need a valid passport to enter France. The passport is valid for a stay of 90 days. All children must have their own passports.

Allow plenty of time before your trip to apply for a passport; processing normally takes 3 weeks but can take longer during busy periods (especially spring). Keep in mind that if you need a passport in a hurry, you'll pay a higher processing fee.

Pharmacies You'll spot French *pharmacies* by looking for the green neon cross above the door. If your local pharmacy is closed, there should be a sign on the door indicating the nearest one open. Pharmacists give basic medical advice and can take your blood pressure. *Parapharmacies* sell medical products and toiletries, but they don't dispense prescriptions. Both the **Pharmacie les Champs** (84 ave. des Champs-Élysées; 📞 **01-45-62-02-41**; Métro: George V) and the **Pharmacie Européene** (6 place de Clichy; 📞 **01-48-74-65-18**; Métro: Place de Clichy) are open 24 hours daily. See also "Emergencies" and "Health."

Police In an emergency, call 📞 **17** for the police, or **112**, the European-Union wide toll-free emergency number. The Préfecture de Police has stations all over Paris. To find the nearest one, call 📞 **17** or go to www.prefecturedepolice.interieur.gouv.fr/English. See also "Emergencies," earlier in this section.

Safety In general, Paris is a safe city and it is safe to use the Métro late at night. However, certain Métro stations (and the areas around them) are best avoided at night: Châtelet-Les Halles, Gare du Nord, Barbès Rochechouart, and Strasbourg St-Denis. The RER can get scary late at night;

try to find alternative transport to and from the airport (such as buses or taxis) late at night or early in the morning.

The most common crime problem in Paris is pickpockets. They prey on tourists around popular attractions such as the Louvre, the Eiffel Tower, Notre-Dame, St-Michel, Centre Pompidou, and Sacré-Coeur, in the major department stores, and on the Métro. Take precautions and be vigilant at all times: Don't take more money with you than necessary, keep your passport in a concealed pouch or leave it at your hotel, and ensure that your bag is firmly closed at all times. Also, around the major sites it is quite common to be approached by a young Roma girl and asked if you speak English. It's best to avoid these situations, and any incident that might occur, by shaking your head and walking away.

In cafes, bars, and restaurants, it's best not to leave your bag under the table or on the back of your chair. Keep it between your legs or on your lap to avoid it being stolen. Never leave valuables in a car, and never travel with your car unlocked.

In times of heightened security concerns, the government mobilizes police and armed forces, so don't be surprised to see soldiers ntrolling around transport hubs and carrying automatic weapons.

Paris is a cosmopolitan city and most nonwhite travelers won't experience any problems, outside of some unpleasant stares. Although there is a significant level of discrimination against West and North African immigrants, harassment of African-American and Asian tourists is exceedingly rare. **S.O.S. Racisme** (51 ave. de Flandre, 19th; ✆ **01-40-35-36-55;** www.sos-racisme. org) offers legal advice to victims of prejudice and will even intervene to help with the police.

Female travelers should not expect any more hassle than in other major cities and the same precautions apply. French men tend to stare a lot, but it's generally harmless. Avoid walking around the less safe neighborhoods (Barbès Rochechouart, Strasbourg St-Denis, Châtelet-Les-Halles) alone at night and never get into an unmarked taxi. If you are approached in the street or on the Métro, it's best to avoid entering into conversation and walk away.

Senior Travel Many discounts are available to seniors—men and women over 60. Although they often seem to apply to residents of E.U. countries, it pays to announce at the ticket window of a museum or monument that you are 60 years old or more. You may not receive a discount, but it doesn't hurt to ask. "Senior," incidentally, is pronounced roonyora in France. Senior citizens do not get a

discount for traveling on public transport in Paris, but there are senior discounts on national trains. Check out www.voyages-sncf.com for further information. Frommers.com offers more information and resources on travel for seniors.

Smoking Smoking is now banned in all public places, including cafes, restaurants, bars, and nightclubs.

Student Travel Student discounts are less common in France than other countries, but simply because young people under 26 are usually offered reduced rates. Some discounts only apply to residents of E.U. countries, who will need to prove this with a passport or driver's license, but if you're not from the E.U. it's worth carrying ID to prove your age and announcing it when buying tickets. Look out for the **Ticket Jeunes** when using the Métro. It can be used on a Saturday, Sunday, or bank holiday, and provides unlimited travel in zones 1 to 3 for 3.75€ (see "By Public Transport," earlier). SNCF also offer 25% off for under-26-year-olds traveling on national trains (www.voyages-sncf.com).

Taxes As a member of the European Union, France routinely imposes a value-added tax (VAT in English; TVA in French) on most goods. The standard VAT is 20% and it is already included in virtually all prices for consumer goods and services (you'll know for sure when you see TTC, which means *toutes taxes comprises*, "all taxes included"). If you're not an E.U. resident, you can get a VAT refund if you're spending less than 6 months in France, you purchase goods worth at least 175€ at a single shop on the same day, the goods fit into your luggage, and the shop offers *vente en détaxe* (duty-free sales or tax-free shopping). Give them your passport and ask for a *bordereau de vente à l'exportation* (export sales invoice), which will have a bar code. Both you and the shopkeeper will sign the slip, and you will choose how you will be reimbursed (credit on card, bank transfer, or cash). Once you get to the airport, scan the code in one of the new "Pablo" terminals (if your airport doesn't have one, just got to the "detaxe" counter). If your reimbursement is a credit to your bank account or credit card, it will be sent automatically once you scan the slip. If you chose cash, you'll need to go to the "detaxe" counter.

Telephones Public phones are a dying breed in France, and may be obsolete by 2016. If you can find one, it will require a phone card (known as a *télécarte*), which at press time could still be purchased at post offices, *tabacs*, and supermarkets, or anywhere you see a blue sticker reading *télécarte en vente ici* ("phone card for sale here").

They cost 7.50€ for 50 calling units and 15€ for 120 units.

The country code for France is 33. To make a local or long distance call within France, dial the 10-digit number of the person or place you're calling. Mobile numbers begin with 06. Numbers beginning with 0 800, 0 805, and 0 809 are free in France, other numbers beginning with 8 are not. Many public service numbers are now four digits, some are toll free.

To make international calls from Paris, first dial 00 and then the country code (U.S. and Canada 1, U.K. 44, Ireland 353, Australia 61, New Zealand 64). Next you dial the area code and number. For example, if you want to call the British Embassy in Washington, D.C., you would dial ✆ **001 202/588-7800.**

Time France is on Central European Time, which is 1 hour ahead of Greenwich Mean Time. French daylight saving time lasts from the last Sunday in March to the last Sunday in October. France uses the 24-hour clock. So 13h is 1pm, 14h15 is 2:15pm, and such For help with time translations and more, download our convenient Travel Tools app for your mobile device. Go to www.frommers.com/go/mobile and click on the "Travel Tools" icon.

Tipping By law, all bills in cafes, bars, and restaurants say *service compris*, which means the service charge is included. Waiters

are paid a living wage and do not expect tips. However, they certainly won't mind if you leave one, and if you are planning on frequenting a certain cafe, it's a good investment to leave a euro or two after a meal. Taxi drivers usually appreciate a 5 to 10% tip, or for the fare to be rounded up to the next euro. The French give their hairdressers a tip of about 15%, and if you go to the theater, you're expected to tip the usher 2€ or 3€. For help with tip calculations, currency conversions, and more, download our convenient Travel Tools app for your mobile device. Go to www.frommers.com/go/mobile and click on the "Travel Tools" icon.

Toilets Paris is full of gray-colored, street toilet kiosks, which are a little daunting to the uninitiated, but free, and are automatically washed and disinfected after each use. If you're in dire need, duck into a cafe or brasserie to use the toilet but expect to make a small purchase if you do so. In older establishments, you can still find Turkish toilets, otherwise known as squat toilets.

VAT See "Taxes," above.

Visas E.U. nationals don't need a visa to enter France. Nor do U.S., Canadian, Australian, New Zealand, or South African citizens for trips of up to 3 months. Nationals of other countries should make inquiries at the nearest French embassy or consulate before they travel to France. If non-E.U. citizens wish to stay for longer than 3 months, they must apply to a French embassy or consulate for a long-term visa.

Visitor Information The **Office du Tourisme et des Congrès** (25 rue des Pyramides, 1er; Ⓒ **01-49-52-42-63;** www.parisinfo.com) has information on hotels, restaurants, monuments, shopping, excursions, events, and transport. From May to October it is open every day from 9am to 7pm (except May 1); from November to April it's open from 10am to 7pm. There are several other offices around Paris: **Anvers** (72 bd. Rochechouart, 9e; daily 10am–6pm except major holidays); **Gare du Nord** (18 rue de Dunkerque, 10e; daily 8am–6pm except major holidays); **Gare de l'Est** (place du 11-novembre-1918, 10e; Mon–Sat 8am–7pm except major holidays); **Gare de Lyon** (20 bd. Diderot, 12e; Mon–Sat 8am–6pm except bank holidays); and **Porte de Versailles** (1 place de la Porte de Versailles, 15e; daily 11am–7pm during trade fairs).

Water Drinking water is safe, if not particularly tasty. To order tap water in a restaurant ask for *une carafe d'eau.*

Wi-Fi See "Internet & Wi-Fi," earlier in this section.

Women Travelers See "Safety," above.

USEFUL TERMS & PHRASES

12

It is often amazing how a word or two of halting French will change your hosts' disposition in their home country. At the very least, try to learn a few numbers, basic greetings, and—above all—the life-raft phrase, *Parlez-vous anglais?* (Do you speak English?). Many Parisians speak passable English and will use it liberally if you demonstrate the basic courtesy of greeting them in their language. *Bonne chance!*

THE BASIC COURTESIES

English	French	Pronunciation
Yes/No	Oui/Non	**Wee/Noh**
Okay	D'accord	**Dah-core**
Please	S'il vous plaît	**Seel voo play**
Thank you	Merci	**Mair-see**
You're welcome	De rien	**Duh ree-ehn**
Hello (during daylight)	Bonjour	**Bohn-jhoor**
Good evening	Bonsoir	**Bohn-swahr**
Goodbye	Au revoir	**O ruh-vwahr**
What's your name?	Comment vous appellez-vous?	**Kuh-mahn voo za-pell-ay-voo?**
My name is	Je m'appelle	**Jhuh ma-pell**
How are you?	Comment allez-vous?	**Kuh-mahn tahl-ay-voo?**
So-so	Comme ci, comme ça	**Kum-see, kum-sah**
I'm sorry/excuse me	Pardon	**Pahr-dohn**

GETTING AROUND & STREET SMARTS

English	French	Pronunciation
Do you speak English?	Parlez-vous anglais?	**Par-lay-voo ahn-glay?**
I don't speak French	Je ne parle pas français	**Jhuh ne parl pah frahn-say**
I don't understand	Je ne comprends pas	**Jhuh ne kohm-prahn pah**
Could you speak more loudly/more slowly?	Pouvez-vous parler plus fort/plus lentement?	**Poo-vay voo par-lay ploo for/ploo lan-te-ment?**
What is it?	Qu'est-ce que c'est?	**Kess kuh say?**

English	French	Pronunciation
What time is it?	Qu'elle heure est-il?	Kel uhr eh-*teel*?
What?	Quoi?	Kwah?
How? or What did you say?	Comment?	Ko-*mahn*?
When?	Quand?	Kahn?
Where is?	Où est?	Ooh eh?
Who?	Qui?	Kee?
Why?	Pourquoi?	Poor-*kwah*?
here/there	ici/là	ee-*see*/lah
left/right	à gauche/à droite	a gohsh/a drwaht
straight ahead	tout droit	too drwah
Fill the tank (of a car)	Le plein, s'il vous plaît	Luh plen, seel-voo-play please
I want to get off at	Je voudrais descendre à	Jhe voo-*dray* day-*sen* drah-ah
airport	aéroport	air-o-*por*
bank	banque	bahnk
bridge	pont	pohn
bus station	gare routière	gar roo-tee-*air*
bus stop	arrêt de bus	ah-*ray* duh boohs
by means of a car	en voiture	ahn vwa-*tur*
cashier	caisse	*kess*
cathedral	cathédrale	ka-tay-*dral*
church	église	ay-*gleez*
driver's license	permis de conduire	per-*mee* deh con-*dweer*
elevator	ascenseur	ah-sahn-*seuhr*
entrance (to a port building or a city)	porte	port
exit (from a building or a freeway)	sortie	sor-*tee*
gasoline	carburant/essence	car-bur-*ahn*/eh-*sahns*
hospital	hôpital	oh-pee-*tahl*
luggage storage	consigne	kohn-*seen*-yuh
museum	musée	mu-*zay*
no smoking	défense de fumer	day-*fahns* de fu-may
one-day pass	ticket journalier	tee-kay jhoor-nall-ee-ay
one-way ticket	aller simple	ah-*lay* sam-pluh
police	police	po-*leece*
round-trip ticket	aller-retour	ah-lay re-*toor*
store	magasin	ma-ga-*zehn*
street	rue	roo
ticket	billet	*bee*-yay
toilets	les toilettes/les WC	lay twa-*lets*/les vay-say

English	French	Pronunciation
I'd like	Je voudrais	Jhe voo-*dray*
a room	une chambre	ewn *shahm*-bruh
the key	la clé (la clef)	la clay
How much does it cost?	C'est combien?/Ça coûte combien?	Say comb-bee-*ehn*?/Sah coot comb-bee-*ehn*?
That's expensive	C'est cher/chère	Say share
Do you take credit cards?	Est-ce que vous acceptez les cartes de credit?	Es-kuh voo zaksep-*tay* lay kart duh creh-*dee*?
I'd like to buy	Je voudrais acheter	Jhe voo-dray ahsh-*tay*
aspirin	aspirines	ahs-peer-*een*
condoms	préservatifs	pray-ser-va-*teef*
a gift	un cadeau	uh kah-*doe*
a hat	un chapeau	uh shah-*poh*
a map of the city	un plan de ville	uh plahn de *veel*
a newspaper	un journal	uh zhoor-*nahl*
a phone card	une carte téléphonique	ewn cart tay-lay-fone-*eek*
a postcard	une carte postale	ewn carte pos-*tahl*
a road map	une carte routière	ewn cart roo-tee-*air*
some soap	du savon	dew sah-*vohn*
a stamp	un timbre	uh *tam*-bruh

NUMBERS & ORDINALS

English	French	Pronunciation
zero	zéro	*zare*-oh
one	un	oon
two	deux	duh
three	trois	twah
four	quatre	kaht-*ruh*
five	cinq	sank
six	six	seess
seven	sept	set
eight	huit	wheat
nine	neuf	noof
ten	dix	deess
eleven	onze	ohnz
twelve	douze	dooz
thirteen	treize	trehz
fourteen	quatorze	kah-*torz*
fifteen	quinze	kanz
sixteen	seize	sez
seventeen	dix-sept	deez-set

English	French	Pronunciation
eighteen	dix-huit	**deez-*wheat***
nineteen	dix-neuf	**deez-*noof***
twenty	vingt	**vehn**
thirty	trente	**trahnt**
forty	quarante	**ka-*rahnt***
fifty	cinquante	**sang-*kahnt***
one hundred	cent	**sahn**
one thousand	mille	**meel**
first	premier	***preh*-mee-ay**
second	deuxième	***duhz*-zee-em**
third	troisième	***twa*-zee-em**
fourth	quatrième	***kaht*-ree-em**
fifth	cinquième	***sank*-ee-em**
sixth	sixième	***sees*-ee-em**
seventh	septième	***set*-ee-em**
eighth	huitième	***wheat*-ee-em**
ninth	neuvième	***neuv*-ee-em**
tenth	dixième	***dees*-ee-em**

THE CALENDAR, DAYS & SEASONS

English	French	Pronunciation
January	Janvier	***jhan*-vee-ay**
February	Février	***feh*-vree-ay**
March	Mars	**marce**
April	Avril	**a-*vreel***
May	Mai	**meh**
June	Juin	**jhwehn**
July	Juillet	***jhwee*-ay**
August	Août	**oot**
September	Septembre	**sep-*tahm*-bruh**
October	Octobre	**ok-*toh*-bruh**
November	Novembre	**no-*vahm*-bruh**
December	Decembre	**day-*sahm*-bruh**
Sunday	Dimanche	**dee-*mahnsh***
Monday	Lundi	***luhn*-dee**
Tuesday	Mardi	***mahr*-dee**
Wednesday	Mercredi	***mair*-kruh-dee**
Thursday	Jeudi	***jheu*-dee**
Friday	Vendredi	***vawn*-druh-dee**
Saturday	Samedi	***sahm*-dee**
yesterday	hier	**ee-*air***

English	French	Pronunciation
today	aujourd'hui	**o-jhord-*dwee***
this morning/this afternoon	ce matin/cet après-midi	**suh ma-*tan*/set ah-preh-mee-*dee***
tonight	ce soir	**suh *swahr***
tomorrow	demain	**de-*man***
summer	été	**aytt-ay**
fall	automne	**aw-*tonne***
winter	hiver	**iv-*erre***
spring	printemps	**prehn-*tawm***

BASIC MENU TERMS

Note: No need to get intimidated when ordering in French. Simply preface the French-language menu item with the phrase *"Je voudrais"* (jhe voo-*dray*), which means, "I would like. . . ." *Bon appétit!*

MEATS

English	French	Pronunciation
beef	boeuf	**buhf**
beef stew	pot au feu	**poht o *fhe***
chicken	poulet	***poo*-lay**
dumplings of chicken, veal, or fish (often pike)	quenelles	**ke-*nelle***
duck breast	magret de canard	**maa-*gray* duh can-*ar***
preserved duck	confit de canard	**con-*fee* duh can-*ar***
goose or duck liver	foie gras	**fwah grah**
ham	jambon	**jham-bohn**
dried sausage	saucisson	**soh-see-*sohn***
leg of lamb	gigot d'agneau	***jhi*-goh dahnyoh**
kidneys	rognons	**row-nyon**
lamb	agneau	**lahn-*nyo***
lamb chop	cotelette d'agneau	**koh-te-*let* dahn-*nyo***
liver	foie	**fwah**
pork	porc	**pohr**
potted and shredded pork	rillettes de porc	**ree-*yet* duh pohr**
rabbit	lapin	**lah-*pan***
steak	bifteck	**beef-*tek***
steak with pepper sauce	steak au poivre	**stake o *pwah*-vruh**
snails	escargots	**ess-car-*goh***
veal stew with white sauce	blanquette de veau	**blahn-*ket* duh voh**
sweetbreads	ris de veau	**day *ree* duh voh**
veal	veau	***voh***

FISH

English	French	Pronunciation
fish	poisson	pwoss-*ohn*
herring	hareng	ahr-*rahn*
lobster	homard	oh-*mahr*
monkfish	lotte	loht
mussels	moules	*moohl*
oysters	huîtres	hoo-*ee*-truhs
pike	brochet	broh-*chay*
sea bass	bar	bar
sea bream	dorade	dor-*ahde*
shrimp	crevettes	kreh-*vette*
smoked salmon	saumon fumé	soh-*mohn* fu-*may*
trout	truite	tru-eet
tuna	thon	tohn

SIDES/APPETIZERS

English	French	Pronunciation
bread	pain	pan
butter	beurre	bhuhr
fries	frites	freet
green beans	haricots verts	*ah*-ri-co ver
rice	riz	ree
salad	salade	sa-*lahd*
vegetables	légumes	lay-*goom*

BEVERAGES

English	French	Pronunciation
beer	bière	bee-*aire*
coffee (long espresso)	café	ka-*fay*
coffee (decaf)	décaféiné/déca	day-kah-fay-*nay*/day-ca
coffee (with milk)	café crème/café au lait	ka-*fay* krem/ka-*fay* o-*lay*
milk	lait	*lay*
orange juice	jus d'orange	zhoo dor-*ahnjhe*
tea	thé	*tay*
tea (herbal)	tisane	tee-*zahn*
tea (w/lemon)	thé au citron	tay o see-*tran*
water	eau	oh
wine (red)	vin rouge	vhin *rooj*
wine (white)	vin blanc	vhin *blahn*
soda	soda	su-*da*
tap water	eau du robinet	oh doo rob-in-*ay*

SPICES/CONDIMENTS

English	French	Pronunciation
mayonnaise	mayonnaise	**may-o-*nayse***
mustard	moutarde	**moo-*tard***
pepper	poivre	***pwah*-vruh**
salt	sel	***sel***
sugar	sucre	***sook*-ruh**
vinegar	vinaigre	**vin-*aigre***
olive oil	huile d'olive	**weele dol-*eeve***

Index